PC/Computing Guide to Excel 3.0

PC Computing

PC/Computing Guide to Excel 3.0

Dale Lewallen

Ziff-Davis Press
Emeryville, California

Editor	Leslie Tilley
Technical Reviewer	Ed Jones
Project Coordinator	Jeff Green
Proofreader	Audrey Baer Johnson
Cover Design	Michael Yapp
Book Design	Laura Lamar/MAX, San Francisco; Steph Bradshaw
Technical Illustration	Cherie Plumlee
Page Layout	Kevin Shafer & Associates Tony Jonick Anna L. Marks Bruce Lundquist
Word Processing	Howard Blechman Kim Haglund
Indexer	Julie Kawabata

This book was produced on a Macintosh IIfx, with the following applications: FrameMaker®, Microsoft® Word, MacLinkPlus®, Aldus® FreeHand™, and Collage Plus™.

Ziff-Davis Press
5903 Christie Avenue
Emeryville, CA 94608

ISBN 1-56276-019-X

10 9 8 7 6 5 4 3 2 1

To the memory of Grandma Crowe. Although she didn't see this book, I'm sure she would have approved.

CONTENTS AT A GLANCE

TABLE OF CONTENTS

ACKNOWLEDGMENTS

A book is rarely the sole work of one author, but rather a lengthy collaboration among the author and a team of professionals. I've had the pleasure to work with such people at Ziff-Davis Press and I extend my sincere thanks to them:

Cindy Hudson for giving me the chance to work with Ziff-Davis Press. Her support and understanding, through both the trying times and normal production hassles, have helped to smooth the waters many times over.

Leslie Tilley for her editing skills and her ability not only to point out opportunities for clarification, but to suggest excellent alternatives.

Ed Jones for his helpful and insightful comments on the technical component of this book.

The staff at Ziff-Davis Press—Jeff Green, Cheryl Holzaepfel, Sheila McGill, and some folks whom I have yet to meet—for their production and copyediting assistance.

The staff of *PC/Computing* for putting up with me toward the end of the process as I became cranky. Thanks for your support.

I'd also like to recognize my family for teaching me the importance of a strong work ethic and that, with perseverance, all is possible. The lessons you taught early on are still with me.

Finally, thanks to my wife Lysa who has put up with more late night and weekend work sessions than any newlywed should have to. Her support and assistance eased this process a great deal.

Who This Book Is For

This book is geared toward readers that have some experience with PCs, and it is assumed that you have had some basic hands-on experience with Microsoft Windows and a mouse.If you have not worked with Windows or a mouse, turn to Appendix A for a quick tour of what you will need to know. A rudimentary knowledge of DOS and file name conventions is also assumed, as well as the DOS subdirectory structure. Again, a brief overview of these topics is given in Appendix A.

How to Use This Book

This book has been designed primarily as a step-by-step tutorial, but once you learn the ropes, you will also find it useful as a reference.

Throughout the book, instructions are given for operating Excel 3.0 using the mouse since most things in Excel are easier to do with a mouse. If you prefer to work with the keyboard, you can just move the cell pointer around with the arrow keys.

Chapter 1 is an introduction to some of the things you need to know as you begin to work with Excel 3.0. Here you will begin to construct a worksheet from the ground up, entering numbers and text labels and then saving your file.

In Chapter 2 you continue with your worksheet and learn how to make it more readable and aesthetically pleasing. In this chapter, you also learn how to insert and remove rows and columns from the worksheet.

Formulas and functions are the foundation of most of the worksheet models you will construct. In Chapter 3, as your worksheet continues to grow in complexity and usefulness, you'll learn how to enter formulas that give your worksheet the power to calculate figures according. In addition, you'll be introduced to the concept of ranges and how to prevent and detect errors.

In Chapter 4 you'll take a detailed look at functions—the predefined building blocks on which you construct a sophisticated worksheet model. Excel provides more than 100 functions, which perform a wide variety of tasks, from calculating the radius of a circle to figuring out the rate of return on an investment.

At that point, after having added formulas and functions to your worksheet model, it's time to embellish it a bit. Chapter 5 shows some advanced formatting and presentation features, such as cell shading, numeric formats, and worksheet styles.

And what good is a worksheet if you can't share it with others? In Chapter 6, after you learn about previewing a worksheet before printing it, you'll see how to print documents from within Excel. This chapter also shows how you can add special characters to your worksheet—non-keyboard symbols such as the Japanese yen or the British pound.

Among Excel's strong points is its ability to create high-quality charts and graphs. You'll build several types of charts and add textual annotation to them as you work through the exercises in Chapter 7.

Chapter 8 describes Excel's ability to place graphical objects—lines, rectangles, and circles—on the worksheet. In addition, you'll see how to add special graphical features such as text boxes and embedded charts.

Chapter 9 explores worksheet outlining, a feature new both to Excel and to the world of electronic spreadsheet products. With worksheet outlining, you can create summaries of all or part of a worksheet. The ability to create worksheet outlines often makes it easier for you to work with a large worksheet. It is also useful for creating reports to share with others.

In Chapter 10 you'll learn to work with multiple files and to protect your data. One of the important benefits of working within the Windows environment is the ability to work with more than one file at a time by having multiple windows showing on the screen. Excel provides features that let you work with multiple worksheet files. You'll also learn about the security features built into Excel that enable you to guard the sensitive data in your worksheets.

Exercises in Chapter 11 help you learn about two of Excel's most important features: the ability to link two or more files and the ability to consolidate data from many worksheets. With linked worksheets, a change to the data in one sheet is automatically reflected in all the worksheets linked to it—so that the data is always current and consistent.

Chapter 12 briefly discusses several tools you can use to perform very sophisticated mathematical calculations. Excel's Solver and Goal Seek features let you solve equations where you need to ask, "What is the appropriate set of values to use in order to achieve a certain result?"

Chapter 13 looks at Excel's rich and flexible programming, or macro, language. With Excel 3.0 macros, you can create complete applications or just build simple macros that handle routine, repetitive tasks automatically. By recording the steps as you execute them, you can create macros without programming experience. As you become more fluent with the language, you can write macros from scratch.

In addition to its ability to calculate numerical worksheets, Excel has a number of features for storing and accessing data in a database format. After performing the exercises in Chapter 14, you will have a solid background for working with Excel's database features. You'll learn how to sort data, extract data to other places on the worksheet, and how to delete data when you are done with it.

Chapter 15 will show you how to bring in data from other computer applications you might use such as Lotus 1-2-3, dBASE, and dBASE-compatible programs. In addition, this chapter contains tutorials on how to share data between Excel and other applications.

Chapter 16 offers a taste of the way Excel can communicate with other Windows applications via the Dynamic Data Exchange protocol (DDE). The true benefit of Windows-based applications is their potential to integrate data from different programs—it's as easy as copying data from one worksheet to another. After reading this chapter, you'll have a solid foundation for further exploration of the potential of DDE.

Appendix A is a brief overview of how to use the mouse and how to work with Windows applications. It also contains a brief review of DOS's file name and subdirectory schemes.

In Appendix B you'll learn how to install Excel—it's important to understand what Excel is doing when you install it on your hard disk.

Appendix C serves as an abbreviated reference to the more than 100 worksheet functions available in Excel 3.0.

Welcome to Excel

The PC revolution isn't too old for many people to remember what it's like to work with numbers—the time-tested flexible storage medium (a ledger) with some good, solid woodware (paper and pencil).

Consider the task facing those who used earlier methods of maintaining a ledger. They worked with a large piece of paper with multiple columns. Once the data was entered into the ledger, it was more or less static—changing the data was often far more trouble than it was worth. Old-fashioned ledgers were less tools for analysis than they were for recording and storage. The time required to make changes limited the usefulness of yesterday's ledgers. Imagine if you didn't discover a mistake you had made further back in the ledger and you had to refigure and recopy by hand all the changes the correction necessitated. The same would apply if you just wanted to change some of the assumptions to see if you could get a better result.

Today, with computers and software such as Microsoft Excel 3.0, you can easily build sophisticated models that can be quickly updated. You can construct and calculate models that were not feasible with pencil, paper, and calculator.

Because the computer never gets tired or complains of eyestrain, it can slavishly calculate as many iterations or variations of the model as you want to devise. Because the computer does math faster and more accurately than most humans, your model can now include complex mathematical formulas. Because the computer is a tireless worker when it comes to manipulating data, you can store and manipulate data of all types—numbers, names, addresses, zip codes, part numbers, and so on.

Excel 3.0 is a combination of features that work together to provide an environment for calculations, data manipulation, and presentation. Built into Excel are tools to store data, perform mathematical calculations on that data, and finally to create charts and graphs to put it all into perspective. The heart and soul of Excel is the worksheet—the foundation around which everything else is built.

The Microsoft Windows Environment

Excel is fundamentally a spreadsheet program that is meant to be used within the Microsoft Windows environment. Windows is a powerful platform from which to run applications that are designed to work on it. Excel 3.0 is just one of a large number of applications that are meant to work under Windows and take advantage of the features the environment offers.

With applications written to work in the Windows environment, and consequently supporting the same integration features, you can do things with more than one Windows-based application that you would not be able to do with the same number of DOS-based applications. For example, all Windows applications support a feature called the Clipboard. The Clipboard is a place where an application can store information—think of it as a scratch pad for applications to temporarily put data. You can cut or copy data from one application, such as Excel, and then paste that data into another application, say Microsoft Word for Windows. Because both applications are written for Windows—they speak the same language, if you will—they can share that data.

Another benefit of Windows-based applications is a feature called Dynamic Data Exchange (DDE). With DDE, one application can talk to another application, using a language called a protocol. At this point, DDE remains limited to rather specialized applications, but later on in the book you'll see some of the ways you might want to use DDE. Every application that is written for the Windows environment automatically gains access to these powerful integration features.

Excel 3.0 lets you open up a number of worksheets, each as a separate window. Multiple windows let you easily move data from one worksheet to another, link one worksheet to another, or just view two different worksheets at once. Excel provides several ways for you to look at multiple windows. You can tell Excel to arrange them so that a part of each window is visible, or you can choose to overlap them and work with just one at a time. You can also split one file into two or four panes that show different parts of the same file.

The Mouse Versus the Keyboard

Because Excel is a Windows-based application, it really shines when you use a mouse. There are, however, some people that are timid around a computer mouse. Although it's possible to use the keyboard to work with Excel, this is probably as good a time as any to get accustomed to using a mouse. Learning to use a mouse is a little like learning to ride a bike. After a bit of practice and some measure of patience on your part, you'll get the hang of it and soon will be wondering why you were so concerned about it in the first place.

Spreadsheet Outlining

Excel is the first spreadsheet program to offer outlining. Once only the domain of word processing programs, Excel has implemented outlining in a useful and productive way. The ability to create spreadsheet outlines makes it easy to do presentations. Say you have to give a presentation to two different groups: executives who need to know the bottom line, and your peers who are more interested in the details. With the worksheet outlining feature, you can print out your detailed data for one group, then click on a couple of buttons with the mouse and present an identically formatted worksheet—but without all the detail.

Database Management

Besides the spreadsheet features, Excel can be used as a powerful database manager. Excel can store any kind of information you want to put into it, including a stock portfolio, sales results from the field, or inventory levels. Once you have entered the data into the database, you can then perform data manipulations such as sorting and adding or deleting records, as well as making queries and creating reports and graphs based on the data.

There are a variety of ways to get information into a database. Excel will accept data from other file formats such as Lotus 1-2-3 or dBASE III and IV. In addition, Excel provides a method to quickly enter data into the spreadsheet manually.

Graphing and Presentation Features

What good are mathematical and data storage functions if you can't present your data to others or use visual tools to help you analyze it? The first version of Excel for Windows offered a wide variety of graphical presentation tools. Excel 3.0 continues in that tradition of worksheet presentation features. Some call this ability to create presentation-quality output directly from the worksheet "spreadsheet publishing."

Excel offers a wealth of individual features to help you make your output look good. You can format your worksheet in a number of ways by changing the font, size, and the layout of your text or numbers. You can add graphical elements such as arrows or borders to your document. You can even change the color of the cells to indicate the type of value stored there.

For example, you can format the cells so that if the result of a calculation is a negative number, it will display in red.

You can also create charts and graphs, and having done so you can modify their appearance. For example, you might decide that your data is better presented as a line chart instead of a bar chart. You can add titles and legends to the chart and even create charts with a three-dimensional look.

Task Automation with Macros

Somewhere in the annals of software development, someone figured out that users might one day want to perform sets of instructions over and over again. Although they probably weren't called macros back then, that's how we know them today. With Excel 3.0, you enter a series of instructions onto a special type of worksheet, called a macro sheet, which knows how to execute commands on your behalf. There are no limitations to the capabilities of the macro feature in Excel 3.0—its power is only limited by your imagination and knowledge.

The Powerful Nature of the Electronic Spreadsheet

Editing and Enhancing the Worksheet

Formulas, Ranges, and Errors

Functions, Moving and Copying Data, and Addressing

PART 1

Excel Basics

CHAPTER

1

The Powerful Nature of the Electronic Spreadsheet

The Integrated Worksheet Metaphor

Navigating in the Excel Worksheet

Entering Information

SPREADSHEET PROGRAMS SUCH AS MICROSOFT EXCEL AND LOTUS 1-2-3 are designed to provide a wide range of flexibility. When you first load a spreadsheet program, you face a blank screen—much as artists see a blank canvas before they begin to paint. It is upon this electronic landscape that you design the model you want, including the mathematical assumptions that you want to make. You are, in a very real sense, programming the computer to perform the calculations, analyses, and presentations you want to see—just as artists paint the picture they want to see upon the canvas.

The malleability of the tool is both a blessing and a curse. Although you enjoy great latitude in the kinds of models you can produce, you are at the same time responsible for creating an accurate model and ensuring that you have not introduced unseen errors into your calculations. Sometimes, the computer will beep insistently if you goof. Other times, it won't make a sound while it blissfully churns out the wrong numbers. Chapter 3 will address the issues of debugging and ensuring the accuracy of your worksheet.

Even though you'll be creating a model from scratch, don't think that the process must be difficult. Taken one step at a time, constructing a model with Excel is very straightforward. This book uses the term *spreadsheets* to refer to a general class of computer program but uses *worksheet* to refer to Excel's specific spreadsheet-like features.

The Integrated Worksheet Metaphor

Although there are several components to the worksheet, including graphics and database modules, at the heart of Excel 3.0 is the integrated worksheet. It is the nerve center around which all other modules operate, and it's the place where you will spend most of your time.

Paper-and-Pencil Method

Consider for a moment what it was like to work with a ledger based on pencil and paper. Once you had entered your information into the rows and columns of the paper-based worksheet, you had to perform a number of calculations, much as you would when calculating your bank account balance. Imagine what it would be like if you discovered a mistake early in your calculations or if you wanted to modify an assumption just to see what would happen if you changed one or more of the values in your model.

With electronic spreadsheet programs, you face none of the tedious recalculation associated with pencil-and-paper methods. Instead, you can perform any number of *what-if analyses*—trying various numbers to see how they affect the bottom line—and let the computer handle all of the difficult mathematical work. Excel even provides tools that facilitate these what-if analyses by letting you create models that can insert a specific value into a formula, calculate the result, and then save that result to another table somewhere else in the worksheet.

Rows and Columns

Excel's worksheet functions, like earlier paper-based ledgers and other modern spreadsheet programs, are based on the concept of rows and columns. Consider the sample worksheet in Figure 1.1. In this example, you see a simple model of a departmental budget for the final quarter of a fiscal year. Across the top, in columns C, D, and E, are the months of the budget. Running down the rows from top to bottom, you can see the individual items that make up the budget each month, arranged by department.

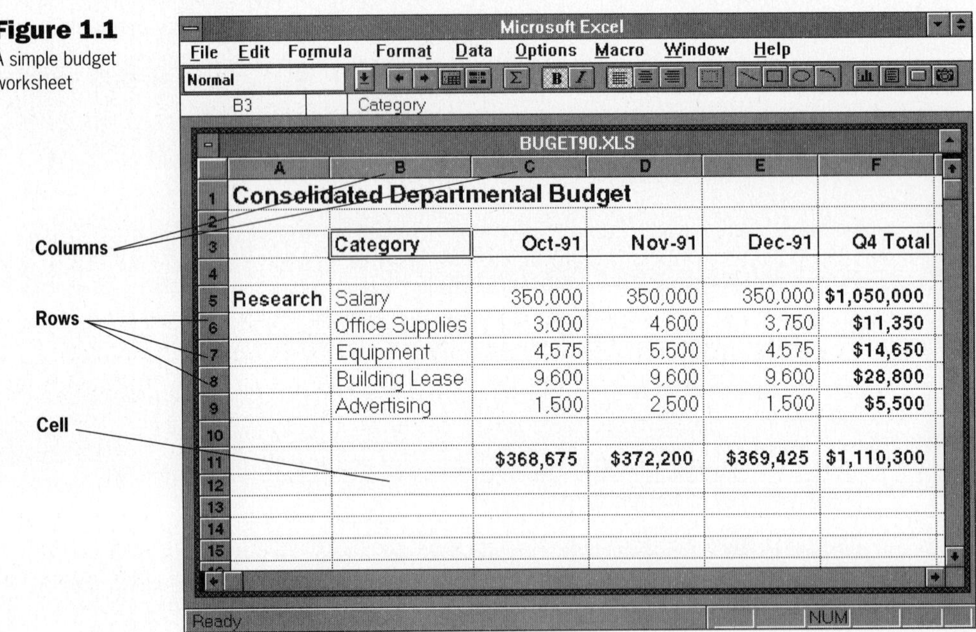

Figure 1.1 A simple budget worksheet

In our sample budget, you can see how much money was spent for office supplies in November. Find "Nov-91" across the top in column D, and look down the rows until you find the entry labeled "Office Supplies" in row 6. The point where a row and column intersect is called a *cell.* A cell generally represents one single number or piece of data. In the cell you just located, you can see just how much the Research Department spent on office supplies that month. The location of the cell is identified as D6. This is known as the cell's *reference.*

Navigating in the Excel Worksheet

In this section, you'll move around a bit within Excel and explore some of the features of the worksheet. First, you need to load Excel and get ready to work with the program.

Starting Excel

If you have not yet installed Excel on your system, turn to Appendix C. Assuming that you have accepted the default installation routine, you'll see a Program Group called Excel 3.0. To begin working with Excel:

1. Select the Excel 3.0 Program Group.
2. If you are using a mouse, double-click on the icon labeled Excel 3.0. If you are using the keyboard, use the arrow keys until the Excel 3.0 icon is highlighted and then press Enter.

After Excel displays its copyright logo, your screen should look like the one in Figure 1.2. Note the labels for the columns across the top (A, B, C, and so on) and the rows running down the left-hand side of the screen (1, 2, 3, and so on).

Before you proceed too far into the exercises, you also need to ensure you are using all of Excel's menus. Excel comes configured to use Short Menus—a subset of the total features available to you. Use the following steps to enable Excel's full menu system:

1. Click on the Options menu selection or press Alt-O.
2. Look at the end of the menu for the Full Menus selection and click on it or move the cursor to it and press Enter. If the last menu item on your Option menu says Short Menus, then you have already enabled the full menu system.

Cell References

By now, you might be wondering how to keep track of where you are and which cell is which. Excel uses two distinct methods of referring to cells. By default, Excel uses the convention of naming the columns starting with A and working through Z, then AA through AZ, then BA through BZ, and so on, all the way to column IV—256 columns in all. Rows are numbered sequentially starting at 1 and proceeding through 16,384. Although it sounds like an awful lot of cells—4,194,304 to be exact—you'll probably never use anywhere near that number. Filling up all of those cells depends mostly on how much memory you have installed in your computer.

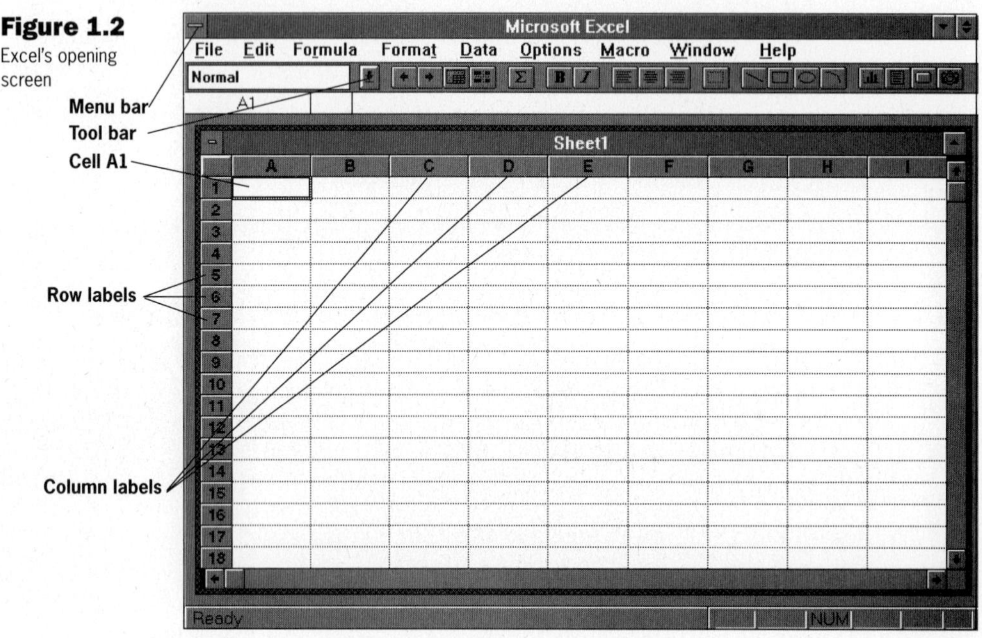

Figure 1.2
Excel's opening screen

Even if you could create one giant spreadsheet, you wouldn't want to; it would be too hard to keep track of everything logically. Instead, Excel offers a number of features designed to encourage you to create more numerous, but smaller, worksheets and link them together. You'll get the same result as you would with a big sheet, but you avoid memory problems and the risk of getting lost.

You can also choose to refer to cells in a worksheet in a different way. Another Microsoft spreadsheet, called MultiPlan, uses a convention of referring to a row number and then a column number, in that order. You can change Excel to use this *R1C1 format* if you wish. R1C1 stands for row 1 and column 1. It corresponds to cell A1 in the default naming method.

Now is a good time to experiment with the worksheet and change it from one display method to another. With your worksheet still on the screen as in Figure 1.2, look for the menu bar across the top of the screen. Then perform the following steps.

1. Click on Options, Workspace, or from the keyboard, press Alt-OW. The Workspace dialog box will appear, as shown in Figure 1.3.
2. Move the cursor to the check box marked R1C1 and click or press Enter.
3. Then click or press Enter on the OK command button.

The dialog box will disappear and the spreadsheet will be redisplayed with the column markers now labeled 1, 2, 3, and so on. Although most people prefer to work with the A1 method of cell references—it's easier to understand when you begin designing spreadsheet models—you might feel more comfortable with the R1C1 convention. Throughout this book, however, the A1 convention will be used.

Figure 1.3
Changing display options

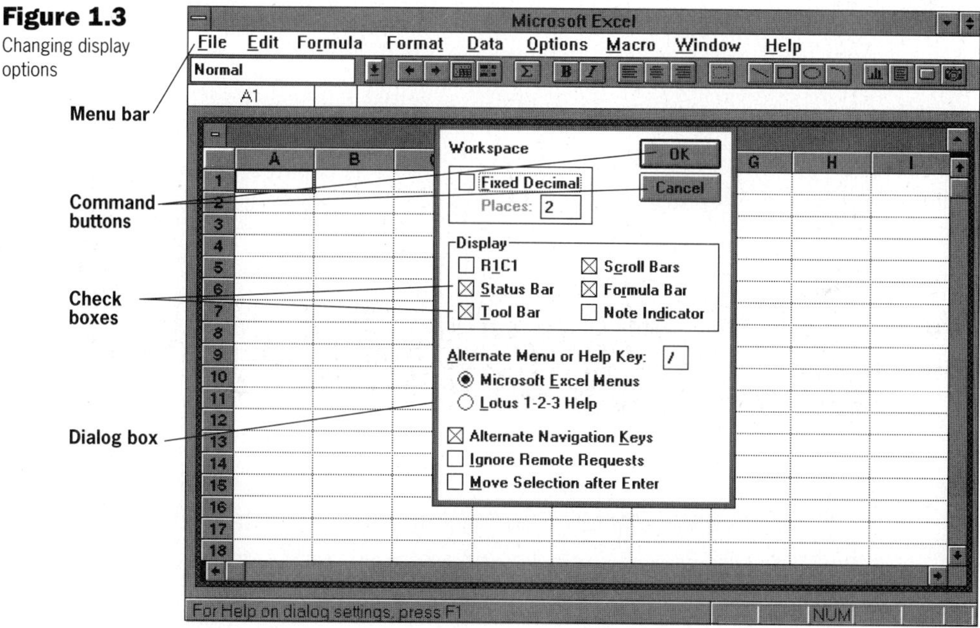

Moving Around the Worksheet

Now that you have selected the way you would like to work with Excel's cell references, it's time to learn how to move around within the worksheet. If you prefer to work with the keyboard, you can just move the cross-shaped cell pointer around with the arrow keys. However, using the mouse is even easier (most things in Excel are easier to do with a mouse). Just move the cell pointer until it is over the cell you wish to highlight and click the left mouse button once. (If you are going to be using the keyboard, refer to Appendix A for a brief explanation of Excel keypresses.)

The Concept of Ranges

Life with Excel (or any spreadsheet, for that matter) would quickly become tedious without the ability to carry out tasks on more than one cell at a time. Fortunately, Excel uses a concept known as ranges to define more than one cell. A *range* is any rectangular group of adjacent cells, including a single column of cells, a single row of cells, or even a single cell. The screen in Figure 1.4 shows several examples of valid ranges. Excel won't let you enter an invalid range, so don't worry about getting something wrong.

Figure 1.4
Valid Excel ranges

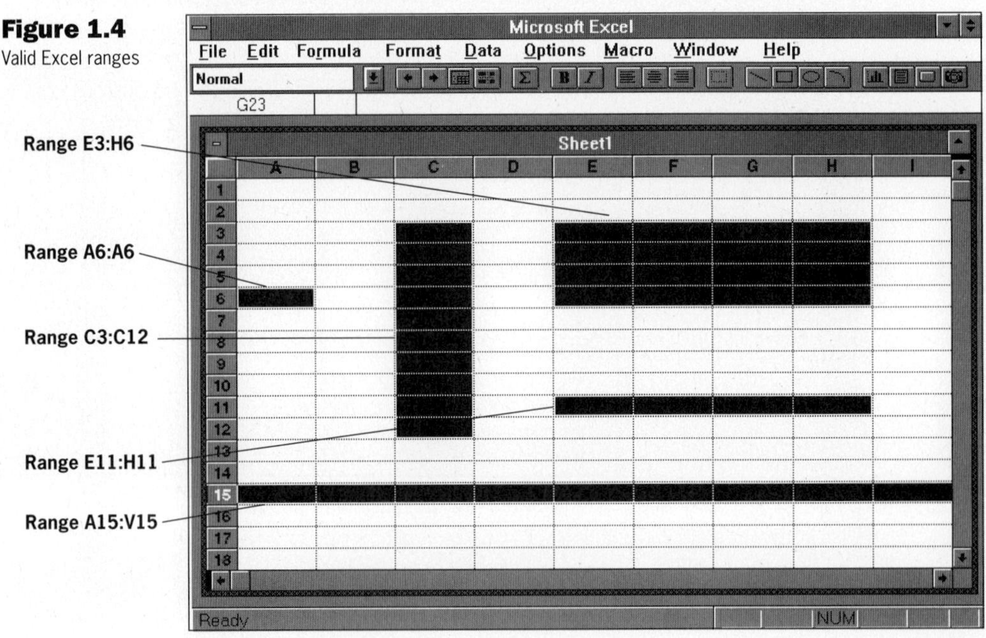

Once you have defined a range, you can copy information into it, format a group of cells within it, delete a group of cells, or apply some type of textual style to it, all at the same time.

Take a few moments to practice selecting ranges. There are two ways that you can select a range. If you use a mouse, you can use the following steps.

1. Place the cell pointer over the cell that you want to be the anchor of your range selection. The *anchor* cell will remain in place no matter how you move the cursor.
2. Click and hold down the left mouse button.
3. Move the mouse pointer (still holding down the left button) in any direction and watch while Excel highlights groups of cells.
4. Once you have selected the cells you want to include in your range, simply release the left mouse button.

If you prefer to use keyboard equivalents, follow these steps to select a range:

1. Use the arrow keys to place the cell pointer in the anchor cell.
2. Press and hold down the Shift key while pressing the arrow keys in the direction of the cells that you want to highlight.
3. When you have painted the range that you want, let go of the Shift key.

The concept of ranges will come up throughout this book. You'll see in Chapter 3, for example, how you can assign a name to a particular range of cells and then refer to that *named range* in calculations and formulas. You'll also see how you can select noncontiguous groups of cells (still rectangular, however) when you want to carry out formatting commands.

You will find it useful from time to time to select entire rows or columns or even groups of rows or columns. Here's an example of how to select one whole column:

1. Move the cell pointer until it is over the C at the top of the column.
2. Click the mouse once. The entire column becomes shaded, indicating that any subsequent action that you choose will be carried out on that entire column.

You can use the same technique to select an entire row. Try it on row 5.

It's just as easy to select a group of rows or columns. Here is an example of selecting a group of columns:

1. Move the cell pointer over column C.
2. Click and hold down the left mouse button.
3. Move two columns to the right, so that your cell pointer is located directly over column E. Watch the highlight move with you.

4. Release the left mouse button.

The same technique applies to selecting groups of rows.

Finally, there will be times when you want to highlight the entire worksheet. You could go to cell A1 and then drag down and to the right until you reached the end of your data. This method isn't always practical, however; you might have your worksheet set up in such a way that you can't see the entire worksheet. The easiest way to ensure that you've highlighted every cell is to use the following method.

1. Position the cell pointer over the blank rectangular box just to the left of column A and directly above row 1.
2. Click on that button. At once, the entire spreadsheet becomes highlighted.

The worksheet is now one giant range.

Entering Information

Now you are ready to begin constructing our budget model by entering some information into the worksheet. Generally, Excel uses two kinds of information: text and numbers (dates and times are treated as numbers by Excel). There are some variations on this theme, but for the most part, text and numbers are what you will use most frequently in Excel. Here's a good rule of thumb: If the cell contains any one of the characters + - = . , ( ) % $, Excel considers it to be a number; otherwise, it is text.

Although there is a large number of cells available in Excel, keep in mind that each cell can hold only up to 255 characters. You won't often use all 255 characters for text, but it's possible to create some pretty complex formulas that come close to bumping up against the limit.

Entering Text Headings

First, you'll add the headings for the departmental budget:

1. Move the cell pointer to cell A1. Use the arrow keys or the mouse to highlight cell A1.
2. Type **Consolidated Departmental Budget** and press Enter.

When you press the Enter key, the text is placed in cell A1. Your worksheet should look something like the one in Figure 1.5. Notice that the text in cell A1 overflows from that cell into two other cells. It's important to remember that the text is not stored in cells B1 and C1—all of the text is stored in cell A1 but is simply displayed in adjoining cells. However,

Excel does not permit numeric data to overflow into other cells. Instead it displays a series of # symbols in the cell, indicating there is more data that can be shown.

Figure 1.5
First text heading

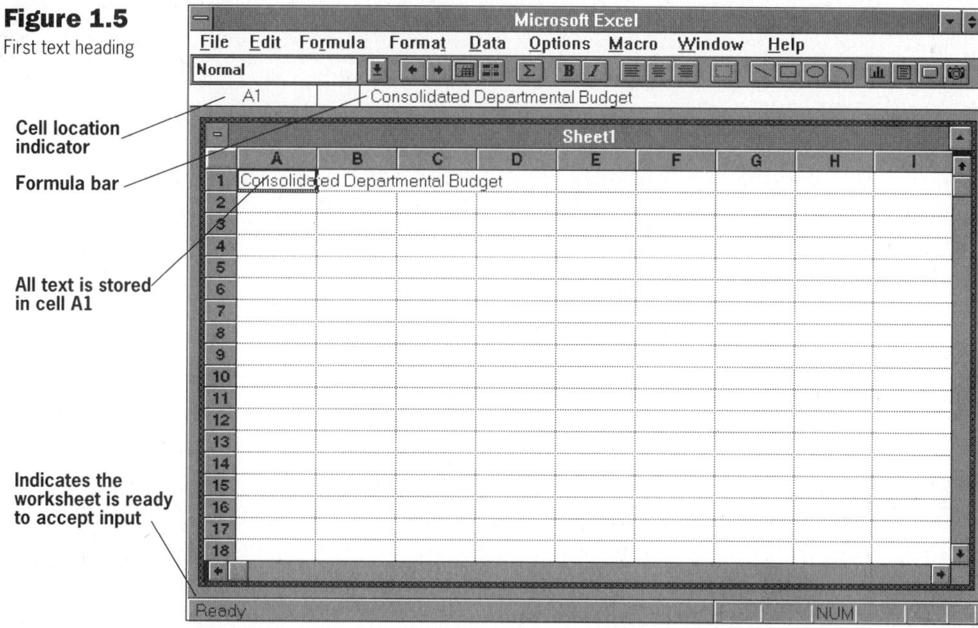

Note. Instead of pressing Enter after each number that you enter, just press the Down Arrow key if you want to go down to the next cell or the Right Arrow key if you want to move to the right.

Also note that the same text is displayed in the formula bar in the center of the upper portion of the screen. The *formula bar* always shows the actual contents of the cells. In the case of text, the contents of the formula bar and the actual cell will be the same. This is not necessarily true of numbers, however. The reason for that will be explained in the discussion of formulas in Chapter 3.

Now, continue to enter textual headings in other cells:

1. Use the mouse or the arrow keys to move the cell pointer to cell A5.
2. Enter the label **Research** and press the Enter key.
3. Enter the remaining headings and labels for the worksheet in the same way. Refer to Figure 1.1 for the contents of cells B5 through B9 and B3 through F3.

When you have finished, your worksheet should resemble the one shown in Figure 1.6.

As you entered some of the headings, you may have noticed that the contents of the formula bar and the actual cell were identical but that when you entered the first of the monthly headings (Oct-91), the contents of the formula bar changed as shown in Figure 1.7.

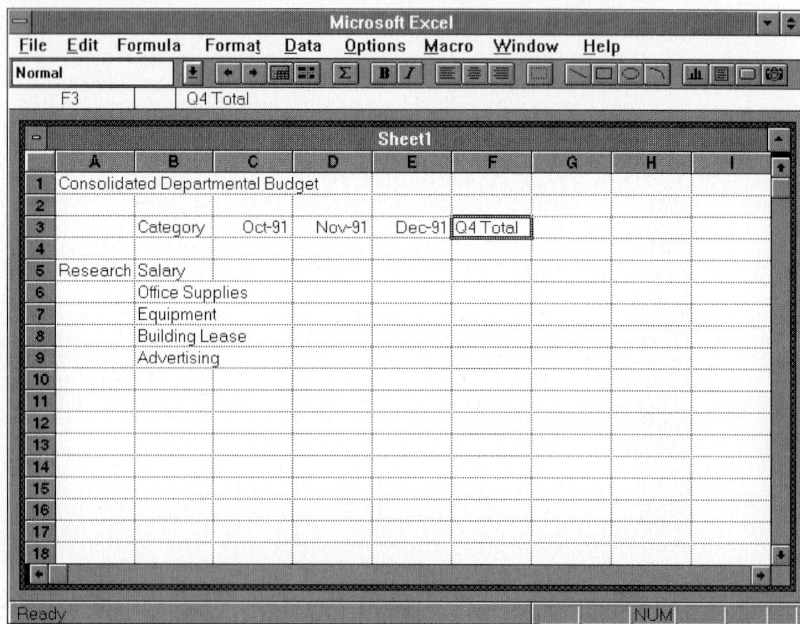

Figure 1.6 All headings and tables in place

Click on one of the cells that contain date headings (C3, D3, or E3) and you'll see the difference. Excel is smart enough to realize that you really wanted to enter a date there instead of regular text. We'll come back to Excel's treatment of dates in Chapter 5.

Entering Numbers

You're almost done with the skeleton of our model. It's time to enter the actual values that you want to model, calculate, and graph. Entering numbers is just like entering text, although Excel stores and displays numbers slightly differently than text.

To enter the numbers, follow these steps:

1. Move the cell pointer to cell C5 and enter the first value: type **350000** and press Enter.

2. Referring to Figure 1.1, enter the remaining values, but only from cells C5 through to E9.

Don't enter the numbers in column F or those in row 11. Those are formulas that calculate totals. We'll get to them in Chapter 3.

Figure 1.7
Formula bar versus cell contents

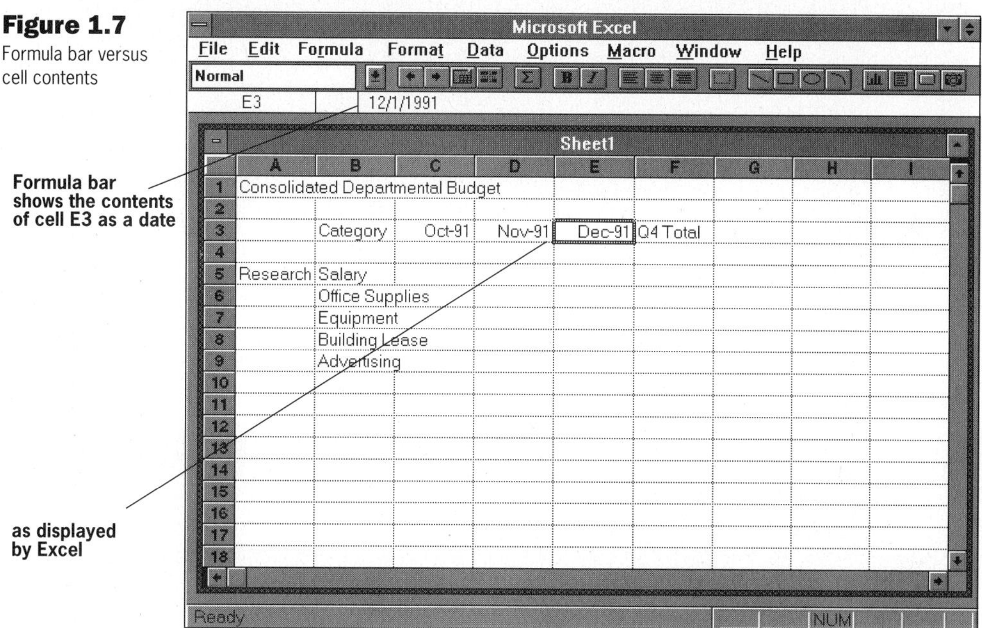

Notice that the numbers don't quite match the ones in our budget worksheet. Be patient—the reasons that Excel often stores and displays numbers differently are explained in Chapter 5, where you'll also learn how to format numbers. When you've finished entering numbers, your worksheet will look something like the one in Figure 1.8.

Correcting Mistakes

As you enter any sort of information—text, numbers, formulas, and so on—into your worksheets, you're bound to make mistakes. Fortunately, with Excel, it's easy to fix your goof.

If you're right in the middle of entering some information into a cell and you have not pressed the Enter key, just use the Backspace key to erase the mistake and retype the correct information. Try the following steps.

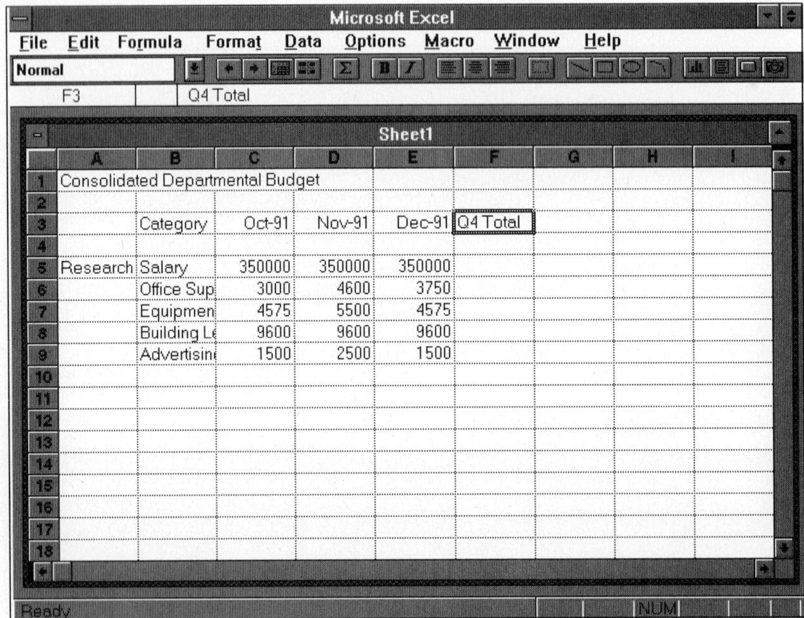

Figure 1.8
Budget worksheet with basic data

1. Place the cell pointer in cell A2.
2. Type **First Qtr.** but don't press the Enter key. Note that what you are typing is visible in the formula bar.
3. Press the Backspace key three times to erase the last three characters that you typed.
4. Complete the word by typing **uarter**.
5. Complete the entry by pressing the Enter key.

Once you have pressed Enter, Excel considers your entry to be done, and you have to use some other method of correcting a mistake. To fix a mistake after you have pressed the Enter key, you need only type over your error. Say you really wanted to enter **Fourth Qtr.** in cell A2. Follow these steps:

1. If you're not there, position the cell pointer over cell A2.
2. Type **Fourth Qtr.**, which is the text you want to replace the contents of A2 with.

3. Complete the entry by pressing the Enter key.

Finally, there are times when it's easier to edit the contents of a cell without having to retype the contents of the entire cell. Perhaps you have a long and intricate formula and all you want to do is change one number. Try this:

1. Move to cell A1 and press the F2 key.
2. Look at the formula bar and note that the cursor now appears at the end of the cell contents.
3. Use the Backspace key or the Arrow keys (depending on whether you want to delete some of the characters) to move within the cell contents.
4. When you finish editing the cell contents, just press Enter to tell Excel that you have finished.

Saving Your Work

The last task to accomplish is to save the model that you've worked hard to create. Excel saves all data files with a number of different file name extensions (see Appendix A). If you do not intervene, it will automatically assign certain extensions to its files. For instance, worksheet files like the one you've been working on are saved with the extension of .XLS, while chart files get an extension of .XLC. Finally, macro sheets (covered more thoroughly in Chapter 13) are given an .XLM extension.

Saving your file is very simple. You haven't yet given Excel a name for your file, but Excel has already named the file on your behalf. Look at the top of the window that you've been working in; Excel has probably put the words "Sheet1" or "Sheet2" up there. It's okay to name your worksheets that way, but these names don't help you remember what is in the files when you want to come back and work on them again. It is better to give your files names that are as descriptive as possible.

If you want to replace the name that Excel uses, just type a new name for the file. Remember that your file name must conform to DOS's restrictive eight-character limit. Do this now:

1. Click on File, Save As. The Save As dialog box appears, as shown in Figure 1.9.
2. Type **Budget1**.
3. Click on OK to complete the command.

Excel will save your file with the name BUDGET1.XLS.

To save your file under the default name, you click on File, Save As, and then on the OK command button. Excel saves the file with that name and an .XLS file extension.

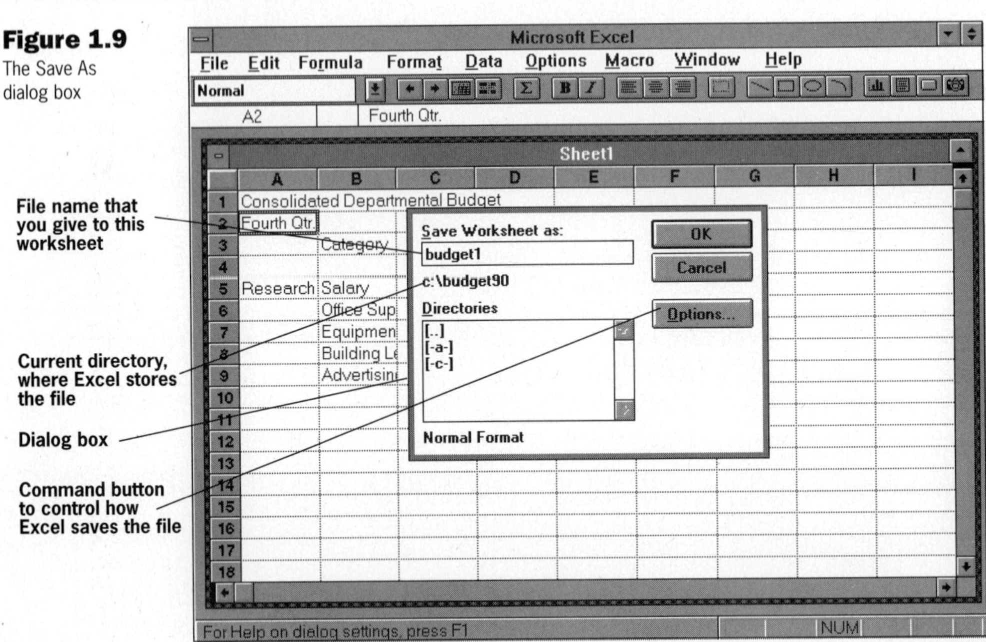

Figure 1.9
The Save As dialog box

Note that Excel displays the current directory just below the file name prompt. If you want to change the destination directory—where Excel will save the file—you can do so here (see Appendix A for more on directories). Finally, Figure 1.9 also shows a command button you can use to change the way Excel saves the file and to indicate whether you want your file to have a password (see Chapter 10).

As soon as you click on OK to save the file, Excel saves the file to disk and alters the name of the file in the worksheet window bar. Now the new name is displayed there to let you know which document you are currently working on. After saving your worksheet for the first time, it should look like the one in Figure 1.10.

Save Versus Save As

Excel makes a slight distinction between two commands on the File menu. If you have already given your file a name or if you have retrieved a file that was already on disk and then click on the Save command, Excel will just write the latest changes to disk without asking for your permission. If, however, you start from scratch or if you want to give a new name to an existing file, Save As lets you save a file to disk with a new name.

Figure 1.10
The worksheet after saving the file for the first time

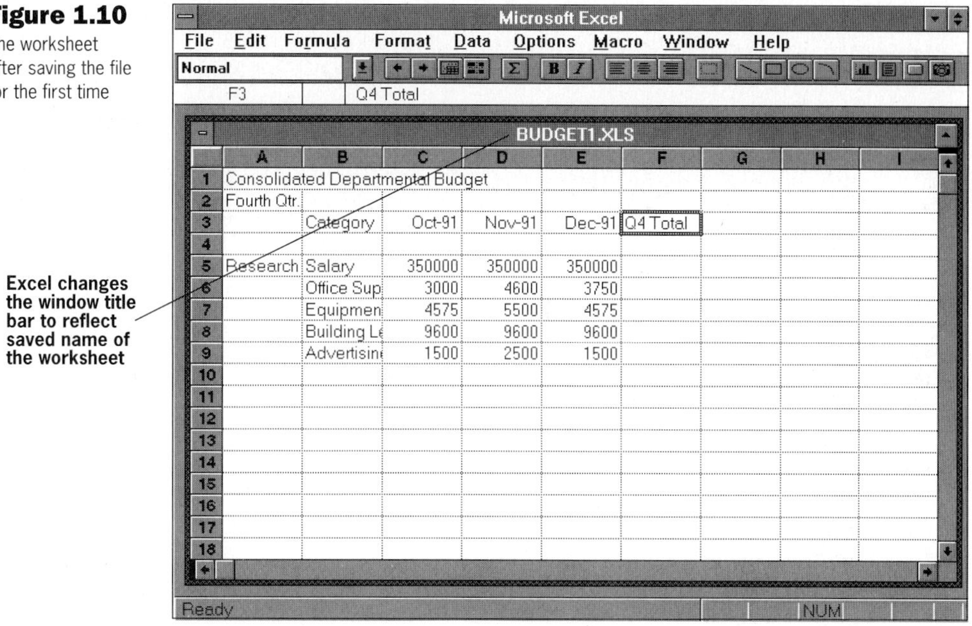

Excel changes the window title bar to reflect saved name of the worksheet

"You can never save your files often enough," is the chant of someone who has lost three hours' worth of data since last saving the worksheet. Why not just pause every once in a while to save the latest version of what you're working on? Once you get used to it, it doesn't take up any time at all.

Creating Backup Files

One way to reduce the risk of lost data is to configure Excel so the program creates a backup file every time you save a new version. If you do so, the first time you save a new file, Excel creates the file on disk with the name that you specify, say, BUDGET1.XLS. The next time you save that file, Excel will first rename BUDGET1.XLS as BUDGET1.BAK and then save the *current* version of the worksheet under the name BUDGET1.XLS. Excel will keep only two versions of the file: the newest version, which carries the name that you assigned it, and the next-to-most-recent version, which has a .BAK file extension.

To configure Excel to use backup files, use the following steps:

1. Click on File, Save As.

2. Choose the Options button.

3. Click on the check box marked Create Backup File.
4. Choose OK.

The screen in Figure 1.11 shows the dialog box that you'll see after you click on the options button.

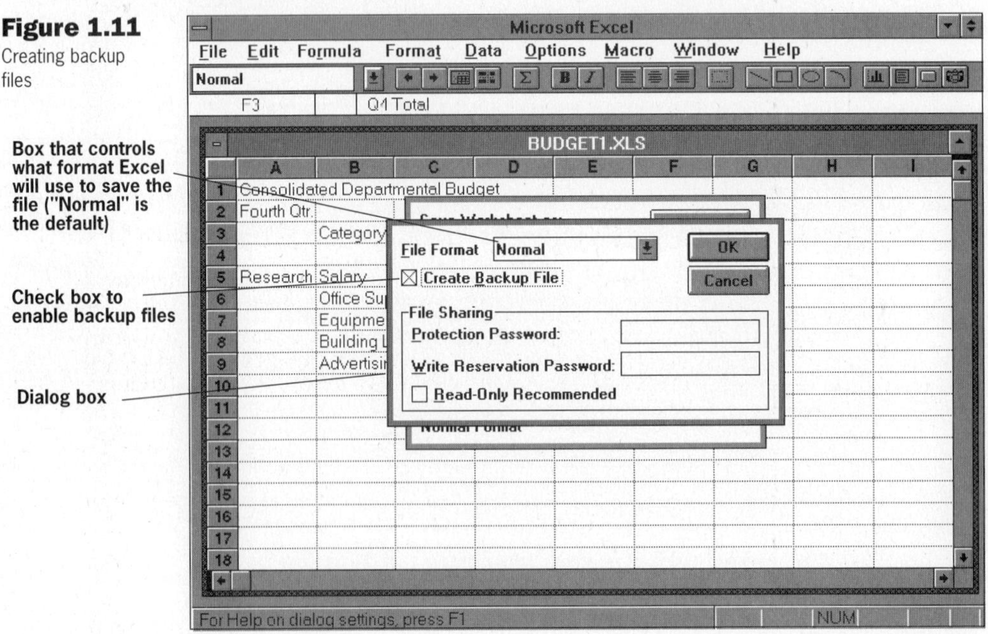

Figure 1.11
Creating backup files

Quitting Excel

When you have finished these exercises, it's time to put Excel 3.0 away and relax. It's easy to exit from Excel, and there is more than one way to do it.

To quit by using the menus, click on File, Exit. If you have done some work on a file but have not saved it, Excel will ask you if you want to save the file or not. If you have not given the file a name and you elect to save it, Excel will bring up the Save As dialog box and prompt you for a name. Figure 1.12 shows the File menu with the Exit command at the bottom of the menu.

You can also quit Excel via a keyboard shortcut. There are a number of these shortcuts within Excel. Many of them are standard to all Windows-based applications, but some are not. One way to quit with the keyboard is to press Alt-F4. You will immediately exit from Excel and whatever worksheet you were working on. If you have done some work on a file but have not saved it, Excel will ask you if you want to save the file or not. If you have not given the file a name and you elect to save it, Excel will bring up the Save As dialog box and prompt you for a name.

There is one other way to exit from Excel. (Note that it, like Alt-F4, will work with any Windows application.) Double-click on the Control menu bar (see Figure 1.12). You will immediately exit from Excel and any worksheet that you were working on. If you have done some work on a file but have not saved it, Excel will ask you if you want to save the file or not. If you have not given the file a name and you elect to save it, Excel will bring up the Save As dialog box and prompt you for a name.

Figure 1.12
First text heading

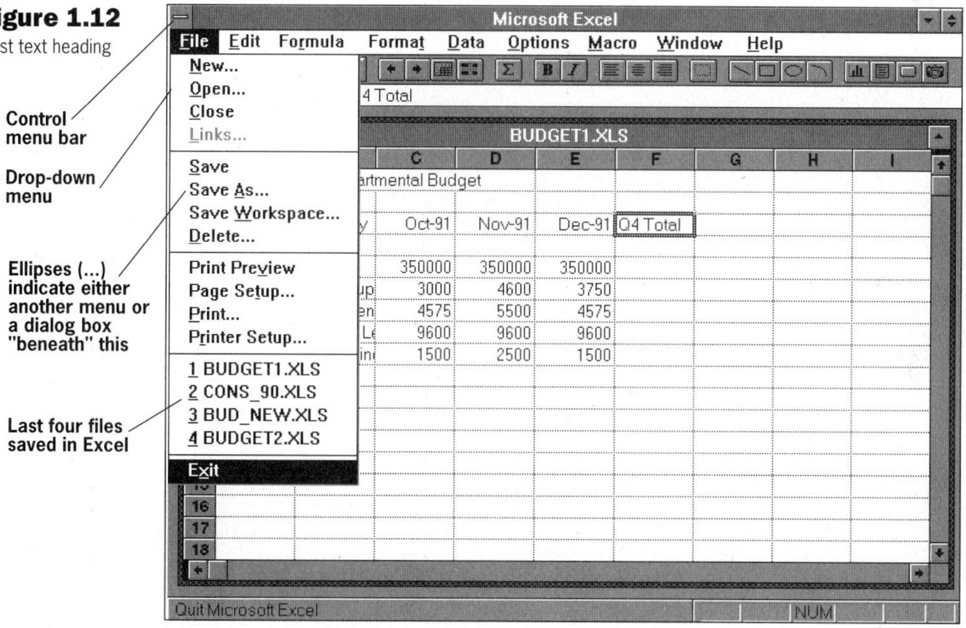

Control menu bar

Drop-down menu

Ellipses (...) indicate either another menu or a dialog box "beneath" this

Last four files saved in Excel

CHAPTER

2

Editing and Enhancing the Worksheet

Editing the Worksheet

Basic Presentation Features

Annotating Cells

Saving Your Work

IN CHAPTER 1 YOU LEARNED THE BASIC STEPS OF CREATING A WORKSHEET in Excel 3.0. In this chapter, and later on in Chapter 5, you'll have a chance to learn new techniques for presenting and formatting your data in a pleasing way. There are a number of things you can do to enhance the appearance of your worksheet, such as changing the text attributes (font, type size, boldface, and so on) and adding shading and borders. As you can see in Figures 2.1 and 2.2, there is a lot of difference between a plain, drab worksheet, and one that has been enhanced.

Figure 2.1
Worksheet (in progress) before formatting and enhancement

Microsoft Excel - BUDGET1.XLS

File Edit Formula Format Data Options Macro Window Help

Normal

F3 Q4 Total

	A	B	C	D	E	F
1	Consolidated Departmental Budget					
2	Fourth Qtr.					
3		Category	Oct-91	Nov-91	Dec-91	Q4 Total
4						
5	Research	Salary	350000	350000	350000	
6		Office Sup	3000	4600	3750	
7		Equipmen	4575	5500	4575	
8		Building Le	9600	9600	9600	
9		Advertisin	1500	2500	1500	

Ready NUM

But before you can have a worksheet that looks like Figure 2.2, you need something to work with. First, you'll retrieve the spreadsheet you created in Chapter 1 from the disk where it was stored. Then you'll spend a bit of time learning some further basic skills that will help you with the material that comes later.

Figure 2.2 Finished worksheet—with shading, borders, and text enhancements

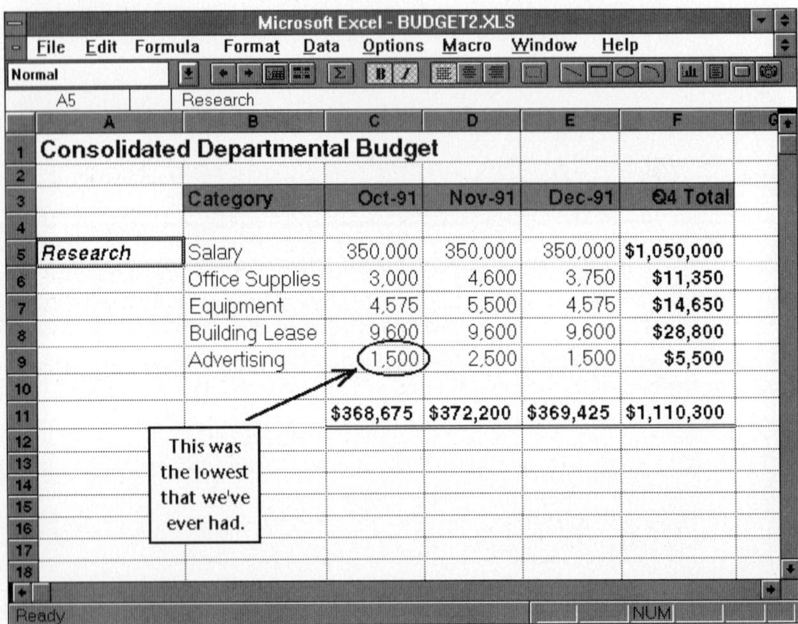

Editing the Worksheet

Remember that at the end of Chapter 1 you saved your file to disk. If nothing has gone wrong in the meantime, it should still be there when you go back to look for it. First you need to start Excel, then you can look for the worksheet.

Opening an Existing Worksheet

To find the worksheet, follow these steps from the opening screen:

1. Click on File.
2. Look at the bottom of the drop-down menu, where the names of recently created files are displayed. You should see the file named BUDGET1.XLS. Figure 2.3 shows this menu.

3. Select that file and either press the Enter key or double-click on the file name. The worksheet will be loaded into memory, where you can work on it. (If BUDGET1.XLS doesn't appear in the list, use the File, Open option to enter the file name and directory path. See Appendix A for information on directory structures.)

Figure 2.3
Listing of the last four files saved

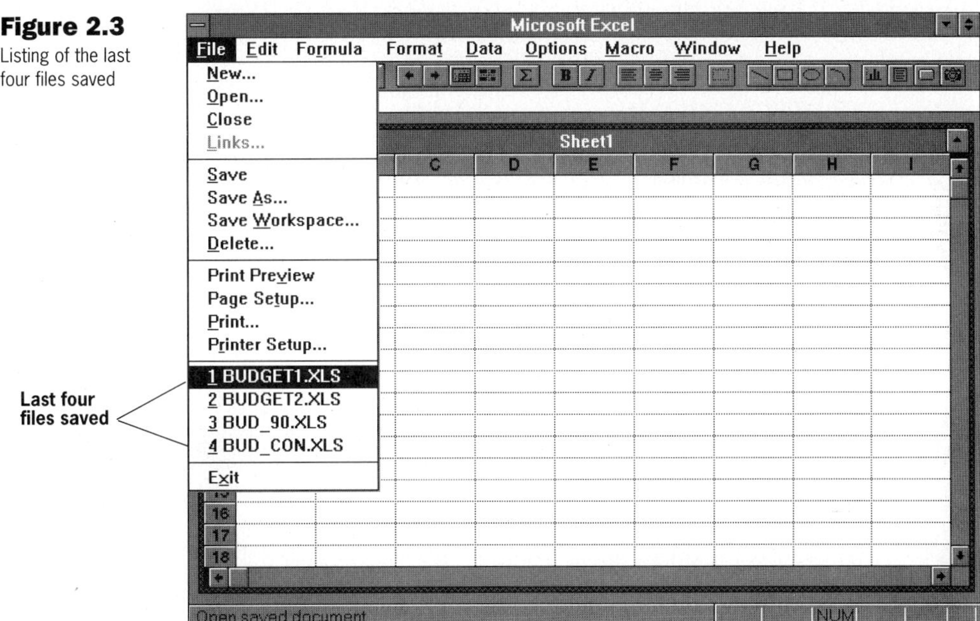

Excel's ability to recall the last four worksheets you created is new to version 3.0. Excel will remember the names and locations of these files, even if they are in different subdirectories.

How Excel Displays Data in Columns

Take a look again at Figure 2.1. You can see that some of the text labels you entered in the last chapter seem to be truncated at the point where they run into the next column. Excel abides by certain rules in displaying data on the worksheet. One of those rules is that text will be displayed in its entirety only if there is nothing in the next cell to the right. Thus, in Figure 2.1 the text in cell A1 displays correctly because there is nothing stored in cell B1. On the other hand, the labels that are stored in column B, starting at B5, are truncated because there are numeric values in the adjacent cells to the right.

With numeric values, Excel will never let one number appear to overlap another because of the possibility of error. Instead, if a number is too big to be displayed in a column, Excel displays # symbols to indicate that you need to widen the column. (This is covered in detail in Chapter 3.) Likewise, when displaying *textual* data (that is, anything but numeric data), where the data is too long to fit into one cell you also need to change the width of the column.

Changing Column Widths

As with many operations in Excel, there are several ways to adjust the width of the columns, both from menus and with the mouse. Remember that when you change the width of the column, you are not changing the contents of the column, only what portion of the column is being displayed.

You can change the column width from a menu by specifying a number that corresponds to the number of characters you want to fit into the cell. By default, every column begins 8.43 characters wide, but they can be as wide as 255 characters and as narrow as less than 1 character.

You can also change the width of a column by selecting Best Fit from the menus. By changing the columns this way, you are asking Excel to calculate how wide it must make the column in order to display the longest piece of data in that column.

Probably the simplest way to adjust columns is with the mouse. Instructions for each of these methods are given below.

Using Menu Commands

Use the following steps to change the width of a column with menu commands:

1. Highlight column A by clicking on the A in the column bar.
2. Click on Format, Column Width. A dialog box appears.
3. Enter the desired width of the column, expressed in the number of characters of text you want to fit. For this exercise, type **13**.
4. Click on OK to complete the command.

Tip. To quickly format a column to have the best fit possible, highlight the column that you want to change. Then, place the cell pointer in the column bar on the dividing line to the right of the column. Double-click and Excel will set the column width of the column to the longest entry in that column.

When you select the column that you want to adjust, you can either highlight the entire column by clicking in the column bar, or you can click on a single cell that lies within the column you want to adjust.

Using Best Fit

Alternatively, you can ask Excel to calculate and apply the optimal column width for your highlighted column by choosing the Best Fit option. Follow these steps to do so:

1. Highlight column B.

2. Click on Format, Column Width. A dialog box appears.
3. Click on the Best Fit button.

Excel will immediately calculate and set the column width necessary to display the largest entry in that column. But note that if you go into the worksheet later and make an entry or label longer than the current column width, you will have to reselect the column, and go through the Best Fit process again. Figure 2.4 shows the worksheet after you have applied Best Fit to column B.

Figure 2.4
Worksheet after selecting Best Fit

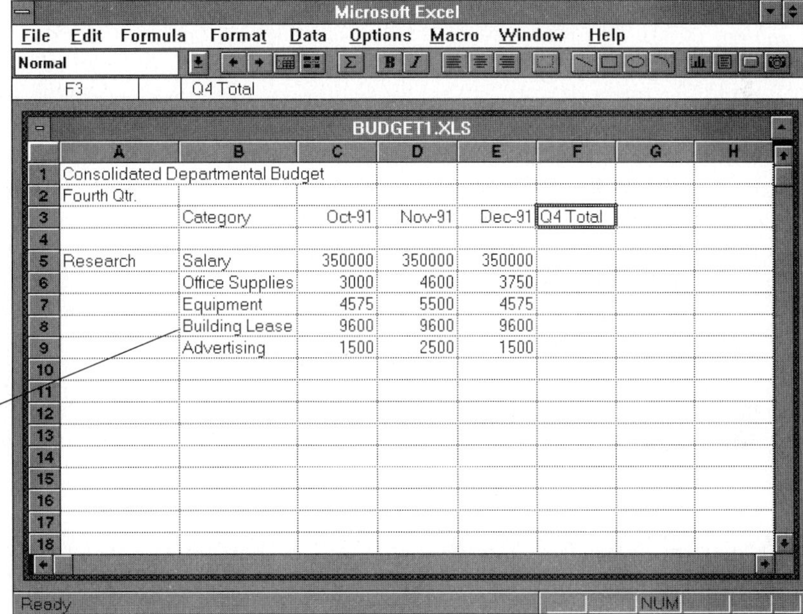

Excel calculates the best column width based on the longest cell contents

Using the Mouse

As already noted, the preferred way to work in Excel is with a mouse. If you would rather use the mouse to change the width of columns, use the following steps to adjust the width of column B:

1. Carefully move the mouse pointer until it is directly over the dividing line between column B and column C in the column labels.

2. When you have correctly positioned the mouse pointer over the column border divider, it changes shape to look like a vertical line with arrows pointing out the right and left sides.
3. Depress the left mouse button and hold it down while you move the column border to the left or right, respectively shrinking or enlarging the column.
4. When the column width is adjusted to your satisfaction, release the left mouse button to complete the command.

Changing a Range of Columns

Remember that you can carry out a set of instructions not only on a single cell or column, but on a range of cells or range of columns. In this case, it's possible to change the column widths on any number of columns at the same time:

1. Highlight the range of columns that you plan to change. For this exercise, select columns C, D, E, and F.
2. Click on Format, Column Width. A dialog box appears.
3. Type **12**.
4. Click on OK to complete your command.

Excel will size each of the columns you selected to the width you entered. Figure 2.5 illustrates the result of setting all four columns to 12 characters wide.

Changing Row Heights

Changing the heights of the rows works basically the same as changing the widths of the columns. You can do it manually or have Excel automatically adjust the height of the row to correspond to the largest font size on that row—much as the Best Fit feature accommodates the largest entry in a column.

Changing a Single Row

First let's see how Excel handles the job of automatically adjusting the row heights to accommodate changes in font size. Unlike column width, which is measured in terms of characters, row height is measured in points, as are fonts. (A *point* is a unit of measure used in typography and printing that is equal to $^{1}/_{72}$ of an inch.) The standard row height is 12.75 points, but you can change this later, if you wish. For now, watch what happens when you change the size of the font.

1. Highlight row 3 by clicking on the row number in the row bar.
2. Click on Format, Font. A dialog box appears.
3. In the dialog box, click on 16 as the font size. Note that the sample box changes to show what the text will look like when you apply the current selection. (Depending on your printer, 16 may not be available. You can either type 16 in the small box above the list or select the next nearest point value, such as 14 or 18 points.)
4. Click on OK to carry out your command.

Figure 2.5
Worksheet after all four columns have been set to 12 characters

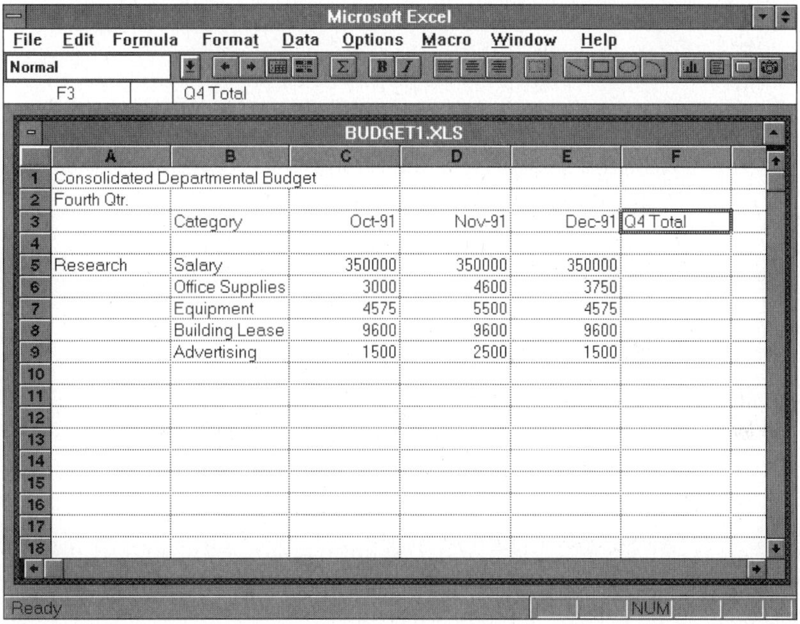

	A	B	C	D	E	F
1	Consolidated Departmental Budget					
2	Fourth Qtr.					
3		Category	Oct-91	Nov-91	Dec-91	Q4 Total
4						
5	Research	Salary	350000	350000	350000	
6		Office Supplies	3000	4600	3750	
7		Equipment	4575	5500	4575	
8		Building Lease	9600	9600	9600	
9		Advertising	1500	2500	1500	
10						
11						
12						
13						
14						
15						
16						
17						
18						

Notice that Excel not only changed the size of the text in your selected row, but also adjusted the row height to accommodate the new text size. Since your choice of point size was larger than Excel's standard row height, the program made the row-width adjustment for you. See Figure 2.6 for an example.

And what if you want to change the row heights manually? No problem. Like most operations and procedures in Excel, there are several ways to accomplish the same thing. Try the following exercise.

Figure 2.6
Listing of the last four files saved

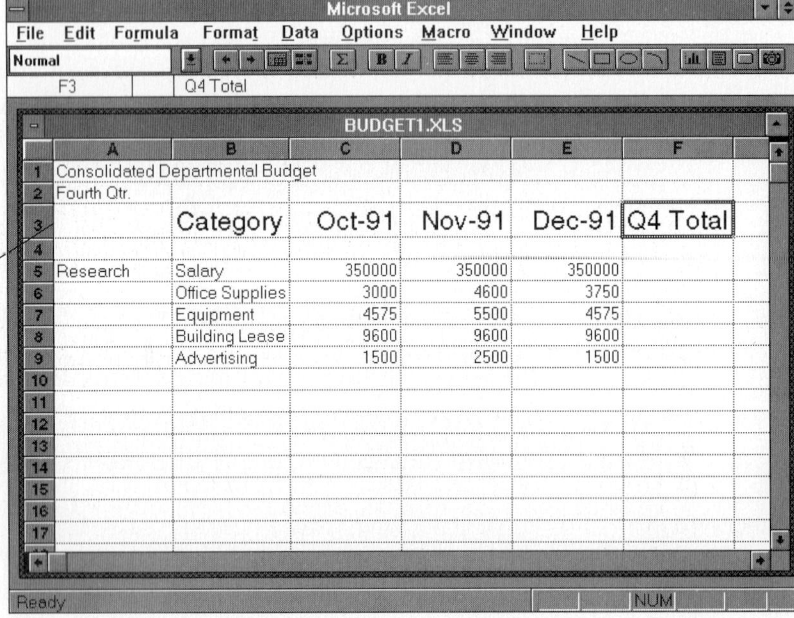

1. Move the cell pointer to the row bar and carefully position it on the dividing line between rows 3 and 4. As when you're changing the column width, watch for the cell pointer to change shape as you slowly pass it over the dividing line between the two rows.

Tip. You don't have to select a range of columns or rows from the column or row bar. Instead, just select a range of cells on the worksheet contained in the columns or rows you want to change. For example, if you wanted to change rows 2, 3, and 4, you would just select a range of cells within those rows, for instance E2 to G4.

2. Depress the left mouse button and, while holding it down, drag the line representing the row height up or down, respectively increasing or decreasing the row height.

3. When the row reaches the height you want, release the mouse button.

The key to getting this trick right is to remember that you must position the mouse pointer on the dividing line *beneath* the row you want to change.

Changing a Range of Rows

You can change the height of a range of rows just as if you were adjusting a single row:

1. Highlight the range of rows you want to adjust. For this exercise, highlight rows 2, 3, and 4.

2. Click on Format, Row Height. A dialog box appears.

3. Type in the new row height that you want. Use **22** for now.
4. Click on OK to complete your command. Figure 2.7 shows the result of this exercise.

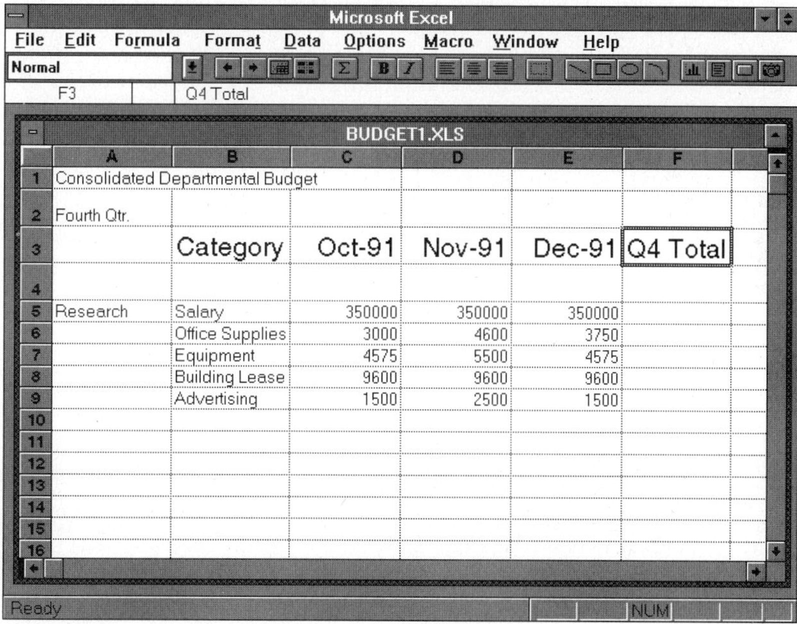

Figure 2.7 Worksheet after changing the row height to 22 points

The Format Row Height dialog box is shown below. If you leave the Standard Height option checked, Excel will automatically adjust the height of each row to fit the point size of the largest font in that row.

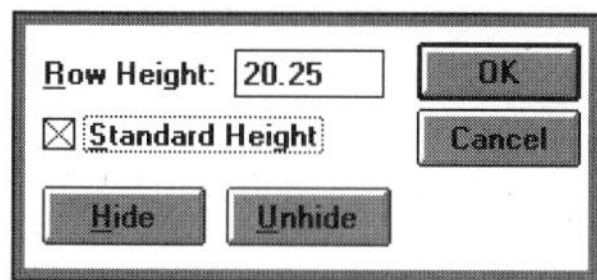

Text Alignment

By default, any time you enter text into an Excel worksheet, Excel will align that text against the left-hand side of the cell. The following exercises will show you how to change this alignment. As with many procedures in Excel, there is more than one way to accomplish the task, and both methods are given here so that you can decide which one is faster and easier for you.

Before you begin, however, you'll need to change the worksheet text back to its original size and change the width of the rows back to the default:

1. Highlight row 3 by clicking on the 3 in the row bar.
2. Click on Format, Font.
3. In the dialog box that appears, click on 10 for the font size.
4. Click on OK to complete the command.
5. Highlight rows 2, 3, and 4.
6. Click on Format, Row Height. Another dialog box appears.
7. Click on Standard Height.
8. Click on OK to complete the command.

Before moving on, make sure your worksheet looks like the one shown in Figure 2.8.

Figure 2.8 Worksheet with default cell alignment

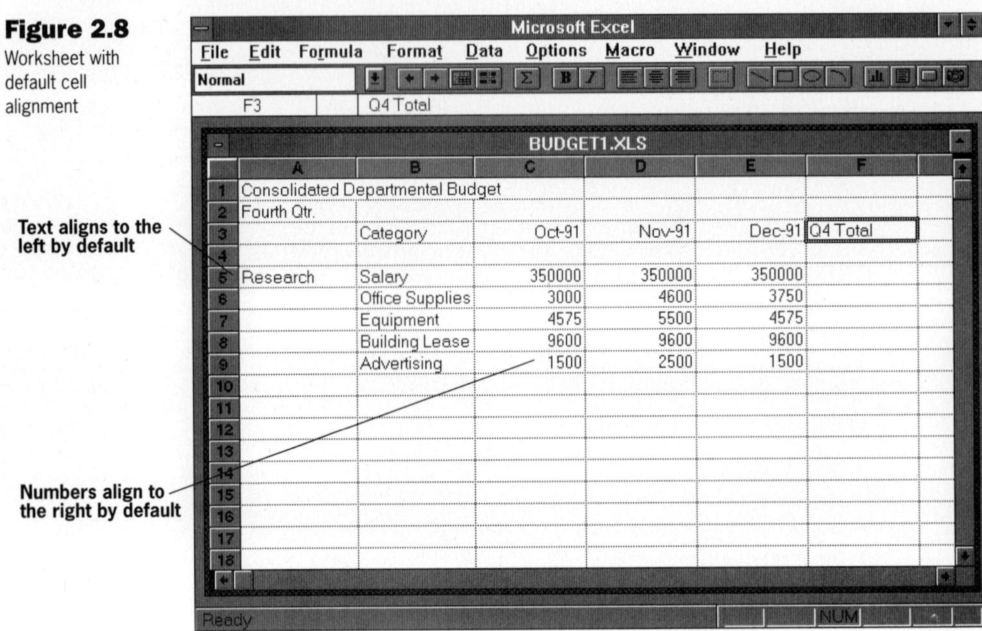

Changing the alignment of the data in the cells is just a couple of menus or a mouse-click away:

1. Highlight cell F3.
2. Click on Format, Alignment. You should see a dialog box like the one shown here:

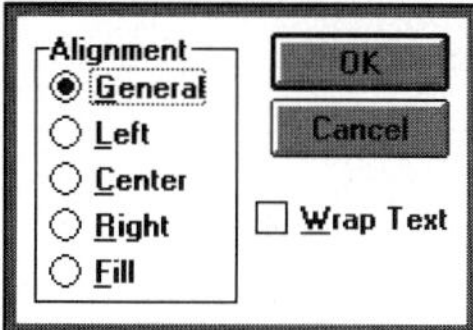

3. Choose Right.
4. Click on OK to complete the command.

You can use this procedure again to set the contents of other cells to be right- or left-aligned or centered, but there is another way to accomplish the same task in Excel 3.0. Remember that Microsoft has placed many frequently used functions on the toolbar. Three of those functions relate to data alignment within a cell or range of cells. Try this:

1. Highlight the range of cells from B5 to B9.
2. Move the mouse pointer into the toolbar and click once on the icon that represents right alignment. A detail of the toolbar is shown here:

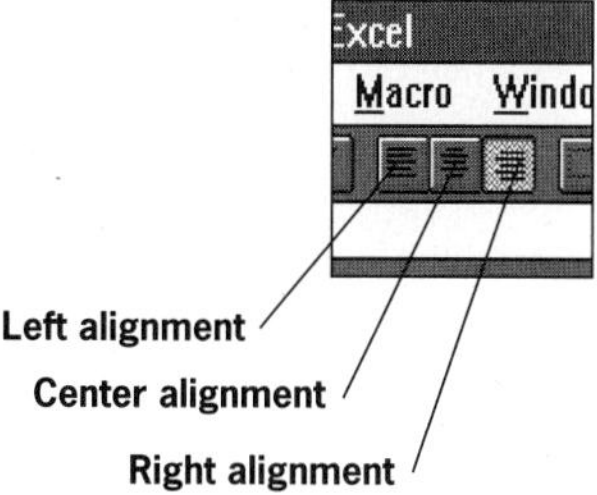

Figure 2.9 shows the results of clicking on the right-alignment icon.

This icon (and many other icons on the toolbar) acts as a *toggle switch,* enabling or disabling a certain action. In the case of an alignment icon this means if you click on it once, the cell contents will be aligned according to the icon. If you click on it again, the contents will revert back to the default left-justification.

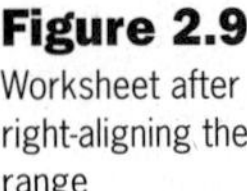

Figure 2.9
Worksheet after right-aligning the range

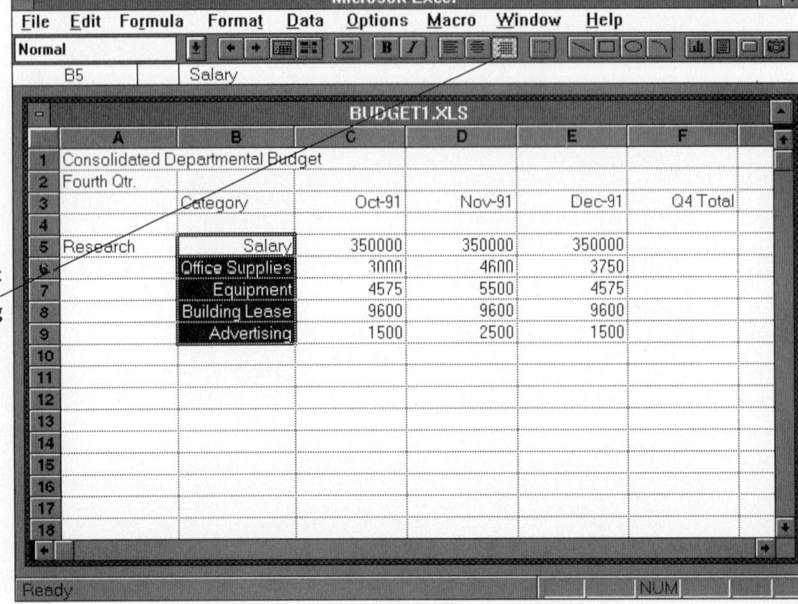

The right alignment icon appears to be depressed, showing that the highlighted cells are aligned to the right

Now is a good time to experiment a bit with the way alignment, column heights, and row widths work. When you're ready, before we move on to more editing commands, make sure that your worksheet looks like Figure 2.10. (Click on the right-alignment icon again, if necessary.)

Also, be sure to save your worksheet at that point. The next section of this chapter will present some techniques for adding and removing rows, columns, and cells. After you complete those exercises, you will be asked to discard the changes you made and load a "clean" version of the worksheet. Thus, you will need the worksheet as it stands now.

To save the worksheet, simply click on File, Save. You choose Save at this point instead of Save As because the worksheet has already been given a name.

Deleting Data, Rows, and Columns

Now—before you get too far into cell formatting and basic presentation features—is a good time to learn some of the commands for removing data from individual cells and ranges of cells, and even how to delete entire rows and columns. First, though, you need to understand the difference between clearing data and deleting data from the worksheet.

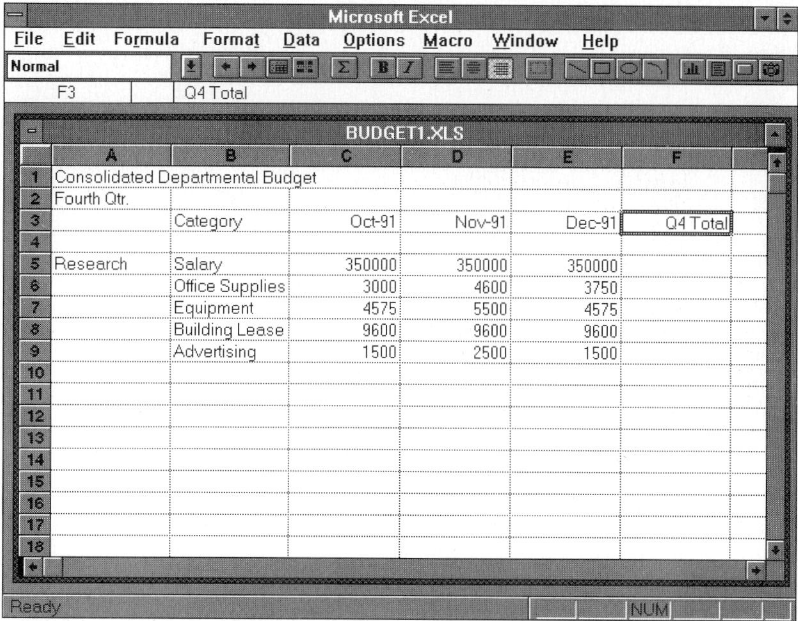

Figure 2.10 BUDGET1.XLS after changing column widths and cell alignments

Tip. Take a quick look back at the Edit menu. Next to many of the menu items are the names of other keystrokes. These are known as *alternate keystrokes* and can be used instead of the commands used in this book. For example, instead of clicking on Edit, Clear, you could just highlight the cells you wanted to clear and then hit the Delete key. Take a look at the other menus to see if an alternate key might save you some time in the future.

Clearing means that you simply want to remove the data from a cell or cells, without affecting the structure of the underlying worksheet. If you clear data from a cell, the cell remains intact—but empty. On the other hand, if you *delete* a cell (or a row or column) the cell itself will be removed from the structure of the worksheet.

The implications of this distinction are important. Suppose you have created a formula that refers to another cell. If you *clear* the contents of the cell, the formula considers that cell to contain a zero, that is, no value. If, however, you *delete* the cell, your formula will be unable to reference that cell, since it has been deleted, and your formula will return an error code. (More information on formulas and functions appears in Chapters 3 and 4, respectively.)

Removing Data from Cells

Now let's remove some data from our sample worksheet. (The word *remove* is used because we'll both clear and delete data from the worksheet in upcoming exercises.) Suppose you wanted to remove the information you previously entered in cell F3. As you saw earlier, it's possible to simply type over the contents of a cell, if you want to change the contents to something else. But how do you remove data from the cell entirely? The answer is shown in the following steps.

1. Use the mouse to select cell F3 or use the keyboard to move the cell pointer to that cell. As always, you first select the cells you want to receive the action that follows.
2. Click on Edit, Clear. The following dialog box appears:

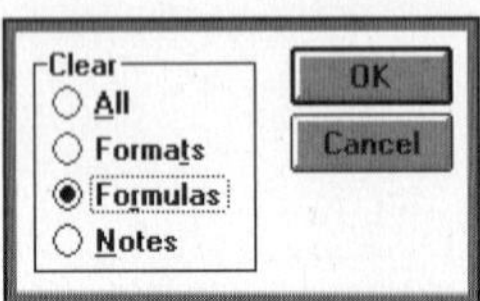

3. Choose the items in the cell you wish to clear. You can choose to clear all the contents of the cell, any formatting you have applied, just the formulas in the cell, or just the cell notes. For this example, choose All.
4. Click on OK to carry out your command.

With the command completed, you can see that the cell is still where it always was, but that it no longer contains “Q4 Total.”

Deleting a cell, instead of clearing it, is also easy, but it requires you to answer one question before you can proceed. Remember that deleting a cell (or a range of cells, or a row or column) means that the selected object actually goes away. Consequently, something else must take its place. To delete cell E5, perform the following steps:

1. Highlight the cell that you want to delete. In this case, pick cell E5.
2. Click on Edit, Delete. The following dialog box appears:

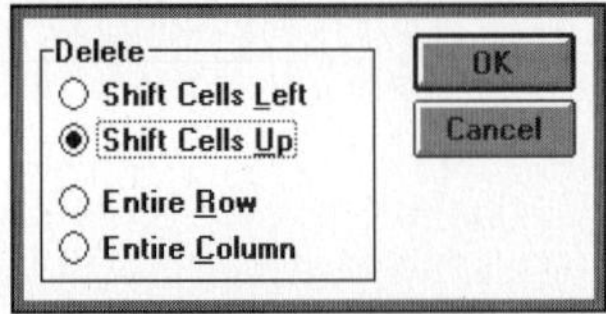

3. Now, choose what you want the worksheet to do in order to compensate for the hole you are about to create. Your choices here are to move the cells up from beneath or to move the cells over from the left. It doesn’t matter which you choose here—just pick one.
4. Click on OK to carry out the command.

In this example, it doesn't really make sense to delete a cell since you can accomplish the same goal by just clearing the cell contents. Whatever choice you make about moving the cells will result in a worksheet with data in the wrong place.

Tip. Be very careful when you are deleting rows and columns. It's important to remember that the worksheet goes out 256 columns to the right (and down for another 16,000 cells or so), so that when you delete a row, you are deleting the contents of some 256 cells. Make sure there are no important cells in the column you are about to delete that you can't see because they are off the screen.

Removing Rows and Columns

What does make sense in this example is to delete an entire row or column or a group of rows or columns. In the following exercise, you will delete (entirely remove) row 9:

1. Highlight the row or column you want to delete by clicking in the column or the row bar. (Remember that you can highlight a range of rows or columns, instead.) For this exercise, select row 9.
2. Click on Edit, Delete.

Notice that Excel immediately performed the delete operation without asking if you wanted to move any cells up or from the left. Excel knew that, since you had selected an entire row, the only way for it to carry out the command was to remove the entire row and move everything else up. If you had elected to delete a column, Excel would have simply deleted the column and moved all subsequent columns over to the left.

TIP. *What if you delete the wrong thing? In many cases, you can reverse any action you have just performed by clicking on Edit Undo* action *(the word* action *changes to show the last thing you did). In this example, the menu choice would read Undo Delete. To reverse the effect, you must carry out this command before you do anything else. Undo also works with clearing, formatting, moving, and so on. In general, if you want to Undo something, just try it. You'll probably be able to do it.*

Inserting Cells

Just as you can delete a cell from the worksheet, you can insert a cell into a worksheet. As you perform this exercise, note that Excel again asks what you want done with the existing cells so that you can insert a blank cell. The choices here are identical to those you saw when you deleted a cell:

1. Highlight cell E5. This is the location that you want to be the home of your new, blank cell. The data that cell currently contains will be moved.
2. Click on Edit, Insert. A dialog box appears.
3. Choose Shift Cells Down. This tells Excel that you want every cell beneath E5 shifted down to make room for the new cell.

4. Click on OK to carry out your command. Figure 2.11 shows the worksheet after you have inserted a cell.

Figure 2.11
Worksheet after inserting a cell

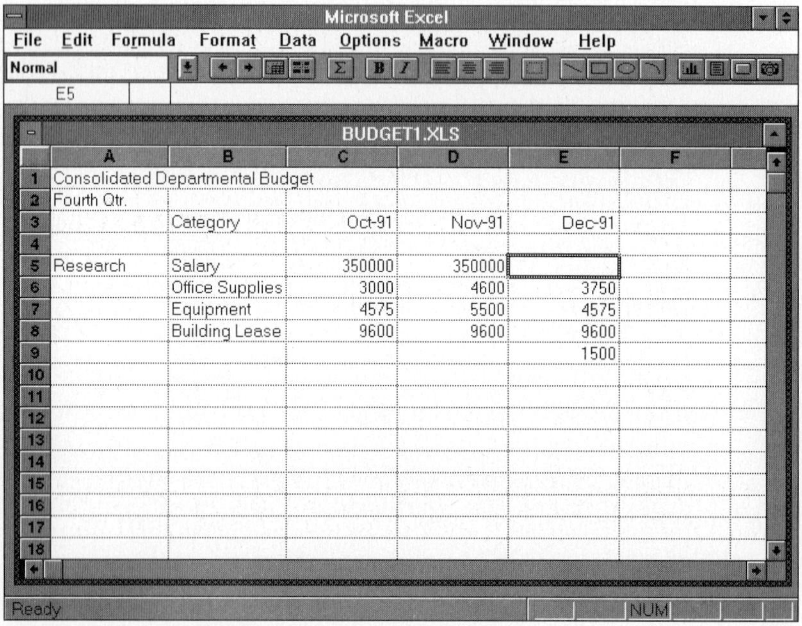

	A	B	C	D	E	F
1	Consolidated Departmental Budget					
2	Fourth Qtr.					
3		Category	Oct-91	Nov-91	Dec-91	
4						
5	Research	Salary	350000	350000		
6		Office Supplies	3000	4600	3750	
7		Equipment	4575	5500	4575	
8		Building Lease	9600	9600	9600	
9					1500	

Inserting Rows and Columns

Inserting rows or columns into a worksheet is very straightforward and follows two basic guidelines: You always highlight the row or column where you want your new row or column to appear, and rows always shift down and columns always shift to the right. Here's an example:

1. Highlight row 7. (You can also highlight a range of rows or columns.)
2. Click on Edit, Insert.

Excel immediately inserts a new row and shifts all the other rows down to accommodate your new row. Figure 2.12 shows the worksheet after you have inserted a row.

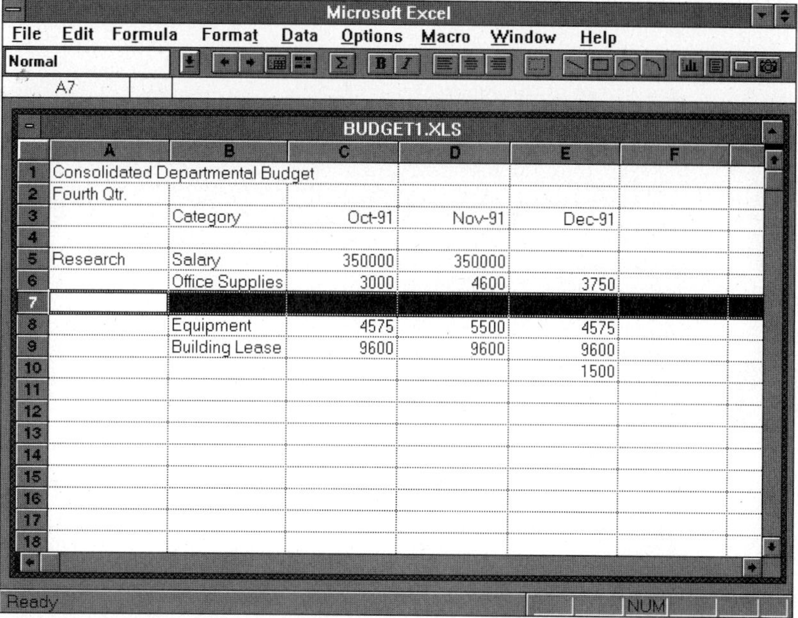

Figure 2.12
Worksheet after inserting a row

Losing Your Changes

Now that you've learned how to remove and insert cells, rows, and columns in the worksheet, it's time to work with some of Excel's basic formatting features. Right now, though, you will need to get your worksheet back to the state it was in at the end of the last section:

1. Click on File, Close to close the current version of the worksheet.
2. When Excel asks if you want to save the current version, click on No. You want to discard the changes that you made during this session and read back into memory a clean version of the worksheet.
3. Click on File to load the File menu.
4. Look at the list of the last four files that you worked on (at the bottom of the menu), find the worksheet titled BUDGET1.XLS, and click on it. Your worksheet should now look like Figure 2.13.

The prompt asking if you want to save your changes demonstrates Excel's built-in safety features. If you had wanted to save the contents of the worksheet and responded Yes to the prompt, Excel's reminder that you had not done so would then give you the opportunity to save your changes. By choosing No, you simply told Excel that you didn't want to keep the contents of that worksheet at all. Excel will always warn you if you have made changes to a worksheet and you try to close the worksheet or exit from Excel without saving them.

Figure 2.13
Worksheet after loading from disk

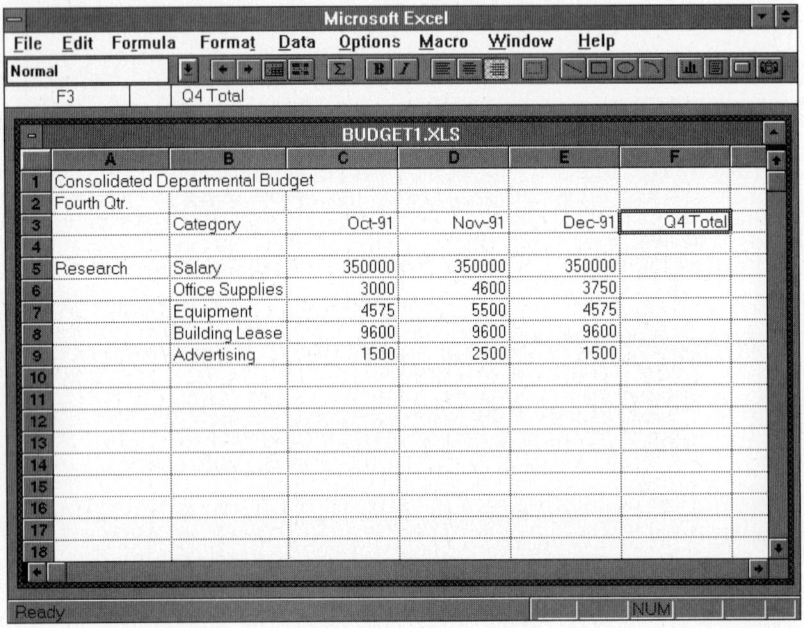

	A	B	C	D	E	F
1	Consolidated Departmental Budget					
2	Fourth Qtr.					
3		Category	Oct-91	Nov-91	Dec-91	Q4 Total
4						
5	Research	Salary	350000	350000	350000	
6		Office Supplies	3000	4600	3750	
7		Equipment	4575	5500	4575	
8		Building Lease	9600	9600	9600	
9		Advertising	1500	2500	1500	

Basic Presentation Features

Long before other spreadsheet vendors caught on, Microsoft had powerful presentation features. And its control over the ways to format and enhance your worksheet remain flexible and impressive in this new version. With Excel's formatting features, you will be able to modify the appearance of the worksheet by adding color and other attributes such as boldface and italic type. Furthermore, you'll learn how to spice up your worksheet by adding graphical elements: text boxes, arrows, charts, and so on. The remainder of this chapter will concentrate on the basics of formatting. More advanced topics in formatting and presentation will be discussed in Chapter 5.

The Toolbar

The toolbar is an optional but very useful area of the Excel spreadsheet program. It allows you, with a click of the mouse, to quickly carry out many of the tasks that go into creating and presenting a worksheet. Among the commands you can perform with the toolbar are assigning styles, adding graphical elements to your spreadsheet (lines, circles, text), and applying formatting commands to selected cells in the spreadsheet.

Although each of these items will be covered later in greater detail, look now at the close-up view of the toolbar shown below. Take a moment here to note what each of the icons means, starting from the left side of the toolbar. Later, when you've forgotten what each does (as many of us have!), you'll be able to turn back here and get a quick summary of each tool.

Style Box Button

Use this button both to apply styles and to define new styles based on some change you have made. For further information on defining and applying styles, see Chapter 5.

Promote and Demote Buttons

These buttons are used when you're working with an outline of the worksheet. The Promote button moves a block up one level, and the Demote button drops the section down one level. See Chapter 9 for more information about outlining within the spreadsheet.

Show Outline Symbols Button

This button is used to turn the outline level symbols on or off. Outlining is covered in detail in Chapter 9.

Select Visible Cells Button

You use this button to show all *visible cells*, those that do not contain hidden data. More information on hiding and displaying hidden cells is available in Chapter 8.

Autosum Button

Use this button to automatically add a row or column of numbers. When you select this option, Excel will look at your data and try to decide the most likely range that you want to sum. Once Excel determines what range you want to sum, it places a valid =SUM statement in the active cell. (In case you're wondering where Microsoft got that icon, it's an uppercase Greek sigma, the mathematical symbol for summation.)

Bold and Italic Buttons

These buttons are useful for quickly applying either bold or italic attributes to a single cell or a range of cells. Simply select a range of cells, then click on either the bold icon or the italic icon to apply the changes.

Alignment Buttons

Use these three buttons to align text or numbers in the cells that you have selected. There is one button each for left, center, and right alignment.

Selection Button

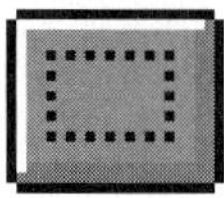

Use this button to select graphical objects that you wish to move, resize, or delete. To learn more about working with graphical objects in a worksheet or a chart, turn to Chapter 8.

Line, Rectangle, Oval, and Arc Buttons

This new feature of Excel 3.0 lets you add four graphical elements to your spreadsheet. Adding a graphical element is simple. Just click on the tool that corresponds to the element you want to add, then place the cursor where you want the object to go, and drag the pointer across the worksheet to create the object. For more information on graphical objects, see Chapter 8.

Chart Button

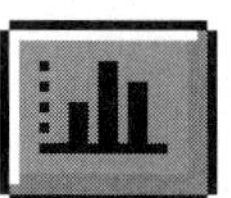

This button is used to begin an embedded chart on your worksheet. See Chapter 7 for more information on charting and data presentation.

Text Box Button

Use this tool to add text objects to your spreadsheets. Once you have entered the text, you can format it to appear in different colors, fonts, and type sizes.

Button Tool

This tool lets you create other buttons. A *button* allows you to build a macro into your worksheet. When you have placed a button on the worksheet, given it a descriptive name, and attached a macro to it, every time thereafter that you click on the button, you execute the macro assigned to it. Use this tool to create stand-alone applications or to help someone who is using your model and may not know how to do a specific task.

Camera Tool

Finally, the camera tool is useful for "taking a picture" of a section of your data. Say that you want to watch a part of your spreadsheet that is located (figuratively) far away in another part of the spreadsheet. With the camera tool, you can capture an image, or *snapshot,* of that other portion of a spreadsheet and display it on the portion of the worksheet that you are currently using. In essence, the snapshot is a link to data in another part of the spreadsheet, so you are always working with up-to-date information.

The Toolbar versus Menus

The toolbar is a new addition to Excel 3.0. When Microsoft was deciding what icons to put on the toolbar, they conducted research to determine which features were used most often. These features were then placed on the toolbar. Even with the toolbar enabled (it's that way by default), however, you can still use the menus to do almost everything you do with the toolbar. Conversely, there are some things that are only accessible via the toolbar, such as the Autosum command and the camera tool.

Status Bar Indicators

By now, you may have noticed some of the indicators in the lower-right and lower-left corners of the screen. These indicators show the state of various options and features of the product. Here is a quick rundown on what each one means.

ADD

The status of the Add key (Shift-F8) is shown by this indicator. The Add key lets you select more than one range while using keyboard commands instead of the mouse.

CAPS

Indicates the status (on or off) of the Caps Lock key.

EXT

The Extend key (F8) lets you extend your selection from the keyboard. Holding down the Shift key and pressing the Right Arrow key is the same as pressing the Extend key (F8) and pressing the Right Arrow key.

FIX

This indicates that the Fixed Decimal option has been enabled from the Options Workspace dialog box. This option adds a fixed number of decimals (user-specified) to each number.

NUM

Displays the status (on or off) of the Num Lock key. If you press Num Lock within Excel, you can enter numbers and certain operators (addition, subtraction, multiplication, and division) from the numeric keyboard.

OVR

This indicator displays the status of the insert/overtype mode while you are editing a cell. As you edit a cell, pressing the Insert key will toggle between inserting characters and overwriting existing characters.

SCRL

The SCRL indicator lights if you have pressed the Scroll Lock key. Once you press the Scroll Lock key, pressing the arrow keys will move the entire worksheet rather than moving the cursor from one cell to another.

READY

In addition to the preceding indicators, which are displayed in the lower-right corner of the screen, Excel also displays useful information along the left side of the status bar. Most of the time, you'll see a READY indicator, which means that Excel is ready for a command.

Help Information

Excel also uses the left side of the status bar to display amplified help information about what the selected menu item does. For example, if you click on any menu item, and hold down the left mouse button, you can see a one-line description of what that menu item does.

Text Attributes

When you apply a format to one or more cells in a worksheet, you are applying a particular attribute to that cell. An *attribute* is associated with a single characteristic about the cell, such as bold, italic, type size, or a color. It's also possible for a cell to have more than one attribute—it could be bold, italic, and red, for example. In the following exercises, you will learn two ways to set the bold attribute. Setting the italic attribute and the cell alignment is just as easy. To do so, try this.

1. Highlight cell A1.
2. Click on Format, Font. A dialog box appears.
3. In the box marked Style, click on Bold.
4. In the list box that shows type sizes, click on 12. This sets your type size to 12 for this cell only. Before you carry out this command, the dialog box should look like Figure 2.14.
5. Click on OK to carry out the command.

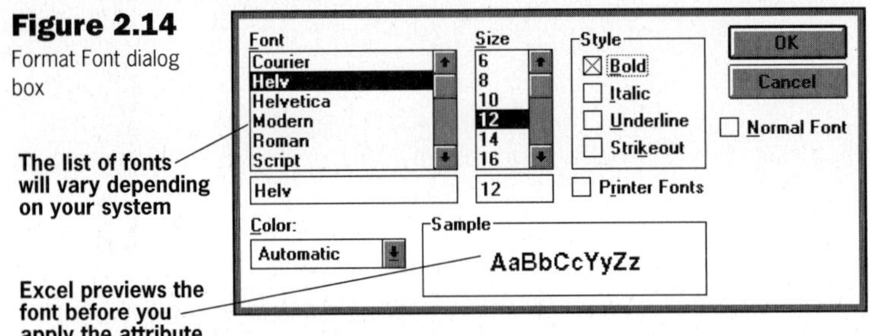

Figure 2.14
Format Font dialog box

Tip. You can format a cell to have one or several attributes even though there is nothing currently visible to you in the cell. This feature is useful if you intend to fill the cell (or some range of cells) with data at some point, and you want it to appear correctly the first time it is shown.

You probably noticed that the Format Font dialog box provided a lot of options for you to change. As you experiment with the attributes you can change in this dialog box, pay close attention to the Sample box at the bottom. Excel lets you see what the text will look like as you set the attributes. Only after you click on OK will Excel change the highlighted range to apply the attributes you have selected.

If all you want to do is to quickly make a cell's text bold or italic, there's a faster way to do it. Let's make the column headings bold:

1. Highlight the range of cells from B3 to F3.
2. Move the mouse pointer up into the toolbar and click once on the B icon.
3. Highlight cell A5.
4. Click on the B icon.

You can see that the highlighted text has shown up as bold. Note that while you still have the range highlighted, you can use the bold icon to turn on and off the "boldness" of a particular cell. This is also true of the italic icon. Practice enabling and disabling the bold and italic attributes by clicking on them until you get the hang of it. After you have finished applying the bold attribute, the worksheet should look like the one in Figure 2.15.

Figure 2.15 Worksheet after bold attribute is applied

Microsoft Excel

File Edit Formula Format Data Options Macro Window Help

Normal

A5 Research

BUDGET1.XLS

	A	B	C	D	E	F
1	**Consolidated Departmental Budget**					
2	Fourth Qtr.					
3		**Category**	**Oct-91**	**Nov-91**	**Dec-91**	**Q4 Total**
4						
5	**Research**	Salary	350000	350000	350000	
6		Office Supplies	3000	4600	3750	
7		Equipment	4575	5500	4575	
8		Building Lease	9600	9600	9600	
9		Advertising	1500	2500	1500	
10						
11						
12						
13						
14						
15						
16						
17						
18						

Ready NUM

Annotating Cells

Although putting notes into worksheet cells doesn't, strictly speaking, enhance the appearance of your worksheet, it does help you remember why you might have formatted the cell a certain way. It might also tell you why you used one number in a calculation instead of another.

Adding notes to certain cells in a worksheet can also serve as a rudimentary debugging tool, both for you and for anyone else who must carry out the maintenance of your worksheet model if you aren't around. If you are in doubt about whether you should use a note, go ahead and use one. It can't hurt, and it's cheap insurance for that day when you can't figure out the flow of the worksheet.

Finally, notes can be used as a documentation tool, as well. Excel provides an option at print time to let you print only the notes from a worksheet. If you have documented all the formulas, assumptions, and tricky math, this will give you a head start on documenting the worksheet or re-creating it if it should be lost or destroyed.

Adding Notes to Cells

The following steps illustrate how to add a note to a cell:

1. Highlight cell B5. This is the cell you will annotate with a cell note.
2. Choose Formula, Note. The Cell Note dialog box appears.
3. In the Note box, type some notes about this cell. (For this exercise, it really doesn't matter what you type. See Figure 2.16 for a sample.)
4. Choose OK to close the dialog box.

Figure 2.16
Cell Note dialog box

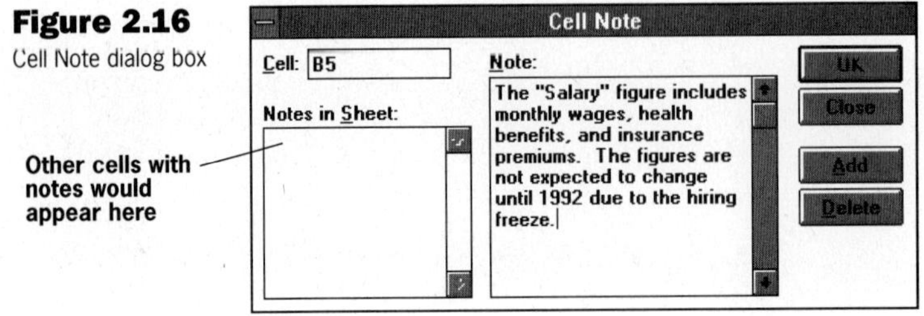

Controlling the Note Display

The notes you add to your worksheet don't display as part of the worksheet. Instead, if you have a note attached to a cell, Excel will display a very small indicator in the upper-right corner of the cell. On a color display, the indicator shows up as a small red dot. If, however, you don't want to see any reference to the notes on the worksheet itself, you can enable or disable the marker like this:

1. Choose Options, Workspace. A dialog box appears.
2. Enable or disable the note markers by turning on or off the Note Indicator check box.
3. Choose OK to close the Options Workspace dialog box.

Removing Notes from Cells

Once you have finished with the notes in a single cell or a range of cells, use the following steps to remove a note from a cell:

1. Highlight the cell or the range of cells that contain the notes you want to remove.
2. Choose Edit, Clear. A dialog box appears.
3. Choose the Notes option.
4. Choose OK to close the Edit Clear dialog box and complete the command.

Saving Your Work

Now that you've worked through a series of exercises to enhance your worksheet, let's make sure that you have brought it up to date before you save it. Your worksheet should look like Figure 2.15. If it doesn't, use the skills you've learned in this chapter to correct the cell alignment and apply formatting attributes to the appropriate cells.

After you have made any necessary changes to the worksheet, follow these instructions to save it before you conclude this chapter:

1. Click on File, Save to save the worksheet.
2. Click on File, Exit to quit from Excel.

CHAPTER

3

Formulas, Ranges, and Errors

Formula Basics

Operators

Range Referencing

Worksheet Errors and Logical Errors

IN MANY WAYS, FORMULAS, ALONG WITH FUNCTIONS (WHICH ARE COVERED in Chapter 4) are the fundamental building blocks of a worksheet. Unless you only want a place to store data, your model will almost always use formulas, functions, or both. These tools give you great flexibility in the way you set up your analytical model. A *model* is really just another name for a worksheet—it refers to the way you want to "model" your decision based on the results of the worksheet.

Consider the budget worksheet you have been constructing. Up to this point, you have only entered actual numbers based on what various departments have spent. By adding a few simple formulas to the worksheet, you can calculate the total amount of money spent by the research division in any given quarter and by any department within the research division. The goal of this chapter is to add a few formulas to your worksheet and to explain some concepts that are required as you move on to Chapter 4 and the concept of functions.

Another concept that you will learn about in this chapter is that of ranges. When you are creating a complex worksheet, it's awkward to continue to work with cell references. It becomes difficult to remember where on the worksheet you have stored the values for salaries, for example, if you can only refer to the values like cell B5 or J10. With ranges, you can refer to any number of cells by using a special notation. In fact, you can even name a range so that it's easier to remember later on. Instead of having to remember that the percentage increase figure is stored in cell B12, you can give a name to that cell (or cells, for that matter) and refer to B12 from then on as 89_Salary, or whatever you want to call it.

Finally, this chapter will introduce you to some of the errors you might see when you are working with formulas and functions on your worksheet. No one likes to see an error occur, but it's helpful to know what to do about solving it when it happens.

Formula Basics

Simply stated, a formula is a series of numbers, cell references, ranges, mathematical operators (+ and –, for example), and worksheet functions (described in Chapter 4) that produces a result based on the contents of cells it references.

The easiest way to describe a formula is to give a couple of examples. First, consider a very simplistic example from elementary school math class. If you wanted to multiply two numbers together, the result you calculated would be based on the values of other numbers. The formula you created to carry out this calculation might look like this:

$$5 * 10 = 50$$

The number 50 is the result of the formula 5 * 10.

Now, let's apply this example to the worksheet metaphor. Suppose you wanted to add together the values stored in cells B1 and B2 and put the result into cell B5. The formula you construct in cell B5 (where you want the result to appear) would look like this:

=B1+B2

Excel formulas always begin with an equal sign so that the program knows you are entering a formula instead of text. In this example, the formula is very simple, consisting only of two cell references and the arithmetic (or mathematical) operator for addition, the + symbol. As you might imagine, there are also operators for subtraction, multiplication, and division, along with some others you may have never heard of, such as exponentiation, concatenation, and comparison operators. (More on these appears later in the chapter.)

For a more concrete example, consider the BUDGET1 worksheet in Figure 3.1. Without any formulas added to it yet, it is only useful up to a point. One calculation you might want to perform is to sum up the expenditures made by all departments during the month of October. The formula that accomplishes this calculation goes in cell C11 and looks like this:

=C5+C6+C7+C8+C9

Figure 3.1 BUDGET1.XLS worksheet without formulas

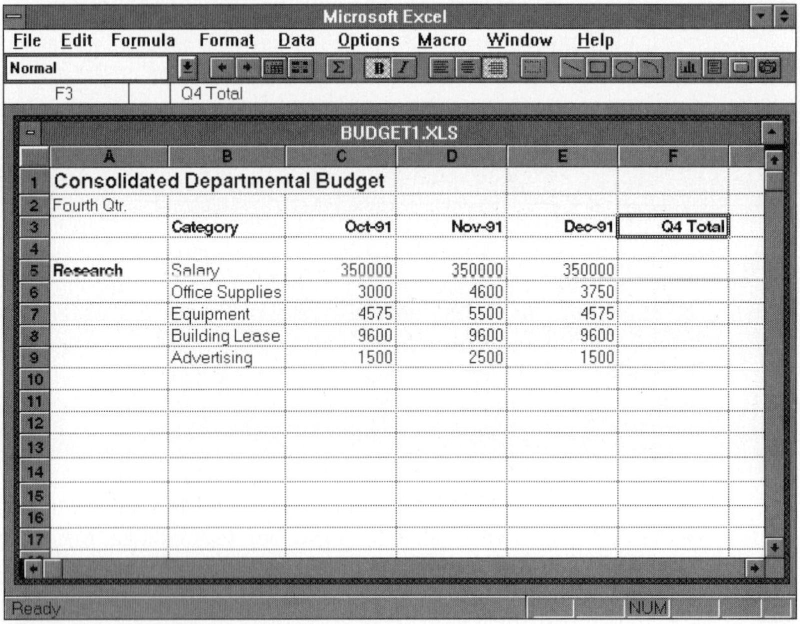

	A	B	C	D	E	F
1	Consolidated Departmental Budget					
2	Fourth Qtr.					
3		Category	Oct-91	Nov-91	Dec-91	Q4 Total
4						
5	Research	Salary	350000	350000	350000	
6		Office Supplies	3000	4600	3750	
7		Equipment	4575	5500	4575	
8		Building Lease	9600	9600	9600	
9		Advertising	1500	2500	1500	

Formulas Versus Functions

Formulas and functions are interrelated in Excel. Both perform calculations and return values based on the contents of other cells. When you write a formula, you will often use a function within the formula. In fact, functions are really like prewritten formulas that perform a specific operation on a group of cells—often a range of cells—and return a value. You can use a function alone, as you'll see in a moment, or you can use functions as building blocks to create complex and powerful formulas. Functions, however, offer more flexibility than formulas. Consider the formula to sum up the total expenditures in October.

=C5+C6+C7+C8+C9

Entering that formula requires 15 keystrokes. Now, compare that to Excel's built-in (that is, prewritten) function that adds that same set of numbers:

=SUM(C5:C9)

Using this function requires 11 keystrokes—not a big difference in this case. But imagine if you needed to sum up the range of numbers from C1 to C50. You could add up these numbers in two ways:

=C1+C2+C3+C4+C5+C6+C7+ ... +C48+C49+C50

or

=SUM(C1:C50)

It's no longer just a small difference!

In any case, there is an absolute limit of 255 characters on the contents of a cell. Thus, at some point it would be impossible for you to enter the formula at all, and you would have to rely on the analogous function to accomplish the same thing.

The latter example is that of a function being used as the formula. The "=SUM" portion is the function, and the rest of the line is the range you want to sum. But what if you wanted to multiply that range of numbers by a number stored in another single cell? Your revised formula might look like this:

=SUM(C1:C50)*B9

There are really two parts to this formula: the function that first sums up the numbers in the range, and the second part that multiplies the sum by the number stored in cell B9.

Syntax Rules of Formulas

The rules for entering formulas are fairly straightforward. Each formula begins with an equal sign (=) and must contain no more than 255 characters. If you use parentheses in your formula to change the order of calculation, you must have a matched set; that is, for every opening parenthesis, there must be a closing one, and vice versa. (See the section "Order of Operator Precedence" later in the chapter.)

Entering Formulas

Excel gives you two ways to enter formulas: with the mouse or from the keyboard. Depending on how long or intricate the formulas you use are, you might want to become conversant with both methods.

Using the Keyboard

Using the keyboard is straightforward. Once you have loaded the BUDGET1 worksheet, simply move the cell pointer to the cell that you wish to hold the formula, and then type in the formula just as you would any other data. Excel will know that you want to perform a calculation because the formula begins with an equal sign. Use the following steps to sum up the total salaries for the three-month period in the BUDGET1 worksheet:

1. Position the cell pointer to highlight cell F5.
2. Enter **=C5+D5+E5**.
3. Press Enter to complete the formula. Figure 3.2 shows the result of the new formula.

Note that the number displayed in cell F5 is different from what Excel is displaying in the formula bar. It's important to remember that Excel will always display the *actual contents* of the cell in the formula bar. What is displayed in the cell is the *result* of what you have entered in the cell. Clearly, if all you entered was text or numeric data, the contents of the formula bar and the cell will be the same. However, if you enter a formula or a function into a cell, the cell will display the result of the calculation performed by the actual contents of that cell. If this concept is a bit confusing now, be patient, it will get better as you become more familiar with Excel.

Using the Mouse

Building a formula with a mouse is also easy, as you might expect, since Excel was designed to be used with a mouse. The advantage the mouse offers over the keyboard is that you don't have to figure out the address of the cell you want to reference and then type that address into the formula.

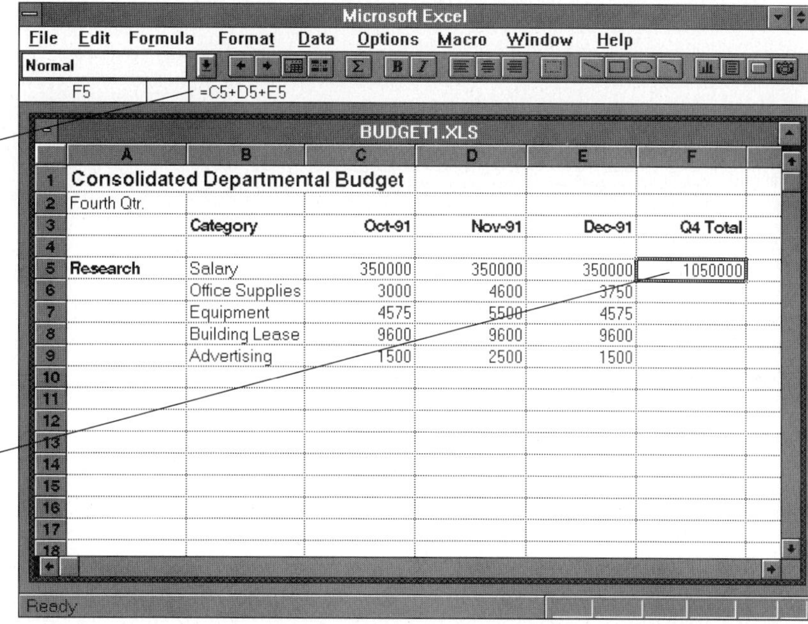

Figure 3.2 Summing the salaries

Tip. If you want to display the actual formulas instead of the formula *results*, click on Options, Display and make sure the Formulas box is checked. Click on OK to complete the command. You'll see the actual contents of the cells.

With the mouse, you can point directly to the cells you want to include in the formula. Try the following exercise to build a formula with the mouse:

1. Highlight the cell you want the formula to appear in. For this exercise, highlight cell F6.
2. Type **=** (an equal sign) to tell Excel you are building a formula.
3. Click on cell C6, the first cell you want to add to the formula. Watch the formula bar closely as you build the formula (see Figure 3.3).
4. Type **+** (a plus sign) to signify that you want to add the first cell to others.
5. Click on cell D6.
6. Type **+** again.
7. Click on cell E6.
8. Complete the formula by clicking on the check mark icon located directly to the left of the formula bar, or just press Enter. Figure 3.4 shows the completed formula.

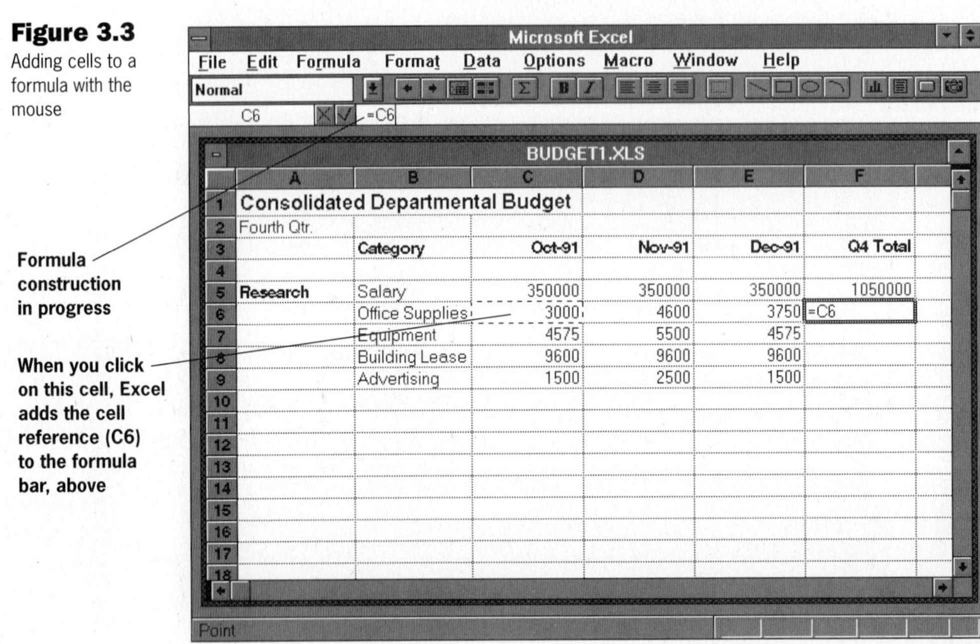

Figure 3.3
Adding cells to a formula with the mouse

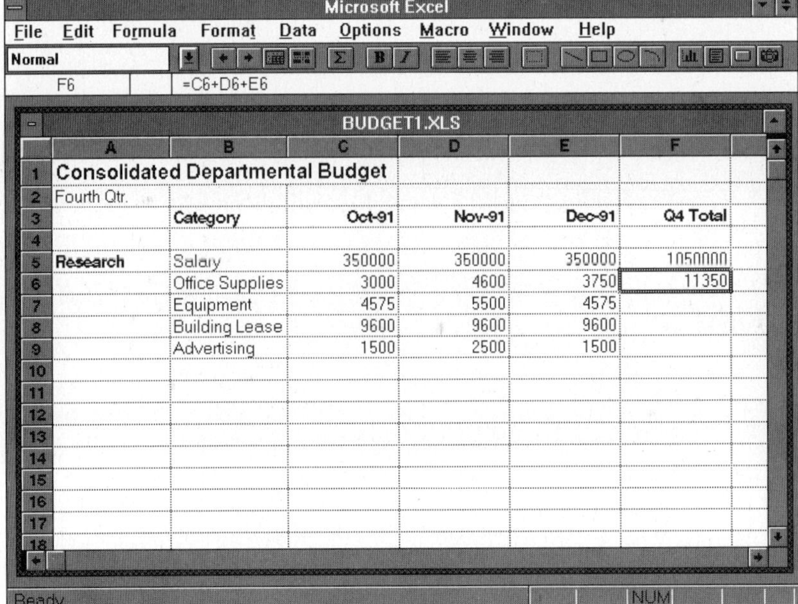

Figure 3.4
The completed formula

Note that both methods of entering the formula produced the same results. Since the mouse method is not entirely based on using the mouse (since you have to type the equal and plus signs), its main advantage is that it enables you to simply point to the cells you know contain the values you want to calculate. In that sense, the mouse method may be more efficient and accurate.

Complete the totals in column F by building formulas to sum the numbers in rows 7, 8, and 9. When you have finished, your worksheet should look like Figure 3.5.

Figure 3.5 BUDGET1.XLS after completing the totals

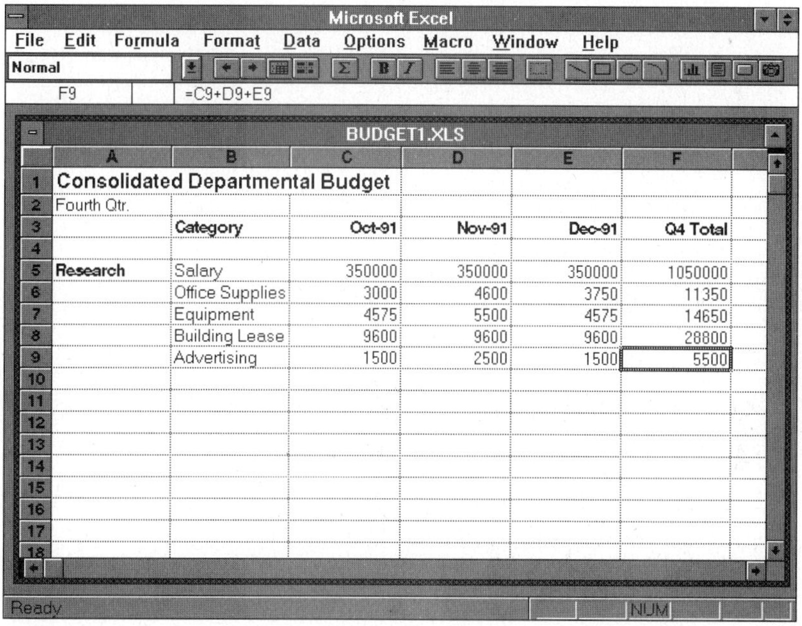

	A	B	C	D	E	F
1	Consolidated Departmental Budget					
2	Fourth Qtr.					
3		Category	Oct-91	Nov-91	Dec-91	Q4 Total
4						
5	Research	Salary	350000	350000	350000	1050000
6		Office Supplies	3000	4600	3750	11350
7		Equipment	4575	5500	4575	14650
8		Building Lease	9600	9600	9600	28800
9		Advertising	1500	2500	1500	5500

Operators

Operators are used to complete the formula by specifying what action is to take place between two or more cell references, which are called *operands* in a formula. You have already seen the plus sign operator used to add two or more cell references. Excel's operators can be generally classified into four categories: arithmetic or mathematical, text, comparison, and reference. You might want to just quickly skim the following descriptions of the operators, and then come back to them after you have had the chance to work a bit more with functions and formulas.

Arithmetic Operators

The most straightforward and familiar of the operators are the arithmetic operators. They are similar to symbols used in mathematics.

Addition (+) Use the plus sign to add two or more values together.

Subtraction (–) The minus sign (–) is used to subtract one value from another. In addition, this operator negates a value if it is used with only one operand. For example, if you precede the number 5 with the subtraction operator, the value becomes –5.

Division (/) Use the forward slash to signify division; it has the same effect as the familiar ÷ symbol. Since the computer keyboard does not contain that symbol, you must use the slash instead.

Multiplication (*) The asterisk (also called a star) is used to indicate multiplication of two operands. The multiplication operator is another one that may not be too familiar. Normally, you would use an x to denote multiplication but it might be confused with the letter x.

Percentage (%) The percent sign is used to translate one operand into its decimal equivalent. For example, if cell A1 contains 1, the formula =A1+5% equals 1.05. Excel translates the value of 5% into its decimal equivalent of .05, while allowing you to represent the number in the more convenient form of 5%.

Exponentiation (^) The caret (Shift-6) is used to represent exponentiation—that is, raising one number to the power of another. For instance, if cell A1 contains 7 and cell A2 contains 3, the formula =A1^A2 returns the value of 7^3 or 7*7*7*=343.

Text Operator

There is only one text operator, the ampersand (&). This operator is used to *concatenate*, or join, text together. For example, if cell A1 contains The and cell A2 contains End, the formula =A1&" "&A2 returns the value The End. (Note the use of the blank space between the quotation marks in the formula to create the space between the two words.)

Comparison Operators

Comparison operators differ from both the arithmetic and text operators in that, instead of returning numbers or text results, they only return TRUE or

FALSE. These comparison operators are often called *Boolean operators*—named after the field of Boolean logic, which deals with true/false conditions.

These operators are useful as ways to control calculation or logic based on the condition of some value. For instance, since Excel will let you control the color of the text in a cell, using comparison operators you could construct a formula that would display negative numbers in red and positive numbers in black. As you learn more about automating the worksheet in Chapter 13, comparison operators will become very handy tools and an integral part of your Excel repertoire.

Equal (=) You use the equal sign to test the equality of one value to another. If cell A1 contains 2, cell A2 contains 2, and cell A3 contains 3, the formula =A1=A2 returns TRUE, but the formula =A1=A3 returns FALSE.

Greater Than and Less Than (> and <) Use the > and < symbols for greater-than and less-than comparisons, respectively. Thus, if cell A1 contains 3 and A3 contains 4, the formula =A1>A3 returns FALSE.

Greater-Than-or-Equal-To and Less-Than-or-Equal-To (>= and <=) These are very similar to the preceding pair, but add equality to the test. For instance, the formula =3>=3 returns TRUE, as does =6>=3.

Not Equal To (<>) This operator is just the opposite of the equal operator. Use the <> to test for items not equal to one another. The formula =4<>4 returns FALSE, for example.

Reference Operators

Reference operators may be the most difficult of the operator types to understand. With these operators, you can create specialized groups of cells.

Range (:) With the range operator, you can specify ranges of cells. For example, the reference A1:A10 refers to the cells A1, A10, and all the cells in between.

Intersection ( ) The intersection operator (a space) returns the cell reference that is common to two ranges. For example, take a look at Figure 3.6, which illustrates one use for the intersection operator.

Note the formula visible in the formula bar: =DEC_91 OFFICE_SUPPLIES. In this formula, both DEC_91 and OFFICE_SUPPLIES are named ranges (named ranges are covered later in the chapter). The space between the two range names (the intersection operator) returns a reference to the single cell where they intersect.

Figure 3.6
Referring to one cell with the intersection operator

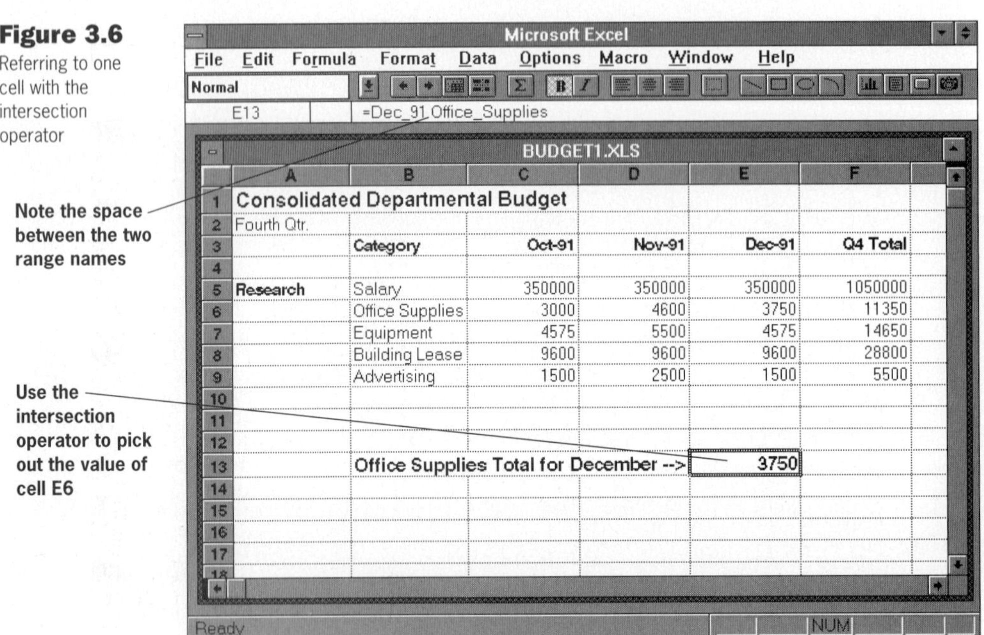

Union (,) The union operator (a comma) is the opposite of the intersection operator. You use it to reference the cells common to two ranges. See Figure 3.7 for a graphical demonstration of how this works. It shows the results of a command to display the reference =DEC_91,ADVERTISING (as before, DEC_91 and ADVERTISING are named ranges).

Order of Operator Precedence

In one of those junior-high math classes so easy to forget about, your teacher undoubtedly covered something called "the order of operator precedence" or something similar. It may not have been very interesting back then, but it's critical here. It is one of the most fertile spots for logical errors to creep into worksheets.

To illustrate this point, take a look at these two formulas:

3*15+2+4/2

3*((15+2)+4)/2

Except for the way the parentheses have been placed, they're the same. But they won't return the same result. It's important to understand how Excel will calculate these formulas if you choose to leave out the parentheses. It's equally important to understand what Excel will do if you include parentheses.

Figure 3.7
Demonstration of the union operator

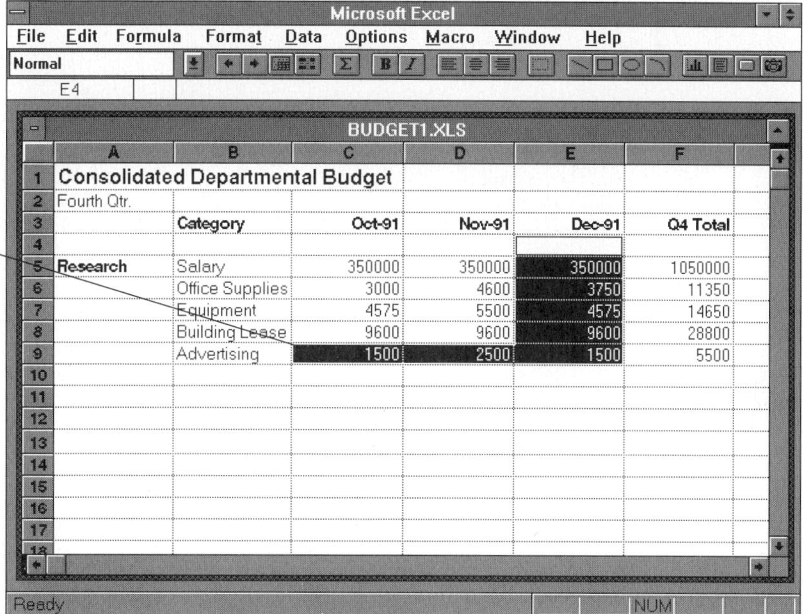

Excel has a set of strict rules regarding the order in which calculations within a formula are carried out. First of all, anything that is within parentheses will be calculated first. If one or more sets of parentheses are included within another set—called *nesting*—Excel performs the innermost set of calculations first, and then begins to work out. Using parentheses gives you complete control over the order of calculation. But you also need to understand the default order in which Excel evaluates the operators. This order is shown in Table 3.1.

Let's work through the two formulas using Excel's default order of operator precedence to see how the results are calculated.

If there are no parentheses, Excel evaluates each operator's expression in the default order. If two or more operators have equal precedence, the leftmost one evaluates first, then the next one to the right, and so on. So, for the first example, here is how Excel would calculate the formula 3*15+2+4/2:

3*15=45

4/2=2

45+2+2=49

Table 3.1 Excel's Order of Operator Precedence

Order of Precedence	Operator Symbol and Name
1	: (range)
2	(intersection)
3	, (union)
4	– (negation)
5	% (percentage)
6	^ (exponentiation)
7	* and / (multiplication and division)
8	+ and – (addition and subtraction)
9	& (text concatenation)
10	=, <, >, <=, >=, <> (comparison)

However, if Excel encounters parentheses, it will first evaluate the items enclosed in the parentheses beginning from the inside out. So the formula 3*((15+2)+4)/2 evaluates as follows:

15+2=17

17+4=21

3*21=63

63/2=31.5

Note that where there are no parentheses, Excel falls back on its default order of operator precedence. Once Excel calculated 15+2 and 17+4, it started on the left and performed 3*21 and finally 63/2.

You might want to take this opportunity to try entering different formulas into the worksheet and see how the placement of parentheses affects the order of the calculation. Something as simple as changing the order in which numbers appear in a formula may also make a big difference. For example, consider these two formulas (refer back to Table 3.1 for the order in which Excel will evaluate the formulas):

3*6+5 = 23

but

6+5*3 = 21

This is where it's important to know what you are trying to accomplish with your formula and to be cautious about what you want Excel to do. Errors like these are the worst kind because Excel will never stop to ask you if you really want the 5 to come before the 3; it will just go ahead and perform whatever calculation you entered into the system.

Here are a few more examples. Try to calculate these yourself and see if you get the same answers:

(3*15)+2^(6/3) = 49

3*15+2^6/3 = 66.333...

12*4/6+4 = 12

12*((4/6)+4) = 55.999...

Range Referencing

The concept of ranges and how they are used by Excel was briefly mentioned back in Chapter 1. Here, you'll learn why ranges are such a useful concept and how they can be helpful as you build and modify the logic of your worksheet.

The concept of ranges becomes more important as you proceed through this book, so now is the time to learn the correct way to reference a range of cells. You saw examples of this earlier. Remember the function to sum up a range of numbers: =SUM(C1:C50). This function would sum up the range with its upper-left corner in C1 and its lower-right corner in C50. In other words, this range is only one column wide but 50 cells deep. Similarly, the range D1:Q1 refers to a range of cells in one row. Finally, note that a range can even be a single cell. Although it isn't very useful, the construction =SUM(A5:A5) is allowed by Excel. It simply sums the single value in cell A5.

Excel refers to a range by its upper-left and lower-right corners. For example, the range of cells named in the range A1:C3 is composed of nine cells: A1, A2, A3, B1, B2, B3, C1, C2, and C3. Figure 3.8 shows several valid ranges in a worksheet along with the *range reference* for each one—for example, G3:H9.

Figure 3.8
Ranges and their references

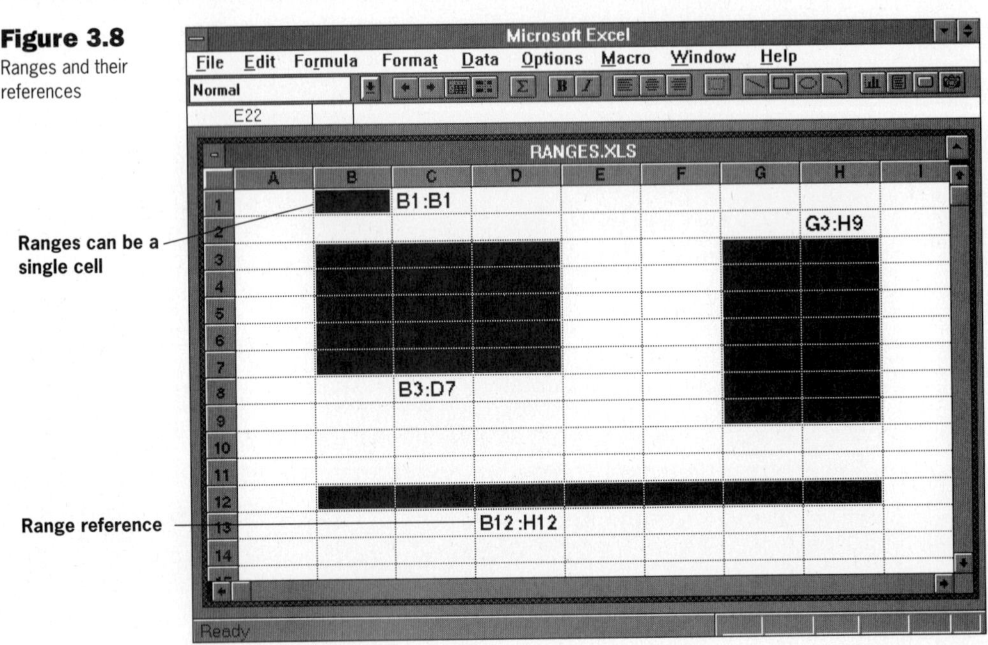

Named Ranges

Although this type of range reference is very useful, since it saves you from referring to each cell in a range individually, ranges are still somewhat cryptic. Fortunately, Excel offers an alternative way for you to refer to ranges. By assigning a name to a range of cells, you can more easily identify the contents and nature of the range. For example, referring to the sample budget worksheet (see Figure 3.1), you might choose to give the name SALARIES to the range C5:E5. Clearly, it's a lot easier to remember SALARIES than it is to remember C5:E5.

If all Excel offered was a way to name a range for future reference, it would be helpful. Even more useful, however, is Excel's ability to use named ranges in both formulas and functions. For example, if the following functions perform the exact same calculation, which one do you immediately know the purpose of?

=SUM(C5:E5)

=SUM(SALARIES)

Named ranges can also be used in formulas. You can, for instance, create a named range that refers to one cell, and then use that named range in a calculation. For example, if you have named cell E4 SALARY_TOTAL and cell E5 COST_OF_BENEFITS, you could create a formula in cell E7 that calculates the total cost of salary and benefits:

=SALARY_TOTAL+COST_OF_BENEFITS

Creating Named Ranges

Returning to our budget worksheet, we can give some of the ranges more descriptive names, which would help us later in expanding the worksheet to do other things. As with most Excel commands, you first select the object on which you want to carry out the action, and then select the action that you want carried out. Use the following instructions to create a named range:

1. Highlight the range C5:E5.
2. Click on Formula, Define Name. A dialog box appears, as shown in Figure 3.9.
3. Either enter the name you want this range to have in the Name box, or accept the name that Excel proposes. For this exercise, just accept the name Salary that Excel has proposed.
4. Click on OK to complete the command.

Excel looked at the cells you selected prior to dropping down the menu and the dialog box. When you told Excel that you wanted to apply a name to that particular range, Excel noted that there was an adjacent name (the label "Salary" you had placed there earlier), and concluded that you might like to name that range Salary.

When the dialog box appears, you can instead choose to name the range something else. You could have named this range Bullwinkle if that name was more meaningful to you. More likely, you will want to give a more descriptive name to this range, such as Research_Salaries_Q4.

Note the use of the underscore (_) character. One of the rules for the use of names in a worksheet is that they cannot contain any spaces. Instead, either an underscore or a period must be used to separate words. The name you choose can be up to 255 characters long and must start with either a letter or an underscore. Note also that Excel does not make a distinction between upper- and lowercase letters in range names. This means that Excel will consider ranges named Salary_87, SALARY_87, sALARY_87, and salary_87 to be the same range.

Creating Multiple Range Names

What do you do if you want to apply range names to several ranges at once? Excel provides a method of naming ranges for you automatically based on the logic that the label adjacent to a range is probably a reasonable name to give to that range. To see how this works, try the following steps.

Figure 3.9
Formula Define Name dialog box

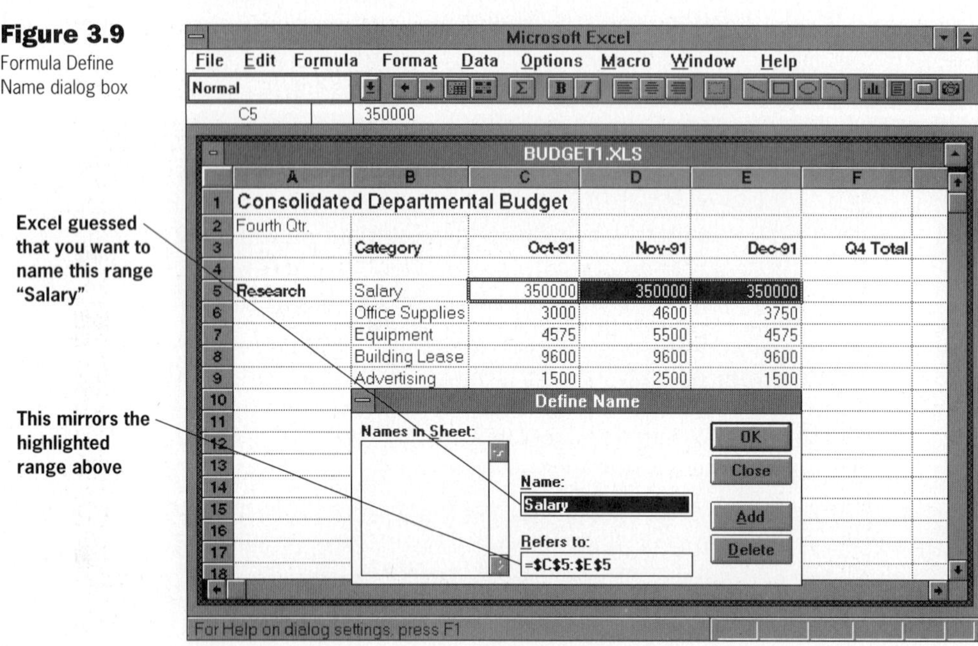

1. Highlight the ranges you want to apply names to, including the labels that Excel will use as the basis for the names. In this case, highlight the cells B3:E9.
2. Click on Formula, Create Names. A dialog box appears.
3. Make sure that the Top Row and Left Column boxes are selected. Figure 3.10 shows this dialog box with the correct selections made.
4. Click on OK to carry out the command. Excel will apply the names to the ranges and then return control of the worksheet to you.

At this point, it doesn't look like anything has happened, but it's easy to see what happened behind the scenes by clicking on Formula, Define Name and looking at the dialog box (see Figure 3.9). The box titled Names in Sheet lists all the named ranges in the worksheet. When you click on a named range, its name will appear in the Name box, and the cells that the name references appear in the Refers to box. (The reason for the dollar signs in the references here is explained in the section "Methods of Addressing" in Chapter 4.)

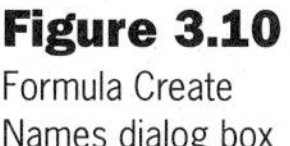

Figure 3.10
Formula Create Names dialog box

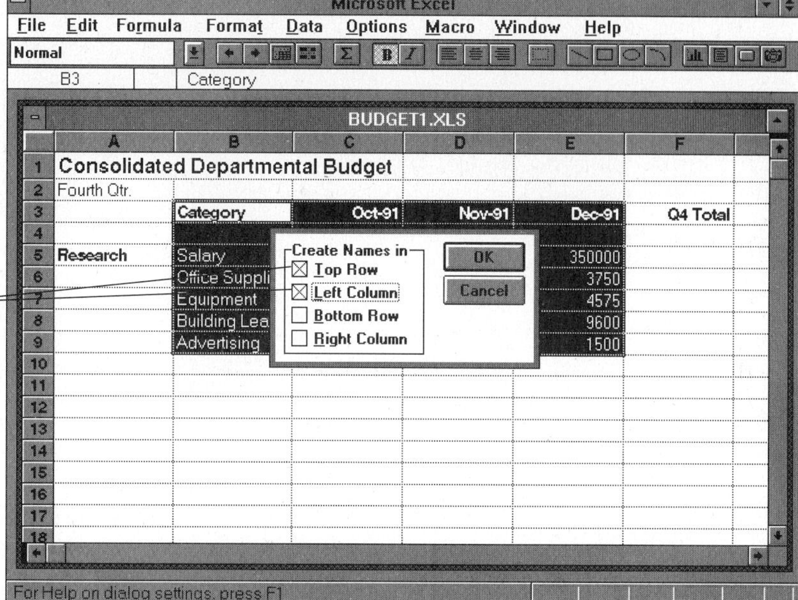

Check these boxes to create range names based on the top row and the left column

Deleting Range Names

Now that you have created several range names, you can delete any you don't like or don't need. For example, in the previous section, Excel created a number of range names for you. One of the range names it created, Category, isn't one you really need. Use the following steps to delete it:

1. Select the name you want to delete by clicking on it. If there is only one name, it will already be highlighted. Find the range name Category and click on it. Figure 3.11 shows the Formula Define Name dialog box with the Category range name selected.
2. Click on the Delete command button (at the lower-right corner of the box) to complete the command.
3. Click on the Close command button to close the dialog box.

Editing Range Names

To change a range's name, you simply assign the range a new name using Formula, Define Name, as you did before. When you do this, however, the range then has two names. If you originally named the range Interest Income, and then gave it the name Interest Earnings, you would be able to refer to it later by either name.

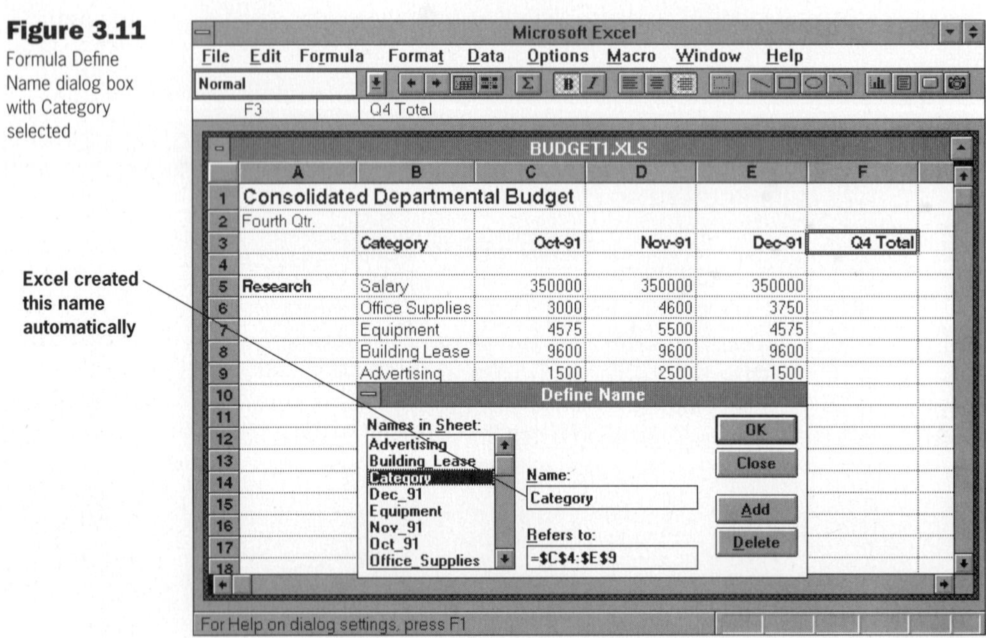
Excel created this name automatically

Figure 3.11
Formula Define Name dialog box with Category selected

For that reason (in the interest of avoiding problems later) it's a good idea to immediately delete the range name you're no longer using, as you did in the preceding section.

Worksheet Errors and Logical Errors

Unfortunately, there will come a time, perhaps sooner than later, when you are going to make an error in Excel. The error's repercussions and the time you spend tracking down the error will depend largely on what kind of error it is. For the most part, errors will fall into two categories: worksheet errors and logical errors.

Excel's Error Detection

By all accounts, it's far easier to solve worksheet errors. Excel has several ways of telling you that your formulas or calculations are erroneous—it will usually beep at you and put a special error message in the cell where the error occurred. Excel will catch a number of different kinds of errors, depending on what you did incorrectly.

The following is a list of Excel's error messages. They all begin with the number sign (#) and are followed by cryptic, yet understandable text noting the type of error. This list includes a slightly expanded description of what each error message means.

#DIV/0! This error occurs if a formula, or a formula that it references, is trying to divide by zero. For example, the formula =5/0 would return a #DIV/0 error (though they usually won't be this obvious).

#NAME? Excel returns this error when you try to reference a name that Excel does not understand. There are several causes of this error, but mostly it occurs if you misspell a reference or do not adhere to all of the syntactical rules. A simple example is forgetting to include a colon when you refer to a range. Thus the function =SUM(B23B38) will fail with a #NAME? error because Excel can't figure out what the range should be.

#N/A More of an informational message than a report of an error condition, the #N/A status is meant to show that a particular value is not available and that any calculation is suspect because not all the data is present. If you are building a model that adds two numbers, and you don't have one of the numbers, enter **#N/A** into the model as a placeholder. The formula that calculates the sum will display #N/A instead of an incorrect value.

#NUM! This error condition appears if you attempt to calculate a number that is too large or too small for Excel to handle. In addition, you will see this error condition if you use a number that is an illegal argument for a function. The function =SQRT(–1), for example, will return a #NUM! error since Excel is not equipped to handle imaginary numbers such as the square root of –1 (more on this in Chapter 4).

#NULL! You will only see this condition if you use an intersection operator with two ranges that do not share any common cells. For example, if SALARIES is the range A1:A10 and BENEFITS is the range C1:C10, then the intersection of =SALARIES BENEFITS returns #NULL!.

#VALUE! This condition occurs when you enter the incorrect operand for a formula or the incorrect argument for a function. For example, using a number where a logical value (TRUE or FALSE) was expected would return this error.

#REF! This error condition occurs if you try to reference cells that are not valid cell references. For instance, if you perform certain types of moving, pasting, or deleting operations, you might erase a cell that another formula points to, creating the #REF! error condition.

Avoiding and Detecting Logical Errors

The other kind of error is much more insidious and difficult to catch. The logical error is the one where you accidentally tell Excel to sum only 11 months of expenses instead of 12, or when you enter the projected growth next year as 50 percent instead of 5 percent (.5 versus .05), and so on. These are dangerous errors because Excel won't tell you about them. In fact, in most cases, Excel will continue to accurately calculate the numbers—the wrong numbers—but Excel doesn't know that.

Logical errors have caused many a worksheet to lose its validity. Excel doesn't have any way of knowing that one year's worth of data should be made up of 12 months, and so it will display the incorrect total. Likewise, Excel can't know that you really mean 5 percent if you entered 0.5 instead of 0.05. If you don't check yourself from time to time, you run the risk of getting caught in a potentially costly logical error.

There are a number of things you can do to catch logical errors. Excel provides several tools, which are covered in depth in Chapter 8. In the meantime, however, there are a few things you can consider as you construct your worksheet models.

Use Cross-Foot Totals This procedure requires you to calculate both down and across a range of numbers. Since the range of numbers will always sum up to the same number, no matter what order in which you choose to add the elements, both of the totals—across and down—should be the same number. If there is a discrepancy, it might be from a formula that does not sum all the numbers that it should. Figure 3.12 shows the BUDGET1 worksheet with cross-foot totals added.

The Common Sense Approach to Worksheet Auditing This is a technique that more people should consider. If you are creating a model and you have a fair guess about what the result should be, consider something to be wrong if the answer is significantly above or below the number you are expecting. If you reasonably guess that your profit next year should be 35 percent based on your calculations, there is probably something wrong with your model if it reports a projected profit of 75 percent.

Visual Clues Use visual clues whenever you can to avoid logical errors. For example, highlighting a range before you perform an action, as opposed to entering cell references, makes it less likely that you will select the wrong range. It's also more difficult to copy a formula to the wrong location if you can see where you are inserting the formula.

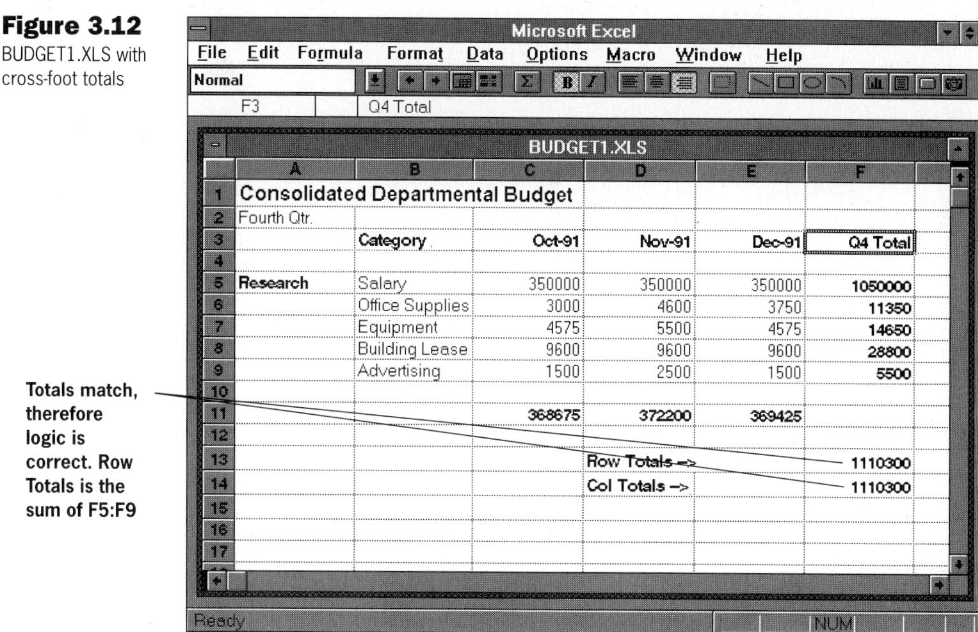

Figure 3.12
BUDGET1.XLS with cross-foot totals

This applies to building formulas, as well. If you point at a cell, you are less likely to make a mistake than if you had to just look closely at the worksheet for the cell address of a given cell.

Check Your Work Check all of your assumptions with a calculator as a backup. Generally, it's fairly easy to verify that a calculation in Excel is working if the same calculation seems to work correctly on a financial calculator.

Also, as a final check, use your common sense. For example, if you're analyzing an investment, and your model shows that your return on the investment is 2,000 percent, you'll probably want to look at your formulas again. It's more likely your investment is returning 20 percent.

CHAPTER

4

Functions, Moving and Copying Data, and Addressing

FORMULAS AND FUNCTIONS TOGETHER ARE THE BUILDING BLOCKS—THE very foundation—of worksheets. It's possible to just enter some labels and data into a worksheet, but without formulas and functions that information is just a list of facts. By adding the tools to calculate and analyze that information, you can solve almost any question you might have.

You've already worked a bit with formulas. In this chapter, you'll learn about functions and how to use them. In addition, you'll learn a few new concepts that you will use over and over as you build your worksheet models. This chapter covers copying and moving information as well as the concept of *addressing*—how you refer to other places on the spreadsheet in your calculations.

Function Basics

As you saw in the last chapter, formulas add a great deal of flexibility to the worksheet. Indeed, the combination of formulas and functions lets you turn almost any kind of numerical analysis into a model that Excel can calculate more quickly and efficiently than you could by hand. A *model*, in this sense, is similar to the word problems from your high-school math class: The toughest part of the problem was describing it in mathematical terms. If you can figure out what has to be done mathematically—that is, the steps you must follow to arrive at the answer to your problem—Excel can do the calculations in the model for you very quickly and efficiently.

Excel's worksheet functions add even more power and flexibility to the modeling process. Microsoft developers have created more than 135 functions in 11 categories, which you can use in worksheet models to perform complicated mathematical analysis, format text to display in a certain way, and execute other actions based on the value of a cell. When you couple the power of the predefined functions with the flexibility of formulas, you truly can perform almost any calculation you can imagine.

Most helpful is the ability to save time as you construct the logic of your model. In the last chapter you saw how it was possible to create a very large formula to sum up a group of numbers. But by using a single function you can reduce summing a range to the keystroke-saving =SUM(*range*).

The SUM() function is one of the most widely used of all the Excel worksheet functions, and it serves to illustrate the structure of a function. In this example, the name of the function is SUM and it requires one *argument*—a range of cells to add up, in this case. Both formulas and functions use arguments. In a formula, the operator performs some action on two or more arguments (sometimes called *operands*). Similarly, in a function, the function name takes the place of the operator and performs some action on one or more arguments. (In some cases, a function will not require an argument, but that's the exception and not the rule.)

Thus, worksheet functions are simply special tools that you can combine with formulas to put into a cell, generally for the purpose of saving you time and effort. Most often, functions will return a value that has been calculated in some way. For example, consider the function that Excel has provided for calculating the absolute value of a number. (Remember that the absolute value of a number is simply that number without its sign.) If cell B3 contains the value –5, the function =ABS(B3) will return the value 5 in the cell where the function is stored.

Functions are also very helpful when you are trying to perform a complex calculation. Consider the function Excel provides to calculate an exponential curve to fit a set of data. Although few people will have a need for this function (or even understand it), it does serve to illustrate the point. The function =LOGEST(*range*) performs the mathematical equation

$$y=(b*(m_1\hat{}x_1)*(m_2\hat{}x_2)*...)$$

which saves you a "few" keystrokes.

Not all worksheet functions in Excel are this esoteric. For example, Excel also provides functions to perform common mathematical calculations such as averages and median values. In fact, not all of Excel's functions perform mathematical calculations. Many perform operations on text strings such as searching for a value and replacing it with another string (the REPLACE() function), converting text to upper- or lowercase (the UPPER/LOWER() functions), or repeating a text string a given number of times (the REPT() function).

Finally, functions are very similar to formulas in the way they are used, and in some cases, the two may be used interchangeably. In real life, most calculations on a worksheet are built with combinations of formulas and functions.

The Ten-Second Function

To give you a taste of Excel's most popular function, let's continue working on the BUDGET1.XLS worksheet. After you retrieve your version of BUDGET1, compare it to the one in Figure 4.1. You will need to make sure that your version looks like that one before you proceed. Your goal here is to add totals to columns C, D, E, and F. You will use several methods to add these totals.

The fastest way to add totals to any worksheet is to use the summation tool on the toolbar. Remember, the purpose of the toolbar is to speed up your access to the most frequently used tools. Follow these steps to add a total at the bottom of column C:

1. Highlight cell C11. This is the cell that will contain the function.
2. Locate the summation icon on the toolbar. It's the one that looks something like a capital E.

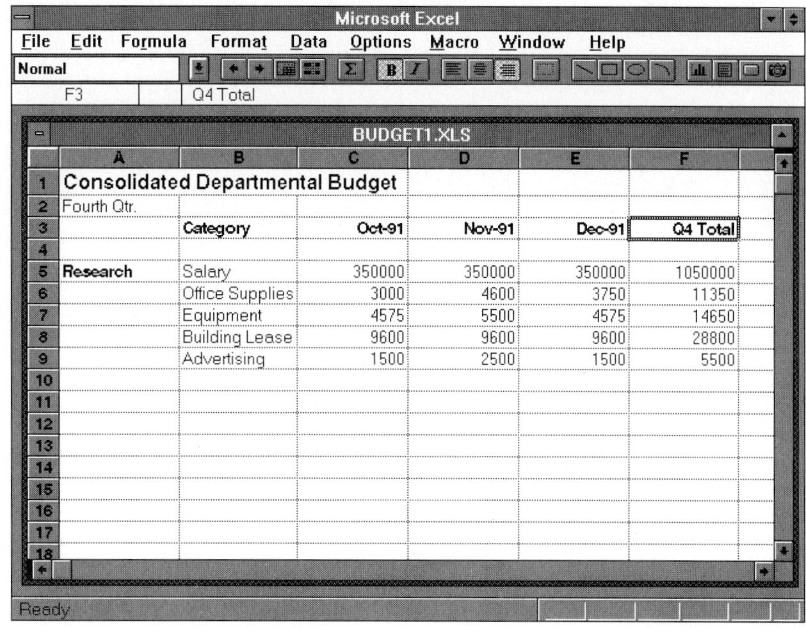

Figure 4.1
BUDGET1.XLS before adding column totals

3. Click once on the summation icon. Notice the dotted box that surrounds the range C5:C10 (see Figure 4.2). This box, called a *marquee*, represents Excel's best guess about what you want to sum.

4. If the range you want to sum is the same one that Excel has guessed on your behalf, click again on the summation icon to complete the command.

Note. You also could have completed the formula entry using one of two other traditional methods within Excel: Either press the Enter key or click on the check mark that appears just to the left of the formula bar.

When you first click on the summation icon, Excel makes a guess about what you want to sum. In this case, Excel correctly guessed that the range C5:C10 was the one you wanted to sum. The flashing, dotted box surrounding its guess is called a marquee because the flashing looks like a movie theater marquee. When you click on the icon the second time, Excel completes the command. Look at Figure 4.3 and see what Excel has entered into cell C11 on your behalf.

Syntax Rules

Like formulas, worksheet functions must follow a certain syntax. Both this chapter and Appendix C (the function reference) will use certain conventions to illustrate the syntax of the worksheet functions. First, all functions begin with an equal sign (=) if the function appears at the beginning of a formula. If functions are nested within other functions, they do not begin with an equal sign. For example, the following set of functions is syntactically correct:

```
=SUM(AVERAGE(A5:A12),B5:B12)
```

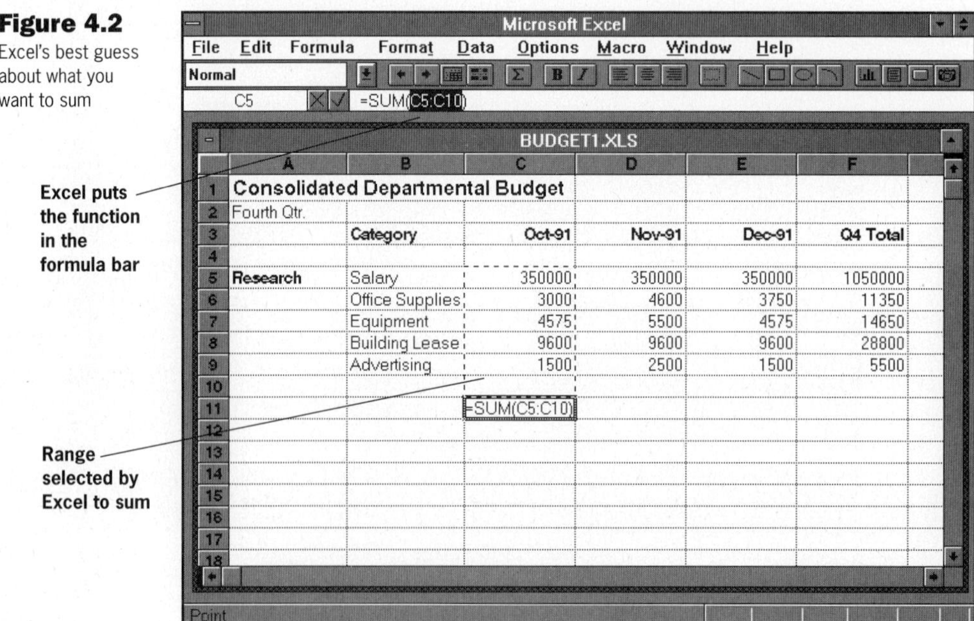
Excel puts the function in the formula bar
Range selected by Excel to sum

Figure 4.2 Excel's best guess about what you want to sum

Tip. Although Excel does not make you pay attention to case when you enter a function, Excel will capitalize a function in the formula bar if you have entered it correctly. If you see a function in lowercase in the formula bar, it means that you have spelled it incorrectly or have otherwise entered a function name that Excel doesn't recognize.

Note that only the first function, SUM(), begins with an equal sign. The other function in this formula, AVERAGE(), doesn't require a leading equal sign because it is not the first statement in the formula.

Although the worksheet functions are presented in uppercase letters, Excel does not care if you use upper-, lower-, or mixed case when you enter functions and formulas. However, you will find that, as you begin to construct more complicated models, it's easier to read your model if you are consistent with the way that you capitalize the functions.

Arguments

As mentioned earlier, almost every one of Excel's worksheet functions requires one or more arguments to do its job. Arguments are those parts of functions that appear in parentheses; they are usually separated by commas. Some functions, such as ABS() (the absolute value of a number), take only one argument, whereas others take more and still others take none. Consider the preceding example of the SUM() function. It takes two *parameters* (another word for arguments). Let's dissect the preceding function to identify all the parts of the full function:

```
=SUM(...)
```

The function name is SUM(). Note the required leading equal sign.

```
AVERAGE(A5:A12)
```

The first argument is another function. Here Excel calculates the average value of the range of numbers A5:A12.

```
B5:B12
```

The second argument is another range, which Excel will sum and add to the average of the first range.

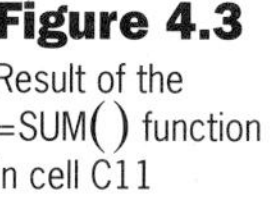

Figure 4.3
Result of the =SUM() function in cell C11

The formula bar

Microsoft Excel
File Edit Formula Format Data Options Macro Window Help
Normal
C11 =SUM(C5:C10)

BUDGET1.XLS

	A	B	C	D	E	F
1	Consolidated Departmental Budget					
2	Fourth Qtr.					
3		Category	Oct-91	Nov-91	Dec-91	Q4 Total
4						
5	Research	Salary	350000	350000	350000	1050000
6		Office Supplies	3000	4600	3750	11350
7		Equipment	4575	5500	4575	14650
8		Building Lease	9600	9600	9600	28800
9		Advertising	1500	2500	1500	5500
10						
11			368675			
12						
13						
14						
15						
16						
17						
18						

Ready

Not all functions accept the same kind of arguments. For instance, the SUM() function will accept either individual numbers, a range of cells containing numbers, a named range of numbers, or a combination of all three, for example:

```
=SUM(12,14,SALARIES,B5:B13,18)
```

On the other hand, the LOWER( ) function only accepts a text argument, which it then converts to lowercase.

To further complicate things, many functions require more than one argument of *different* types. Consider the LEFT( ) function, which returns a portion of a text string. This function takes two arguments: a string of text and a number that represents how much of the text string you want to use.

Finally, there are a few functions that do not take arguments. The PI( ) function, for example, simply represents the value of pi to 15 digits of accuracy. By using this function, you don't have to remember (or research) what the value of pi is if you need it in a calculation. Another example is the NOW( ) function, which simply inserts the current date and time into the worksheet.

All of this may seem complicated at first look, but it will become quite logical after you work with Excel for a while. Appendix C contains a table showing all 135 functions grouped into 11 categories. (These categories are described later in this chapter.) Appendix C also contains a detailed reference to the most important functions in Excel.

Entering Worksheet Functions

You have already seen the fastest way to sum a range of numbers. Unfortunately, although the summation icon is very useful, it can only be used to calculate sums. For all the other functions you might want to use as the logic of your worksheet unfolds, you will need to use one of three methods to enter functions into your worksheet. First, you can simply type the function into a cell. But unless you're proficient with the various arguments the function requires, you might have to dip into the manual to get some guidance about the syntax of the arguments.

An easier way to enter functions is with the Formula, Paste Function command. This command displays a dialog box that contains the names of all the functions. Once you have scrolled to the function that you want to use, just click on it and it will appear in the formula bar, complete with the arguments listed for you to fill in.

Finally, if the functions you use most often contain a number of range names as arguments (many of them do), you can also use the Formula, Paste Names command in concert with the Formula, Paste Function command. With the Formula, Paste Names feature, you can pick from a list of all the named ranges in the worksheet, again eliminating the chances of mistyping a name and suffering a beep from Excel. Let's take a look at all three methods.

Typing a Function

The most straightforward way to enter functions is to type them into the worksheet, just as you would any other label or number. Enter a function to sum column D using the following steps:

1. Highlight the cell where you want the sum to appear—in this case, cell D11.
2. Enter the function **=SUM(D5:D9)**.
3. Press Enter to complete the command.

Figure 4.4 shows the results of this command. If you move the cell pointer back and forth between cells C11 and D11, you'll note that the results of typing the function directly are the same as using the summation icon, even though the ranges you summed differ.

Figure 4.4
Worksheet after typing in the =SUM( ) function

Microsoft Excel
File Edit Formula Format Data Options Macro Window Help
Normal
D11 =SUM(D5:D9)
BUDGET1.XLS

	A	B	C	D	E	F
1	Consolidated Departmental Budget					
2	Fourth Qtr.					
3		Category	Oct-91	Nov-91	Dec-91	Q4 Total
4						
5	Research	Salary	350000	350000	350000	1050000
6		Office Supplies	3000	4600	3750	11350
7		Equipment	4575	5500	4575	14650
8		Building Lease	9600	9600	9600	28800
9		Advertising	1500	2500	1500	5500
10						
11			368675	372200		
12						
13						
14						
15						
16						
17						
18						

Ready

Using Formula, Paste Function

Now try the following steps to sum the contents of column E using the Formula, Paste Function command.

1. Highlight cell E11. This is where you want the function to be placed.
2. Click on Formula, Paste Function. The dialog box shown in Figure 4.5 appears.
3. Scroll through this list until you find the SUM( ) function.
4. Highlight the SUM( ) function if it is not already highlighted.
5. Click on OK to paste the function into the formula bar. Figure 4.6 shows what cell E11 and the formula bar look like at this point.
6. Click on the formula bar. Then edit its contents so that the SUM( ) function shows the range E5:E9 between the parentheses.
7. Press the Enter key to finish editing the formula bar and enter the completed function into cell E11.

Tip. Instead of scrolling through a long list of function names, just type the first letter of the function; Excel will go to the first item in the list that starts with that letter. If you want to look for other items that start with the same letter, just keep pressing that letter.

Figure 4.5
Formula Paste Function dialog box

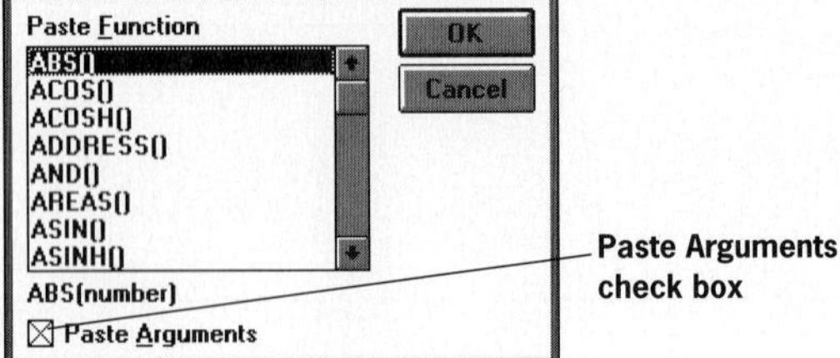

Note the Paste Arguments check box in Figure 4.5. By default, this box is checked when you paste a function into Excel. As long as it's on, you will be reminded of the required arguments.

Using Formula, Paste Name

Before you sum the contents of column F, quickly add a range name for the row totals you added in Chapter 3. This way, you can take advantage of Excel's ability to use a range name in a function. Follow these steps to create the named range:

1. Highlight the range F5:F9.
2. Click on Formula, Define Name.
3. Enter **Q4_Totals** in the Name box.
4. Click on OK to complete the command.

Figure 4.6
Worksheet after pasting the =SUM( ) function into the formula bar

Excel will paste placeholder arguments in the function if you wish

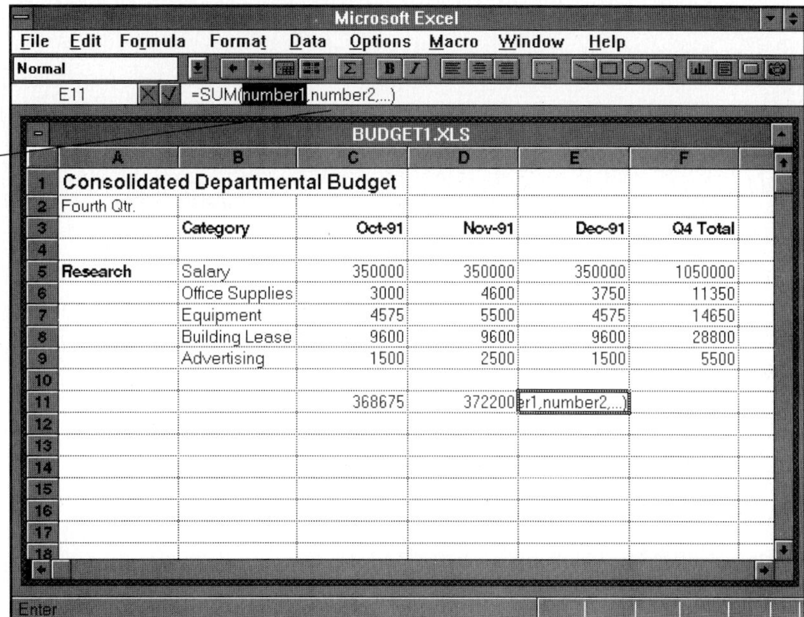

Now that you have added the range name, you can use the following steps to total column F by pasting a named range into the function:

1. Highlight the cell that you want to contain the contents of the calculation—cell F11.
2. Click on Formula, Paste Function.
3. Highlight the SUM() function as you did in the previous example.
4. This time, turn off the Paste Arguments check box.
5. Click on OK to paste the function into the formula bar. Note that there are no sample arguments this time. Your screen should look like Figure 4.7.
6. With the cursor still in the formula bar, click on the Formula, Paste Name command. A dialog box like the one shown in Figure 4.8 appears.
7. Highlight the range named Q4_Total.
8. Click on OK to paste the range name into the function in the formula bar.

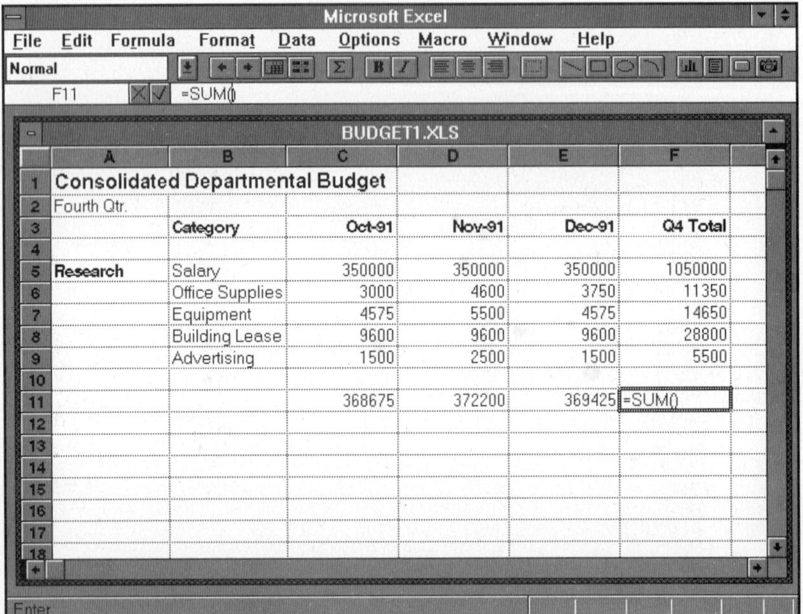

Figure 4.7
Pasting a function into the formula bar without arguments

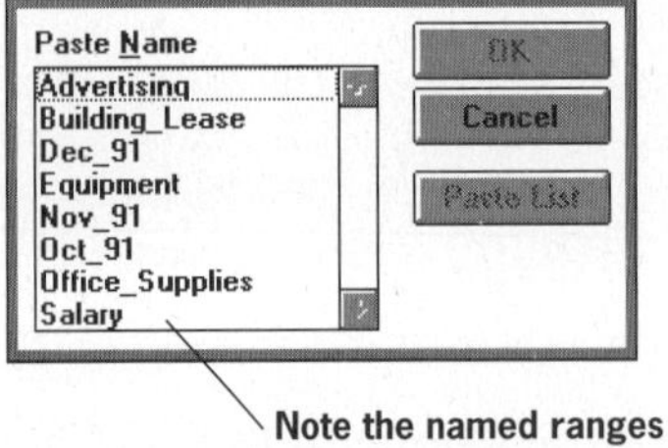

Figure 4.8
Formula Paste Name dialog box

9. Click on the check mark icon just to the left of the formula bar to complete the command.

When you have completed these steps, your worksheet should have totals at the bottom of each column containing numbers and should look very similar to the one shown in Figure 4.9.

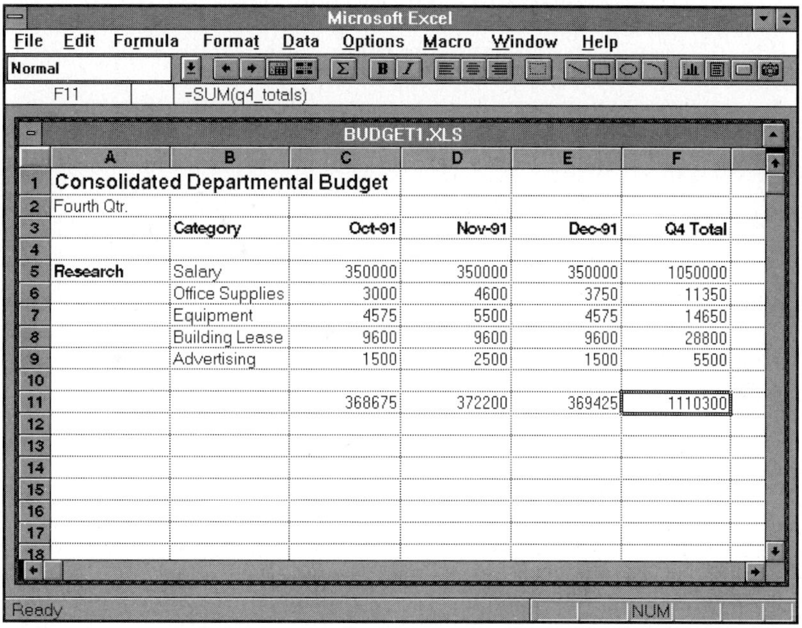

Figure 4.9
BUDGET1.XLS after adding sums to all the columns

Excel's Function Categories

The following descriptions are designed to give you an idea of how the worksheet functions are grouped by category. Each of the 11 categories contains several predefined functions, which you can use to accomplish a wide variety of tasks. All the worksheet functions are listed in Appendix C and many of them are fully described there.

Database Functions

The database functions are used, as the name implies, when you are using Excel more as a repository of data than as a complex worksheet full of calculations. Databases in Excel use special range designations to refer to parts of the database, for example, where the data is stored or where any records that you might extract should be put. (You'll learn more about databases in Chapter 14.) These functions use the special database range designations as arguments to calculate sums, averages, standard deviations, and so on for values that satisfy certain criteria.

Consider a database of employee addresses with a field called Salary that contains the employee's salary. With the DAVERAGE() function, for example, you could compute the average salary of a selected subset of the database records.

Date and Time Functions

Excel's date and time functions are quite useful for displaying dates and times in a variety of formats and styles. Since Excel stores dates and times as a special kind of number, you can also do arithmetic on dates and times.

For example, you could create a worksheet that showed the correct number of days between your birthday and the current date. The NOW() function always returns the current date and time as reported by your computer's clock.

Other date and time functions help you determine what day, month, or year it is, and to calculate the number of days between two dates.

Financial Functions

The financial functions are those that perform very complicated mathematical equations to help you calculate models generally related to business. You would use financial functions, for example, if you wanted to depreciate an item using the double declining balance method, or if you wanted to calculate the future value of an annuity. Anyone with a need to calculate investment or lending-related questions will find these functions invaluable.

Financial functions generally require a number of arguments to work. Consider the RATE() function. It requires three arguments and accepts another three optional ones. So, a typical RATE() function might look like this:

```
=RATE(48,-300,10000,0,0,.09)
```

This function calculates the monthly interest on a 4-year (48 months) $10,000 loan that will have a future value of 0 with payments of $300 per month due at the beginning of each period. (The answer, by the way, is 1.6 percent per month, or 19.19 percent per year. Pretty steep.)

Informational Functions

The informational functions perform a number of tasks that relate to specific information about parts of the worksheet. For example, the CELL() function can give you information about the formatting, contents, and location of a particular cell. These functions are important if you want to build more complicated models and you need to take certain actions based on a condition within the cell.

Logical Functions

The logical functions are, at first glance, not entirely logical at all. It takes some time to get used to the concept of a function that only returns a value of TRUE or FALSE. These functions are very important, however, because they let you make comparisons between two or more conditions. Once you know whether the conditions are equal or not, you can choose a different action based on the results of the test.

Here's an example of the logical function IF( ):

```
=IF(YEAR(NOW())=1991,"It's 1991!","It's not 1991")
```

The purpose of this function is to compare the current year (found by determining the year value of the current time) with the text string "1991". If the values are equal, then the words "It's 1991!" appear in the cell. Otherwise (that is, if the test is FALSE) the words "It's not 1991" appear in the cell.

Lookup Functions

Lookup functions are a bit more difficult and for the most part fall outside the scope of this book. Basically, lookup functions are used to point to data in tabular form. These functions have application in those worksheets where it makes sense to store data in lookup tables.

An example of this might be in a tax accountant's worksheet. A lookup table would be used to determine the tax based on another value, in this case, the taxable income. Once the table is set up correctly, Excel scans the table, finds the value of the taxable income, and then finds the matching amount of tax to pay in the lookup table.

Mathematical Functions

The mathematical functions do just what they sound like they do. These functions perform calculations of all sorts. For instance, the ABS( ) function returns the absolute value of a number, and the ROUND( ) function is useful for rounding off numbers. Here's an example of how easy it is to nest these functions:

```
=ABS(PI()*PRODUCT(2,3,2))
```

Remember the order of precedence for this exercise. Calculation begins in the innermost set of parentheses and works outward. This function first multiplies 2 times 3 times 2, to give you 12. Then, Excel computes 12 times the value of pi, and finally takes the absolute value of the result: 37.699.

Matrix Functions

Far beyond the scope of this book, the matrix functions perform mathematical calculations on matrices of numbers. These calculations perform such tasks as computing the inverse of a matrix or transposing a matrix to have different dimensions.

Statistical Functions

Excel's statistical functions are useful for performing calculations of basic statistics such as the arithmetic mean, median, standard deviation (population and sample), and variance (population and sample).

In addition, Excel provides several different methods of calculating multiple regression equations. These calculations, when used with experience and caution, help you to determine the future performance—the trend—of something through time.

String (Text) Functions

The string functions are very useful for working with text on your worksheet. There are a number of these functions, and they perform a variety of tasks. For example, the PROPER() function capitalizes the first letter of text arguments, and the UPPER() function converts each letter of the text argument to uppercase.

In addition, there are functions that can extract a designated number of characters from the right or left end of a string (the RIGHT() and LEFT() functions), as well as a function that can replace one string with another (the REPLACE() function).

Trigonometric Functions

Finally, the trigonometric functions are for those who need fairly complex mathematical functions. You can use these functions to calculate all sorts of neat things such as the cosine, the arcsine, and my favorite, the inverse hyperbolic tangent of a number.

Copying and Moving

Excel would not be very flexible if it didn't have a way to move or copy data from one part of the worksheet to another. And, in fact, Excel does provide a way to either move or copy any range of cells to another range. But first, let's spend a moment on the difference between moving and copying.

When you *move* data from one part of the worksheet to another, the data is deleted from the *source range*; that is, the original data is no longer where it was. Instead it appears at another location—the target range. On the other hand, to *copy* data is exactly what the word implies—data is duplicated from one spot and inserted in another, leaving the original data intact and resulting in two ranges that contain the same exact information.

In practice, copying data and moving data are similar. Excel makes use of something called the *clipboard* as a temporary place to save information. You issue a command that temporarily stores information on the clipboard, and then you give another command that places that information elsewhere within the worksheet or even in other Windows-based applications.

When you want to move data, you *cut*—or remove—data from the worksheet. That data is then automatically stored on the clipboard until the next time you either cut or copy an item to the clipboard. You then *paste* the data back to the worksheet at the point that you want it to appear.

Copying data involves nearly the same steps. Instead of cutting the data, you *copy* it to the clipboard, and then paste it where you want it to go. The difference is that cutting to the clipboard means that the data is removed from the source cells, whereas copying to the clipboard only puts a copy of the source cells on the clipboard. The whole process sounds more complicated than it actually is. After you practice a couple of times, it will seem like second nature.

Before you proceed, make sure your worksheet is saved. That way, as you copy and move data around, you won't have to worry about messing something up if you make a mistake—you'll be able to reload the saved worksheet if you have a problem.

As with many other operations in Excel, copying and moving data can be done with the keyboard, once you get the hang of the concept. For these exercises, however, we'll use the mouse to perform the moving and copying commands. First, use the following steps to delete some of the column totals in order to make room to practice moving and copying some formulas and functions:

1. Highlight the range D11:F11.
2. Click on Edit, Clear.
3. Click on OK to complete the command.

Moving Formulas and Data

At this point, you only have the formula that is left in cell C11. Use the following commands to move the function from cell C11 to cell F11:

1. Highlight cell C11. This is the cell whose contents you want to move to the new location.
2. Click on Edit, Cut. Remember that cutting removes the data from the source and puts it onto the clipboard.

3. Highlight cell F11. This is the target cell, the one you want to receive the data from the clipboard. Note the marquee around the source cell. This serves to remind you what cell (or range) you have selected to be either copied or moved. The target cell (F11 in this case) is also called the *paste range.* At this point, check that your worksheet looks like Figure 4.10.

Figure 4.10
Moving a function

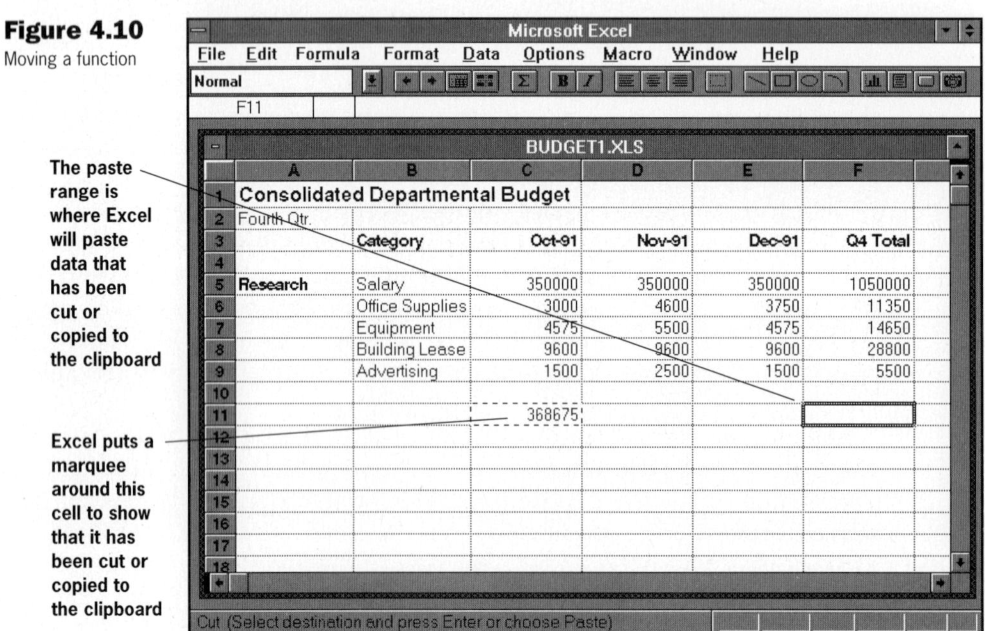

4. Click on Edit, Paste to paste the contents of the clipboard into the paste range.

After you finish these steps, your worksheet should look like Figure 4.11.

Look closely at Figure 4.11. The formula bar shows the contents of cell F11, but note that Excel has not automatically adjusted the contents of the cell to reflect the fact that it has moved. If you look closely at the formula bar, you'll see that the contents of cell F11 still refer to summing column C—obviously an error. This points out an important lesson: Watch carefully what Excel does as you move or copy data from one place to another. In the next section, you'll see a method that works a bit better for what we are trying to do here.

Figure 4.11
Worksheet after moving the function from cell C11 to F11

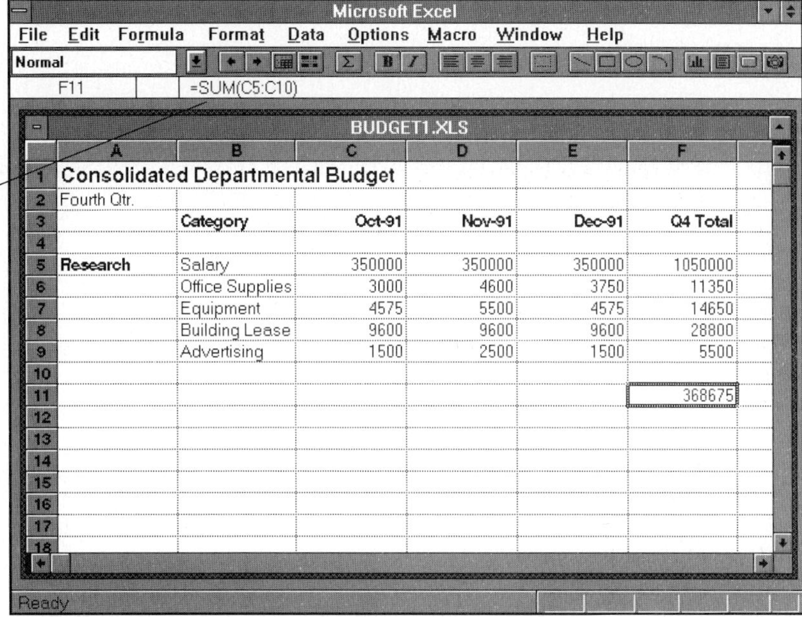

Formula still shows the sum of column C

Copying Formulas and Data

Now suppose you want to reinsert the function in cells C11 through E11. Instead of reentering the function at the bottom of each column, it makes sense to simply copy it from cell F11 to the range of cells C11:E11.

But wait a moment! You already saw that when Excel moved the formula from cell C11 to F11 it didn't automatically adjust the contents of the cell to reflect its new position on the worksheet. Before you can perform a successful copy operation, you need to replace the wrong function in cell F11 with one that will automatically adjust as you copy it across the C11:E11 range. The following steps simply sum the range of values in a column using the Autosum feature:

1. With cell F11 highlighted, click on the Autosum icon on the toolbar.
2. Click again on the Autosum icon to accept Excel's guess about what to sum and complete the command.

OK. *Now* you are ready to quickly copy the contents of cell F11 (the SUM() function) to the rest of the columns. Use the following steps.

1. With cell F11 still highlighted, click on Edit, Copy. Notice the marquee around the cell. The contents of cell F11 have now been copied to the clipboard.
2. Highlight the cell or the range where you want the contents of the cell inside the marquee to appear. In this case, highlight the range C11:E11. Your worksheet should now look like Figure 4.12.
3. Click on Edit, Paste to paste the contents of the clipboard into the paste range.
4. Finally, press the Esc key to remove the marquee from cell F11.

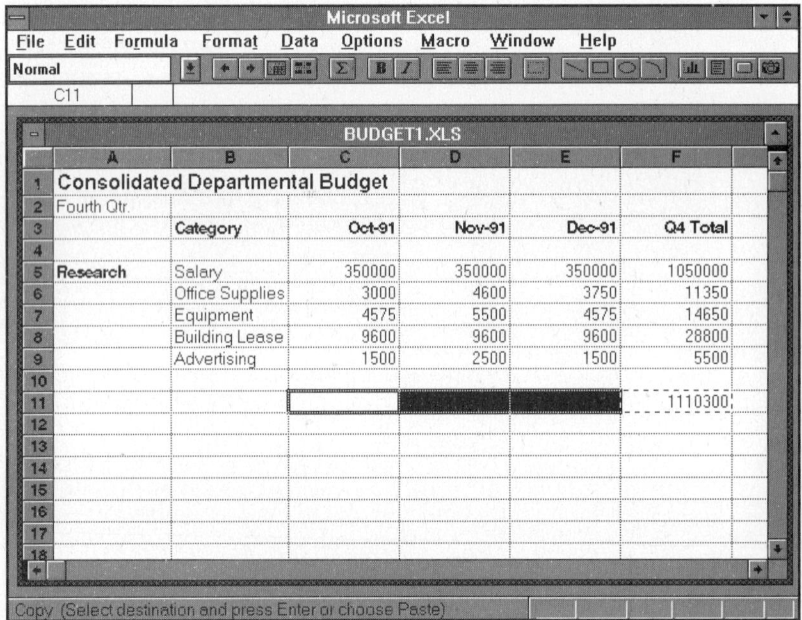

Figure 4.12
Highlighting the paste range

After completing the process, the worksheet should look like Figure 4.13.

This time, Excel correctly made the adjustments to the functions as you copied data from one cell to another. This illustrates the difference between the relative cell addresses, used here, and absolute cell addresses, which were used before. If the function in F11 had contained absolute references to that column, the moved function in cell C11 would not have summed the values in column C, but those in column F. (More on addressing in a moment.) This kind of accident is another way to get yourself into logical errors.

Figure 4.13
Worksheet after completing the copy operation

	A	B	C	D	E	F
1	Consolidated Departmental Budget					
2	Fourth Qtr.					
3		Category	Oct-91	Nov-91	Dec-91	Q4 Total
4						
5	Research	Salary	350000	350000	350000	1050000
6		Office Supplies	3000	4600	3750	11350
7		Equipment	4575	5500	4575	14650
8		Building Lease	9600	9600	9600	28800
9		Advertising	1500	2500	1500	5500
10						
11			368675	372200	369425	1110300

Saving Your Work

As always, you should save your work before moving on to something else. Check to make sure that your worksheet looks like Figure 4.13, since that's what we'll continue to use in the next couple of chapters.

This time, instead of using the menu to save your files, why not try one of Excel's keyboard shortcuts to help speed the process? To save your current worksheet with its current name, just press Shift-F12. Once you get the hang of this keystroke combination, it's a very speedy way to save your file.

Note, however, that some keyboards don't have the F11 and F12 keys, and even on some that do various system incompatibilities might preclude their use. If you face this situation, use the mouse command File, Save, or the equivalent keyboard command Alt-FS.

Methods of Addressing

Addressing refers to the way you tell Excel to look for values in your formulas throughout the worksheet. Whether you think about it or not, each time you construct a formula, you use the concept of addressing. You have seen that Excel is able to adjust a formula automatically when you copy it. It's also possible to move a formula and have it adjust correctly. The way you approach addressing determines whether your formulas will still perform correctly as you move and copy data around the worksheet.

As you copy formulas and functions from their original locations, Excel needs to know where to go to get the information. For example, if cell A1 contains 3 and A2 contains 2, the formula =A1+A2 will total 5. Say that this formula is in cell A4. Now, what happens if you copy that formula to cell B4? Where will Excel look to find the two numbers to add together? Will Excel look in cells A1 and A2, or will it look in cells B1 and B2? The answer depends totally on how you choose to set up the cell addressing. The common sense answer to this simple example seems to be that the formula should look in cells B1 and B2, but there are some cases in which you want a formula to look specifically in one place, and one place only, for a particular value.

By way of analogy, consider two ways to give directions to a specific location within a city. If someone asks you where the police station is, you could tell them that it's located at 1212 Main Street. This example corresponds to *absolute addressing,* because from any part of the city, the person would have the information needed to find the police station. On the other hand, you could tell the individual that the police station was "down to the first light, turn left, go two blocks, turn right, third building on the left." This example corresponds to *relative addressing,* because it depends on where you are for the directions to work. From any other place in the city, the instructions, *relative to your current position*, would be useless.

The topic of addressing is one of the more difficult to comprehend the first time around. It requires that you understand what the formulas and functions you use are doing, and it forces you to examine exactly what it is that you want to present with your model.

Relative Addressing

Most addressing you will do as you first begin to work with Excel will be relative addressing. And, in fact, most of the exercises you have performed up to this point used relative cell addresses. Take a look Figure 4.14. It's a version of the budget worksheet that you've been working on, but modified to show the actual contents of the cells. In this case, it makes sense that if you copy the contents of cell F5 to cells F6 through F9, you would want Excel to adjust the references for each row, and, in fact, that's what happens when you copy the formula down.

Excel uses relative addressing by default. However, with absolute addressing and mixed addressing (a combination of absolute and relative), you can change this behavior to suit your special purposes.

Figure 4.14
Actual cell contents

	A	B	C	D	E	F
1	Consolidatec					
2	Fourth Qtr.					
3		Category	33512	33543	33573	Q4 Total
4						
5	Research	Salary	350000	350000	350000	=C5+D5+E5
6		Office Supplies	3000	4600	3750	=C6+D6+E6
7		Equipment	4575	5500	4575	=C7+D7+E7
8		Building Lease	9600	9600	9600	=C8+D8+E8
9		Advertising	1500	2500	1500	=C9+D9+E9
10						
11			=SUM(C5:C10)	=SUM(D5:D10)	=SUM(E5:E10)	=SUM(F5:F10)

Absolute Addressing

Absolute addressing is used when you want Excel to look for values in precisely the same place no matter where you move or copy them around the worksheet. An example will illustrate this. If cell B5 contains 12 and cell B6 contains 12, the formula =$B$5+$B$6 will *always* return the value 24 (unless you change the contents of B5 and B6, of course) regardless of where on the worksheet you enter the formula.

You have already seen a few examples of absolute addressing. Do you recall earlier in this chapter when you worked with the Formula Define Name dialog box to name a range? Click on Formula, Define Name to pop up that dialog box again. You can see that the contents of the box labeled "Refers to" show cell references as absolute addresses.

To turn a relative reference into an absolute address, you simply edit the cell reference to include a dollar sign ($) before both the column number and row number. For example, A5 is a relative address, and $A$5 is the same cell simply expressed as an absolute address. Thus, any time you want to change a relative cell address to an absolute address, you move to the cell that contains the formula, press F2 to edit the contents of the cell, and insert the $ character in front of each element of the cell address.

Mixed Addressing

Mixed addressing is the logical middle ground between relative addressing and absolute addressing. When you use mixed addressing, you tell Excel that as you copy or move formulas or functions it can adjust some part of the reference but not the rest.

For example, if you wanted to multiply all your profit predictions by a certain percentage figure, you would want all the calculations in one column to be multiplied by a single cell—in this example, the growth figure. By constructing your formulas to use mixed addressing, part of the formula is free to be adjusted, but the other always refers to a specific place. For instance, the address $A5 always refers to column A, but can refer to any row. Conversely, A$5 can refer to any column, but always references row 5.

Worksheet Formatting and Presentation

Printing the Worksheet

Charting and Graphing

Graphical Objects on the Worksheet

Worksheet Outlining

PART 2

Data Presentation and Graphing

CHAPTER

Worksheet Formatting and Presentation

AS YOU SAW BACK IN CHAPTER 2, EXCEL IS VERY FLEXIBLE ABOUT THE way you can format worksheets. In this chapter, you'll learn some techniques for constructing an aesthetically pleasing worksheet by using a variety of Excel's formatting and presentation tools. This chapter also points out another area of Excel's flexibility. Much as worksheet functions give you the flexibility to design whatever logic you wish into your worksheet, custom number formats give you the ability to create any type of format you want for numbers. It's this flexibility and programmability that set Excel apart from most of its competitors.

Working with Fonts

Because Excel is based on the Microsoft Windows environment, it is possible to take advantage of a wide variety of type styles and sizes in order to enhance the appearance of your worksheet. Windows, as the operating environment, provides a number of services to those programs that run under it. Fonts are one type of service Windows provides to all Windows-based applications. You have already seen a few examples of how to change the size and attributes of text. Now let's take another look at what you can do with Excel's font-handling functions.

First, load the BUDGET1.XLS worksheet you have been preparing. Then use the following instructions to change the characteristics of a range of cells.

1. Highlight the range B5:B9. This is the range of cells that you will change to another size and style.
2. Click on Format, Font to pop up the dialog box.
3. Find the Font list box and move through the available fonts until you come to one called either Times or Tms Rmn. When you have found one of them, highlight it.
4. Make sure that 10 is selected in the Size list box.
5. Check to be sure that none of the special attributes such as Bold or Italic have been selected. The dialog box should look like the one in Figure 5.1. (Remember that your font list might be different, depending on the fonts installed on your computer system.)
6. Click on OK to complete the command and apply your changes to the selected range.

Once you have finished these commands, your worksheet should resemble Figure 5.2.

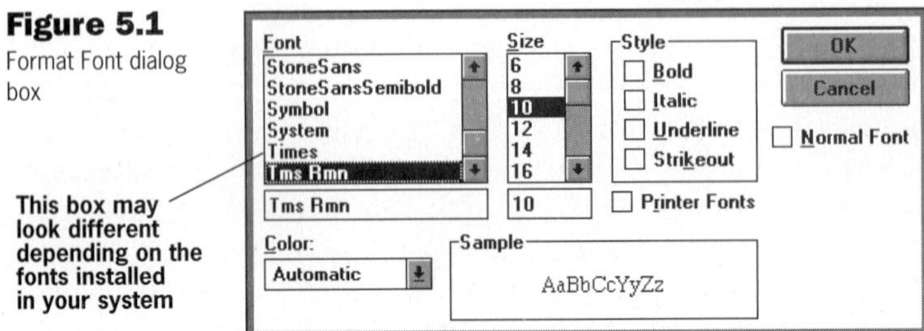

Figure 5.1
Format Font dialog box

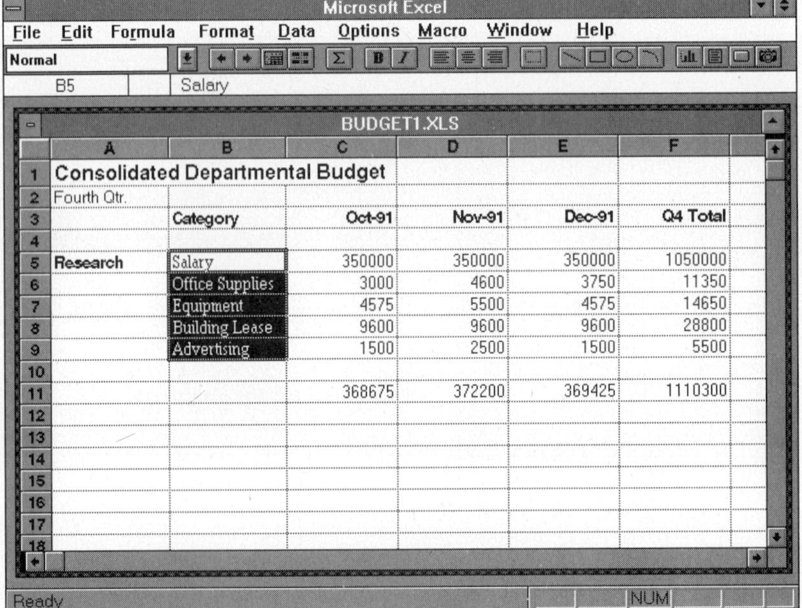

Figure 5.2
Worksheet after applying a new font style

Sizes and Fonts

Let's look at the elements of the Format Font dialog box (Figure 5.1). This dialog box lets you control several aspects of the text you use in your worksheet. The first of these is the typeface you use. In this book, the term *typeface* is used to refer to the style of the text, such as Helvetica Bold, Times Roman Italic, and so on. The term *font* is used to refer to a specific size of text in a particular typeface, for instance, Helvetica Bold 12-point, Times Roman Italic 24-point, and so on.

If you look at the Font list box in the Format Font dialog box, you'll see that Excel gives you a number of typefaces to choose from. This list will vary greatly, depending on the type of printer you have installed, as well as whether you are using any third-party type enhancement products such as Bitstream's FaceLift or Adobe Systems' Adobe Type Manager (ATM). These products allow you to add many more typefaces than are originally shipped with Windows 3.0. If you have one of these products installed, you will have a more substantial list of typefaces than the user who didn't install this third-party product.

The other important aspect of the type that you can control is the size. Use the Size box to control how large the text in a cell or range will be, measured in points. A *point* is a text measurement. One point corresponds to $^1/_{72}$ of an inch; so, 36-point type is $^{36}/_{72}$ or $^1/_2$ inch tall.

The numbers that you see in the Size box show the size of text that you can print with the installed fonts. However, if your printer or software configuration supports it (PostScript printers, for example), you need not choose one of these point sizes. Instead, you can simply type in the point size you want at the bottom of the Size box. Excel can handle typefaces ranging in size from 1 point up to 409 points, although your printer may not be up to the job.

By default, 10-point Helvetica is the font Excel will use when you enter new data—label text or numbers—into the worksheet. If you are working with a worksheet and you want to format some text to whatever font is defined by the Normal style (more on styles later in this chapter), just click on the Normal Font check box, and then click on OK to complete the command.

Type Attributes

Besides the style and size of text in a worksheet, you can use other formatting enhancements. Other attributes you can control from the Format Font dialog box include the color of the cell contents, as well as more traditional text formats such as bold, italic, underline, and strikeout.

You can use colors on your worksheet, but to produce color presentations you must, of course, have a color output device. Whether in print or simply on screen, the ability to use colors is very handy in a worksheet. For example, as you'll learn later in this chapter it's possible to choose from a list of predefined numeric formats so that the number will appear in black if it is zero or a positive number and will appear in red if it is negative. The red color serves to immediately show you that a part of the worksheet is negative. For the most part, however, you'll leave the color attribute set to Automatic, which instructs Excel to use the system-wide colors you set in the Windows Control Panel.

How to Undo (and Repeat) Your Mistakes

Excel has a nice feature that you can use if you get into trouble as you are building a worksheet. Suppose you are trying to format some data and you accidentally apply the wrong formatting commands. The trouble is, you might not remember what the format was previously set to. In fact, you don't really care what attributes the entries had before—you just want them back the way they were. Fortunately, you can use Excel's Undo command to quickly reverse the effects of a number of commands.

To test this, you'll first need to make a mistake—that's easy enough. Use the following instructions to create a situation that requires the use of Undo:

1. Highlight the range C11:F11.
2. Click on Format, Font to pop up the dialog box.
3. Choose a very large font size, such as 40.
4. Click on OK to complete the command. Your worksheet should look like the one in Figure 5.3.

Notice that Excel tried to format the numbers to your specifications, but was unable to display the numbers in the amount of space provided by the cell. If you wanted to correctly display the numbers at this point, you'd have to widen the columns until the numbers displayed correctly.

At this point, you realize you've made a mistake, but you can't recall what attributes were set before you made the change. Consequently, you can't re-enter the correct size. Clicking on Edit, Undo Font, however, will quickly put the worksheet back to its former status—as it was before you made the error. The menu item is shown in Figure 5.4.

Note that the Undo option has a word following it that tells you just exactly what it is that Excel is about to undo—in this case "Font." The word that comes after Undo on the menu bar will change dynamically depending on what it is you are trying to undo, which must be the last thing you did. Excel does not have a multi-level undo feature. That is, you cannot first change a cell attribute and then delete some cells and ask Excel to undo the formatting change. Excel can only undo the very last thing that you did to the worksheet.

Also in Figure 5.4, note the menu item that follows Undo. The Repeat menu item is there in case you want to do the same thing that you just did in another part of the worksheet. For example, say you have just applied a change that involved the typeface size, and color, and applied boldfacing. If you wanted to apply those same changes to some other area of the worksheet, you would just highlight the new area and click on Edit, Repeat. Excel would then repeat the command you had just carried out.

Figure 5.3 Worksheet after formatting the text incorrectly

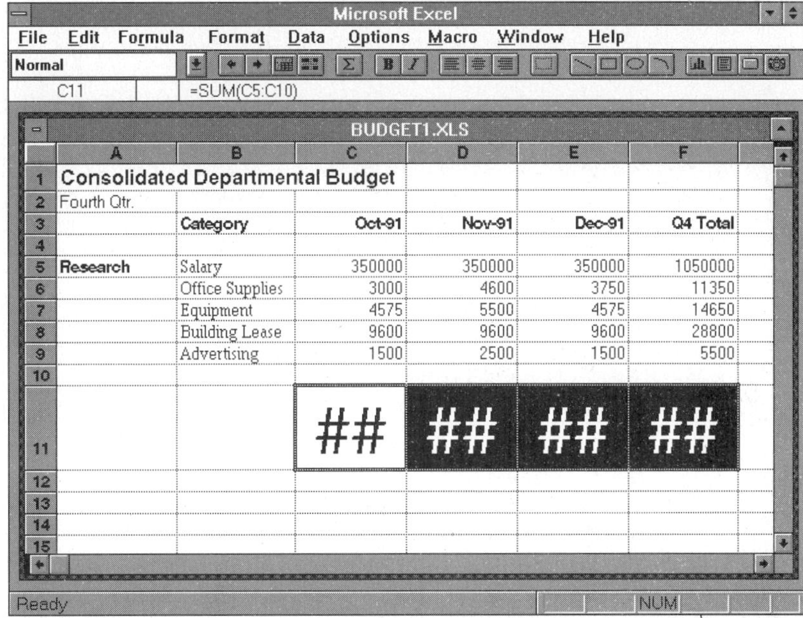

Excel displays this symbol if the column is too narrow to display the whole number

Figure 5.4 Edit menu with Undo highlighted

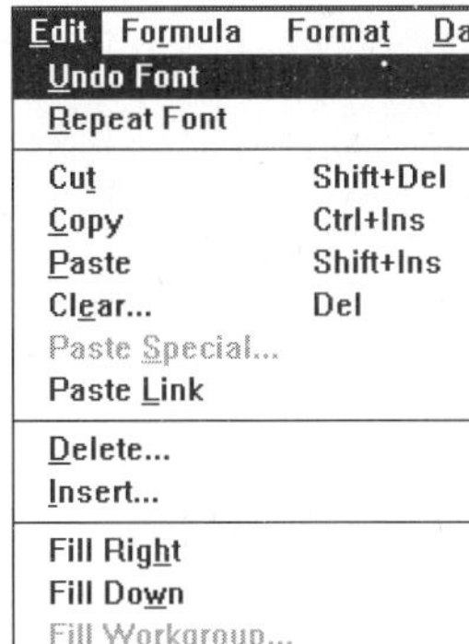

Like Undo, however, Repeat will only repeat the last action you performed. Likewise, the word that follows Repeat will change depending on what you have most recently done. For example, if you most recently performed a sort of some data on the worksheet, you would see Repeat Sort here. Or, if you had just cleared several numbers from a worksheet, you would see Repeat Clear.

Using Borders and Shading

Borders and shading are two other ways you can enhance your worksheet. Generally, borders are used to create lines around cells, and shading is used to change the color and texture of the background of each cell in the selected range. In this section, you will format two different areas of the worksheet, one with borders, and the other with shading.

Adding a Border

The following steps create a border around the numbers that make up the main portion of the worksheet:

1. Highlight the cells B5:F9. This is the range that will receive the borders.
2. Click on Format, Border to bring up the dialog box shown in Figure 5.5.
3. In the Style area of the dialog box, click on the box containing a double line. This sets the type of line Excel will use when you tell it to place the border.
4. Then, in the Borders section, click on the boxes next to the options Outline and Right.
5. Click on OK to complete the command. After you finish, your worksheet should look like Figure 5.6.

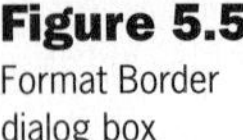

Figure 5.5
Format Border dialog box

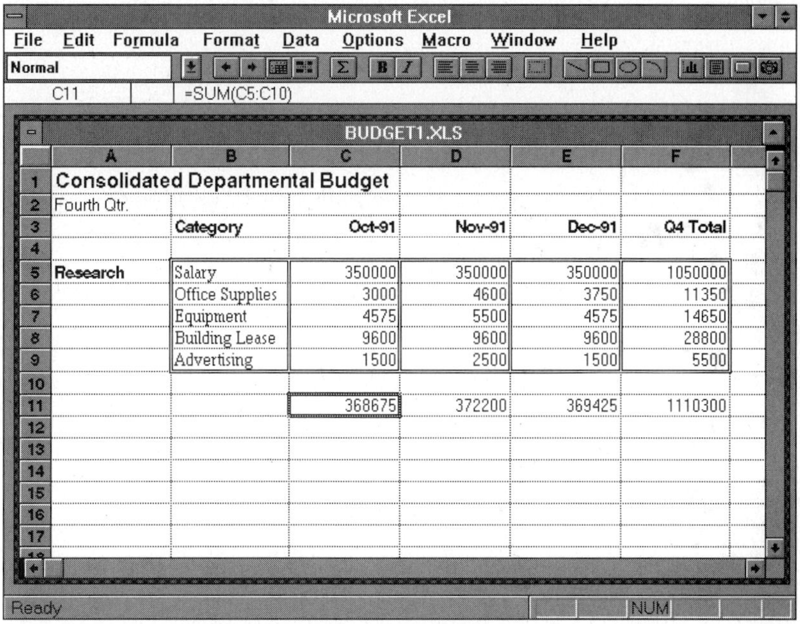

Figure 5.6
Worksheet after applying borders to a range

	A	B	C	D	E	F
1	Consolidated Departmental Budget					
2	Fourth Qtr.					
3		Category	Oct-91	Nov-91	Dec-91	Q4 Total
4						
5	Research	Salary	350000	350000	350000	1050000
6		Office Supplies	3000	4600	3750	11350
7		Equipment	4575	5500	4575	14650
8		Building Lease	9600	9600	9600	28800
9		Advertising	1500	2500	1500	5500
10						
11			368675	372200	369425	1110300

When you apply borders, you use the Border area of the dialog box to select what parts of the cell you want to show a border. The last four options in this area are reasonably self-explanatory. If you choose either Top, Bottom, Left, or Right, each cell in your selected range will get a border on the edge you select. In the example, setting Right puts in the Vertical lines dividing the columns.

The top item in the list, Outline, is what placed the outer border around the entire range. When you select Outline, each cell along the outer edge of the selected range gets a border along its outer side. And of course, the type of border the cells end up with depends on what you select from the Style area of the dialog box.

Adding Shading

You can also experiment with shading to create some interesting effects. The following steps add shading to highlight the column titles and the totals at the bottom of the report:

1. Highlight the range B3:F3.
2. Click on Format, Patterns.

3. In the dialog box that appears, click on the arrow to the right of the Foreground list box, and scroll down to the end of the list. Find the light gray color that is the second one from the bottom. (There are two grays at the bottom: one light and the other one dark. Choose the lighter one of the two.)

4. Click on OK to apply the changes.

If everything went correctly, your worksheet should now look like Figure 5.7.

Figure 5.7 Worksheet after applying shading from the Format Patterns dialog box

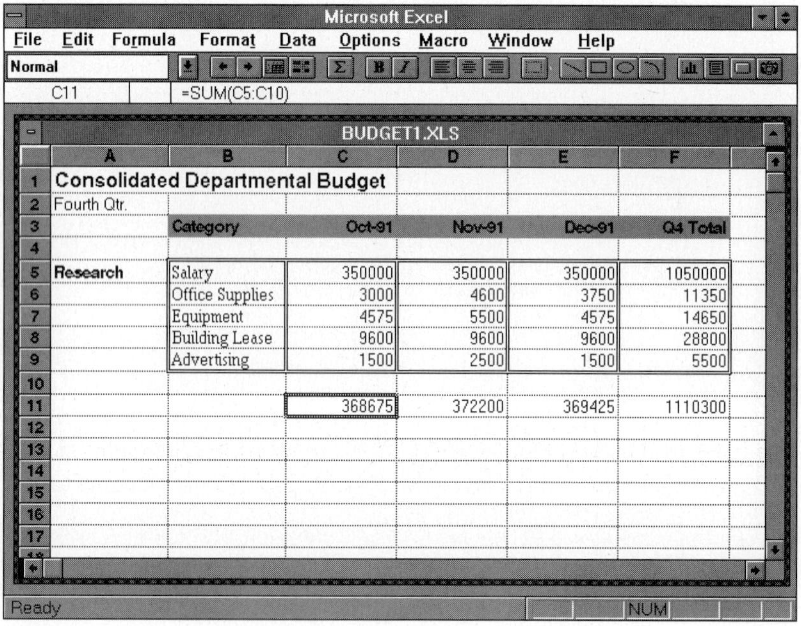

	A	B	C	D	E	F
1	Consolidated Departmental Budget					
2	Fourth Qtr.					
3		Category	Oct-91	Nov-91	Dec-91	Q4 Total
4						
5	Research	Salary	350000	350000	350000	1050000
6		Office Supplies	3000	4600	3750	11350
7		Equipment	4575	5500	4575	14650
8		Building Lease	9600	9600	9600	28800
9		Advertising	1500	2500	1500	5500
10						
11			368675	372200	369425	1110300

Tip. Borders and shading changes usually show up best if you turn off the gridlines. Click on Options, Display, and then remove the check mark from the Gridlines option. Click on OK to return to the worksheet—this time without gridlines.

Now you can put into practice what you read earlier about the Repeat command. Since you also want to shade the totals at the bottom of each column, use the following steps to learn a shortcut:

1. Highlight the range of cells C11:F11.

2. Click on Edit, Repeat Patterns.

Remember that the word following "Repeat" changes depending on what you are doing. In this case, the last thing you did was format a range of cells with a particular pattern. Thus, Excel lets you repeat that formatting command on other ranges.

Finally, you might decide that the worksheet would look better if the totals were in boldface type. To round out this exercise, apply boldfacing to the range you just shaded—C11:F11. (Remember, you can use the Bold icon on the toolbar as a shortcut.) At the end of all of this formatting, check to make sure that your worksheet matches the one in Figure 5.8.

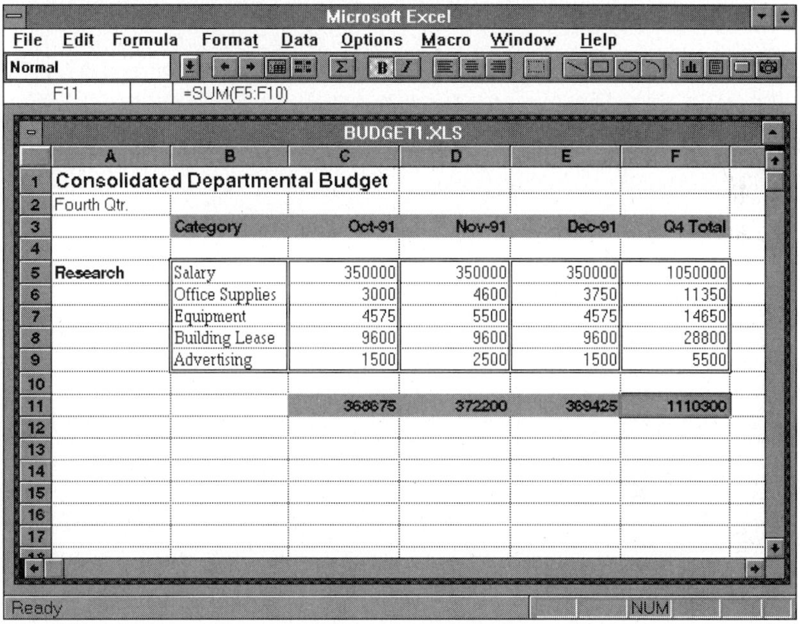

Figure 5.8 BUDGET1.XLS with enhanced formatting

There are no practical limits to what you can do with shading, borders, colors, and text styles. Consider the three screens shown in Figure 5.9. The underlying worksheet is identical, and the only tools used to change its appearance are those that you have learned thus far.

Working with Numerical Formats

So far, you haven't done anything with the way the numbers appear in the BUDGET1 worksheet. Now it's time to change that. In this section, you will learn how Excel stores numbers and how to change the way they appear in a worksheet.

Figure 5.9 Worksheet formatting alternatives

BUDGET1.XLS

	A	B	C	D	E	F
1	Consolidated Departmental Budget					
2	Fourth Qtr.					
3		Category	Oct-91	Nov-91	Dec-91	Q4 Total
4						
5	Research	Salary	350000	350000	350000	1050000
6		Office Supplies	3000	4600	3750	11350
7		Equipment	4575	5500	4575	14650
8		Building Lease	9600	9600	9600	28800
9		Advertising	1500	2500	1500	5500
10						
11			368675	372200	369425	1110300

BUDGET1.XLS

	A	B	C	D	E	F
1	Consolidated Departmental Budget					
2	Fourth Qtr.					
3		Category	Oct-91	Nov-91	Dec-91	Q4 Total
4						
5	Research	Salary	350000	350000	350000	1050000
6		Office Supplies	3000	4600	3750	11350
7		Equipment	4575	5500	4575	14650
8		Building Lease	9600	9600	9600	28800
9		Advertising	1500	2500	1500	5500
10						
11			368675	372200	369425	1110300

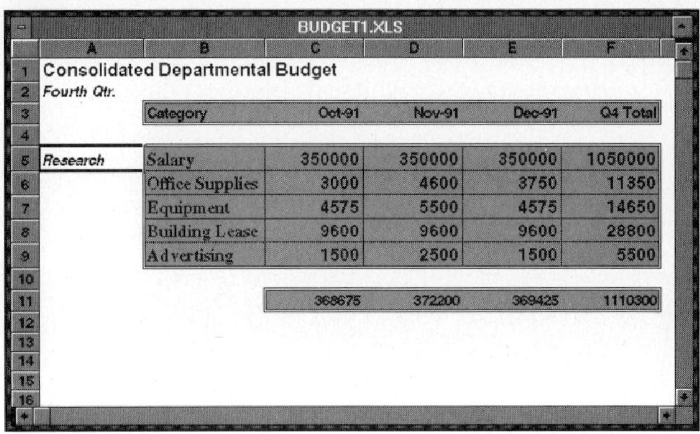

BUDGET1.XLS

	A	B	C	D	E	F
1	Consolidated Departmental Budget					
2	*Fourth Qtr.*					
3		Category	Oct-91	Nov-91	Dec-91	Q4 Total
4						
5	*Research*	Salary	350000	350000	350000	1050000
6		Office Supplies	3000	4600	3750	11350
7		Equipment	4575	5500	4575	14650
8		Building Lease	9600	9600	9600	28800
9		Advertising	1500	2500	1500	5500
10						
11			368675	372200	369425	1110300

Excel uses a symbolic notation to represent how a number will be displayed when you apply a particular numerical format to the number. Figure 5.10 shows the dialog box that lists all the predefined numeric formats that are available in Excel. The first numeric format listed is simply a 0. This is called the *digit placeholder.* With this format selected, Excel will display any leading zeros the number might have, but will not display any numbers to the right of the decimal point.

Figure 5.10
Format Number dialog box

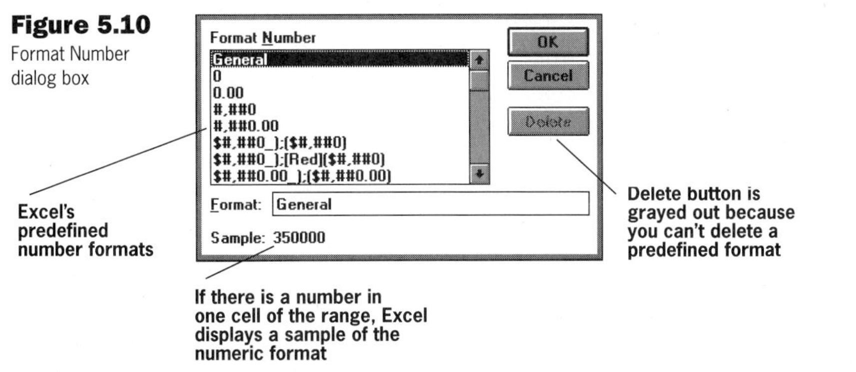
Format Number
General
0
0.00
#,##0
#,##0.00
$#,##0_);($#,##0)
$#,##0_);[Red]($#,##0)
$#,##0.00_);($#,##0.00)
OK
Cancel
Delete
Format: General
Sample: 350000
Excel's predefined number formats
Delete button is grayed out because you can't delete a predefined format
If there is a number in one cell of the range, Excel displays a sample of the numeric format

In contrast, the format 0.00 will display any leading zeros in the number and two digits to the right of the decimal place. To illustrate, if you formatted the number 1234.337 with the 0 format, it would appear in the worksheet as 1234. But if you used the 0.00 format, it would appear as 1234.34 (rounded off).

Another numeric format you will see on the list of predefined formats is the 0.00% format. As you might guess, this one displays a number in a percentage format with two places to the right of the decimal. For example, the number 0.347 displays as 34.70% when formatted with 0.00% (but this would be rounded up to 35% when displayed with the 0% format).

There are other symbols used to determine exactly how Excel displays numbers in the worksheet. In fact, using that symbology, you can even create your own custom number formats. However, the entire list of the description and syntax of the symbols is rather complex and falls outside the scope of this book. In any event, the Microsoft engineers have already defined a wide range of useful numeric formats that you can use right away. Table 5.1 shows all these formats with examples of how they cause numbers to display.

Table 5.1 Excel's Predefined Numeric Formats

Format	Number You Type:			
	6230.79	6.79	–6.79	0.079
	Number as Displayed:			
General	6230.79	6.79	–6.79	0.079
General format, integer, fractional, decimal, leading minus sign				
0	6231	7	–7	0
Numbers only to the left of the decimal point, leading minus sign				
0.00	6230.79	6.79	–6.79	0.08
Numbers to the left of the decimal and two digits to the right of the decimal, leading minus sign				
#,##0	6,231	7	–7	0
Numbers over 999 displayed with comma, only numbers to the left of the decimal, leading minus sign				
#,##0.00	6,230.79	6.79	–6.79	0.08
Numbers over 999 displayed with comma, two digits to the right of the decimal, leading minus sign				
$#,##0_);($#,##0)	$6,231	$7	($7)	$0
Numbers over 999 displayed with comma, leading dollar sign, negative numbers displayed in parenthesis, only numbers to the left of the decimal				
$#,##0_);[Red]($#,##0)	$6,231	$7	($7)	$0
Numbers over 999 displayed with comma, leading dollar sign, negative numbers displayed in red, only numbers to the left of the decimal				

Table 5.1 ***(Continued)***

Format	Number You Type:			
	6230.79	6.79	–6.79	0.079
	Number as Displayed:			
$#,##0.00_);($#,##0.00)	$6,230.79	$6.79	($6.79)	$0.08
Numbers over 999 displayed with comma, leading dollar sign, negative numbers displayed in parenthesis, two digits to the right of the decimal				
$#,##0.00_);[Red]($#,##0.00)	$6,230.79	$6.79	($6.79)	$0.08
Numbers over 999 displayed with comma, leading dollar sign, negative numbers displayed in red, two digits to the right of the decimal				
0%	623079%	679%	–679%	8%
Numbers displayed as percent,trailing percent sign, leading minus sign, numbers only to the left of th decimal point				
0.00%	623079.00%	679.00%	–679.00%	7.90%
Numbers displayed as percent,trailing percent sign, leading minus sign, two digits to the right of the decimal				
0.00E+00	6.23+03	6.79E+00	–6.79E+00	7.9E–02
Numbers displayed in scientific notation, leading minus sign				
# ?/?	6230 4/5	6 4/5	–6 4/5	0
Numbers displayed as fractions, fractional part is displayed with one digit of accuracy, leading minus sign				
# ??/??	6230 15/19	6 64/81	–6 64/81	3/38
Numbers displayed as fractions, fractional part is displayed with two digits of accuracy, leading minus sign				

Stored Numbers versus Displayed Numbers

When you type a number into Excel, or when Excel calculates a number for you, that number is stored internally with 15 digits of accuracy (to the right of the decimal). You simply control what Excel displays on the worksheet. For example, if you enter the number 4.118118, but you have formatted the cell to only display two decimal places, it will display 4.12. However, Excel will still use the full number, stored internally, for any calculations you make using that number. Keep this in mind as you build worksheets. There may be times when a result will appear to be wrong because rounded-off numbers appear on the worksheet, but, in fact, the result is correct.

You can if you choose, however, have Excel use only the precision of numbers as they are displayed for its calculations. This is useful if you work a lot with dollar-and-cents figures. Since you wouldn't normally calculate costs to more precision than the penny, it's often useful to have the ability to work with only two digits to the right of the decimal point. If you want to select this option, click on Options, Calculation and turn on the Precision As Displayed check box by clicking on it. This is discussed in more detail in Chapter 12.

Applying Excel's Basic Number Formats

When you first enter numbers into an Excel worksheet, they appear in the General format by default. The General format is the one used by Excel whenever you enter a number and do not otherwise specify a format for that number. It delivers Excel's best guess about how to display a number based on what you typed. For example, when you type in a number, Excel will display that number using the General format if the number resembles any of the following: 123 (integer format), 123 1/2 (fractional format), 123.23 (decimal-fraction format), or 123E+04 (scientific notation format). If you want to change the number's format and have your numeric data appear some other way, you can use the Format Number dialog box to apply different formats to your numeric data.

Use the following instructions to set the numeric formats of the data on the BUDGET1.XLS worksheet:

1. Highlight the range you want to format. In this case, select the range C5:F9.
2. Click on Format, Number to pop up the dialog box (see Figure 5.10).
3. Select the formatting option that you want for the data. For this exercise, choose the third item from the top: #,##0. This format will display any number larger than 1,000 with a comma and round it off to the nearest integer.

4. Click on OK to apply the formatting that you've chosen.

Note that in the dialog box, if you have selected cells that contain numeric data, Excel will display a sample at the bottom showing what your selection will look like once you apply the format. Let's format the total for column C with a different numerical format, using the following steps:

1. Highlight cell C11.
2. Click on Format, Number.
3. Select the format that looks like this: $#,##0_);($#,##0). This format will display any number larger than 1,000 with a comma, a leading dollar sign, and the entire number in parentheses if it is a negative number. Note the example at the bottom of the dialog box.
4. Click on OK to apply the numeric format to the cell.

When you've finished with both of these format exercises, your worksheet should look like Figure 5.11.

Figure 5.11
Applying numeric formats

Microsoft Excel

File Edit Formula Format Data Options Macro Window Help

Normal

C11 =SUM(C5:C10)

BUDGET1.XLS

	A	B	C	D	E	F
1	Consolidated Departmental Budget					
2	Fourth Qtr.					
3		Category	Oct-91	Nov-91	Dec-91	Q4 Total
4						
5	Research	Salary	350,000	350,000	350,000	1,050,000
6		Office Supplies	3,000	4,600	3,750	11,350
7		Equipment	4,575	5,500	4,575	14,650
8		Building Lease	9,600	9,600	9,600	28,800
9		Advertising	1,500	2,500	1,500	5,500
10						
11			$368,675	372200	369425	1110300
12						
13						
14						
15						
16						
17						

Ready NUM

Date and Time Formats

Until now, you have not worked with dates, except for the column headings in BUDGET1.XLS. Times and dates are handled differently from other data in Excel. Excel stores time and date information using a *serial number,* which records the number of days that have passed since January 1, 1900. For example, the serial number that corresponds to April 1, 1992 is 33695, and serial number 33696 (one number greater) corresponds to April 2, 1992.

Whereas the integer portion of a serial number represents the date, the fractional portion represents time. Excel stores times internally as the portion of a serial number to the right of the decimal point. For example, if you put the function =NOW() into a cell, the cell will contain the serial number of both today's date and the current time, say 33279.6934. The portion of the serial number to the left of the decimal represents the date, February 10, 1991, and the four-digit portion to the right of the decimal represents the time, 4:38:26 P.M. Table 5.2 shows Excel's default date and time formats.

Table 5.2 Excel's Date/Time Formats

Format	Date and Time Displayed
m/d/yy	2/10/91
d-mmm-yy	10-Feb-91
d-mmm	10-Feb
mmm-yy	Feb-91
h:mm AM/PM	4:38 PM
h:mm:ss AM/PM	4:38:30 PM
h:mm	16:38
h:mm:ss	16:38:30
m/d/yy h:mm	2/10/91 16:38

Because Excel uses serial numbers, it's very easy to do *date arithmetic*. Remember that Excel performs calculations on numbers the way they are entered, not as they appear. Thus when you perform date arithmetic, you are doing math on the serial numbers stored internally. They just happen to be displayed as dates and times.

Note. The NOW() function will change the date it displays any time the worksheet is opened—even if you don't make any changes to it.

Here's a final exercise to put this information to use. When you prepare a report, it's always helpful to know when the report was last calculated and printed. Use the following instructions to enter some text and a formula that will let the recipients of this report know when it was printed:

1. Highlight cell A14.
2. Type **Worksheet last updated on:** in cell A14.
3. Highlight cell C14.
4. Type **=NOW()** into cell C14. Or use the Formula Paste Function dialog box to first select and then paste this function into cell C14.
5. With cell C14 still highlighted, click on Format, Number and choose the last of the predefined formats (m/d/yy h:mm) in the dialog box.
6. Click on OK to complete the command.

When you finish, your worksheet will look similar, but not identical to, the one in Figure 5.12—your date will be different. Remember that the NOW( ) function returns the *current* date and time. Also, you might have to adjust the width of column C a bit if the data does not quite fit correctly.

In addition to its predefined formats, Excel gives you the flexibility to create custom formats for both numbers and dates and times. You could, for example, create a numeric format that takes a ten-digit number and formats it as a phone number—displayed complete with parentheses and hyphens in the right places. Custom formats are beyond the scope of this book, but the Excel documentation offers all the information you need to do this.

Formatting with Styles

Many word processing software programs have among their features a tool called a *stylesheet.* With stylesheets, you can create a document that looks just the way that you want it, with margins, tabs, fonts, character attributes, and so on, all in place. Then you save just the styles you have applied in a separate, named stylesheet file. The next time you want a document to look the same way, you just tell the word processor to apply a named stylesheet; the document immediately assumes the overall appearance set forth by the stylesheet.

Excel brings the notion of stylesheets to spreadsheets. With Excel's style features, you can define a look for a particular cell and then tell Excel to use that look for other cells. You can then name the styles you create so that they are available to all your worksheet models. In this section, you will have the opportunity to work with Excel's styles. With styles, Excel gives you control over six of the attributes you can use to control the appearance and behavior of a cell: number format, font and attributes (bold, italic, and so on), alignment, borders, patterns, and cell protection. (The last is covered in more detail in Chapter 10.)

Figure 5.12
BUDGET1.XLS with update information

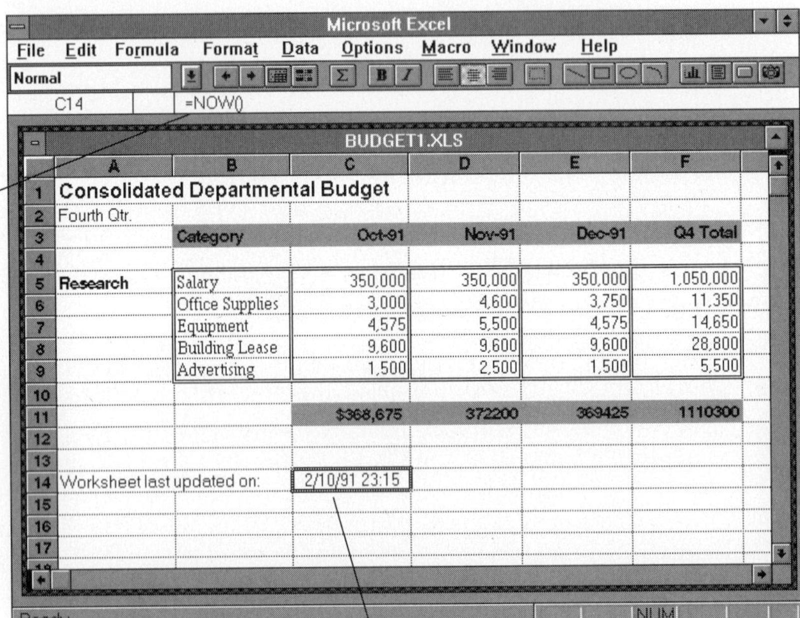

Applying a Predefined Style

As with the predefined numeric formats, Excel is shipped from Microsoft with several predefined styles. If you don't like the default styles provided with Excel (there aren't that many to begin with), you can easily add custom styles of your own.

To try out the predefined styles, just highlight the range or cell you want to change, and then pull down the list of predefined styles by clicking on the downward-pointing arrow at the left end of the toolbar (to the right of the style box). There are four predefined styles: Comma, Currency, Normal, and Percent. Simply click on the one that you want and your highlighted range will be changed.

You might find that the predefined styles are all that you need. However, if you want to add some of the other possible enhancements to a style, such as a different font or a border, you'll need to use custom styles.

Creating Your Own Style

Creating a style with Excel is simply the process of identifying to Excel what combination of the six elements mentioned above should be used to change the appearance of a cell. There are three ways to create a style. First, you can create a style by example. If you have already formatted a cell in a way that you want to repeat, you can simply highlight that cell and tell Excel that you want to give a name to the combination of formats already in place in the cell. You can also create a style by definition. In this process, you work with a dialog box to assign several attributes to a named style. And finally, you can copy styles from other worksheets.

Example Method

First, try out the following steps to create a style by example:

1. Highlight cell C11. This is the cell that will serve as the example of the combination of styles you will give a name to.
2. Click on Format, Style. Figure 5.13 shows the dialog box that appears. Note the six formatting attributes that make up a style. The first five attributes you will recognize right away as numeric format, typeface and size, alignment of text within the cell, borders, and shading. The Locked attribute at the end refers to the status of cell protection, a topic you'll revisit in Chapter 8.
3. Type a new name for the style. In this case, type **Shaded With Currency**.
4. Click on OK to complete the command.

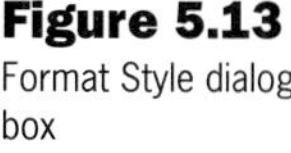

Figure 5.13
Format Style dialog box

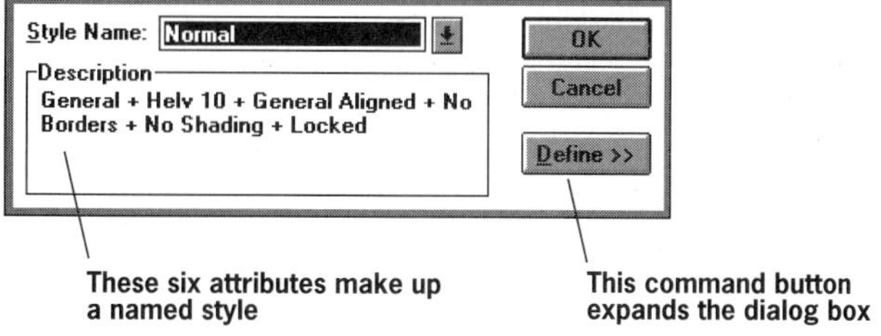

Figure 5.14 shows the dialog box after you enter the new name of the style. Note that as soon as you begin to type the new name of the style, Excel fills in the status of the six attributes that go into this style name. You can see that the numeric format is the one you selected earlier and that the cell is shaded and without borders. If you were to redefine that style (which we'll do in a moment), any cell formatted with the named style will reflect the changes you make to that style.

Figure 5.14
Dialog box after entering the new style name

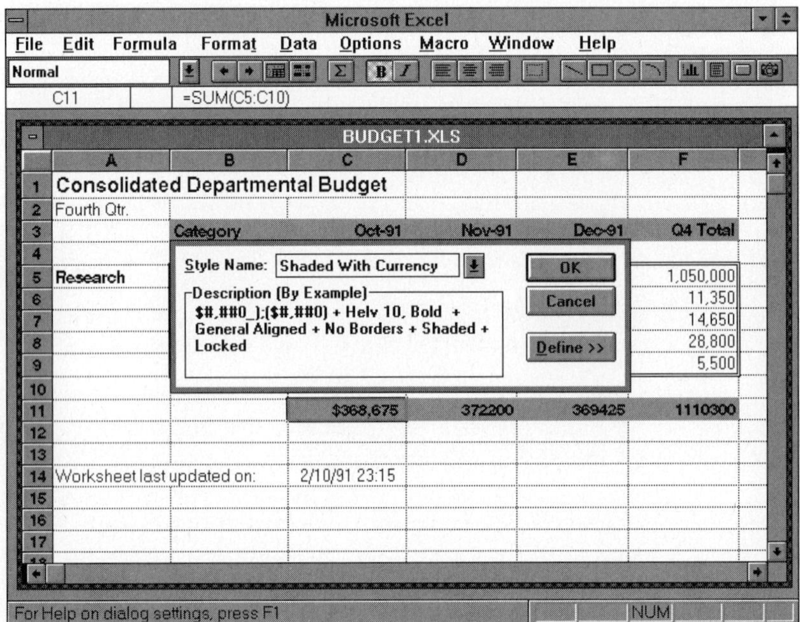

Definition Method

Now let's create a style by definition. In the following exercise, you will define a brand new style and then apply it to a range of cells.

1. Highlight cell C11.
2. Click on Format, Style.
3. Enter the name of the new style. In this case, enter **Currency With Italic**. (This name is arbitrary—you could have called it anything you wish.)
4. Click on Define to pull down a new dialog box, shown in Figure 5.15.

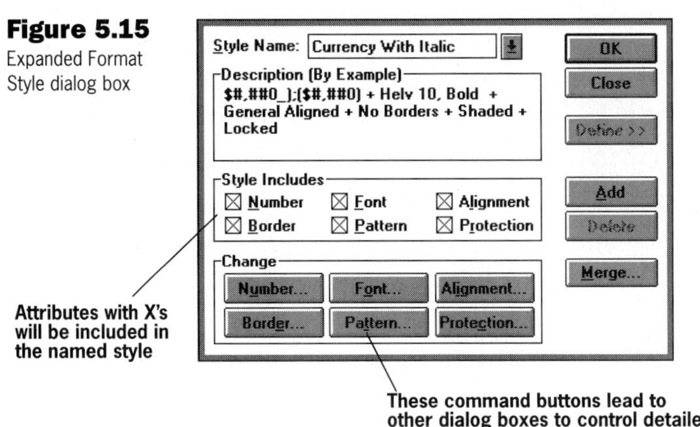

Figure 5.15
Expanded Format Style dialog box

5. Use the six command buttons at the bottom to bring up corresponding dialog boxes. Then use those boxes to set the following attributes:
   - Set the numeric format to the first currency format. It's the one that looks like this: $#,##0_);($#,##0).
   - Set the font to Helvetica 10, Italic and Bold.
   - Set Patterns to None.
   - Set the alignment to Right.
   - Leave the settings for Border and Protection as they are for now. If you don't change them, the normal Excel defaults will be used.

   With the exception of the Protection feature, you have seen each of these dialog boxes before. When you finish, your dialog box should look like the one in Figure 5.16.
6. Click on OK to complete the command.
7. Now highlight the range you want to apply this new style to. In this case, the range of cells is C11:F11.
8. Click on the arrow to the right of the Styles box in the toolbar to drop down a list of available styles. Look for the one you just defined, Currency With Italic, and click on it. When you have finished, your worksheet should look like Figure 5.17.

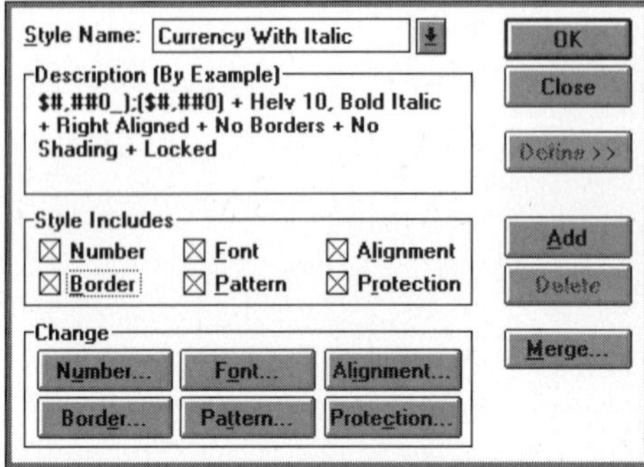

Figure 5.16
Expanded dialog box with attributes set

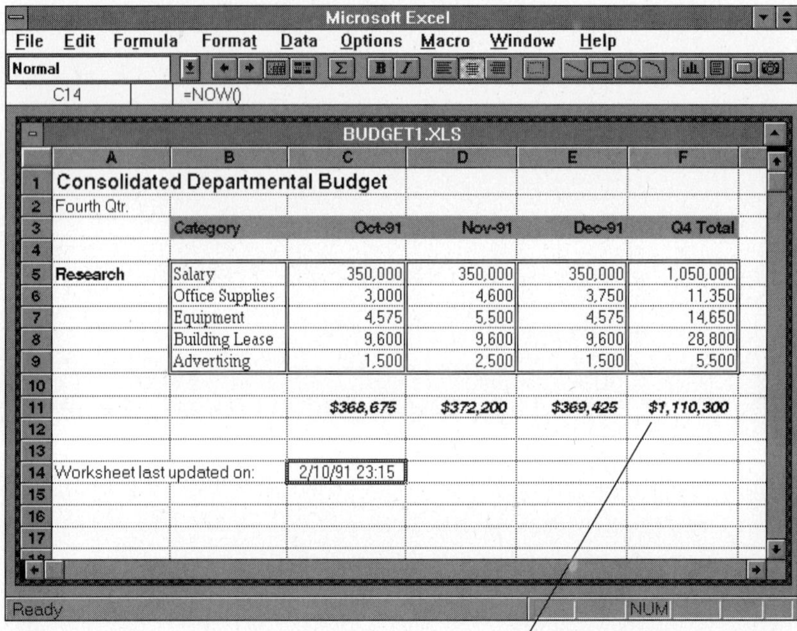

Figure 5.17
Worksheet after defining and applying a new style

You might find this operation causes one or more of the columns to grow too wide, so that you see a row of number signs (#####) in a cell. This means the column is too narrow to display the whole number in the format you requested. Just widen the column until the numbers are all displayed as numbers. Recall from Chapter 2 that you can also select the Best Fit option, and Excel will widen the column just enough to show the longest cell in the column.

When you are working with the Format Style dialog box (Figure 5.16), note the group of six boxes that are checked by default. These boxes indicate those attributes included in the style definition. If you click on one of those boxes, you remove the description of the state of the attribute and consequently the inclusion of that attribute in the style. For these exercises, you might want to remove protection from the style definition by just clicking on the Protection check box.

Copying Method

Finally, it's possible to copy existing styles from other worksheets if you want to use that style definition in your current worksheet model. Although you have not created styles in other worksheets yet, here are the steps for your future reference:

1. First open the worksheet that contains the styles you want to copy, and then open the worksheet you want to receive the copied styles.
2. Click on Format, Style.
3. Click on the Define button.
4. Click on the Merge button.
5. From the list of worksheets Excel gives you, select the name of the worksheet that contains the style definitions you want to use.
6. Click on OK to copy the style definitions from the first worksheet to the second.
7. Finally, click on the Close button to close the dialog box and return to the worksheet.

Once the style definitions are copied over to the second worksheet, you can access them just as you would any other style: After you select the range to apply the style to, pull down the Styles list from the toolbar and click on the style you want.

Redefining a Style

Now that you have created a new style, what happens if you want to change all the cells that have been formatted with that style? It's a straightforward process to simply redefine the style from the Format Style dialog box. Once you have done so, Excel will change all the cells that have been formatted with that style. As you can imagine, this is a real time-saver if you want to quickly change the appearance of a number of cells.

The following exercise shows you how to add a border to the range of cells C11:F11 by simply redefining the style called Currency With Italic. Remember that you just formatted C11:F11 with that style name, so that once you redefine the style, the whole range will change in appearance.

1. Highlight cell C11.
2. Click on Format, Style to pop up the dialog box.
3. Make sure the named style Currency With Italic is shown in the Style Name box. If it is not the currently selected style, click on the arrow to the right of the Style Name box to pull down a list of the defined styles.
4. Click on Define to expand the dialog box.
5. Click on the Border command button to pop up the Borders dialog box.
6. Click on the box that contains the double line in the Style section of the dialog box.
7. Click on the Top, Bottom, Right, and Left boxes. The dialog box should look like Figure 5.18.
8. Click on OK to complete the border style.
9. Click on OK to complete the style redefinition.

Figure 5.18
Border dialog box with border attributes selected

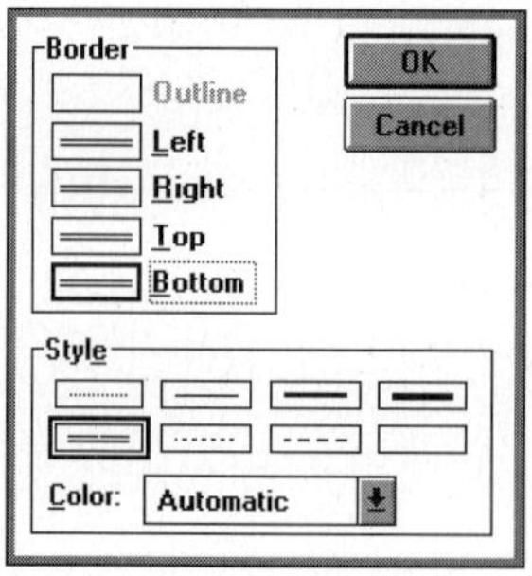

As soon as you click on OK to complete the style name redefinition, Excel automatically adjusts all the cells in the worksheet that have been formatted with the style you just redefined. Once you have finished these steps, your worksheet should look like the one in Figure 5.19.

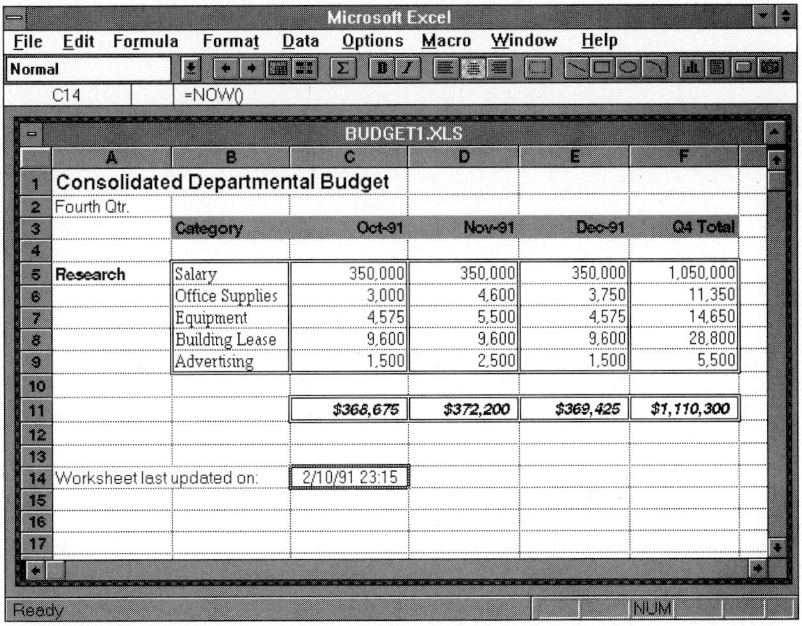

Figure 5.19
BUDGET1.XLS after redefining a named style

Microsoft Excel

File Edit Formula Format Data Options Macro Window Help

Normal

C14 =NOW()

BUDGET1.XLS

	A	B	C	D	E	F
1	Consolidated Departmental Budget					
2	Fourth Qtr.					
3		Category	Oct-91	Nov-91	Dec-91	Q4 Total
4						
5	Research	Salary	350,000	350,000	350,000	1,050,000
6		Office Supplies	3,000	4,600	3,750	11,350
7		Equipment	4,575	5,500	4,575	14,650
8		Building Lease	9,600	9,600	9,600	28,800
9		Advertising	1,500	2,500	1,500	5,500
10						
11			*$368,675*	*$372,200*	*$369,425*	*$1,110,300*
12						
13						
14	Worksheet last updated on:		2/10/91 23:15			
15						
16						
17						

Ready NUM

Deleting a Style

If you have defined a lot of styles in your worksheet, you may decide you don't want to keep all of them. It's easy to delete styles, although there's no reason to do so unless you just don't want them cluttering up the list of style definitions. Here are the steps for deleting a style from the worksheet:

1. Click on Format, Style to pop up the dialog box.
2. Click on Define to expand the dialog box.
3. Either type the name of the style or click on the arrow next to the Style Name box to pull down a list of the defined styles in the worksheet. For this exercise, select the one named Shaded With Currency.
4. Click on the Delete command button to remove this named style from the worksheet.
5. Click on the Close command button to close the dialog box.

Using Templates

Templates are another way to save time when you are creating a number of similar worksheets, or if you would like all your worksheets to have a consistent look. With a template, you can keep all the formulas, range names, defined formatting styles, and text that does not change from one worksheet to the next.

Consider, for example, the BUDGET1 worksheet you've been working on. Say you had to create a new one every month, containing substantially similar data, and you wanted it to look the same for the sake of consistency. Since you'd rather not go to the trouble of recreating all the styles, numeric formats, font attribute changes, formulas, and so on if you don't have to, you could decide to save BUDGET1.XLS as a template and then use its basic formatting again and again.

A template is really just another kind of worksheet. It differs from other worksheets only in the way that Excel treats it when you use it and save it. When you open a template file and make some changes to it, Excel will force you to save it under a different name later on so that the template file remains the same as it was before. (You don't want to save these changes back over the template file, so Excel won't let you.)

Before creating a template, save your BUDGET1.XLS file so that you can pick up from this point in the next chapter.

Creating a Template

You can create a template either from scratch or from an existing worksheet. Although we don't do so here, to create a template you first need to make any changes that you want to appear in the new template: text formatting, *boilerplate text* (text that is always used in your worksheets), defined ranges, style names, and so on. Since you have already made these changes to the BUDGET1 worksheet, use the following steps to save it as a template file:

1. Click on File, Save As to pop up the dialog box.
2. Click on the Options command button.
3. Click on the arrow next to the File Format box to pull down a list of the available file formats.
4. Select the Template file format.
5. Click on OK to return to the first dialog box.
6. Click on OK to complete the command.

Using a Template

You open a template just as you would any other worksheet in Excel. The only difference is the extension for a template—XLT instead of the normal XLS extension for worksheet files.

When you open a template, Excel makes a copy of the existing template and gives a different name to the copy—the file you are currently working on. This way, if you make some changes and then choose the Save command, you won't save the changes back to the template. At that point, Excel would prompt you for a new name for the worksheet and would then save the file with that new name. By default, Excel will use the template's name and add a 1 to the end, but you are free to call the saved file anything that you like.

For example, if you opened this template—the one you just created based on BUDGET1.XLS—Excel would give the worksheet in memory the name BUDGET11.XLS. You could either accept that name or choose an entirely different name when it came time to save the new worksheet.

Editing a Template

Because the idea of templates is that they are standardized models, they are protected from being easily modified or overwritten. Consequently, you have to follow one extra procedure if you want to edit the actual template and not just a copy of it in memory. To edit a template file on disk, follow these steps:

1. Click on File, Open to pop up the dialog box.
2. Select the BUDGET1 template file that you just saved. Remember that template files have an .XLT file extension to distinguish them from normal worksheet files, which have an .XLS extension.
3. Hold down the Shift key and then click on the OK command button to load the actual template instead of just a copy.
4. Make your changes.
5. Click on File, Save to save the template file as you would any other worksheet file.

CHAPTER

6

Printing the Worksheet

The Benefits of Print Preview
Getting Ready to Print
Printing the Document
Printing Special Characters

ALL THE OPTIONS AND FEATURES YOU HAVE SEEN SO FAR ONLY HELP you to create your model on the screen. You have not yet had the opportunity to turn your model into something you can share with others. In this chapter, you will learn how to prepare your worksheet for printing, set up your printer, and finally print out your worksheet.

The Benefits of Print Preview

Before you print your opus, take advantage of Excel's ability to preview the worksheet. The *Print Preview* feature will give you an overall view of the worksheet, enabling you to check the margins, the size of the type, and other elements before you print. This will save you a good deal of paper and even more frustration in the long run.

When you preview your document (that is, your worksheet) before printing, you have the opportunity to see exactly what it will look like before you commit it to paper. *Exactly* means that you will see the correct margins, page breaks, and header and footer contents. (*Headers* and *footers* are lines that appear on every page at the top and bottom, respectively. Setting up headers and footers is covered later in this chapter.)

Let's take a look at the BUDGET1 worksheet in Print Preview mode and examine some of the options available to you. First, recover the worksheet that you saved from the last chapter. Then, click on File, Print Preview to see your copy of the worksheet in preview mode. Your screen should look like Figure 6.1.

Full Page versus Actual Size

Notice that the look of Excel has changed significantly. The menu bar and formula bar you have grown accustomed to have disappeared, to be replaced by a menu composed of buttons. The mouse pointer, too, is a different shape when it's over the document—it now looks like a magnifying glass instead of an arrow.

When you first tell Excel to preview the page, you see a full-page representation of your worksheet. In this view, it is difficult to read text unless it is in a large font. Thus the full-page view is useful in that it gives you an idea of what your page will look like when it is printed out.

If at this point you want to see a portion of the worksheet up close, you can use the Zoom feature to do so. With the magnifying glass pointer positioned over the section of the worksheet you want to see up close, click once with the mouse and then watch as Excel zooms in on that area of the worksheet. Now you can see the cell contents at the size you were working with before.

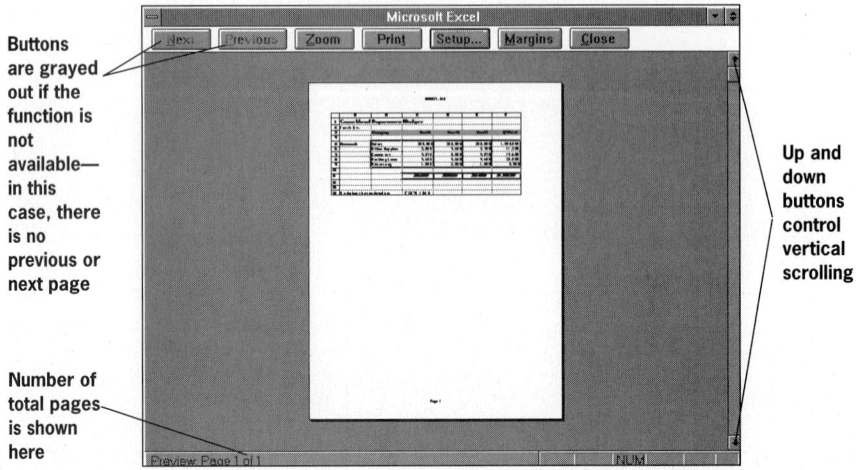

Figure 6.1
BUDGET1 worksheet in preview mode

Note, however, that you cannot edit the contents of the cells in preview mode. You have to exit the Print Preview feature in order to change the contents of a cell.

When you have finished looking at a section of the worksheet up close, just click the mouse button again and you will be back in full-page preview. You can also switch back and forth from full-page to actual-size mode by clicking on the Zoom button at the top of the page. This button acts as a toggle, alternating between full-page and actual-size mode each time you click on it.

Scrolling within the Document

How you move around in the document when you are previewing it depends on the mode (actual-size or full-page) that you are working with.

If you are working in full-page mode (the default mode), moving around is straightforward. When you are previewing a single-page document, such as BUDGET1, there's nowhere to go in this mode because there are no other pages. However, if you are previewing a multipage document, you can just use the vertical scroll bar (on the right side of the screen, see Figure 6.1) to move between pages. Simply click on the up or down arrow to move from page to page. Alternatively, you can click on the Next and Previous buttons to move from one page to the next. The total number of pages in the document and the current page number are displayed in the status bar in the lower-left corner of the screen.

Moving around in the actual-size view is also easy. Since you are not seeing all of the page, you will need to click on both the horizontal and vertical scroll bars in order to move around the document. In actual-size mode, the Next and Previous buttons continue to move you from page to page, not from one section of the current page to another section of the same page.

Adjusting the Margins

Although you can control the margins manually (as explained later in this chapter), it's often easier to do so when you can immediately see the results of the change. Fortunately, the Print Preview feature enables you to do this. While previewing, you have the option of changing both the document margins and the widths of individual columns. This is a very handy feature since you might not know that a column is too wide or too narrow until you see the document in its entirety.

The way to view document margins is to simply click on the Margins button at the top of the screen. Make sure you are in full-page mode by clicking on the Zoom button until your worksheet looks like Figure 6.1. Now click on the Margins button—your document should look like Figure 6.2. Note that the margins are indicated by dotted lines that run down both sides of the page as well as across the top and the bottom.

Figure 6.2
Print Preview with margins visible

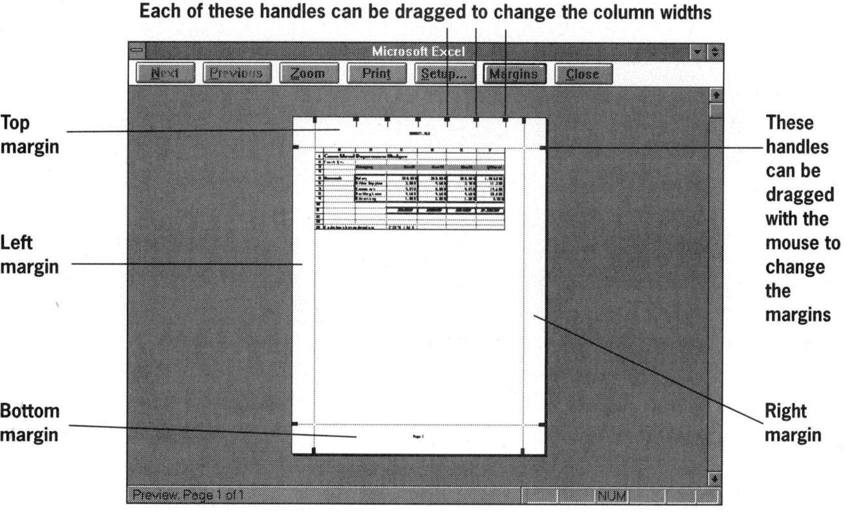

Now that the margin boundaries are visible, you can see that the document is not quite centered between the margins. To make your document more aesthetically pleasing, move the document over a bit to the right to center it horizontally and move it down more toward the center of the page vertically. Use the following steps to do this.

1. Grab the *handle* (the small black box at the left side of the top margin line) and drag it down. Note that as soon as you move the pointer over the handle, it changes shape to let you know that you can click and drag. This operation is much like changing a column width on the worksheet.
2. While still holding the left mouse button down, drag the handle down until the Top Margin indicator in the status bar changes to approximately 2.5. When you are dragging a margin, the status bar changes to reflect the distance from the margin to the nearest edge of the paper. In the case of the top margin, the distance is measured from the top of the paper to the margin. For an example of this, see Figure 6.3.
3. Release the mouse button when the Top Margin distance equals approximately 2.5. When you have finished, your document should look like Figure 6.4.

Figure 6.3
Dragging the margin line

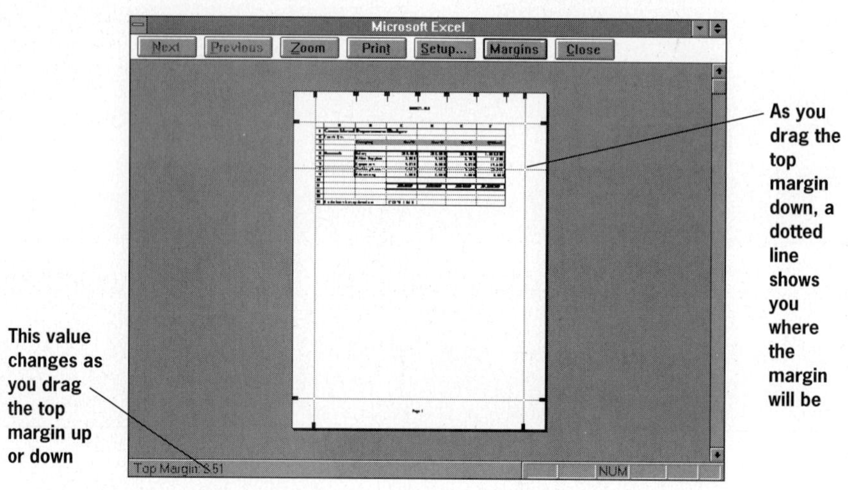
Microsoft Excel
Next
Previous
Zoom
Print
Setup...
Margins
Close
As you drag the top margin down, a dotted line shows you where the margin will be
This value changes as you drag the top margin up or down
Top Margin: 2.51
NUM

Now follow the same steps to move the left margin to approximately 1.20 inches. (You may or may not be able to set the margins exactly to the measurements suggested here depending on the sensitivity of your mouse.) Once you have finished, your document should look like the one in Figure 6.5.

When you have finished with the margins, you can turn off the display of the margin lines by clicking on the Margins button at the top of the screen. Like the Zoom button, the Margins button acts as a toggle, displaying and removing the margin lines each time you click on it. For now though, leave the margin lines on the screen so that you can move on to changing the column widths.

Figure 6.4
Document after setting the top margin to approximately 2.5 inches

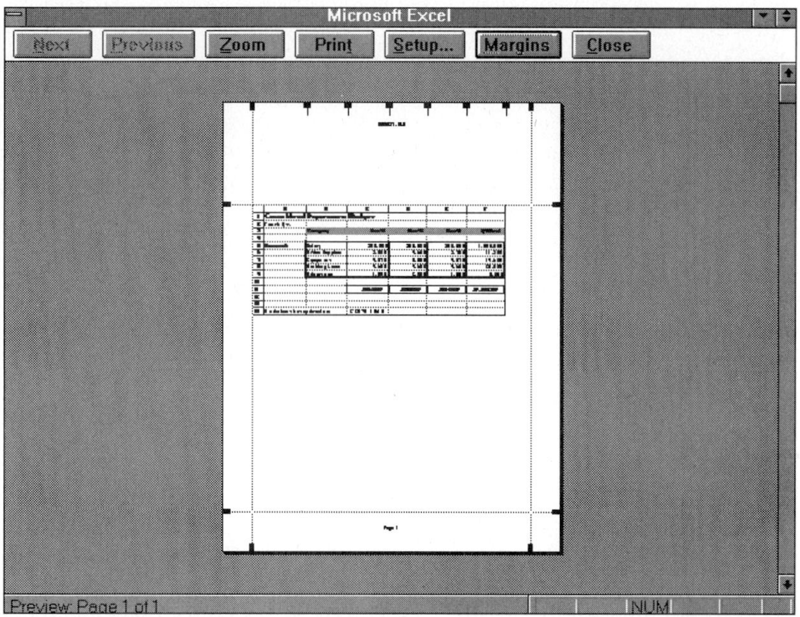

Figure 6.5
Document after setting both margins

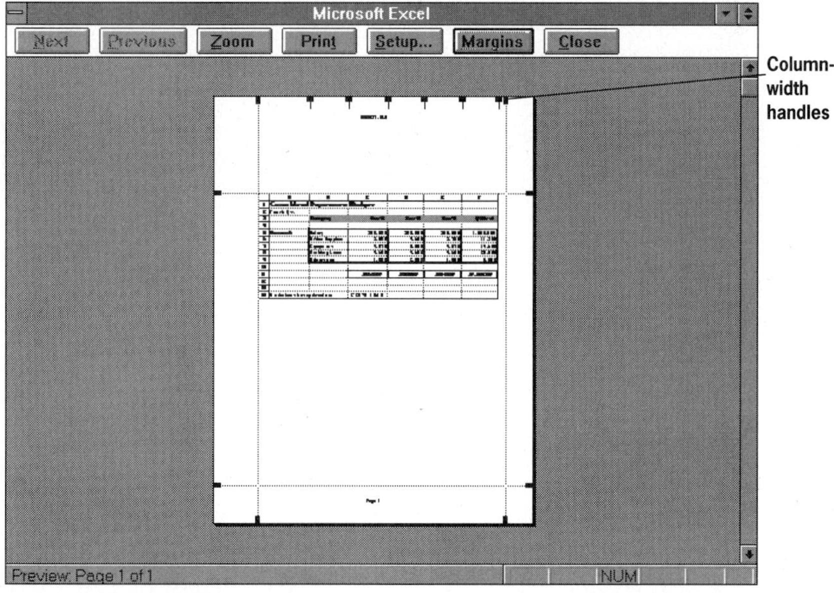

Adjusting the Column Widths

Just as you have the ability to change the margin dimensions once you have your document previewed on the screen, you can also adjust any of the column widths during the Print Preview process.

With the screen as you left it at the end of the previous exercise, note that you can see some handles along the top edge of the page while in preview mode (see Figure 6.5). As with the margins, you can click and drag on any of these column-width handles to make a particular column wider or narrower.

Finally, when you have finished with both the margins and the column widths, turn off the display of these items by clicking once on the Margins button at the top of the screen.

Closing the Preview Window

When you have completed all your manipulations of column widths and margins, it's time to close the preview window and prepare to print the document. To close the preview window, simply click on the Close button at the top of the screen. Excel will return you to the ready mode, where you have been working all along. Any changes you have made to your worksheet, perhaps to the column widths or margins, will remain set as you switch back and forth between modes.

Getting Ready to Print

After you have worked with the Print Preview mode for a while and have completed any last-minute changes you want to make to the worksheet, it's time to print out the document. There are a couple of things, however, that you will need to think about before you actually press the key that begins the whole process. First, you must make sure your printer is set up correctly.

Setting up the Printer

Configuring the printer to work correctly is somewhat of a gray area in a book about Excel. After all, the device-independent nature of Windows was designed so that once you set up your printer for one application, any other application written for Windows can use it correctly. But even though that's mostly true, let's spend a couple of minutes on the concept of setting up the printer.

Figure 6.6 shows the printer setup panels of three popular output devices: an Epson FX-85 dot-matrix printer, a Hewlett-Packard LaserJet III laser printer, and a Hewlett-Packard 7475A plotter. Although each individual device requires slightly different information, there are certain things common to all printers that you will need to know when you configure your own printer. Here are some of the terms you will see in these printer setup dialog boxes, along with their meanings:

Printer This is the model of printer or other output device you want to use. In many cases, Windows uses the same printer driver for several different output devices. For example, Windows uses a single driver for the Hewlett-Packard IIP and 23 other printers that work very much like the IIP does.

Paper Source Here you tell Windows where it should be able to find paper for the printer. If you don't have paper installed where you say it will be, Windows will balk and be unable to complete your request.

Paper Size Here's where you tell the printer driver what size of paper you work with. This choice could be Letter, Legal, A4, or even a custom size, depending on the complexity of the printer driver.

Installed Memory This setting tells Excel and the printer driver how much memory is installed in the printer. Note that many printers will not have this setting. Only certain printers—mostly laser printers and some high end dot-matrix models—have the ability to use more memory. Consequently, the printer driver needs to know how much memory is installed in the printer.

Orientation This refers to the way that your worksheet is printed out. If it is set for *landscape* orientation, the page will be oriented with the longer edge horizontal, the way paintings of landscapes usually are. On the other hand, *portrait* orientation refers to a page that is aligned vertically, like the pages in this book.

Graphics Resolution This controls the resolution the printer will use when it prints out your worksheet. Resolution is usually expressed in dots per inch (dpi) and is stated in terms of a square inch. For example, an HP LaserJet is capable of three resolutions: 75, 150, and 300 dpi. Of the three, 300 dpi is the highest resolution and produces the most detailed and realistic images.

Some laser printers may not have enough memory to produce a full page of graphics at the 300 dpi resolution. Some printers are shipped with only 512k of memory and would not be able to print a full page of graphics without additional memory.

Cartridges This specifies whether you have any font cartridges installed in the printer. Most dot-matrix printers and plotters do not use cartridges, so you might find this option not available on some output devices.

Figure 6.6
Printer setups

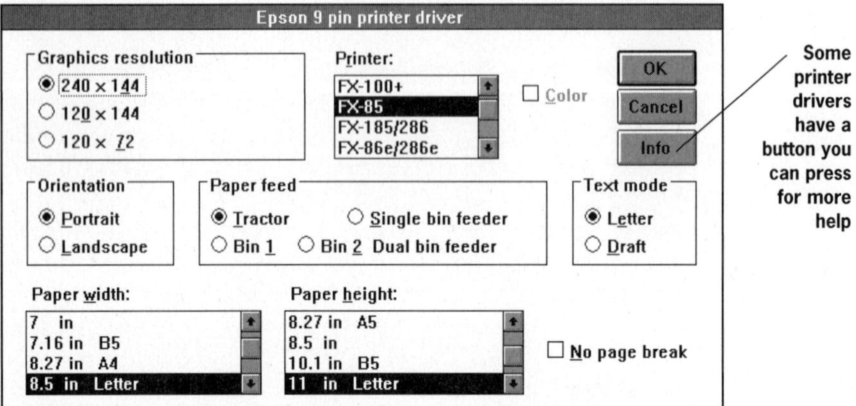

Some printer drivers have a button you can press for more help

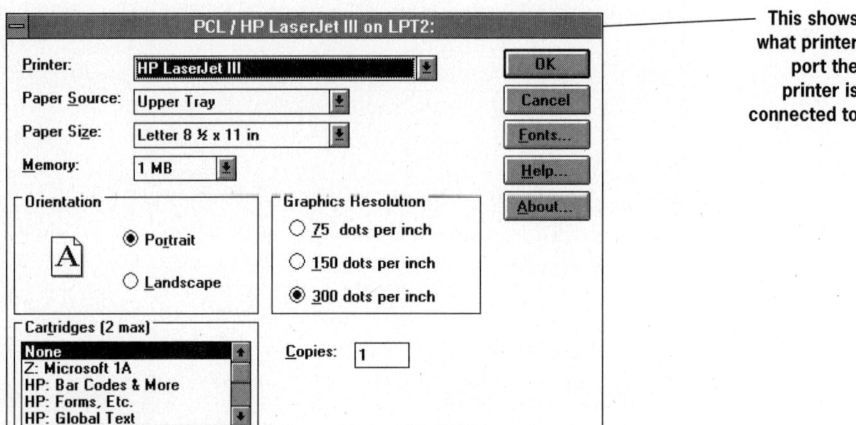

This shows what printer port the printer is connected to

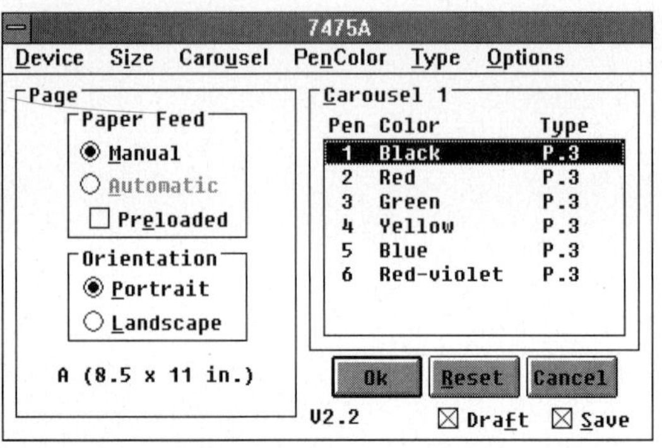

Copies This lets you set how many copies of a particular document you want printed. Note that many applications also provide some method of specifying the number of copies of a document that are to be printed out.

Fonts This option lets you control the soft fonts installed, if any, in your printer.

To look at the Printer Setup dialog box on your computer system, follow these steps:

1. Click on File, Printer Setup to bring up the dialog box.
2. Select the printer you want to view, if you have more than one printer installed. Then, just click on the Setup command button.

You will then see a dialog box specific to your printer that contains many of the options discussed above. It probably isn't necessary to make any changes here, since you wouldn't have been able to print from any other Windows application if the printer wasn't set up correctly. You may at some time in the future, however, choose to change some of the options here.

When you have finished, click on OK as many times as it takes to get back to your worksheet—probably two or three.

Page Layout

Now that you have looked at the printer setup information and made any changes, continue to work through the following exercises to alter the appearance of the Excel worksheet to your satisfaction.

Selecting File Page Setup gives you access to a dialog box that offers additional control over the appearance of the printed page (see Figure 6.7). It's here that you will set up and edit the headers and footers and choose whether to print gridlines and row and column headings. In addition, the File Page Setup dialog box gives you the option of changing the page margins if you prefer to do it from here rather than in Print Preview mode. Any changes you make to this dialog box will be saved when you save the worksheet.

Setting Up Headers and Footers

Headers and footers can be very useful for adding information to the worksheet. Many people like to put a header with a title at the top of the printed page, along with the date. Footers are often used for page numbers and sometimes for the name of the file.

By default, Excel 3.0 places the file name at the top of the document and the page number at the bottom. Although both are centered by default, it's possible to align them to the right or left instead, depending on your preference. In fact, each header and footer can have three elements: one aligned to the left, another centered, and the last aligned to the right.

In the following exercise, you will add a new header and footer to the worksheet before you print it out.

Figure 6.7
File Page Setup dialog box

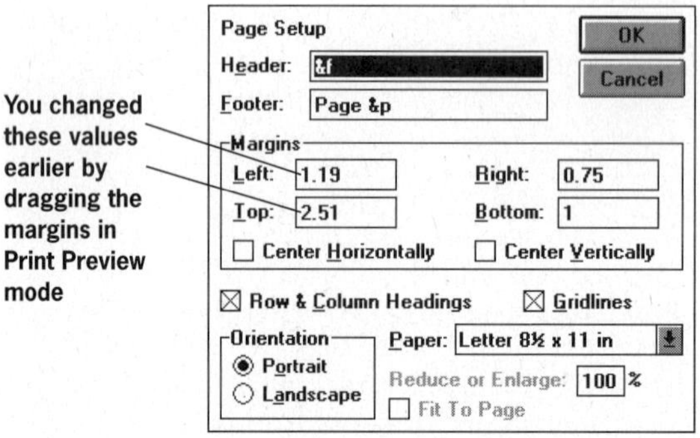

You changed these values earlier by dragging the margins in Print Preview mode

Excel uses a system of codes to define not only what information is to be displayed in the header or footer, but also how that information is to be displayed. See Table 6.1 for these codes.

Follow these steps to change the default headers and footers:

1. Click on File, Page Setup. The resulting dialog box is shown in Figure 6.7.
2. In the Header box, enter the following code: **&L1990 Budget&C&F&R CONFIDENTIAL**. This code places "1990 Budget" in the upper-left corner, centers the file name, and puts "CONFIDENTIAL" in the upper-right corner of the document.
3. In the Footer box, enter the following code: **&L&D&CPAGE &P of &N&R&T**. This code tells Excel to left-align the date, center "PAGE 1 of 5", and right-align the time.
4. Remove any X's from both the Row & Column Headings and the Gridlines boxes by clicking on them.
5. Click on OK to complete the command.

If you like, you can now click on File, Print Preview to get an idea of how your worksheet is going to look printed on paper. When you finish there, click on Close to bring you back to this point. This is also a good time to save your worksheet before you continue making changes to it.

Other Print Features

You can also control whether gridlines and row and column headers print. Generally speaking, most worksheets look more polished when the gridlines and the row-number and column-letter headings are turned off. There will be times, however, when you want to have the flexibility to leave them on. Click on either of the corresponding check boxes in the File Page Setup dialog box to choose whether or not to print these items.

Table 6.1 Header and Footer Codes

Code	Action
&&	Prints a single ampersand
&*nn*	Prints the characters that follow, in the current font, using the point size specified by *nn*
&"*font*"	Prints characters that follow in the font specified in *font* (remember to include the quotation marks)
&B	Prints characters that follow in boldface
&C	Centers the characters that follow
&D	Prints the current system date
&F	Prints the DOS file name of the current document
&I	Prints the characters that follow in italic
&L	Left-aligns the characters that follow
&N	Prints the total number of pages in the current document
&P	Prints the page number
&P+*number*	Prints the page number plus *number* (e.g., &P+4 starts the numbering at page 5)
&P-*number*	Prints the page number minus *number*
&R	Right-aligns the characters that follow

Note that this dialog box only controls the appearance of the printed document. If you want to turn off the gridlines for the worksheet on the screen, you need to use the Options Display dialog box to enable or disable both the gridlines and the row and column headings.

Setting Row or Column Print Titles

Often you will have a worksheet whose columns extend for more than one page. In these cases it is easier to follow the columns from page to page if you can refer to a repeated column heading. Excel provides a feature for printing one row at the beginning of each page—after the header but before the data begins to print.

Use these steps to set up row or column print titles:

1. Make sure you are looking at the worksheet itself and not at a preview version of the document.
2. Select the row or column that you want to serve as the printed titles by clicking on the row or column label. You must select the entire row or column. In this case, highlight row 3.
3. Click on Options, Set Print Titles.

You can preview these titles before printing as you do other features. There is also one more step you need to take before printing. See "A Note about Printing Titles," later in this chapter.

To remove the print titles when you no longer need them, follow these steps:

1. Highlight the entire worksheet by clicking on the small rectangle at the upper-left where the row header meets the column header.
2. Click on Options, Remove Print Titles.

Tip. You can use more than one row or column for your print titles. If you want to do so, however, they must be contiguous rows or columns. For example, you can select rows 4 and 5 for your titles, but you cannot use rows 4 and 7.

Identifying the Range to Print

By default, Excel 3.0 will print the entire document. If you choose to only print a portion of the worksheet, you must first set up what Excel calls a *Print Area.* The Print Area is a range or group of ranges that Excel uses to specify what part or parts of the worksheet to print. Use the following instructions to set up the Print Area:

1. Highlight the portion of the worksheet that you want to print. For this exercise, highlight the range A1:F14.
2. Click on Options, Set Print Area. Note the dotted lines in Figure 6.8 that define the print area.
3. Proceed to print the document as described below.

When you are ready to remove the print area—when either you have already printed the document or you decide that you want to print another range—use these instructions to remove it:

1. Highlight the entire worksheet.
2. Click on Options, Remove Print Area.

Figure 6.8 Worksheet after setting the print area

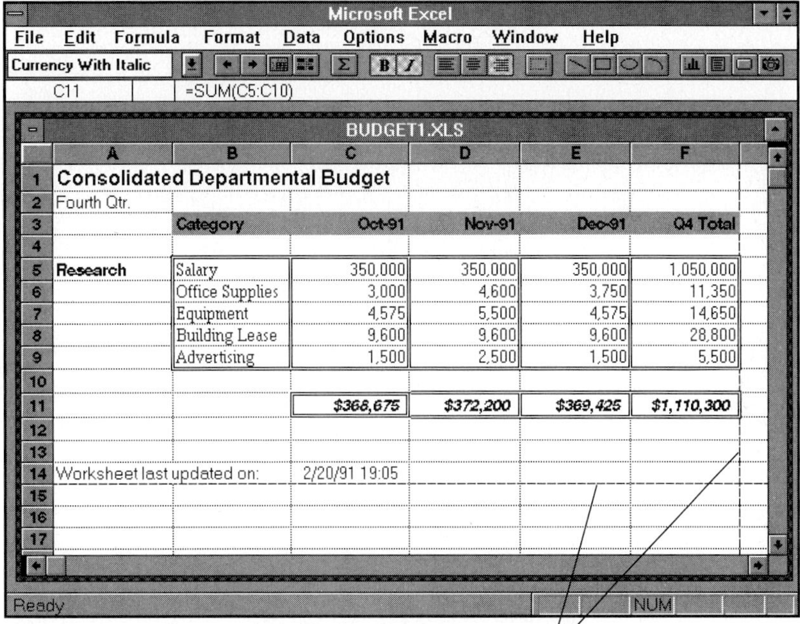

Setting Manual Page Breaks

When you print a worksheet that is longer or wider than one page, Excel will automatically control where the pages break so that everything fits as well as possible. You can override this automatic action, however, by setting manual *page breaks*. By setting a page break, you control how Excel will print a page.

Excel will let you set page breaks in either the row or column dimension—or both. For example, to tell Excel to manually break a page at row 12, you would put the cell pointer beneath the row where you wanted the break to appear. Likewise with the column page breaks: If you want to break the page at column F, you would start with the cell pointer in column G—one column to the right. In the case of placing manual page breaks for both a row and a column, make sure that the cell pointer is located to the right and beneath the cell where you want the breaks to occur. Follow these instructions to see how this works:

1. Highlight cell A10.
2. Click on Options, Set Page Break. Note how Excel put a dotted line between rows 9 and 10.

To remove this page break, you need to ensure that the cell pointer is below the break you want to remove. To remove the page break between rows 9 and 10, follow these steps:

1. Highlight cell A10.
2. Click on Options, Remove Page Break.

To add a page break in both the vertical (columns) and horizontal (rows) dimensions at the same time, use the following instructions:

1. Highlight cell D15. (Remember, this is *below* and *to the right* of the place where you want the page break to appear.)
2. Click on Options, Set Page Break. Once you have finished, your worksheet should have a dotted line that represents the page break in both dimensions. Your worksheet should look like the one in Figure 6.9.

Figure 6.9
Worksheet after adding two page breaks

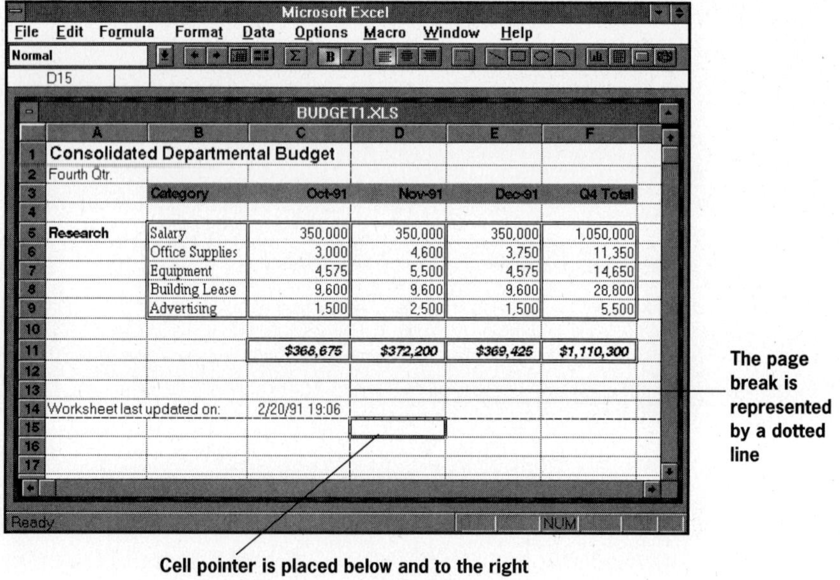

Finally, to remove all the manual page breaks in a document, follow these steps:

1. Highlight the entire document by clicking on the button where the row and column headings come together.
2. Click on Options, Remove Page Break.

You can add more than one manual page break in a document. Each time you add a manual page break, Excel will automatically adjust the automatic page breaks (the ones that Excel sets on your behalf) so that the document prints out correctly. The manual page breaks you include in the worksheet are saved with the worksheet.

Printing the Document

Tip. There might be times when you don't want to either print or display zeros. To turn zeros off, click on Options, Display and remove the X in the box labeled "Zero Values." When you click on OK to complete the command, all cells that either contain zero, or that resolve (by some calculation) to zero, show as blank.

OK, it's finally time to print out the worksheet you have been building for some time now. Remember that what you get from your printer might be a bit different from the result here, due to differences in printers. (The sample document you will see here was printed on a Hewlett-Packard LaserJet IIP printer.) Perform the following steps to print the final document on your printer:

1. Click on File, Print. The dialog box that pops up is shown in Figure 6.10. The dialog box you see may look just a bit different because of the installed and active printers on your system.
2. Verify that the number of copies is set to 1.
3. Verify that the Pages section is set to All. This is where you select to print only a group of pages of the worksheet.
4. Verify that an X doesn't appear in the Draft Quality field.
5. Make sure you have selected Sheet in the Print section.
6. Click on OK to carry out your command.

Figure 6.10
File Print dialog box

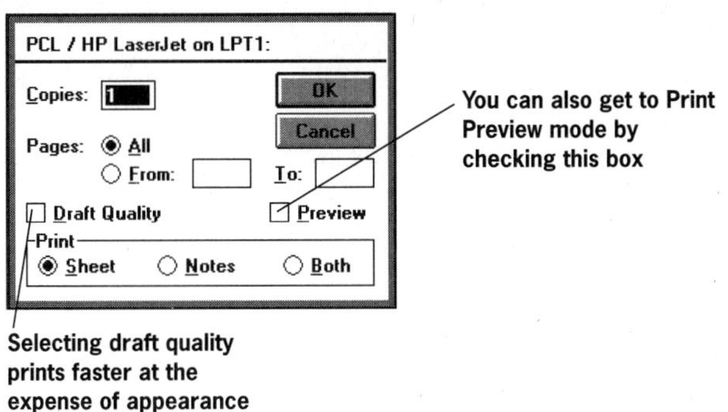

When your printer finishes printing, you should have a document that looks more or less like the sample in Figure 6.11.

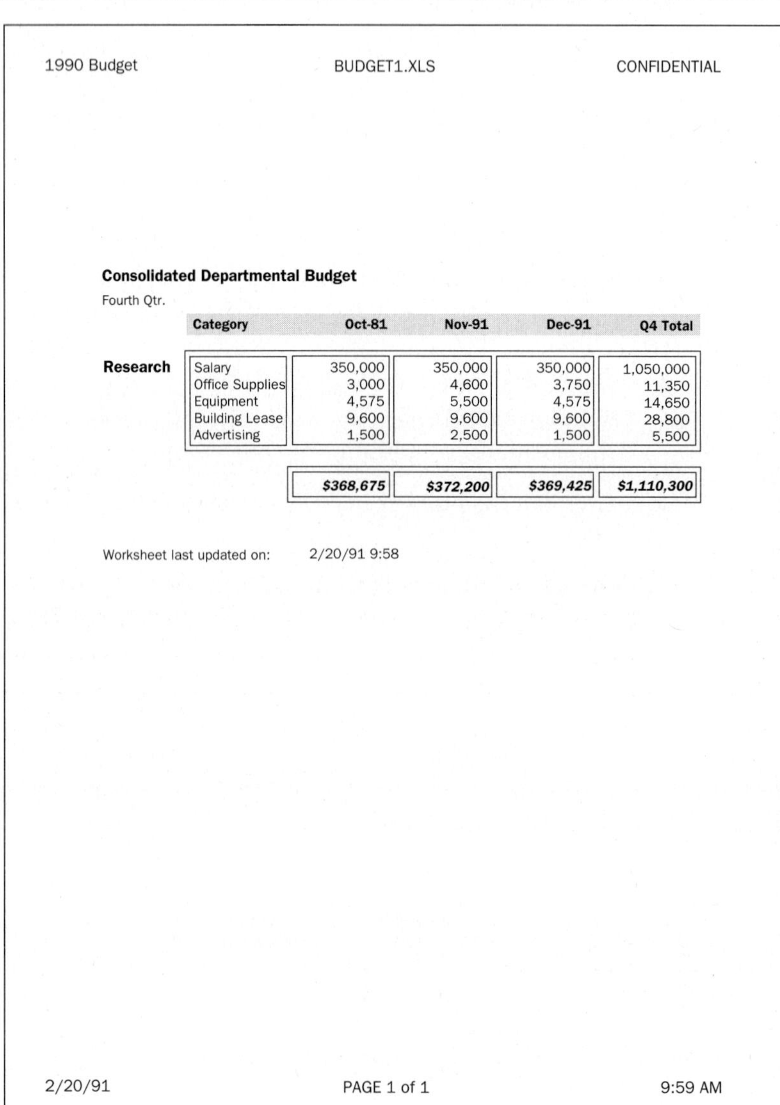

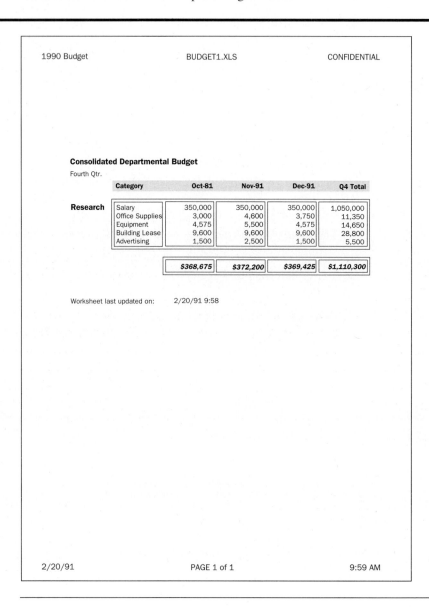

1990 Budget BUDGET1.XLS CONFIDENTIAL

Consolidated Departmental Budget

Fourth Qtr.

	Category	Oct-81	Nov-91	Dec-91	Q4 Total
Research	Salary	350,000	350,000	350,000	1,050,000
	Office Supplies	3,000	4,600	3,750	11,350
	Equipment	4,575	5,500	4,575	14,650
	Building Lease	9,600	9,600	9,600	28,800
	Advertising	1,500	2,500	1,500	5,500
		$368,675	*$372,200*	*$369,425*	*$1,110,300*

Worksheet last updated on: 2/20/91 9:58

2/20/91 PAGE 1 of 1 9:59 AM

Figure 6.11 Printed BUDGET1.XLS worksheet

A Note about Printing Titles

There is one thing to watch out for if you use Print Titles often. Whenever you use Print Titles, you must be sure to also use the Set Print Area and define the print area as one that *excludes* the titles. If you fail to do this, the first page of your printout will have duplicate sets of print titles at the top of the page.

Printing Notes

In the last exercise, you printed out the contents of the worksheet. Recall, however, that you also had added some annotations to one of the cells of the worksheet back in Chapter 2. Cell notes are very useful as reminders of why you might have used a certain formula or a particular assumption in the worksheet. Here's how to print the notes you have put into a worksheet:

1. Click on File, Page Setup. A dialog box appears.
2. Put an X in the box marked Row and Column Headings. This step is necessary so that each note will be identified by its cell location.
3. Click on OK to close this dialog box.
4. Click on File, Print.
5. In the Print section of the dialog box, click on Notes. Alternatively, you can click on Both to tell Excel to print both the Worksheet and the Notes that it contains.
6. Click on OK to carry out the command. When you finish printing out the cell notes, your printout should look more or less like Figure 6.12.

Figure 6.12
Printout of the cell notes in BUDGET1.XLS

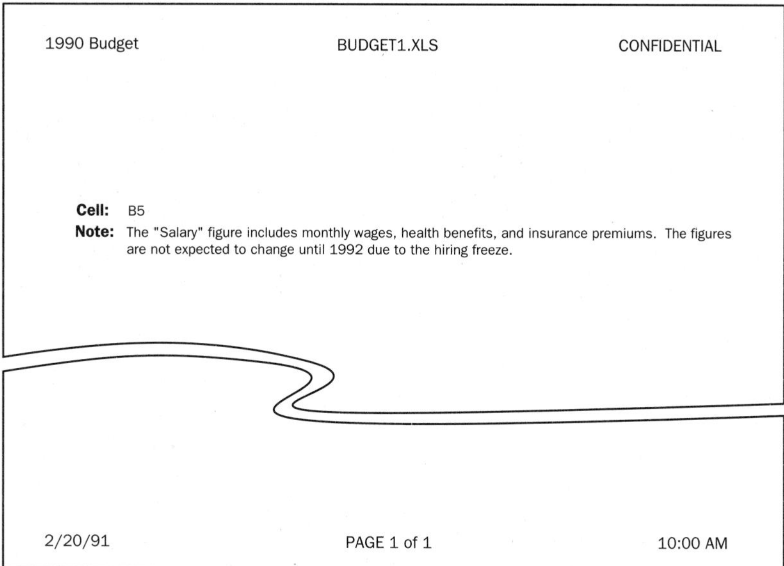

1990 Budget BUDGET1.XLS CONFIDENTIAL

Cell: B5
Note: The "Salary" figure includes monthly wages, health benefits, and insurance premiums. The figures are not expected to change until 1992 due to the hiring freeze.

2/20/91 PAGE 1 of 1 10:00 AM

Printing Cell Formulas

As you construct ever more complicated worksheets, it might become difficult to debug them and maintain the correct logic. Chapter 3 discussed the concept of logical errors and ways to avoid them. One step you can easily take is to print out the worksheet with the formulas displayed instead of the calculated values. It's often helpful to look at a worksheet from this perspective—you can frequently find logical errors just by looking at the formulas.

Excel provides an easy method for you to display the formulas—that is, the actual contents of the cells instead of their calculated values. When you change the display, Excel by default will left-align all the cell contents and double the width of each column in order to accommodate the formula. The following exercise, however, includes approximate instructions on how to get the entire worksheet all onto one screen (which the default wouldn't do). You might have to play around a bit with the width of the columns in order to see other worksheets on a single screen.

Use the following steps to display and print the formulas in the cells in BUDGET1.XLS:

1. Click on Options, Display.
2. Place an X in the box marked Formulas in the dialog box that appears.
3. Click on OK to complete the command.
4. Set the width of columns A and B to 4.5.
5. Set the width of columns C, D, E, and F to Best Fit. You might need to make small adjustments to your column widths to get them to fit onto the screen and match the sample output, but your worksheet should look like Figure 6.13 when you finish.

To print out the full worksheet now, just follow the earlier steps for printing a regular worksheet, making sure that Sheet is selected as the print source in the Print dialog box. The printed worksheet should look like Figure 6.14.

There are a couple of things to note here. First, the date headings you had included at the top of each column of numbers are now displayed as serial numbers corresponding to the dates you entered. Also, note that numbers you explicitly entered (in the range C5:E9) are shown as they are stored by Excel (unformatted), not as they are displayed.

With the worksheet displayed this way, you can see how you would be able to spot discrepancies in the way you constructed the logic of the worksheet. For example, if you had neglected to correctly sum a column of numbers, it would be relatively easy to spot in the =SUM() functions in row 11.

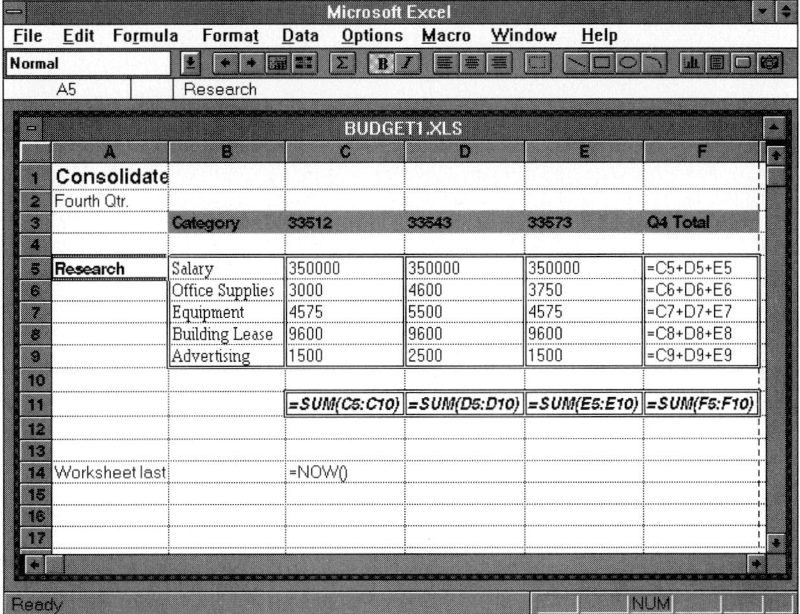

Figure 6.13
Displaying the cell contents

Printing Special Characters

The Microsoft Windows environment, and the applications that run under it, provides a number of benefits if you want to work with special characters such as foreign currency symbols or copyright symbols. The Windows environment makes it easy for you to use special characters with your worksheet. This is very important for financial analysis work where the worksheet might need to include calculations based on the British Pound (£) or the Japanese Yen (¥). Even if your worksheet will not include these international currencies, you might find it useful to be able to display the cents symbol (¢) from time to time.

Entering these symbols is fairly simple. Just follow these instructions to enter and use special symbols on your worksheet:

1. Pick an empty spot on your worksheet. With BUDGET1, highlight cell C16.

2. Press the Alt key, and, while holding it down, type **0162** on the numeric keypad. You must use the numeric keypad; the numbers across the top of the keyboard won't work.

3. Release the Alt key. The cents character should appear in cell C16.

Figure 6.14

Printout of the BUDGET1.XLS worksheet with formulas displayed

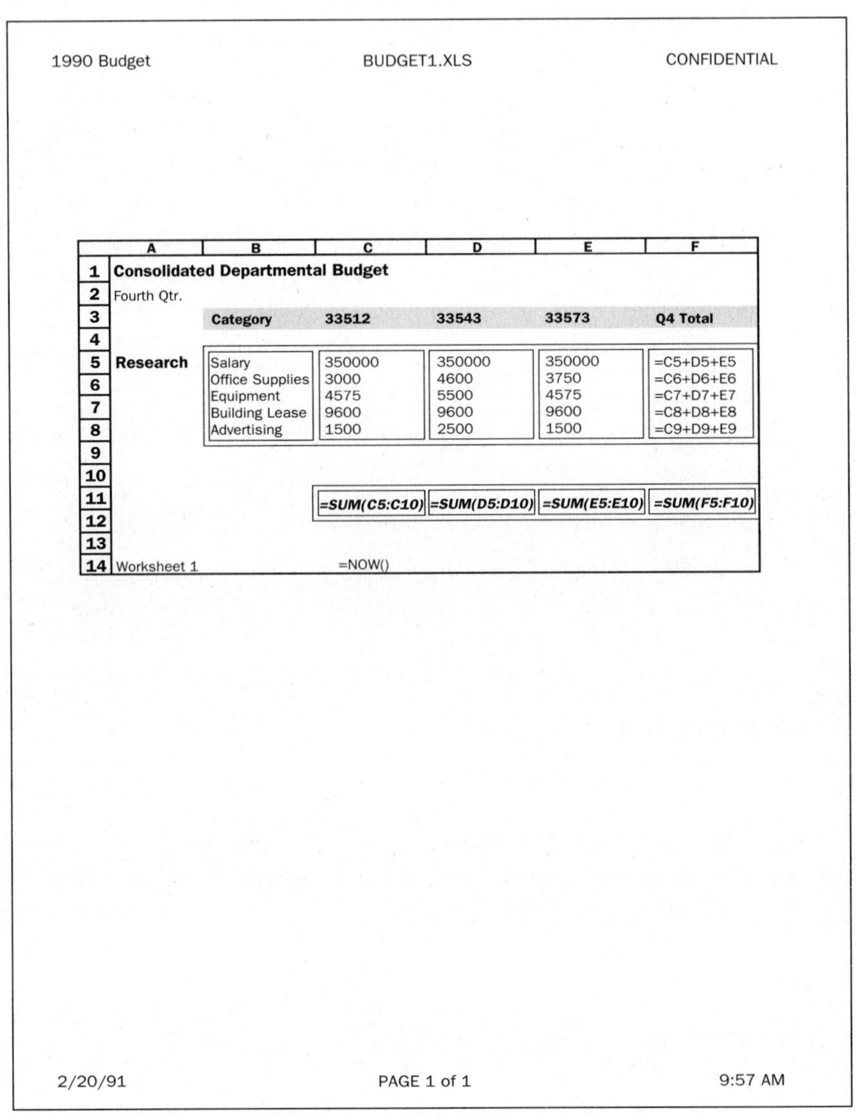

1990 Budget BUDGET1.XLS CONFIDENTIAL

	A	B	C	D	E	F
1	**Consolidated Departmental Budget**					
2	Fourth Qtr.					
3		**Category**	**33512**	**33543**	**33573**	**Q4 Total**
4						
5	**Research**	Salary	350000	350000	350000	=C5+D5+E5
6		Office Supplies	3000	4600	3750	=C6+D6+E6
7		Equipment	4575	5500	4575	=C7+D7+E7
8		Building Lease	9600	9600	9600	=C8+D8+E8
9		Advertising	1500	2500	1500	=C9+D9+E9
10						
11			***=SUM(C5:C10)***	***=SUM(D5:D10)***	***=SUM(E5:E10)***	***=SUM(F5:F10)***
12						
13						
14	Worksheet 1		=NOW()			

2/20/91 PAGE 1 of 1 9:57 AM

Once you have entered a special character, Excel treats it just like any other character—you can format it, move it, make it bold, delete it, and so on.

There are other special characters that might interest you. Some of the other characters that you can use are shown in Table 6.2, along with the four-digit code you use to access them. Experiment with these characters if your application calls for the use of foreign language characters or other special symbols.

Table 6.2 **Selected Special Characters and Their Codes**

Code	Character	Code	Character	Code	Character
0161	¡	0193	Á	0225	á
0162	¢	0194	Â	0226	â
0163	£	0195	Ã	0227	ã
0164	O	0196	Ä	0228	ä
0165	¥	0197	Å	0229	å
0166	/	0198	Æ	0230	æ
0167	§	0199	Ç	0231	ç
0168	¨	0200	È	0232	è
0169	©	0201	É	0233	é
0170	ª	0202	Ê	0234	ê
0171	«	0203	Ë	0235	ë
0172	¬	0204	Ì	0236	ì
0173	–	0205	Í	0237	í
0174	®	0206	Î	0238	î
0175	—	0207	Ï	0239	ï
0176	°	0208	D	0240	d
0177	±	0209	Ñ	0241	ñ
0178	≥	0210	Ò	0242	ò
0179	3	0211	Ó	0243	ó
0180	´	0212	Ô	0244	ô
0181	µ	0213	Õ	0245	õ
0182	¶	0214	Ö	0246	ö
0183	·	0215	x	0247	÷
0184	C	0216	Ø	0248	ø
0185	1	0217	Ù	0249	ù
0186	º	0218	Ú	0250	ú
0187	»	0219	Û	0251	û
0188	1/4	0220	Ü	0252	ü
0189	1/2	0221	Y	0253	y
0190	3/4	0222	P	0254	p
0191	¿	0223	ß	0255	ÿ
0192	À	0224	à		

One final note on the use of special characters. If your printer does not support the character, it will substitute something else—something you didn't want—when it encounters the special character. In this case, what you see on screen is not necessarily what you get.

Once again, be sure to save the worksheet so that you can continue to work with it in later chapters. Before you save this version, be sure to remove the special characters that you have created so that your worksheet is consistent with the examples in upcoming chapters. Then choose File, Save, and Excel will store the latest version of the BUDGET1.XLS worksheet.

CHAPTER

7

Charting and Graphing

Chart Basics

Creating a New Chart

Formatting the Chart

Printing Your Charts

Saving Your Charts

IF YOU SUBSCRIBE TO THE SAYING "A PICTURE IS WORTH A THOUSAND words," then Microsoft Excel 3.0 is the package for you. Excel has long been the leader in the field of presenting information in aesthetically pleasing and visually stimulating ways. Even in earlier versions, Excel's graphical data presentation capabilities outstripped other spreadsheet products on the market. With version 3.0, however, the choices multiply—so much so that this book cannot cover all the charting and graphing options. Instead, it strives to present a general look at how charting and graphing works with Excel 3.0, and reluctantly leaves the advanced issues to a work with a corresponding scope. (For the purposes of this book *charting* and *graphing* are synonymous, so the terms will hereafter be used interchangeably.)

Conceptually, producing a basic chart is very simple. First, you highlight the ranges you want Excel to graph, then you tell Excel to create a new chart. Excel will create a basic chart from the data. You can then modify and enhance the chart to better visually present your data.

Later in this chapter, you will have the opportunity to create some simple charts based on the data in the BUDGET1.XLS worksheet. Chapter 8 will show you how to add graphical elements to your charts and worksheets and how to make a chart part of your worksheet. The first order of business, however, is to spend a few minutes discussing the various chart types available and which is best suited to a particular situation.

Chart Basics

Before you select the type of chart that will best display the data contained in the worksheet, take a few moments to learn Excel's vocabulary for charting. Locate the following elements on Figure 7.1 to help you better understand Excel's terminology.

Data Marker Usually a marker or a bar that marks a single data point (value). Excel will let you customize the marker object in most cases.

Chart Menu Bar This is similar to the normal menu bar, but the items on the bar are different when you are working with charts. All of the chart menu items work just like the normal menu items.

Data Series These are the items (also called *data elements*) that you will graph. They are related items and usually form one row of data on the worksheet. If you were graphing some data from the BUDGET1.XLS file, for example, each of the categories is a data series: Office Supplies, Building Lease, Salaries, and so on.

Figure 7.1
The parts of a chart

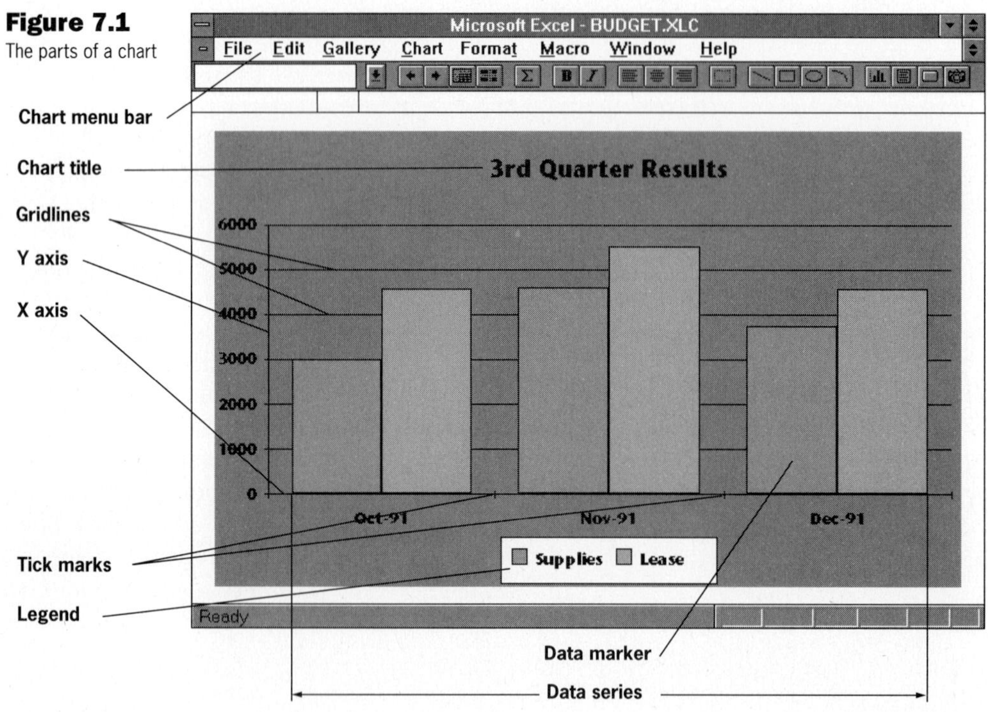

Axes These are the major lines on a chart, which are used as references for plotting the data. If the chart is two-dimensional, there will usually be two axes: the x-axis, which runs horizontally across the bottom of the graph, and the y-axis, which runs vertically along the left side of the graph. There are variations on this, but most two-dimensional graphs conform to this standard. If you have trouble remembering which axis is which, you can remember the little ditty that goes "the y-axis reaches to the sky."

Text Most charts will have some kind of chart text. This text usually includes a title and x- and y-axis labels. Often, other text is also used. Excel offers several ways to place chart text.

Tick Marks These are the small marks that extend from one or both of the axes to help you identify a value on the axis.

Gridlines Gridlines are just extensions of tick marks—gridlines go all the way across the chart. They make it easier to compare values.

Legend The legend is usually a box that contains some type of key used to identify patterns or colors that represent data series.

Choosing the Correct Chart Type

All chart types are not created equal—different chart types serve different purposes. In the following sections, you'll see not only what kinds of charts Excel provides, but also what kinds of charting are best performed by those chart types.

Excel uses what it calls the *Gallery* to present its basic chart types. Within each of these chart types, you can pick from up to eight variations. The variations range from fundamental differences to simple labeling and grid line choices. In the following sections, the Gallery is shown for each type of chart.

Line Charts

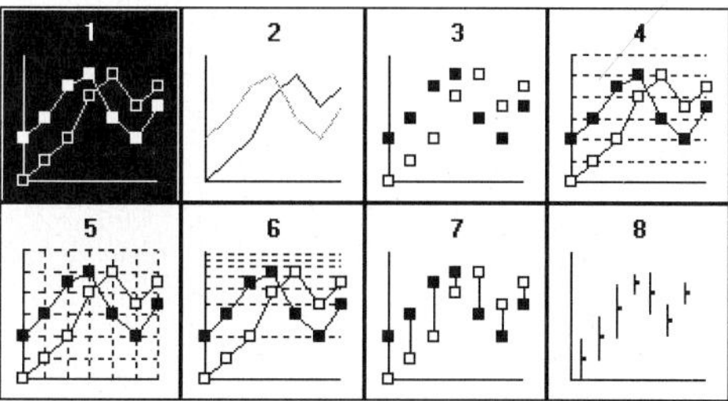

Line charts are most often used to illustrate performance over time. Generally, time periods are shown across the x-axis, and numeric values are shown on the y-axis. For example, if you want to examine the population figures of a country over the last 25 years, a line chart is probably the best way to illustrate that (although a column chart would also be a good choice; see the section on column charts).

The line chart type offers some interesting variations on the basic style. One of the variations of particular interest in financial analysis is the *high-low-close* chart type, which shows both the high and low prices of a stock or other investment instrument as the top and bottom of a vertical line. The closing price of the stock is shown as a tick mark on the line. (Don't confuse the vertical line in a high-low-close chart with the line in a regular line chart. The line in a line chart is the more or less horizontal one that connects the data points.) A sample high-low-close chart is shown in Figure 7.2.

Another variation of the line chart is the *high-low* chart, which is useful for anything that has two data points during a particular time span. This type of chart is useful for displaying extremes in temperature, for example, or a high- and low-pressure measurement within a chosen time frame.

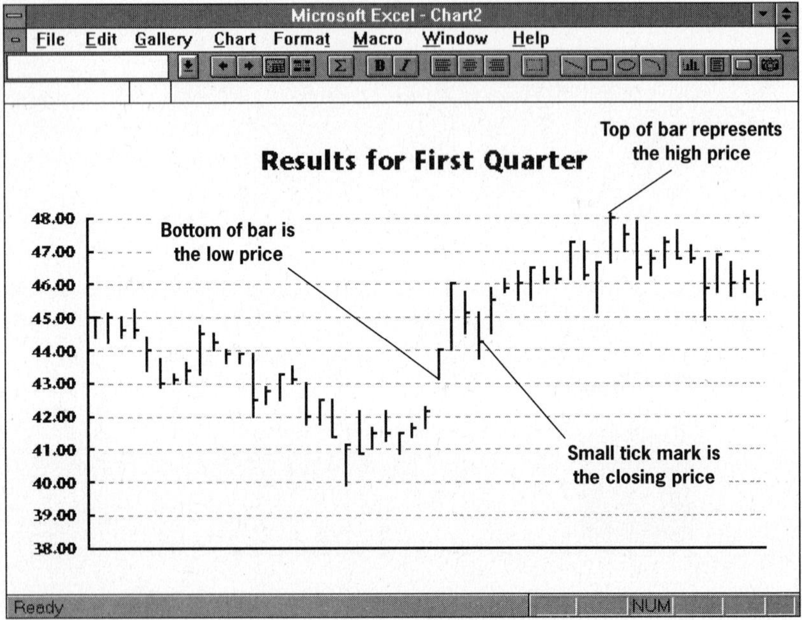

Figure 7.2 High-low-close chart showing stock prices

Finally, other variations of the line chart include logarithmic scales for scientific and mathematical analysis.

Area Charts

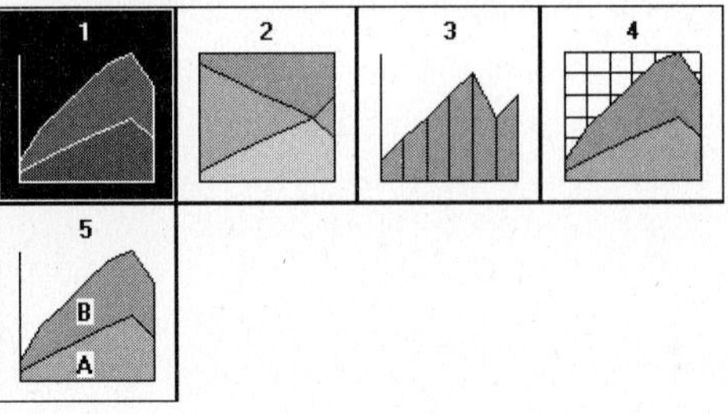

Area charts are best suited for showing the magnitude of change over time. These charts are similar to line charts in that they show the values in relation to one another, but since the areas between the data series are solid, you get a sense of the magnitude of the change not only from one item to the other, but to the cumulative total. Excel offers several variations on the simple area chart, including an area chart that shows each data element as a percentage of the total. Other variations include different ways to label the data elements.

Column Charts

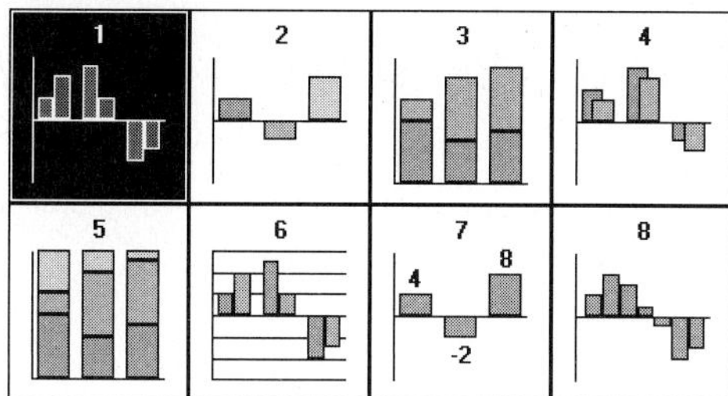

Excel's *column chart* is what is usually called a bar chart. Column charts are useful for illustrating two or more data elements. For example, a column chart could be used to show the performance of two departments over a span of time.

You'll use the column chart for some basic graphs of the BUDGET1.XLS data later on in the chapter. Variations of the column chart include the *100% stacked column*, which shows the data elements as percentages of a total, and the *stacked column* chart, which stacks the data elements one on top of the other to show a cumulative total.

Bar Charts

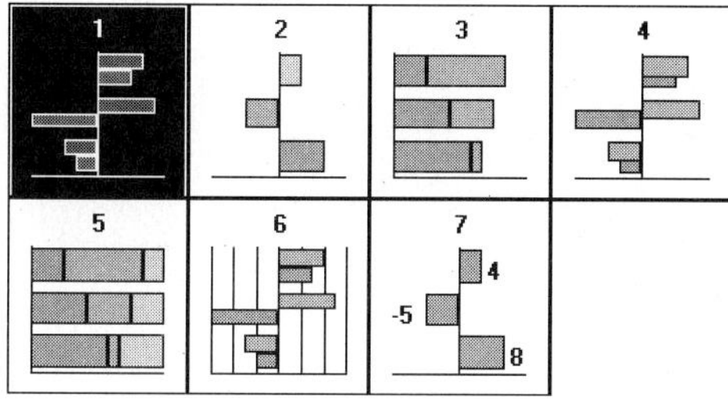

Excel's *bar chart* is not the type of chart that you expect to see when you hear the word *bar*. The bar charts in Excel are composed of *horizontal* bars, which can be used to show the value of two or more items at the same point in time. Variations on this chart type include the *stacked bar* chart, which shows several data elements stacked one on top of the other to show a cumulative total, and the *100% stacked bar*, which shows all the data elements as percentages of a total.

Pie Charts

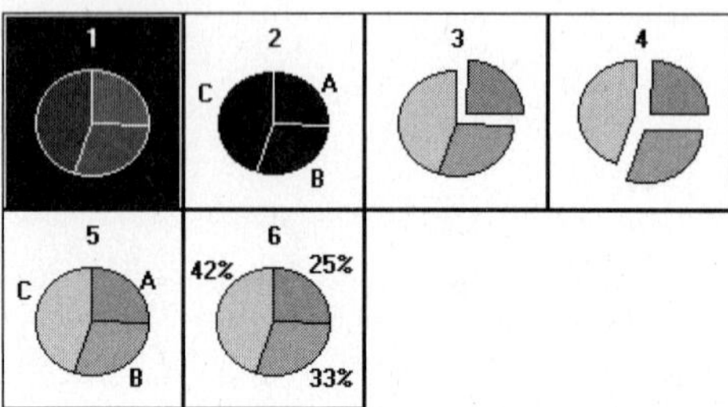

Pie charts are useful as a way to show the data elements as a percentage of some total. Each data element is represented as a slice of the pie, and the whole pie represents the sum of the slices. When you produce a pie chart, Excel will automatically add the numbers together and calculate the proportion that each element contributes to the total.

Variations on the basic pie chart allow you to display the pie chart with the slices labeled either with text or with the percentage figure that slice represents. Excel even lets you *explode*, or move away from the rest of the pie, one or more of the slices. This is a useful feature if you want to add emphasis to a particular slice of the pie.

XY Charts

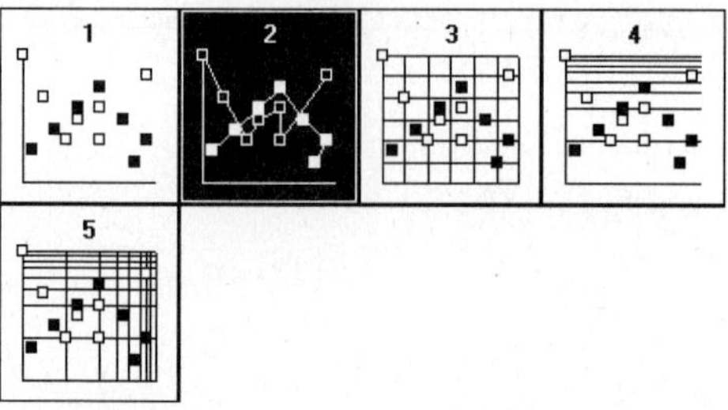

XY or *scatter charts* are useful for plotting two separate variables to show possible relationships. For example, suppose you wanted to know if there is a correspondence between the number of letters in people's names and the number of pairs of shoes they own. If there were a direct relationship, the points would cluster around one line. If there were an inverse relationship, the points would cluster on another line. And if there were no relationship, there would be no cluster.

In addition, you could graph two or more different populations with a scatter chart by using different shapes or colors of points, and thus see if the relationships differed for, say, men and women.

Combination Charts

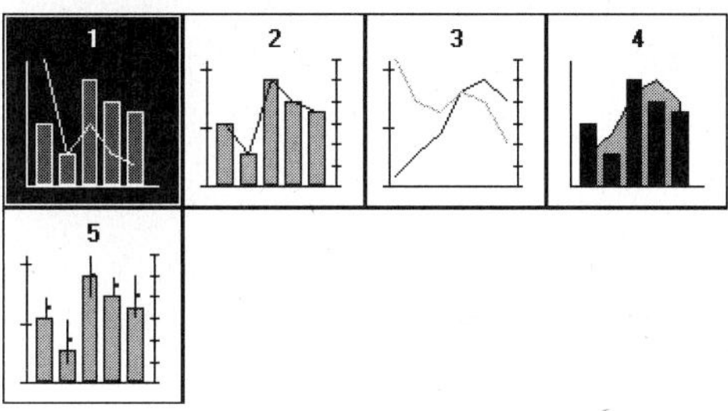

Combination charts, also called *overlay charts*, give you the option of laying one type of chart over another. Use this feature to create charts that compare one type of number to another, perhaps actual sales versus projected sales.

Combination charts are also very useful if you want to show two different types of data that use two different scales. An example of this might be a stock performance chart showing the stock price that varied between $15 and $30, overlaid onto another chart that showed the corresponding stock sales volume, a figure that is normally measured in the millions of shares. If you used the same scale for both, the $15 stock would be invisible compared to a trading volume of 200 million shares.

Although you can create combination charts just by overlaying one chart with another, Excel provides five combination chart types for you to start out with and modify to suit your needs.

Three-Dimensional Charts

Excel 3.0 adds new chart types to the already extensive features of the spreadsheet product. New to the 3.0 version of Excel are three-dimensional (3-D) charts in several different flavors.

3-D Line Charts

For the most part, Excel's 3-D line charts are similar to its standard line chart. However, there are some types of charts that just don't work in three dimensions. For example, there is no 3-D equivalent to the high-low-close chart because it would be cumbersome to implement in three

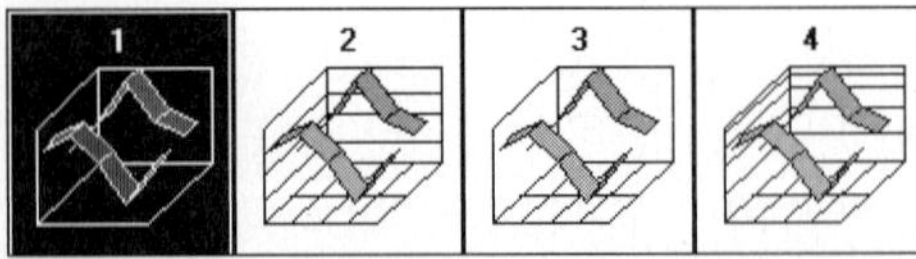

dimensions. Likewise, there is no 3-D equivalent to the high-low style of chart.

3-D Area Charts

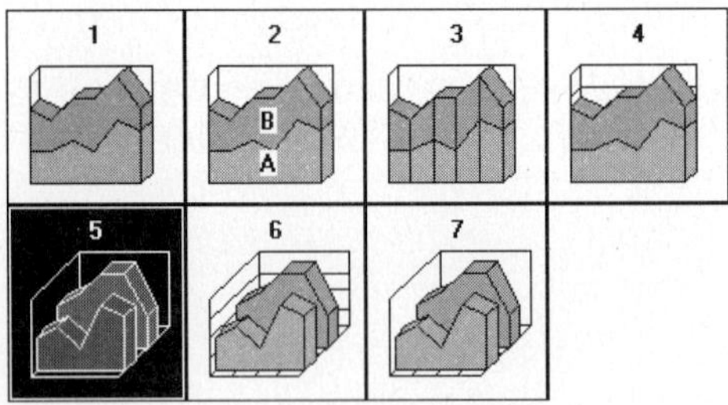

3-D area charts are similar to the basic area charts but have 3-D effects and can be rotated in three axes of motion to produce just the effect you are looking for.

3-D Column Charts

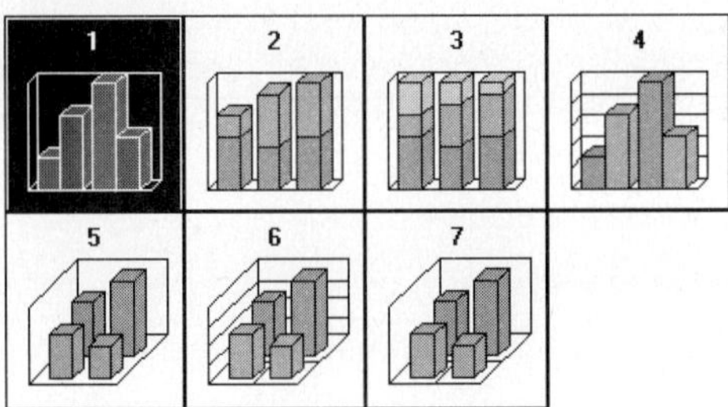

Excel's 3-D column charts are identical to the standard column chart, but feature 3-D effects and can be rotated to change the chart's perspective.

3-D Pie Charts

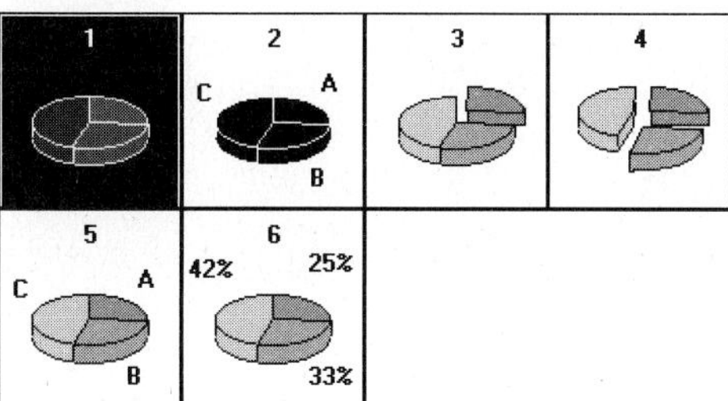

Finally, Excel also offers a 3-D version of the pie chart type. Like the area and column charts, the 3-D pie chart is similar to the two-dimensional version except for the 3-D effects and the ability to rotate the chart to your liking.

Creating a New Chart

As mentioned before, setting up a new chart in Excel is very straightforward. In fact, this section contains several exercises for you to create charts based on the data contained in the BUDGET1.XLS worksheet.

When you create a new chart, Excel will build it based on what is defined as the *preferred chart*. This is the chart that Excel will use by default when you first create a chart. Of course, you can later change the type of chart you want, and you can even change the type of the preferred chart, so that when you create new charts they will initially appear in the format you specify.

To begin creating a chart, reload the BUDGET1.XLS worksheet from the last chapter. Then, use the following instructions to quickly create a new chart from the BUDGET1.XLS worksheet:

1. Highlight the range B6:C9.
2. Click on File, New.
3. Select Chart.
4. Click on OK to complete the command.

Excel immediately creates a default chart based on the data you highlighted. Your chart should look like the one in Figure 7.3. The first chart Excel creates is based on the preferred settings discussed previously. You will learn how to change the preferred chart type shortly, so that Excel will default to your choice of chart.

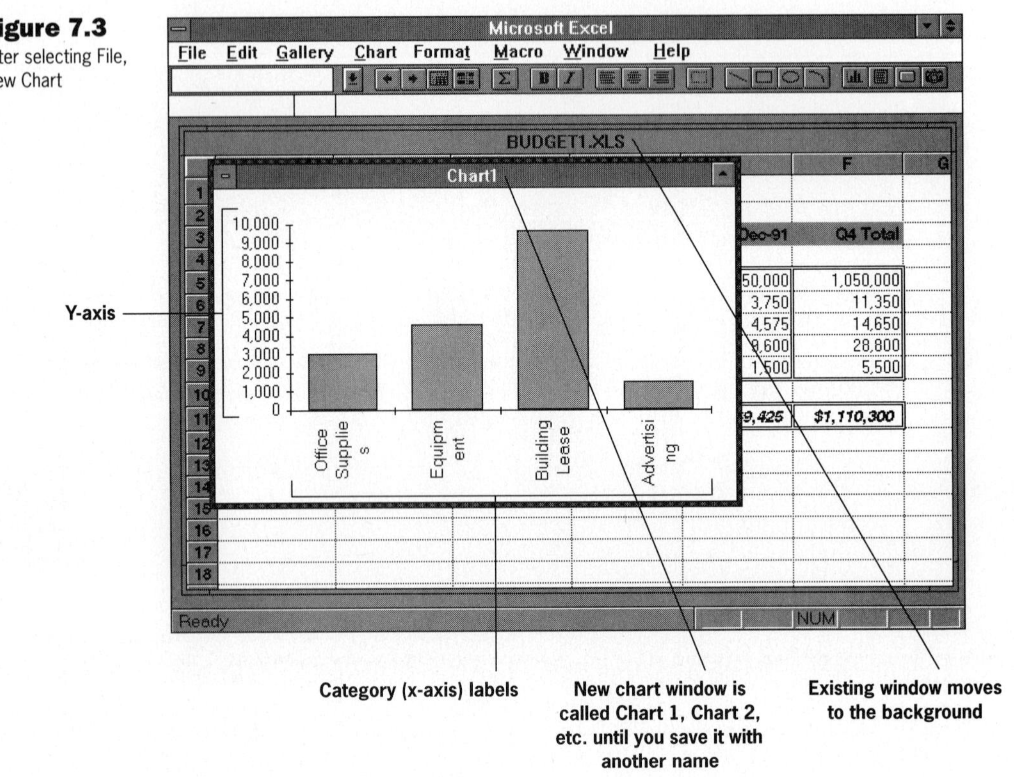

Figure 7.3 After selecting File, New Chart

Moving Between Windows

When you tell Excel to create a chart, Excel opens up a new window. Unlike what you've seen up until now, however, the new window is a *chart window.* Recall that there are three kinds of sheets that Excel uses: worksheet, chart, and macro. A chart window is just another kind of sheet. You can move it around the screen, resize it, close it, save it, and so on, just as you would any other window. In fact, you can easily switch between any open windows by using the following instructions:

1. Click on Window. Notice the brief list of the open windows (see Figure 7.4).
2. Click on BUDGET1.XLS. The chart window disappears and you're back at the worksheet.
3. Click on Window again.

4. Click on Chart1 (yours might be Chart2 or Chart3) to return to the default chart you created.

Figure 7.4
List of open Excel windows

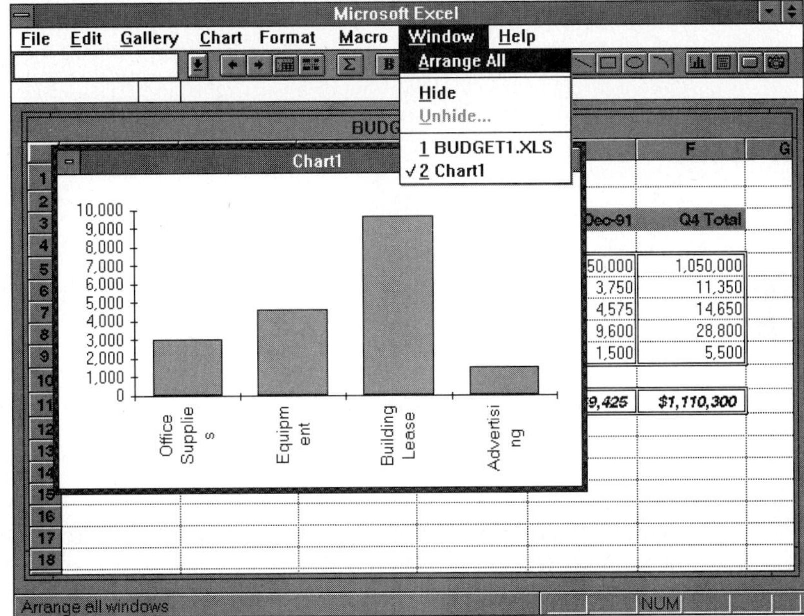

Tip. Another way to quickly switch windows is to click anywhere in the window you want to activate. The Windows environment will make that window the active one.

The Window menu will show the windows you have open at the time, regardless of type. Excel indicates unnamed sheets by giving them names like Sheet3, Macro2, or Chart4. Once you name a sheet, of course, its name appears at the top of the window.

Selecting the Ranges

You have seen that to carry out most actions in Excel, you must first specify what area the command should act upon, and then tell Excel what command to execute. In the case of charting, you first highlight the range of cells you want to chart and then tell Excel to create a new chart based on the information you have highlighted.

Normally, Excel can determine what you want to graph, including the category names, just from the range that you've highlighted. There are times, however, when Excel needs further clarification from you. From time to time you will see the following dialog box pop up.

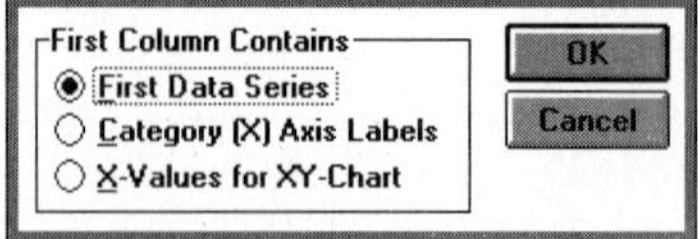

This dialog box is asking for clarification about how to handle the information it found in the first row of your highlighted data. When you are charting two or more rows of numbers, use this dialog box to tell Excel if the first row contains a separate data series or the x values in a scatter chart.

Changing the Chart Type

With your default chart still on the screen, it's time to change the chart to something a bit more interesting and useful. In this case, you are interested in seeing graphically what portion of the expenses paid in October were allocated to each department. (This chart omits the salary figures because they comprise such a large part of the total that they would completely dominate the scale of the chart.) The best type of chart for this is a pie chart because it shows each item's value as a percentage of the total. Use the following instructions to change the default chart to a 3-D pie chart that better illustrates the information you're trying to convey:

1. Click on Gallery and then click on 3D Pie.
2. Choose the type of three-dimensional pie chart you want to create. In this case, choose format 6 by either double-clicking in the box where the sixth pie format is shown or by highlighting it and clicking on OK. When you are finished, your chart will look like Figure 7.5.

But what if you don't like the pie chart and think this data would look better if it were formatted into a column chart? No problem. Just click on Gallery, 3D Column (using the first chart format) to change the pie chart into a column chart. Notice that, although the column chart is fairly standard, the 3-D effects give it some flair. After you change to a 3-D column chart, your screen should look like Figure 7.6.

Changing the Preferred Chart Type

Assume that you plan to do a number of these charts in the future. It doesn't make sense to always start from one type of chart and then change to another, especially if you know what chart type you will be using most often. The way around that problem is to simply change the default chart type. Unless your settings have already been changed, the default chart type is a standard two-dimensional column chart. (Remember that Excel uses the term *bar chart* to refer to a horizontal bar chart—*column* is Excel's term for what you would normally call a bar chart.)

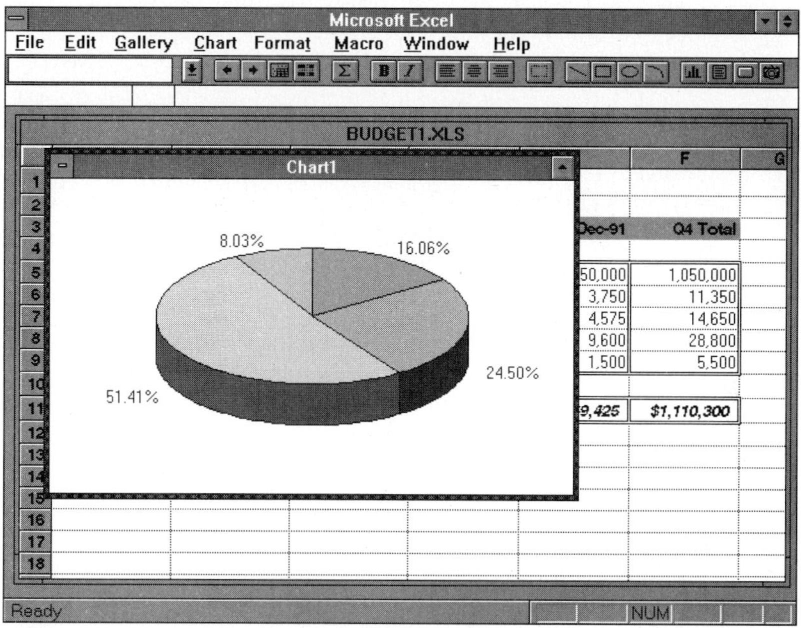

Figure 7.5
3-D pie chart with calculated percentages

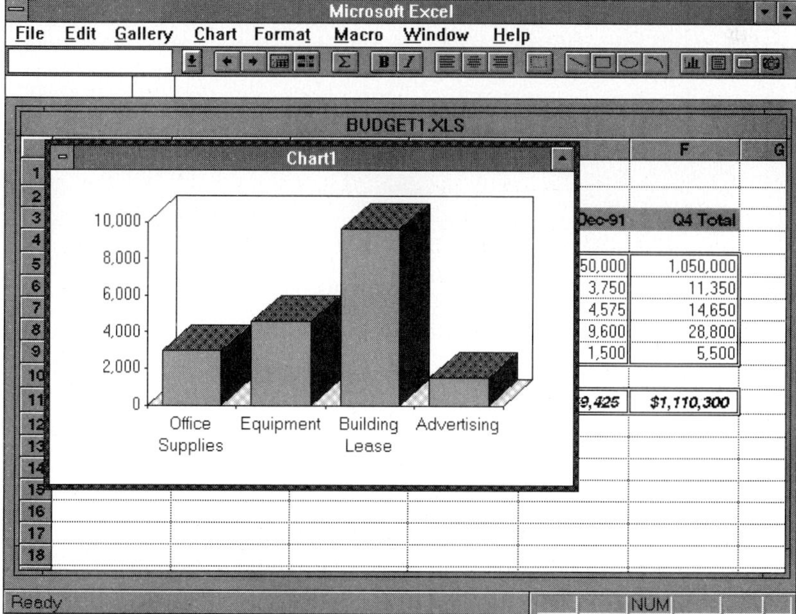

Figure 7.6
3-D column chart

If you want to use a snazzier 3-D column chart like the one you just created as your default, simply click on Gallery, Set Preferred. Nothing will appear to happen to the chart or to the worksheet, but the next time you create a chart, Excel will use the new settings that are in effect.

In addition, if you have customized a chart but then decide you'd like to return it to the default settings, just click on Gallery, Preferred. Excel will reset all the options back to that of the chart type you have defined as the default.

Formatting the Chart

There are literally hundreds of things you can do to format an Excel chart, many of which are outside the scope of this book. However, you should know about some of the basic things you can do to make your charts look better and present more information. (For more information about the numerous options you can control on a chart, consult the Microsoft Excel 3.0 documentation.)

Titles

Foremost on the list of enhancements to a chart is a title. Before you add a title to your chart, however, you should understand the way Excel defines attached text and unattached text. Text is considered to be *attached* to the chart if you cannot move it around after you put it on the chart. For example, a chart title is considered to be attached—once you add it, you won't be able to move it around.

The opposite state is *unattached* text, which can be moved around as your whim dictates. An example of unattached text might be an arrow that is used to call out important parts of the worksheet. Another example of unattached text is a free-floating text box that contains descriptive information about the worksheet. (See Chapter 8 for more on text boxes.)

Axis labels fit into neither of these categories. Once you create the chart they are no longer treated as text.

Use the following steps to add a title to your chart:

1. Click on Chart, Attach Text. A dialog box appears.
2. Make sure the button labeled "Chart Title" in the Attach Text To box is selected.
3. Click on OK.
4. Excel adds the placeholder "Title" on the worksheet and surrounds the word with little white boxes. The fact that the boxes are white means it is in attached text and cannot be moved. Now add a title of your own. Type **Research Div./Oct. '91**

5. Press the Enter key to complete the command. When you have finished, your chart should look like Figure 7.7.

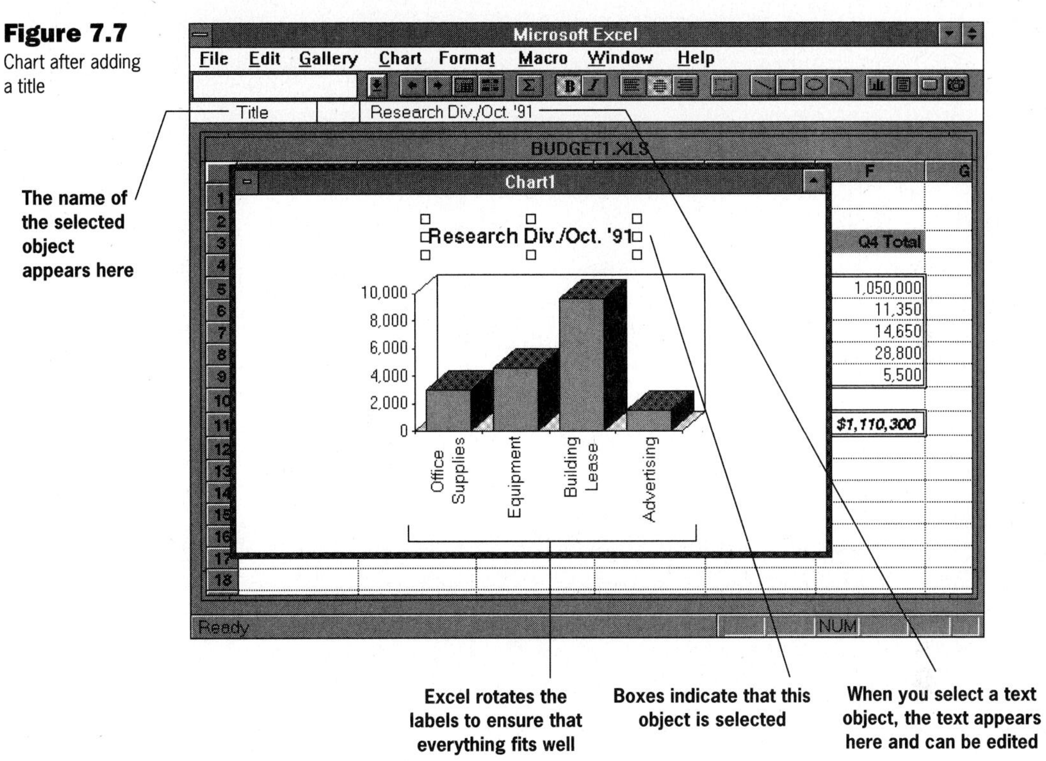

Figure 7.7 Chart after adding a title

Note that when you first add the title text placeholder, Excel automatically adjusts the chart to account for the addition of the text at the top of the chart. When you format the text of the title, as you will do in the next exercise, watch as Excel makes any necessary adjustment to keep everything displayed correctly. To format the title, follow these steps:

1. Make sure that the title text is selected—you can tell by looking for the white boxes that surround the title text. If it is not selected, just click on it once.

2. Click on Format, Font and proceed to format the text as you have done in the past. You will recognize the Format Font dialog box from previous exercises. For this exercise, format the text to 14-point Helvetica Bold or something similar.

3. Click on OK to complete the command. Your chart should now look like Figure 7.8.

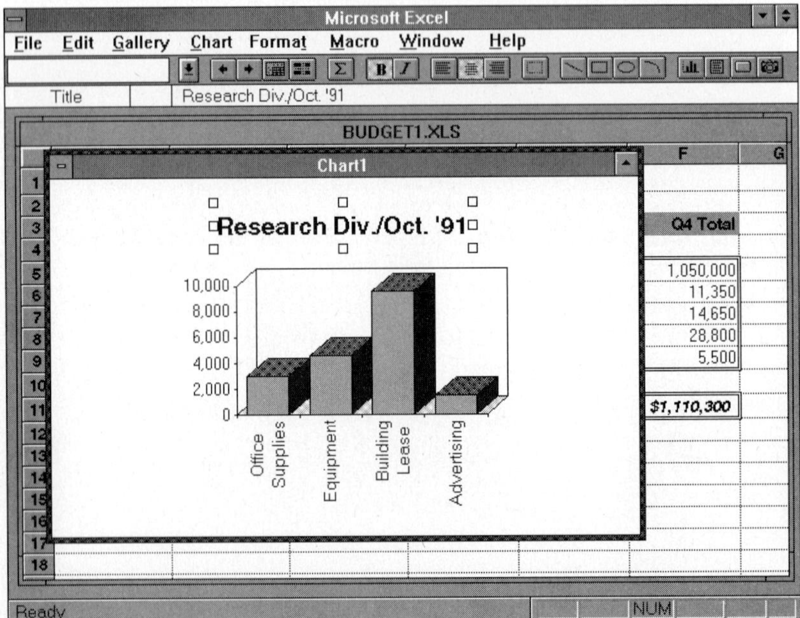

Figure 7.8
After changing the size of the title

Adding Unattached Text

Unlike those text elements that are fixed in position, unattached text is "free to roam." In this exercise, you will create a short block of explanatory text that can be moved around the chart at will. Follow these steps to create a block of unattached text:

1. Ensure that no object is selected on the chart. Simply press the Esc key once to deselect whatever might be selected.
2. Now begin typing the text you want to add. For this exercise, type **Estimated Data...** and then press Enter to complete the text entry. Excel will immediately place your text on the chart as a selected object surrounded by black boxes (which signify that it is movable).
3. Click anywhere within the group of black boxes and hold the mouse button down. Note how the boxes disappear and an outline of the space required for the text appears.
4. Use the mouse to drag the box around until you find a good spot for it—perhaps below the chart or off to one side.

5. Release the mouse button to tell Excel that this is where you want this block of text to appear. Note that the little black boxes reappear. After you finish this exercise, check to make sure that your chart looks something like the one in Figure 7.9.

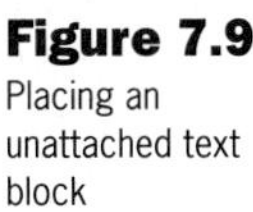

Figure 7.9
Placing an unattached text block

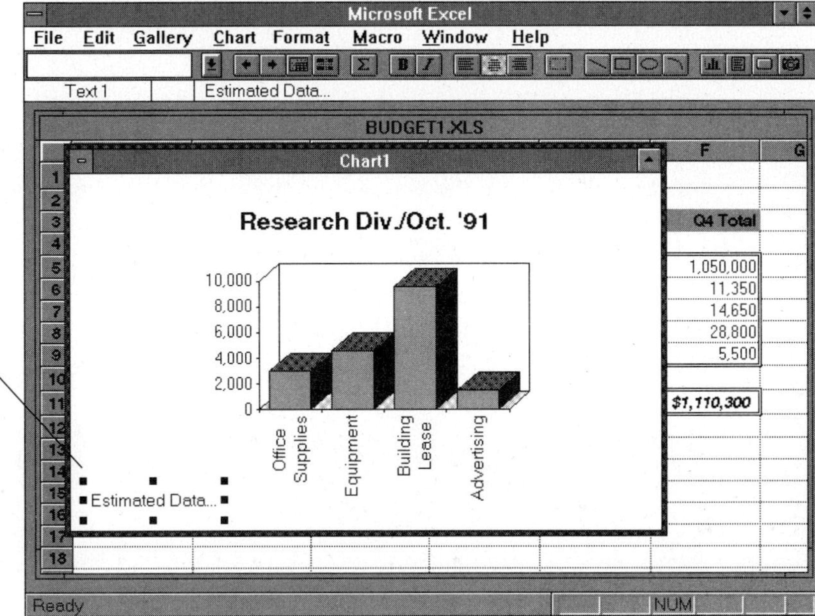

Black boxes mean the object can be moved

Although you don't have to delete the text now, here are the steps to follow if you decide to delete an unattached text block:

1. Select the text block by clicking once on the text. You will know when you have made the right selection because the text block will again be surrounded by small black boxes.
2. Press the Backspace key once to clear out the contents of the formula bar, that is, the text in the block.
3. Press the Enter key to complete the command.

Axis Labels

Look back at Figures 7.6 and 7.7 and notice what happened when Excel didn't seem to have enough room to display the category labels. Instead of running them all together so that the chart was unreadable, Excel elected to rotate the labels 90 degrees so that they wouldn't crash into each other.

On the way toward learning how you can manipulate those category labels, you'll learn several things about formatting charts with Excel. For example, there are a number of places where you can click the mouse button to bring up different dialog boxes. For starters, now it's time to correct the labels that were turned sideways. Use the following steps to bring up the appropriate dialog box:

1. Position your mouse pointer directly over the line that forms the x-axis (the horizontal axis).
2. Click once on that line to select it. You will know you have been successful if a small white box appears at each end of the x-axis.
3. Double-click on the x-axis or on one of the white boxes to bring up the Axis dialog box. Figure 7.10 shows this box.

Figure 7.10
Axis dialog box

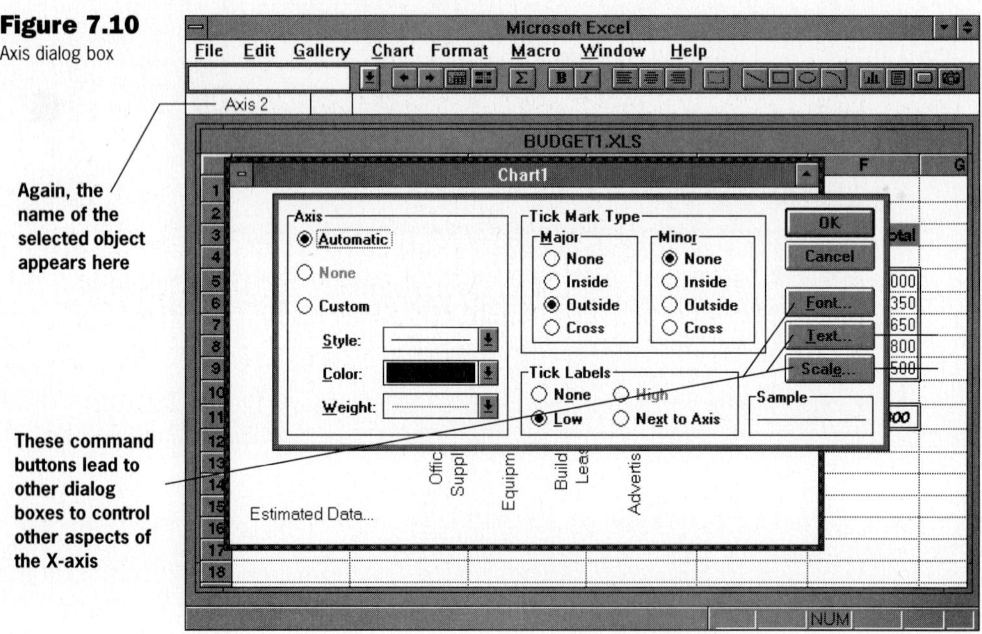

Some elements of this dialog box are already familiar to you. For example, you have already used the Fonts dialog box to change the size and attributes of text. You could make changes in the Axis dialog box to the text of the chart if you wanted to. However, the command button you want now is the one labeled "Text...." Follow the next steps to rotate the text back to horizontal.

1. With the dialog box still showing on your screen, click on the Text command button. The dialog box that appears looks like this:

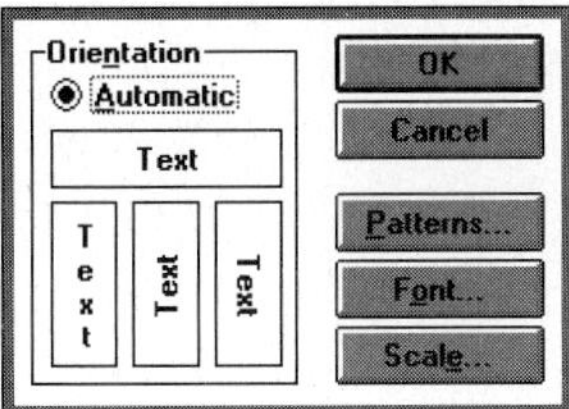

2. Click on the box that corresponds to horizontal text—the second box down from the top in the Orientation section.

3. Click on OK to complete the command.

As soon as you press the OK command button, Excel rotates the text 90 degrees, back to the standard position. Your chart should now look like Figure 7.11.

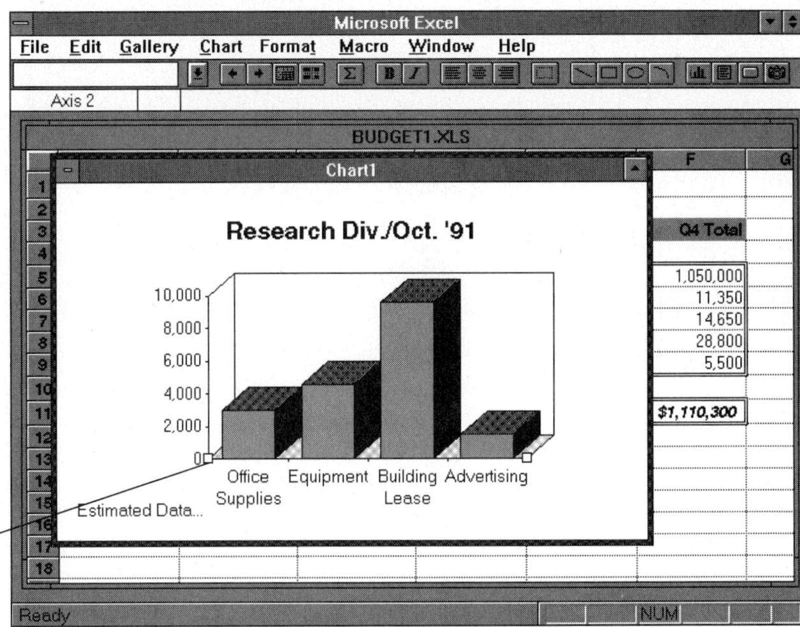

Figure 7.11
Chart after rotating the text

If the labels on your chart run together, or if the chart doesn't match the one here for any reason, you might have to resize the chart window. For a quick reminder of how to do that, turn to Appendix A.

Notice the small white squares at each end of the x-axis. These indicate that the x-axis is still the selected object on the chart.

Tick Marks

Tick marks are another item on the x-axis that offer you quite a bit of flexibility. In Excel, tick marks can be either *major tick marks* or *minor tick marks*. There really isn't any difference between major and minor tick marks. Major tick marks are used for larger intervals than minor tick marks, but they are otherwise identical. For example, if the values to be charted fall between 0 and 10,000, you might elect to have major tick marks at each 2,000 interval and use minor tick marks for each 1,000 or 500 interval.

Both types of tick marks are used to define the category along the axis. When you format the axis, you have four choices for where the tick mark should go: inside the axis, outside, crossing the axis (with some of the tick mark on either side), and none. In the following exercise, you will simply change the tick marks from the outside to the inside. Although the visual difference is not very striking, the exercise will illustrate the versatility and flexibility of Excel 3.0.

1. Double-click again on the x-axis of your chart. A dialog box appears (see Figure 7.10).
2. On the Major tick portion of the dialog box, click on Inside. This moves the tick mark from the outside position to the inside position.
3. Click on OK to complete the command.

Changing the Scale

A more visible and useful item to change on both the x- and y-axes is the way that the axis labels are displayed. One of the command buttons you have seen is the Scale button. The next exercise will demonstrate how to change the format of the numbers along the y-axis (vertical axis).

Before you do the exercises, however, it's important to understand how Excel chooses to display the numbers along the y-axis. Excel determines the format of the numbers along the chart axis based on the numerical format used in the worksheet. This is a handy fact to know. Consider a case where you create a small chart, perhaps just to see the effect that changing one number has on the overall model, and find that the axis numbers are too crowded because of the size of the chart. The way to solve the problem is to just go back into the worksheet and alter the numeric format of the numbers (see Chapter 5 for details) so that Excel can display the chart more neatly.

For example, your worksheet might be formatted so that all the numbers appear with a leading dollar sign and two digits of accuracy. If the chart is small, or if there is a lot of information to be shown on the chart, it might make more sense to simply format the numbers on the scale with no leading dollar sign and no decimal places.

In spite of your inability to directly change the numeric format of the chart axis, you can change the font attributes of the axis labels. This includes size, type style, and other attributes such as bold and italic. (Refer to Chapter 5 for more information on formatting text).

Now it's time to change the way the numbers are displayed along the y-axis. Use the following steps to open a dialog box and change the scale of the y-axis:

1. Highlight the y-axis by clicking once at any point along the axis. Small white boxes will appear at either end when it has been selected. The selected item's name (in this case Axis 1) also appears in the location bar in the upper-left corner of the worksheet.
2. Either double-click on the y-axis and then click on Scale, or simply click on Format, Scale from the Excel main menu. Figure 7.12 shows the resulting dialog box.
3. Change the Maximum value to **12000**.
4. Change the Major Unit to **4000**.
5. Click on OK to complete the command.

Figure 7.12
Format Scale dialog box

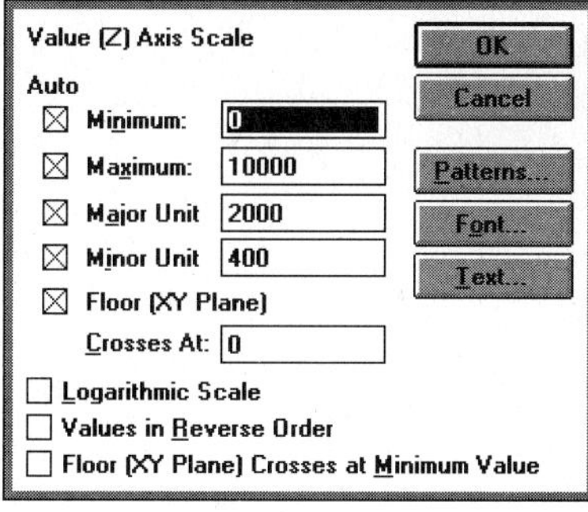

This dialog box has several options that are of interest to you. The Minimum and Maximum values specify the smallest and largest values you want displayed on your chart axis. Excel will format the chart according to what you use here, so be careful that you don't enter values that are obviously too large or too small for the values of the data. Both of these values have a check box to the left of them labeled "Auto." If you turn on the Auto check box, Excel will automatically scale the chart to best display all the data. Remember that in no case is the data on the *worksheet*—the underlying data—affected by changes that you make to the format of the chart.

The Major and Minor Unit options specify the interval between major and minor tick marks. Again, if you enable the Auto check boxes, Excel will automatically scale both the numbers and the chart to best display the data values.

The rest of the items in the dialog box are generally reserved for more specialized charting uses and are outside the scope of this chapter. After you complete the above exercise, your worksheet should look like Figure 7.13.

Figure 7.13
Chart after changing the y-axis scale

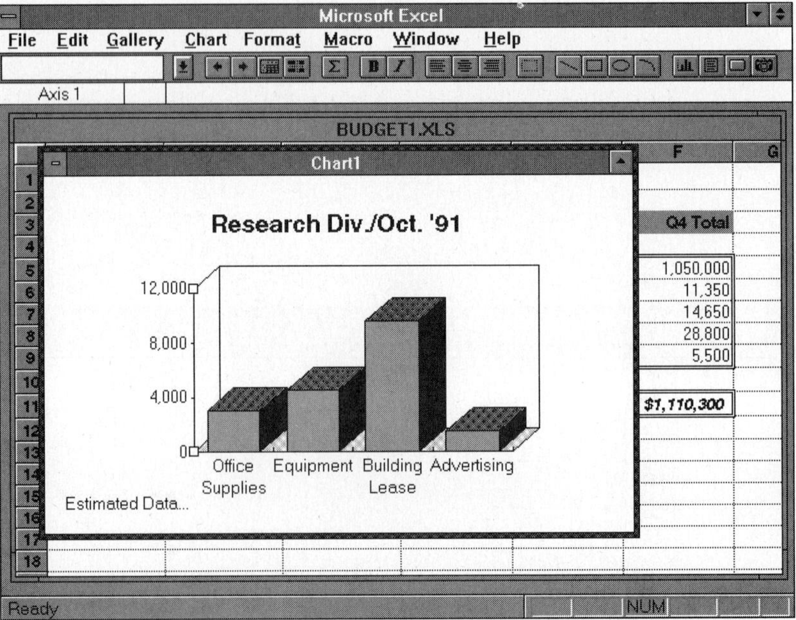

Gridlines

Gridlines are useful for helping to establish a context for the data values. Excel gives you the option of adding and formatting grid lines, which extend the axis across the chart and thus make it easier for the reader to understand the chart. The following steps demonstrate how to add gridlines to your chart:

1. Click on Chart, Gridlines.
2. In the section labeled "Value (Z) Axis," turn on the Major Gridlines box.
3. Click on OK to complete the command. The result is shown in Figure 7.14.

To delete a gridline, simply click on Chart, Gridlines again, and use the mouse to select the gridline(s) that you want enabled or disabled. As always, clicking on OK completes the command and takes you back to the active chart.

Figure 7.14
Chart after adding major gridlines

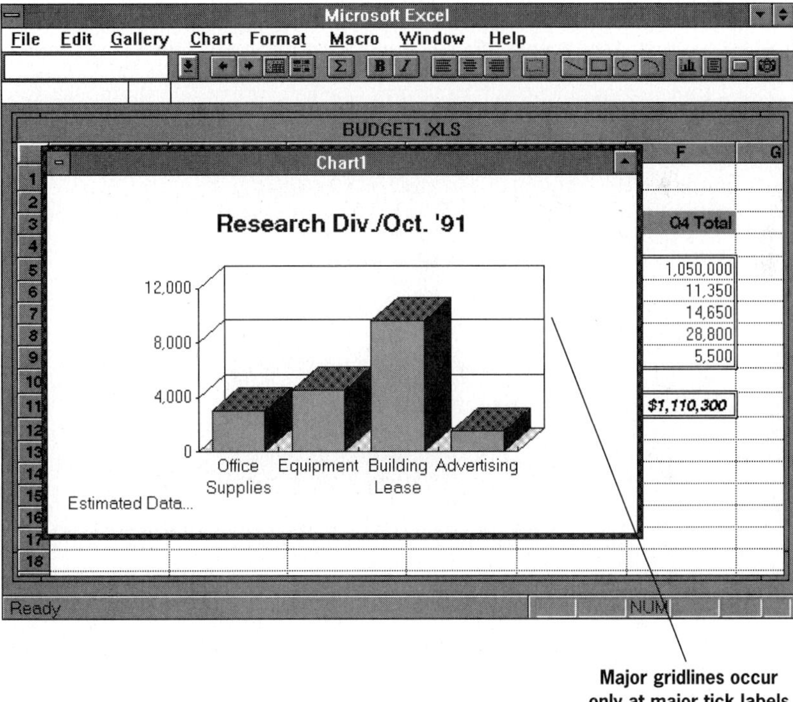

Chart Enhancements

There are quite a few things you can do to enhance the appearance of a chart. One nice feature is the ability to explode one or more pieces of a pie chart in order to emphasize that category.

Use the following steps to change the current chart into a three-dimensional pie chart and then explode one of the pieces of the pie:

1. Choose Gallery, 3D Pie.
2. Select the sixth type of pie chart. Either double-click in that box or select it and then click on OK. (You might have to move your unattached text block if it gets in the way of the new chart.)

Excel immediately changes the format of the chart (keeping the title, unattached text, and any other addition and changes that make sense with the pie chart type) and displays a chart like the one in Figure 7.15.

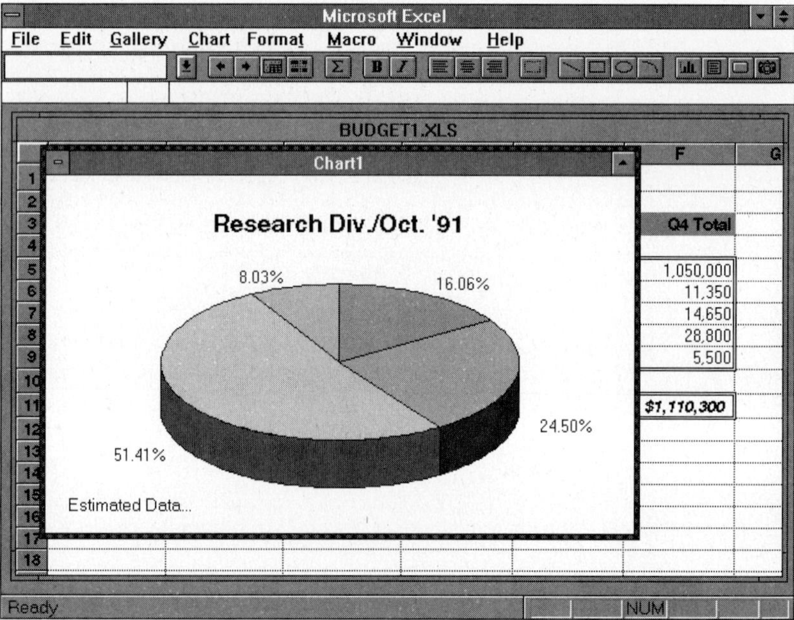

Figure 7.15 Chart after selecting Gallery, 3D Pie

3. Select and drag one of the pie slices. Then watch as Excel displays an outline of the slice as you move the mouse pointer. When you have exploded the pie slice to your taste, just release the mouse button to redraw the pie chart.

Note that you can explode any or all of the slices from the pie. See Figure 7.16 for an example of what a pie chart looks like after a piece has been exploded.

Figure 7.16
3-D pie chart with exploded slice

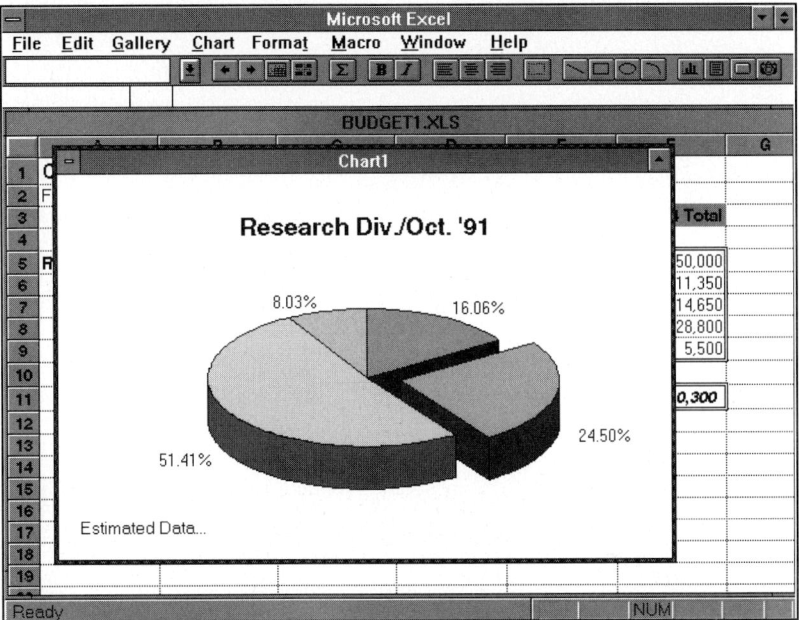

Another thing you can do to a chart is to change the patterns and colors in each of the bars, columns, areas, or pie slices. On the current pie chart, just double-click on one of the pie slices, and you'll see a dialog box, similar to ones you've worked with before, that allows you to change the colors and patterns, among other things.

When you have finished experimenting, move the exploded slice back into the pie so that you will have plenty of room for adding a legend. Your chart should again look like Figure 7.15.

Legends

Legends are very helpful in those cases where it is not clear what chart items represent which data items. For instance, you might have realized in the preceding pie chart example that there was no easy way to tell what each slice of the pie represented. However, in the case of the column chart you worked with, there is no question what each of the data items represents because they are labeled along the x-axis.

Note that each slice of your pie chart is labeled with the proportion of 100 percent that it represents. This is only helpful to a point, since those viewing this chart still don't have any idea what each of the slices represents. For example, what item claimed 51.41 percent of the total October budget? Here's how to add a legend and find out: Simply click on Chart, Add Legend. Excel will create a legend for you and display it to the right of the existing chart. Now it's much easier to tell which item was so costly in October. See Figure 7.17 for an illustration of the default legend.

Figure 7.17
Excel's default legend for pie charts

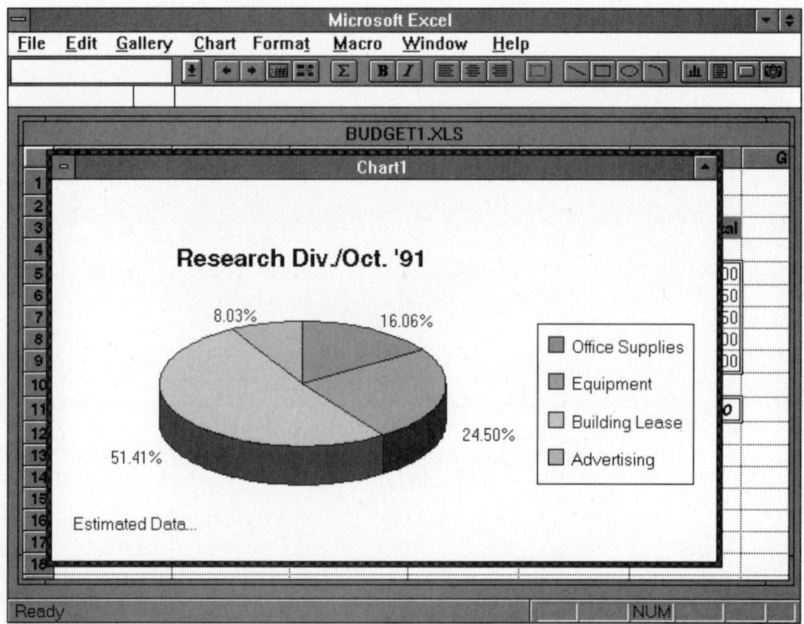

You can also tell Excel to move the legend to other locations, depending on how you want your chart laid out. Note that when you first place the legend it remains selected. You can see this from the small black boxes at each of the corners of the legend. With the legend selected, you can click on Format, Legend to bring up a dialog box that lets you control where you want the legend to appear: at the bottom, top, corner, left, or right. For example, Figure 7.18 shows what the legend looks like on the bottom.

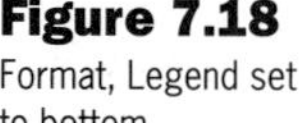

Figure 7.18
Format, Legend set to bottom

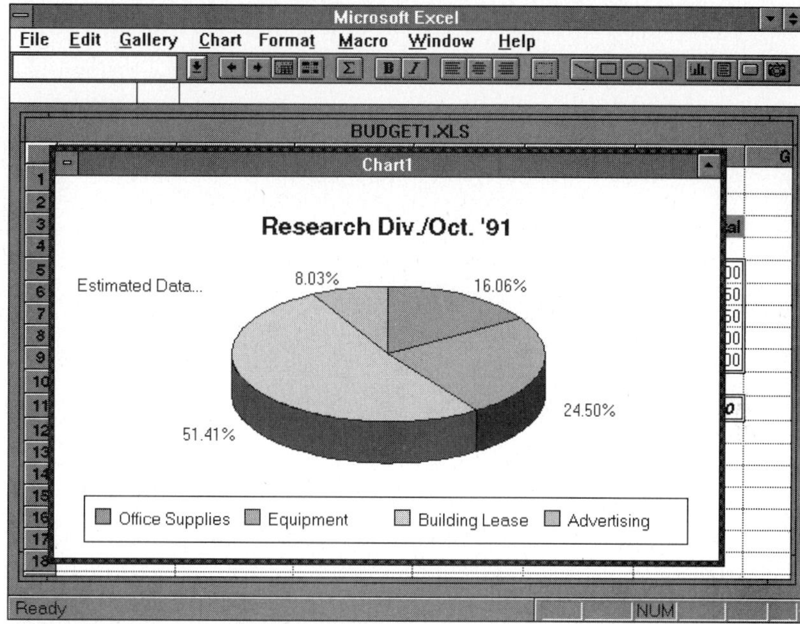

Printing Your Charts

Printing a chart is almost exactly like printing a worksheet (see Chapter 6). With the chart window active (just click in the chart window, if necessary), click on File, Print. Excel will present a dialog box asking how many copies you want, what page range to print, and whether or not you want to preview it first before printing.

Saving Your Charts

You've been working for some time on your chart, but you still haven't saved it or given it a name. Charts are like worksheets in that any power loss or equipment failure will cause all your work to be lost if you don't save from time to time. In this case, since you will not be working with this chart anymore, you can discard it if you want. To throw the chart away, simply choose File, Close from the main menu and answer No when Excel asks if you want to save your changes.

If you want to save your chart, just answer Yes, and Excel will give you a familiar-looking dialog box that gives you the opportunity to save the chart just as you save your worksheets. Note that Excel uses the extension .XLC for charts instead of the .XLS extension it uses for worksheets.

It's important to note at this juncture that you have only begun to explore the myriad ways to customize a chart or a worksheet. Some of the things you can do are clearly outside the scope of this book, and others are simply variations on some of the things that you've done in this chapter. For example, you'll see later that it's possible to embed a chart into a worksheet and make the chart and the worksheet one entity that can be printed or distributed. Embedded charts can be edited just like any other chart but are actually part of the worksheet.

You are encouraged to continue to experiment with the various features of this powerful program and try different things. Venture down the paths of uncharted (so to speak) dialog boxes and see what they do—if it's only test data, you've nothing to lose.

CHAPTER

8

Graphical Objects on the Worksheet

ONE OF THE NEW FEATURES IN EXCEL 3.0 IS THE ABILITY TO PLACE graphical objects on the worksheet. Creating and using graphical objects gives you the flexibility to further enhance your worksheet beyond what you can do with shading and cell formatting.

There are several different kinds of graphical elements that you can place on a worksheet. Figure 8.1 shows some of the basic elements in use. You can format these elements so that they have different colors or pattern fills. You can even assign a set of commands to a graphical object so that Excel will run those commands when you click on that object. (A set of instructions is called a *macro*; macros are covered in Chapter 13.)

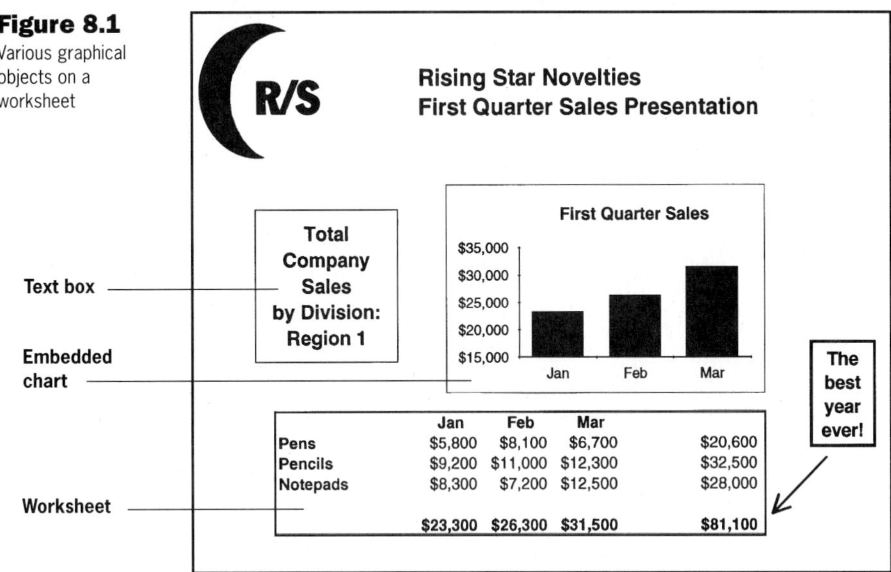

	Jan	Feb	Mar	
Pens	$5,800	$8,100	$6,700	$20,600
Pencils	$9,200	$11,000	$12,300	$32,500
Notepads	$8,300	$7,200	$12,500	$28,000
	$23,300	$26,300	$31,500	$81,100

Figure 8.1 Various graphical objects on a worksheet

Another type of graphical element you can use on the worksheet is a *text box*. The text box feature lets you place a graphical object on the spreadsheet and then fill it with text. You can format the text and use different colors and fonts, just as you can text in the worksheet. Figure 8.1 shows a couple of different text boxes.

Finally, another useful graphical object is the *embedded chart*. You've already seen how you can highlight a range of data in the worksheet and then create a chart. It's also possible to embed a chart in the worksheet so that the chart is printed whenever you print the worksheet. Figure 8.2 shows an example of an embedded chart.

Figure 8.2
Worksheet with an embedded chart

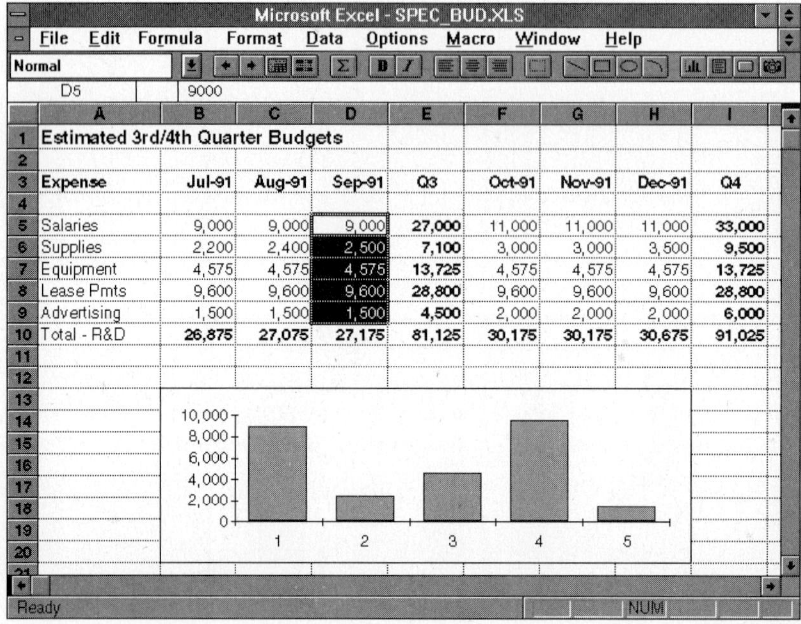

	A	B	C	D	E	F	G	H	I
1	Estimated 3rd/4th Quarter Budgets								
2									
3	Expense	Jul-91	Aug-91	Sep-91	Q3	Oct-91	Nov-91	Dec-91	Q4
4									
5	Salaries	9,000	9,000	9,000	27,000	11,000	11,000	11,000	33,000
6	Supplies	2,200	2,400	2,500	7,100	3,000	3,000	3,500	9,500
7	Equipment	4,575	4,575	4,575	13,725	4,575	4,575	4,575	13,725
8	Lease Pmts	9,600	9,600	9,600	28,800	9,600	9,600	9,600	28,800
9	Advertising	1,500	1,500	1,500	4,500	2,000	2,000	2,000	6,000
10	Total - R&D	26,875	27,075	27,175	81,125	30,175	30,175	30,675	91,025

For comparison, Figure 8.3 shows the same worksheet but with the chart as a separate file. The commands used to edit the chart are the same in each case, but the end result is different.

Graphics Basics

Your work with graphical objects begins with simple geometric shapes such as lines, circles, and squares. In this section you will learn how to create and manipulate these basic objects before combining them to make more complex elements later in the chapter.

Drawing Simple Objects

Begin by opening a blank worksheet. If you have just started an Excel session, you will be working with the blank Sheet1. If you have already been working with Excel, however, and want to open a blank chart, click on File, New, and then select Worksheet. Click on the OK button to complete the command.

For these exercises, you will use a number of tools available on the toolbar. Refer to Figure 8.4 for a close-up of the toolbar and a guide to the buttons you will be using in this exercise.

Figure 8.3
A worksheet with a separate chart

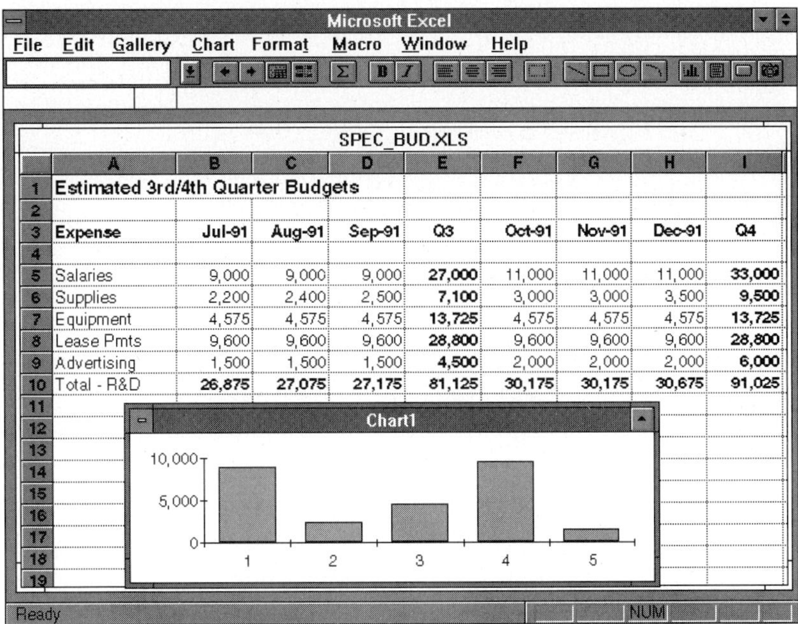

	A	B	C	D	E	F	G	H	I
1	Estimated 3rd/4th Quarter Budgets								
2									
3	Expense	Jul-91	Aug-91	Sep-91	Q3	Oct-91	Nov-91	Dec-91	Q4
4									
5	Salaries	9,000	9,000	9,000	27,000	11,000	11,000	11,000	33,000
6	Supplies	2,200	2,400	2,500	7,100	3,000	3,000	3,500	9,500
7	Equipment	4,575	4,575	4,575	13,725	4,575	4,575	4,575	13,725
8	Lease Pmts	9,600	9,600	9,600	28,800	9,600	9,600	9,600	28,800
9	Advertising	1,500	1,500	1,500	4,500	2,000	2,000	2,000	6,000
10	Total - R&D	26,875	27,075	27,175	81,125	30,175	30,175	30,675	91,025

Figure 8.4
Toolbar's graphics buttons

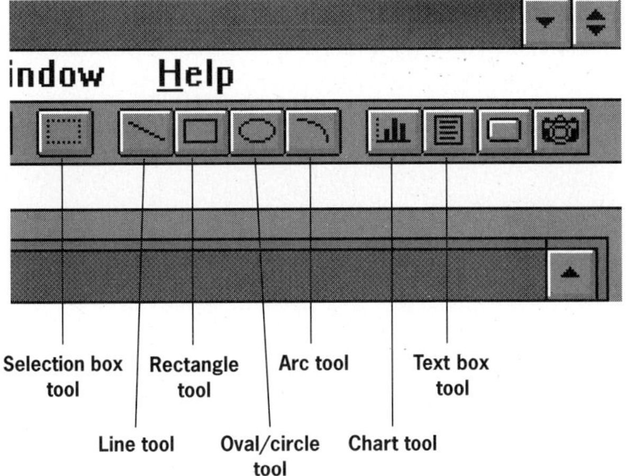

Use the following instructions to add a rectangle to the blank worksheet:

1. Click on the rectangle tool button on the toolbar (see Figure 8.4).
2. Move the mouse pointer to approximately cell B3.
3. Press and hold down the mouse button.
4. Drag the mouse down and to the right to create the outline of the rectangle.
5. Drag the outline to approximately cell E9 and then release the mouse button. When you've finished, your worksheet should look like Figure 8.5.

Figure 8.5
Worksheet after placing a rectangle

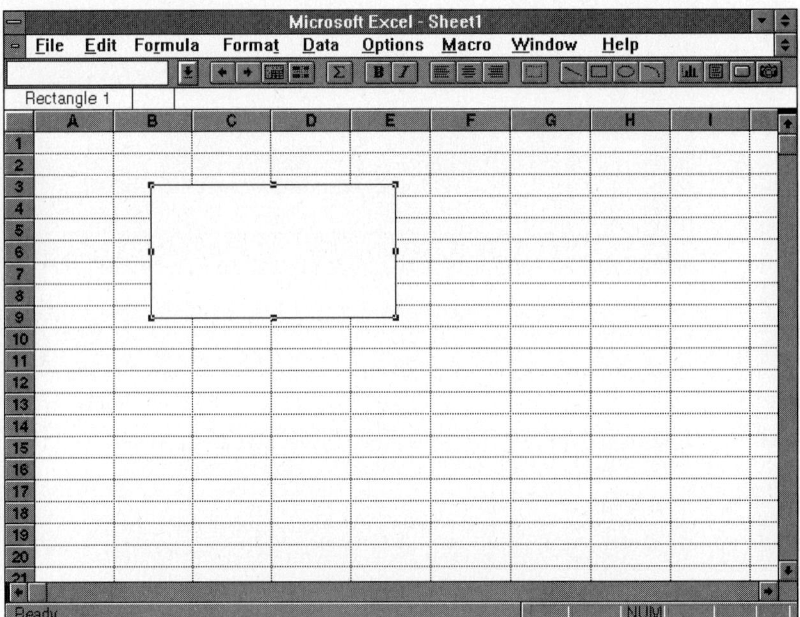

Placing an oval is also simple:

1. Click once on the oval tool in the toolbar.
2. Position the mouse pointer over cell G6.
3. Click and drag the mouse until it is over cell I15. Note that the outline of the oval will not necessarily stay lined up with the mouse pointer. This is normal.
4. Once the cell pointer is over cell I15, release the mouse button. When you've finished, your worksheet will contain two graphical elements, just like Figure 8.6.

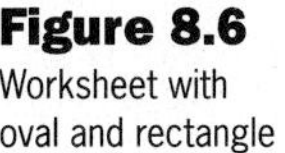
Figure 8.6
Worksheet with oval and rectangle

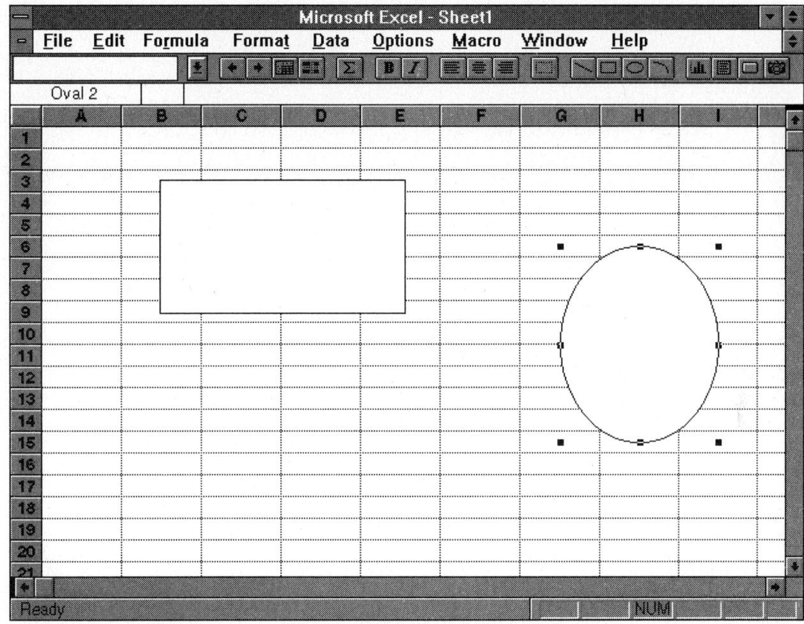

Finally, to round out the basic graphical elements, use the following steps to add a line to your worksheet:

1. Click once on the line tool on the toolbar.
2. Position the mouse pointer over cell B12.
3. Click the mouse button and drag the cell pointer to approximately cell E15.
4. Release the mouse button once you are over the cell.

If all went well, you should see a set of objects like those in Figure 8.7.

Perhaps you've noticed that each time that you finish placing a graphical element on the worksheet, some odd black marks remain, as shown in Figure 8.7. These marks are handles, analogous to the ones used to move unattached text in charts (see Chapter 7). Here, handles are used for resizing and moving graphical objects on the worksheet. The uses of handles will be covered more thoroughly later on in the chapter.

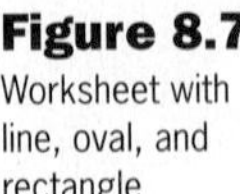

Figure 8.7
Worksheet with line, oval, and rectangle

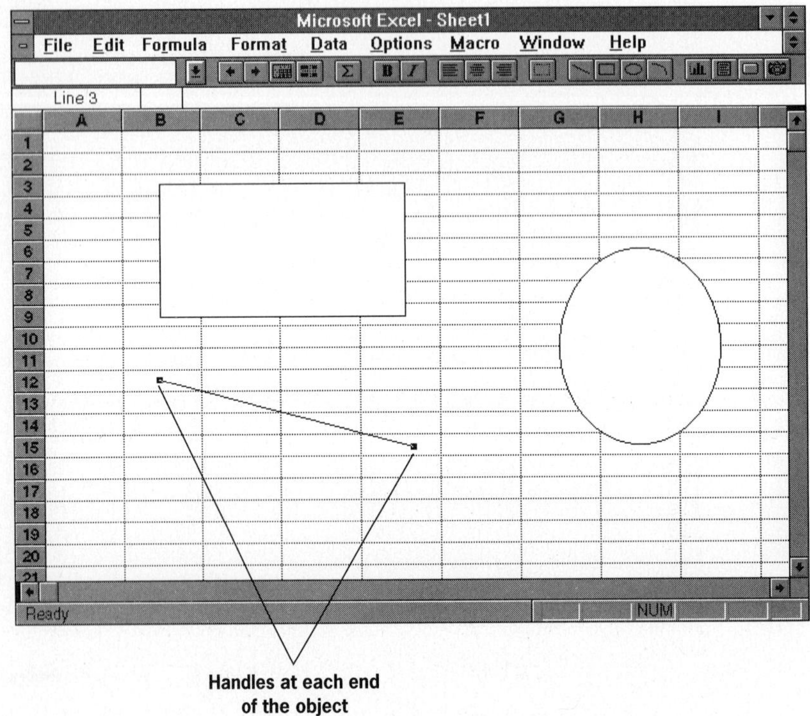

Constraining Graphical Objects

As you placed the graphical elements, perhaps you noticed that you didn't have a lot of control over the shape. For instance, it would be difficult, if not impossible, to draw a perfect circle or a perfect square. And what if you wanted to have the line follow an exact up-and-down path?

Fortunately, Excel 3.0 provides a feature called *constraining* (or *restraining*), which lets you restrict a graphical element to a particular direction or to set proportions. With the constraining feature, you can create perfect squares and geometrically correct circles. Additionally, you can use this feature to draw lines at 45-degree increments.

As an example, use the following steps to draw a line straight up and down on the worksheet:

1. Click once on the line tool in the toolbar.
2. Position the mouse pointer over cell F3.
3. This time, hold down the Shift key before you click and drag the line down.

4. Drag the line down to F12. As you drag the line (keeping the mouse button depressed the whole time) experiment with pressing and releasing the Shift key to see how Excel constrains a graphical object. (You must hold down the Shift key to constrain the object—the Caps Lock key will not work in this situation.)

Now add a circle to the worksheet. The steps to draw the circle are very similar to those for adding a line:

1. Click once on the oval tool.
2. Hold down the Shift key.
3. Position the mouse pointer over cell C10.
4. Depress the mouse button and drag the mouse pointer up and to the right to cell E5.
5. Release the mouse button. When you finish adding these elements, your worksheet will look like Figure 8.8.

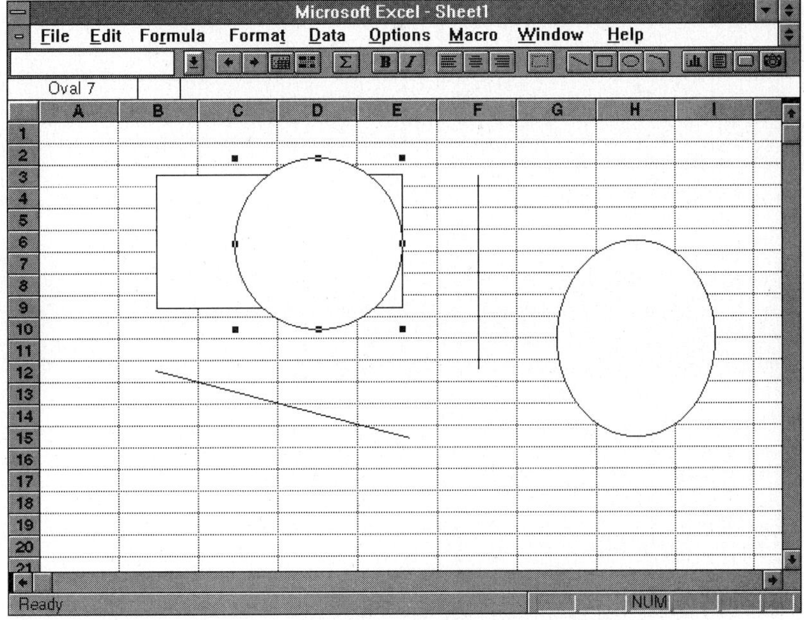

Figure 8.8 Adding a constrained line and circle

As you can see, constraining works differently on different objects.

Another type of constraining is offered as well. Using the Ctrl key, you can constrain a graphical object so that it aligns with the cell borders. This is useful if, for example, you want to line up several graphical objects either horizontally or vertically. Use the Ctrl key as you do the Shift key. If you hold down the Ctrl key as you place a graphical object, the object will "snap to" the cell borders.

Experiment with this now, if you like, using the Ctrl key by itself or in combination with the Shift key to create shape- and placement-constrained objects. You can put these objects anywhere you like, but don't overlap any of the existing objects.

The different effects are listed in Table 8.1.

Table 8.1 How the Shift and Ctrl Keys Constrain Graphical Objects

Object	Unconstrained	Constrained with Shift Key	Constrained with Ctrl Key
Line	Can be at any angle	Constrains to vertical, horizontal, or nearest 45-degree angle	Snaps to cell corner nearest point of origin
Rectangle	Can be any relative height and width	Constrains to square	Snaps to nearest top and left-hand cell borders
Oval	Can be any relative height and width	Constrains to circle	Leftmost point snaps to nearest border to left
Arc	Can be any simple curve	Constrains to 90 degrees of a circle	Ends snap to nearest cell corners

Selecting Graphical Objects

Once you have placed a number of graphical objects on your worksheet, it's important to be able to select one or more of them. You might change your mind and want to move or change them, you might want to perform some type of formatting, or you might simply want to delete a number of graphical objects at one time.

There are two main methods used for selecting graphical objects. You can either use the *selection box* (a box that you can drag with the mouse to select everything inside it) or you can use mouse clicks. You'll learn both methods in this section.

The easiest way to select graphical objects is by clicking on them with the mouse. Follow the next steps to select and deselect several graphical objects.

1. Begin with the large oval positioned in columns G, H, and I (or thereabouts). Position the mouse pointer over the object.
2. Click once to select it. Note how the black handles appear to let you know that you have selected that object.
3. To deselect an object, simply press once on the Esc key, or click on another object to deselect the first one while selecting the second one.

Selecting graphical elements using the selection box is also straightforward. Here you will select a group of objects by dragging the mouse:

1. Click once on the selection box button (immediately to the left of the line tool).
2. Position the mouse pointer in the right-hand side of cell I1.
3. Hold down the mouse button while dragging down and to the left, so that the selection box completely surrounds both the large oval and the vertical line. Before you release the mouse button, your screen will look like Figure 8.9.

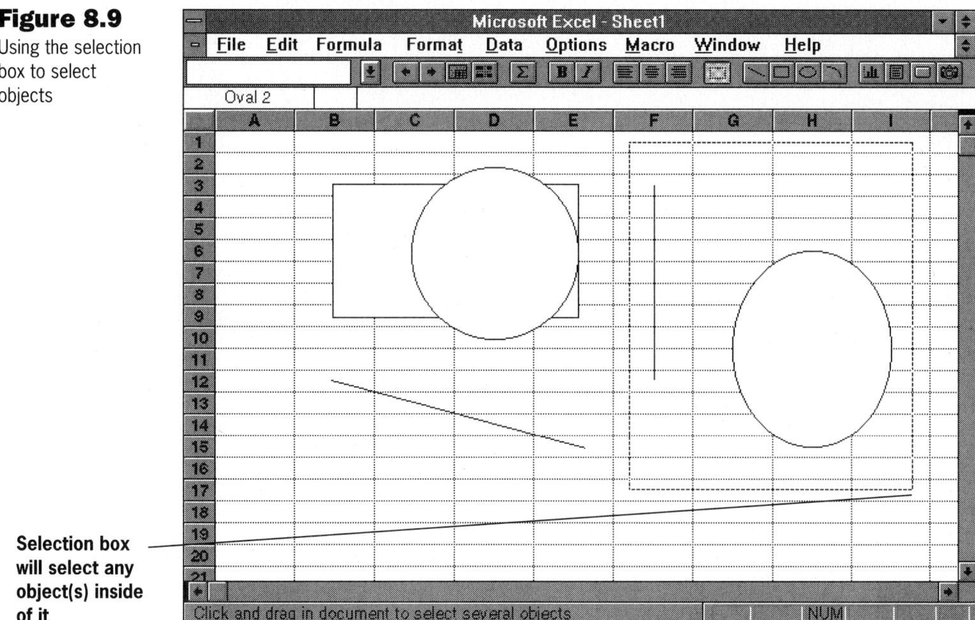

Figure 8.9 Using the selection box to select objects

4. When you have surrounded the objects you want to select, release the mouse button. The objects that were contained in the selection box will be selected. Note the small black handles surrounding the oval and sitting at the ends of the vertical line. Your worksheet should look like Figure 8.10.

Figure 8.10
Selecting multiple objects with the selection box

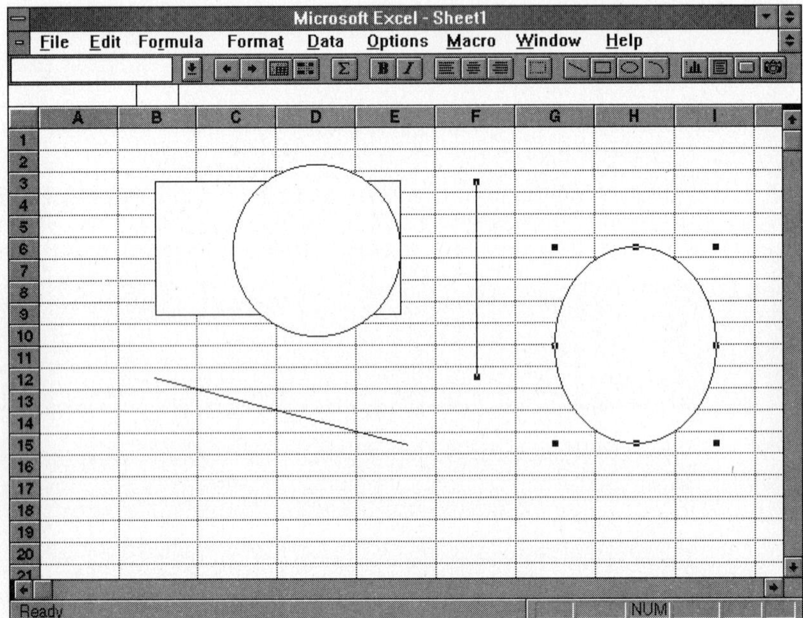

Finally, there is one more way that you can select multiple objects. The following instructions show how to select several graphical objects using mouse clicks:

Tip. To quickly select all the graphical objects on the worksheet, click on Formula, Select Special and then click on the Objects box. Click on OK to complete the command and Excel will select all the graphical objects in the worksheet.

1. Make sure none of the objects are selected. If items remain selected from the previous exercise, simply deselect them by hitting the Esc key once.

2. Click once on the large oval.

3. Hold down the Shift key and then click once on each of the single lines on the worksheet.

4. Release the Shift key. When you finish, your worksheet should look something like Figure 8.11.

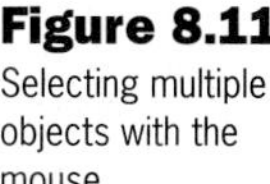

Figure 8.11
Selecting multiple objects with the mouse

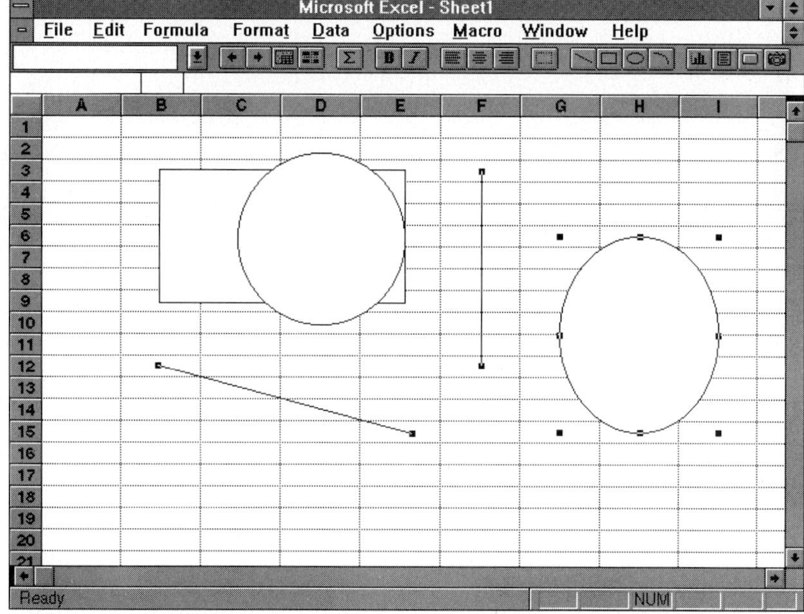

Deleting Graphical Objects

Deleting graphical objects is very simple. Just select the objects that you want to delete, and then remove them by clicking on Edit, Clear. You can also remove selected objects by pressing the Del key. Try this now to delete any additional objects that may be cluttering your screen, so that it resembles Figure 8.11.

Working with Graphical Objects

You can do several things with graphical objects once you have placed them on your worksheet. For instance, it's possible to group multiple objects together so that they can be moved around the worksheet as one object instead of several.

You can also move and resize graphical objects so that they appear exactly where you want them and at the exact size you want them to have. If you like the way one object turned out and you want to make copies of it, you can do that as well.

Finally, you can add some flair to the graphical objects by changing their appearance.

Moving and Sizing Graphical Objects

Moving objects and changing their size is again an area where you have some experience. The concepts are similar to operations you learned in graphing data. Moving is the easiest of the two concepts to work with. These steps show you how to move a graphical object:

1. Select the circle that is on top of the rectangle. Note the *frame* of handles that surrounds the circle.
2. Position the mouse pointer somewhere in the circle and then hold down the mouse button and drag the circle anywhere you want on the worksheet. Note that an outline of the circle shows exactly where it would be placed if you were to release the mouse button.
3. Find a spot for the circle that overlaps the rectangular object. When you finish this exercise, your worksheet should look something like Figure 8.12.

Figure 8.12
Worksheet after moving the circle

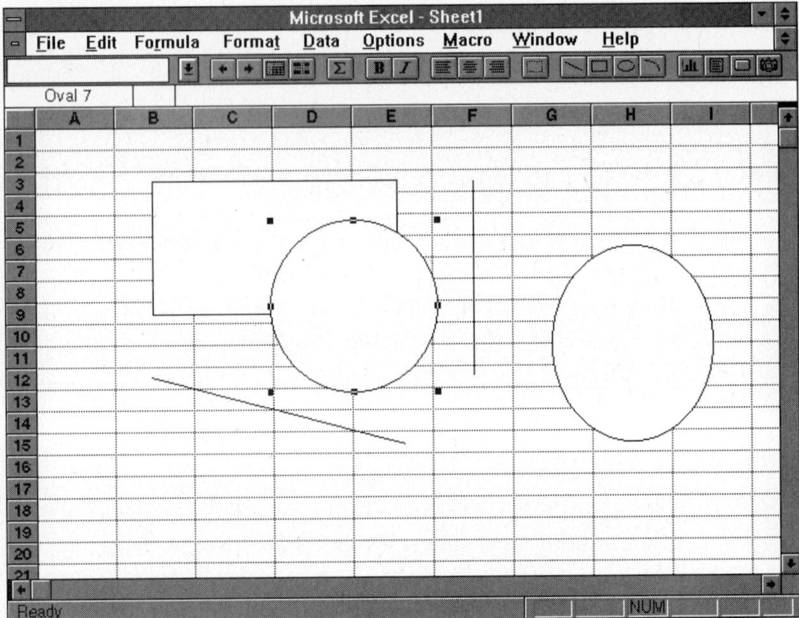

If you want an object to be constrained to cell borders (whether it was originally created that way or not), hold down the Ctrl key as you drag the object. The leftmost side or point of the object will align to the nearest border or intersection to the left.

Sizing a graphical element is also fairly simple, but there are several options that you have to understand in order to resize objects the way you want to:

- If you want to resize an object in one dimension only, click and drag on the handle in the *middle* of one of the sides.
- If you want to resize an object in two dimensions, use a handle at one of the corners of the frame.
- To resize a shape-constrained object, hold down the Shift key as you move the handle, otherwise it will become unconstrained.
- To resize an object constrained to cell borders, hold down the Ctrl key as you resize it.

Two images will quickly illustrate these points. In Figure 8.13, the oval is resized in only one direction, by dragging the middle handle. In Figure 8.14, the oval is resized in two dimensions, by dragging the corner handle.

Figure 8.13
Dragging the middle handle—one dimension

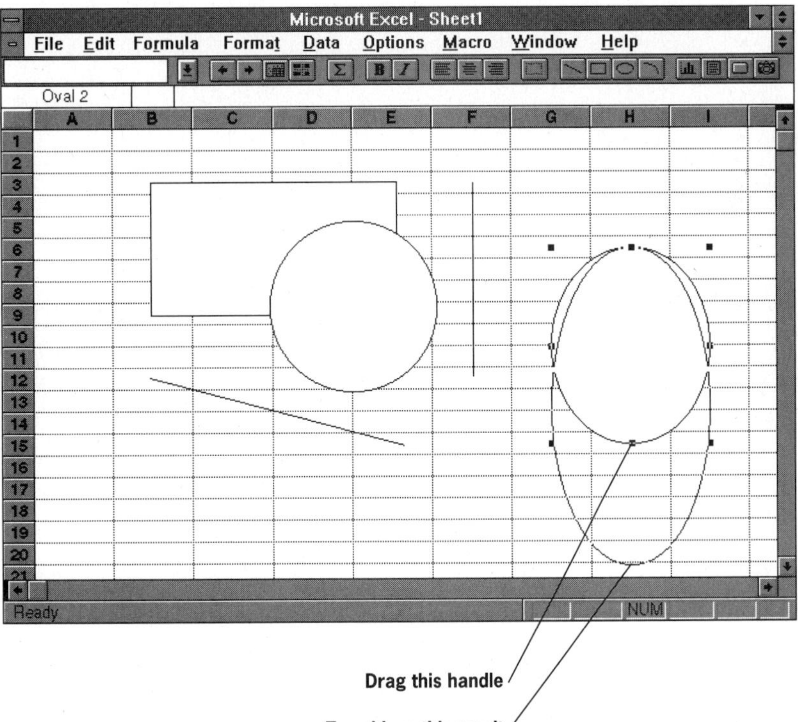

Figure 8.14
Dragging the corner handle—two dimensions

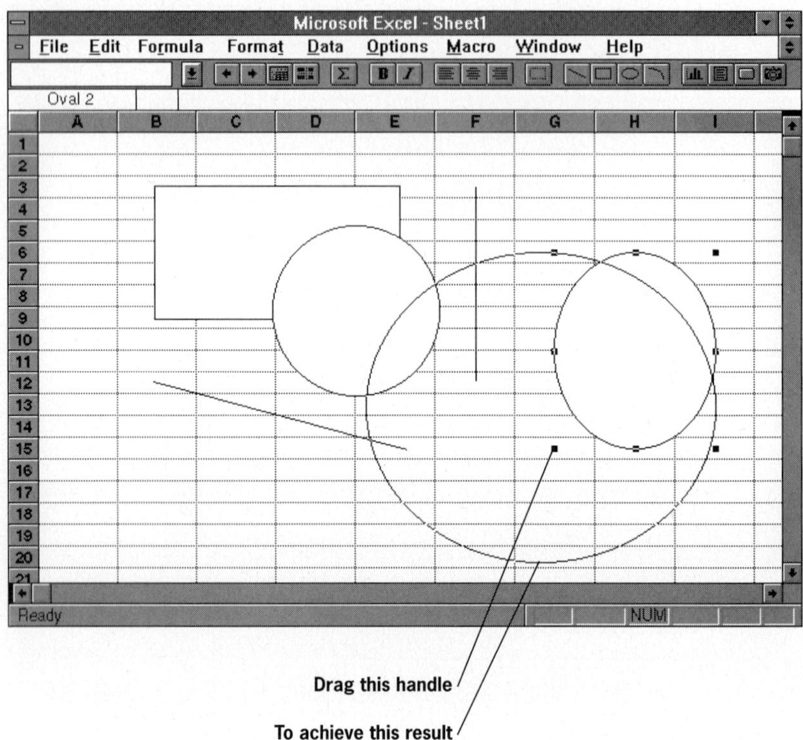

It's easy to see when you have moved the mouse pointer over a handle because the normal thick cross shape is replaced by a cursor that looks like thin crosshairs.

When you finish experimenting with these activities, make sure you place the circle back on top of the rectangle so that you can work with another concept of graphical objects—front and back.

Right now, the circle is in front and the rectangle is in back—the circle covers part of the rectangle. It's quite easy to change this, however:

1. Select the circle by clicking on it once.
2. Click on Format, Send to Back and watch as the circle is moved behind the rectangle (see Figure 8.15).
3. Note that the circle remains selected. Click on Format, Bring to Front to move the circle back where it was, on top of the rectangle.

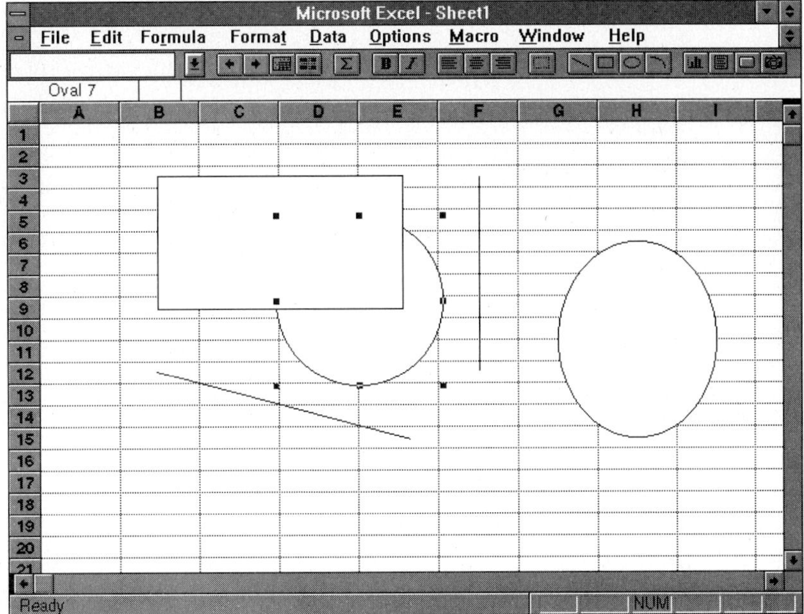

Figure 8.15
Worksheet after moving the circle to the back

Grouping and Separating Graphical Objects

Sometimes you'll find it easier to move multiple objects around on the worksheet if you can treat them as a group. Fortunately, Excel provides an easy way for you to do that. These steps show you how:

1. Using either the selection box method or clicking with the Shift key depressed, select both the rectangle and the circle that is in front of it.

2. Click on Format, Group and watch how Excel immediately changes the way the handles are arrayed around the two objects. These two objects have become one and can be moved, resized, and so on as if they were a single object. Figure 8.16 shows what the handles should look like after you finish this exercise.

As you might imagine, ungrouping objects is pretty simple. Just select the group of objects and then click on Format, Ungroup to command Excel to treat the group as separate, multiple objects. Do so now so that you can move each of the objects independently.

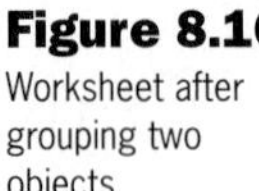

Figure 8.16
Worksheet after grouping two objects

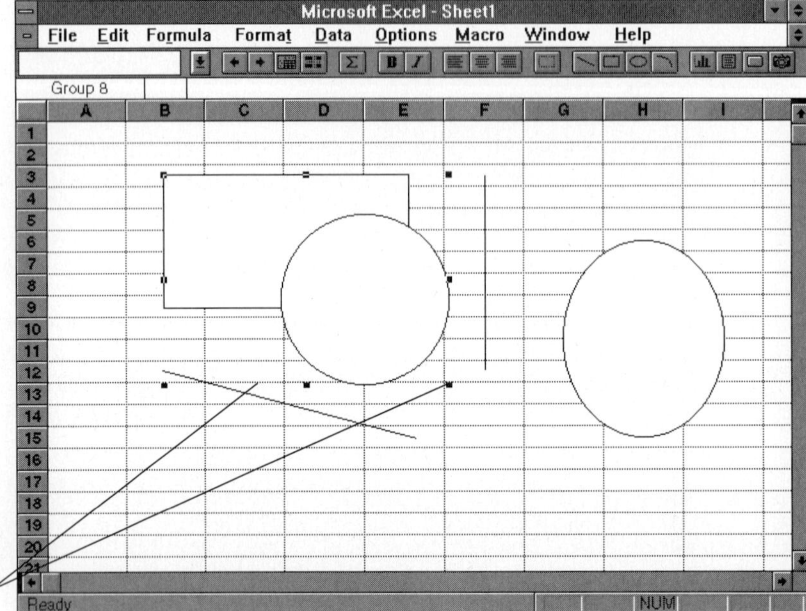

These handles now control the resizing of both grouped objects

Copying Graphical Objects

You can move and copy graphical objects the same way you cut and pasted text and formulas in earlier chapters. This method of moving an object is especially useful if you want to move it from one place in the worksheet to another place that is too far away to make dragging the object feasible.

Once you select the item that you want to either copy or move, just click on the corresponding choice on the Edit menu—Copy if you want to create a duplicate of the object or Cut if you want to remove the object from where it is and place it somewhere else. Once you have found the right place for it, click on Edit, Paste to paste the object back onto the worksheet.

Formatting Graphical Objects

The objects you can create would be pretty boring without the ability to change their appearance. Excel offers a wide variety of options to enhance the look of graphical objects. This section offers a glimpse at what you can do with formatting commands.

As always, the first step in any operation is to select the object that will be the recipient of the action. Double-clicking on a graphical object will give you a dialog box with options for different colors and patterns. The following is but one of a wide variety of things you can do with these features:

1. Double-click inside the circle. Figure 8.17 shows the dialog box that appears.
2. Click on Shadow so that an X appears in the box.
3. Change the Fill, Foreground option so that the circle is colored with the gray color listed last in the foreground colors. Use the up and down arrows to scroll to the color.
4. Click on OK to complete the command. The result is shown in Figure 8.18.

Figure 8.17 Dialog box to format objects

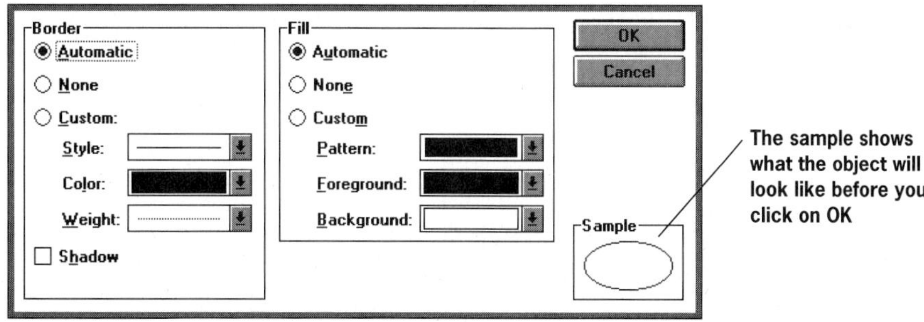

Now try experimenting with some of the hundreds of other different color and pattern combinations available.

Lines are treated a bit differently by Excel. If you double-click on a line, you get a slightly different dialog box, which lets you add arrowheads to the line as well as control its thickness and whether it's solid or dotted. Figure 8.19 shows the dialog box that pops up when you double-click on a line.

Like the dialog box that pops up to help you format a square or a circle, this one features a sample window that shows you how the object will appear before you click on OK to apply the format to the object.

Special Graphical Objects

Excel features two kinds of special graphical objects that you can place on the worksheet. Both embedded charts and text boxes are powerful features in their own right and can greatly enhance the effect of your worksheet if used judiciously.

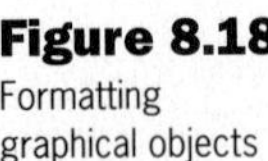

Figure 8.18
Formatting graphical objects

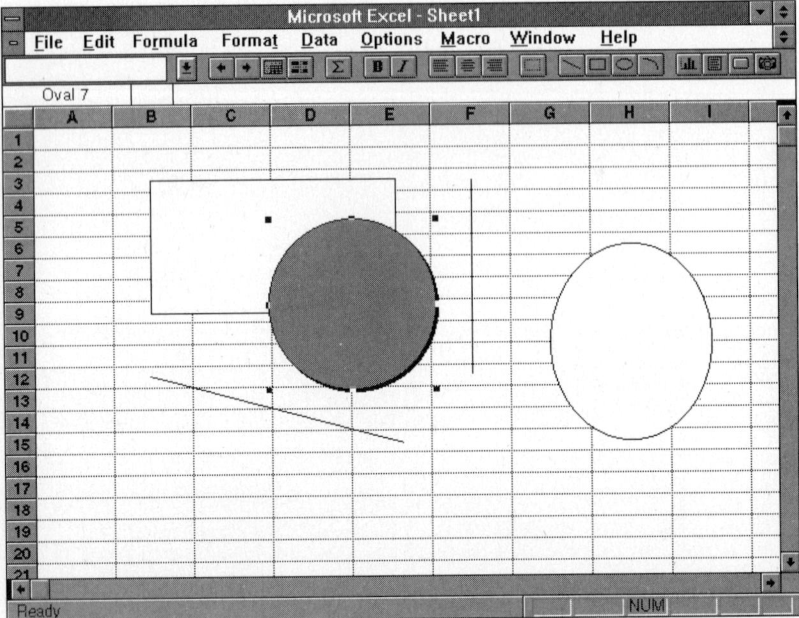

Figure 8.19
Dialog box to format a line

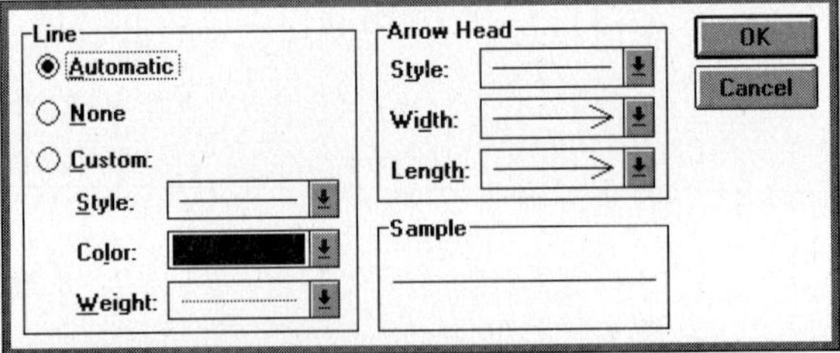

Text Boxes

A text box is initially treated exactly like a rectangular graphical object. When you create a text box, you can make it into a rectangular shape, or you can choose to constrain it with the Shift key to be a perfect square. In either case, you can use the Ctrl key to constrain it to cell borders.

Once you have created and placed a text box, however, you can add text to it. The text will automatically wrap around within the boundaries of the text box. If you enter more text than the text box can hold, however, the extra text will not be visible. You must choose to enlarge the text box in order to accommodate the remaining text—it won't do so automatically.

Use the following steps to add a text box to your worksheet:

1. First, delete the large oval object to the right of the worksheet by selecting it and pressing the Del key.
2. Click on the text box tool from the toolbar (the third one from the right).
3. Position the mouse pointer over cell G3.
4. Click and drag a box outline until your mouse pointer is in cell I11.
5. As soon as you release the mouse button, Excel draws a box and puts a text cursor in the box waiting for you to type in whatever you want.
6. Type some text into the text box and watch as Excel automatically flows the words so that everything fits inside the text box. Figure 8.20 shows an example of a finished text box.

You might also want to experiment with adding more text than the text box can hold, so that you can see what happens and how you can remedy the situation simply by enlarging the box in any direction.

Figure 8.20
An Excel text box

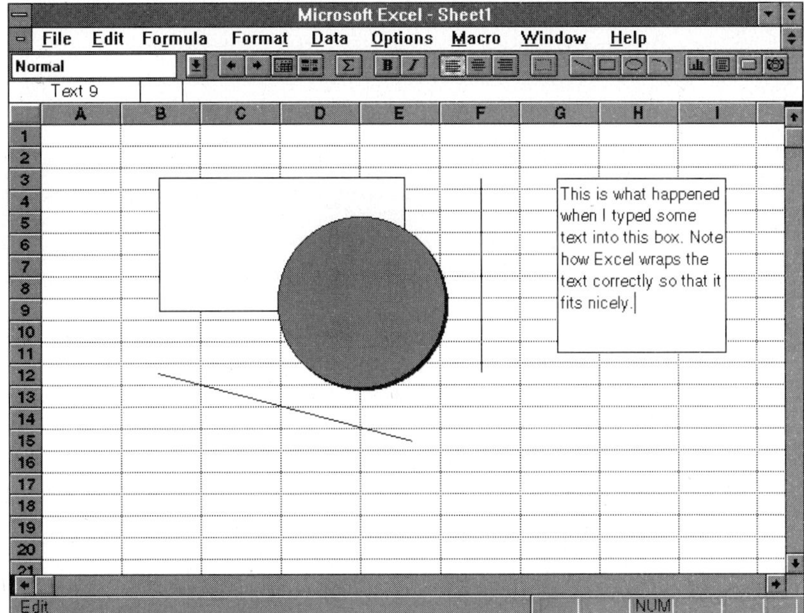

You can format the text in a text box using any of the standard formatting conventions in Excel. You can use the alignment tools to center the text if you wish, or use the Format, Font dialog box to change the typeface or point size of your text.

Embedded Charts

The second special type of graphical object is the embedded chart. It's called *embedded* because the chart is part of the worksheet, instead of being a separate file. You're already familiar with charts as separate files from Chapter 7. Much of how you work with embedded charts is similar to the way you work with charts in separate files.

Embedded charts are very useful if you want to print out a chart as part of a worksheet. If you are working with the chart and worksheet in separate files, printing both of them can be pretty messy. However, if the chart is embedded on the worksheet like any other graphic, it becomes much easier to print out.

Let's again use the BUDGET1.XLS file you have been working with to create a simple embedded chart. First, close the file you have been working on. You can save it if you like, or just respond No when Excel asks if you want to save it. Then, open the BUDGET1 file you saved back in the last chapter.

Once you have that file open, follow these steps to create an embedded chart:

1. Move to an empty part of the spreadsheet so that you will have room for the embedded chart. In this case, just click on the down arrow in the scroll bar several times so that you have some room at the bottom of the worksheet.
2. Highlight the range of cells you want to chart (as discussed in Chapter 7). For this exercise, highlight the range D6:D9.
3. Click on the chart tool in the toolbar.
4. Click and drag a rectangular area around the range of cells B13:F21. Release the mouse button. Note how Excel immediately creates an embedded chart at the place that you specified. After you finish, your worksheet should look something like Figure 8.21.

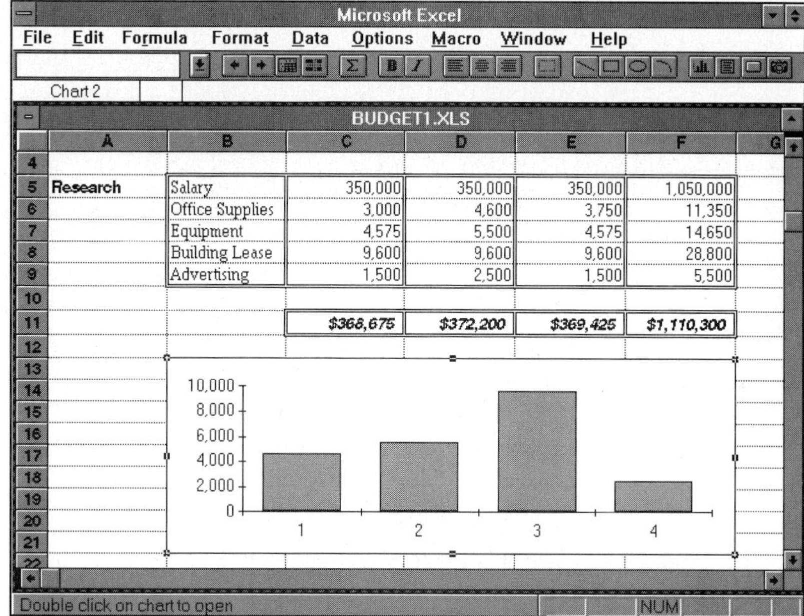

Figure 8.21
Simple embedded chart

As with other graphical objects, Excel leaves the object selected after you place it. You can verify this by looking for the small black handles that surround the chart. As you might guess, you use the chart handles to move and resize the chart the same way you would a graphical object. To see for yourself, experiment with moving and sizing the embedded chart.

While a chart is embedded, however, you can't do much with it. In order to modify the embedded chart, you must double-click anywhere inside it. When you do, the chart will change appearance to look as if it is one of the charts you had worked with before—that is, it will look like a separate file. Compare Figures 8.21 and 8.22 to see the difference.

Once the chart is in this state, you can make any modifications to it that you would have made if it had been created as a separate file. As proof of this, note how the menu bar changes when you double-click on the chart, giving you access to the charting menu functions rather than the normal worksheet menu functions.

When you are ready to put the chart back in place on the worksheet (to "re-embed" it), simply double-click on the chart window's control menu bar (see Figure 8.22) and the chart will return to its embedded state.

Figure 8.22
Embedded chart ready for modifications

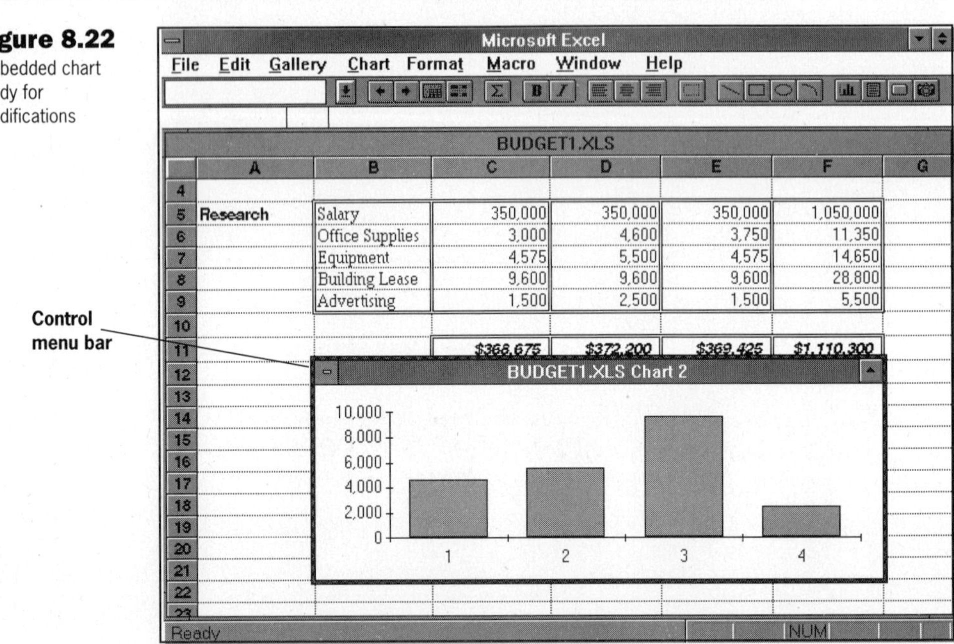

All in all, the graphical enhancements added to the new version of Excel give you much more flexibility when you are designing worksheets and presentations based on the worksheet. Having these graphical functions at your fingertips means that you might not have to use another program to do many of the things that Excel 3.0 allows you to do.

CHAPTER

9

Worksheet Outlining

Creating the New Worksheet

Creating an Automatic Outline

Using the Outline

Creating the Outline Manually

WHAT IS OUTLINING? AND WHAT DOES IT HAVE TO DO WITH A spreadsheet program like Microsoft Excel? Worksheet outlines are similar to the outlines you probably did in school, which showed the structure of your paper and summarized its contents. Many word processing programs have an outlining feature that creates an outline out of headings within a document. These outlines can then be expanded and collapsed as needed, to show more or less material.

Similarly, you can create outlines in Excel 3.0 in which some data is subordinate to other data. You can also expand or contract these levels of data in order to better view or organize your worksheet.

As an example of how this works with a word processing document, say you have an outline of topics you want to discuss in a presentation. It might look something like this:

I. Introduction
    A. Welcome to new members
II. Summary of new business activity
    A. Trends in factory output
        1. Effect of interest rates
        2. Problems with fuel costs
    B. Distribution problems in the Midwest
III. Introduction of new product lines
    A. Demo by head of R&D
    B. Marketing plan for new products

This outline shows all the items to be discussed, but because of the structure of the outline, it's possible to collapse the outline so that only the first level items are visible:

I. Introduction
II. Summary of new business activity
III. Introduction of new product lines

Now imagine that the items in this outline are instead financial figures that you need to present to several different groups of people. It would be helpful, for example, to be able to display all the detailed numbers for a presentation to a group of your peers, but to "roll up" the outline to only show the summary numbers to a group of upper-level managers. This group only wants to see the bottom line. With a correctly designed model, you can use the same worksheet for both groups, by simply showing different levels to each one.

In an outline created by a word processor, if you move one heading, all the subordinate headings move as well. Similarly, in Excel all the data in the worksheet is "live"—all the time. If any number changes—whether the number is visible or not—any results higher up the outline that are based on that number will change as well.

Another twist integral to outlining in a worksheet is the ability to collapse or expand data not only in a vertical dimension—as a word processor does—but also horizontally. Think of it this way: Word processors only have the equivalent of a worksheet's rows—line after line of information. Since spreadsheet products such as Excel have both rows and columns, outlining really takes place in a new dimension.

For example, suppose you have a worksheet that displays budget data by month, with quarterly and annual totals. If you set up the worksheet correctly, you can display either all the detailed data, just the quarterly summaries, or just the annual total.

Creating the New Worksheet

Before you begin the process of creating an outline, it's time you put aside the venerable BUDGET1.XLS worksheet that has been your companion up to now. (You'll come back to it in Chapter 10.) You are going to need a worksheet with a little more information in order to construct a useful outline. Using the skills you have learned up to this point, carefully recreate the worksheet in Figure 9.1 and save it as ESTBUD91.XLS. Enter the numbers as accurately as possible—and check them when you're done. You will use this worksheet in later chapters for linking and consolidation exercises. If your numbers disagree with the book's in later exercises, it may prove confusing.

Tip. One way to ensure consistency in the way your worksheet is designed is to enter your data from left to right and then use the Autosum function to add the numbers. Done this way, your data will be entered consistently and will therefore work correctly with Excel's outlining feature.

Here are a few suggestions regarding the spreadsheet you will create:

- All figures in boldface are calculated sums, and all the calculations are consistent in their direction of reference. That is, each row total is derived by summing items to the left, and column totals are derived by summing items above.

- You'll get the best fit of the whole worksheet (assuming you have a standard VGA screen) if you set the font to 10-point Helvetica and if you set the width of columns B through I to 8.0 using the Format, Column Width command. If you have a different monitor or are running Windows at other than the default VGA resolution, you might have to adjust these values up or down for best results.

Figure 9.1
ESTBUD91.XLS when completed

	A	B	C	D	E	F	G	H	I
1	**Estimated 3rd/4th Quarter Budgets**								
2									
3	**Expense**	**Jul-91**	**Aug-91**	**Sep-91**	**Q3**	**Oct-91**	**Nov-91**	**Dec-91**	**Q4**
4									
5	Salaries	9,000	9,000	9,000	**27,000**	11,000	11,000	11,000	**33,000**
6	Supplies	2,200	2,400	2,500	**7,100**	3,000	3,000	3,500	**9,500**
7	Equipment	4,575	4,575	4,575	**13,725**	4,575	4,575	4,575	**13,725**
8	Lease Pmts	9,600	9,600	9,600	**28,800**	9,600	9,600	9,600	**28,800**
9	Advertising	1,500	1,500	1,500	**4,500**	2,000	2,000	2,000	**6,000**
10	Total - R&D	**26,875**	**27,075**	**27,175**	**81,125**	**30,175**	**30,175**	**30,675**	**91,025**
11									
12	Salaries	4,500	4,500	4,500	**13,500**	5,300	5,300	5,300	**15,900**
13	Supplies	2,000	2,000	2,000	**6,000**	2,500	2,500	2,500	**7,500**
14	Equipment	8,000	8,000	8,000	**24,000**	8,000	8,000	8,000	**24,000**
15	Lease Pmts	8,200	8,200	8,200	**24,600**	8,200	8,200	8,200	**24,600**
16	Advertising	2,500	2,500	2,500	**7,500**	2,000	2,000	2,000	**6,000**
17	Total - Admin	**25,200**	**25,200**	**25,200**	**75,600**	**26,000**	**26,000**	**26,000**	**78,000**
18									
19	**Grand Totals**	**52,075**	**52,275**	**52,375**	**156,725**	**56,175**	**56,175**	**56,675**	**169,025**

The Importance of Organization

Before you ask Excel to create an automatic outline, pay attention to how you lay out your data so that Excel doesn't get confused about how to create the outline. When you are creating formulas and functions, make sure that the direction of reference is consistent—that is, have all your references refer to cells in only one direction within the rows and column.

Figure 9.2 is a screen shot of the completed ESTBUD91.XLS worksheet with the direction of the references labeled so you can see what it means to keep references consistent. Note that you can use any direction of reference as long as you are consistent within rows and within columns.

Creating an Automatic Outline

After you have created the new worksheet file (and saved it to disk), you are ready to create an outline. There are two primary ways to create an outline: manually and automatically. The easiest way to create an outline is to let Excel try to do so automatically. Use the following steps to automatically create an outline from the ESTBUD91.XLS file:

1. Highlight cell A1. This tells Excel that you want to outline the entire worksheet.

Figure 9.2
ESTBUD91.XLS with direction of references shown

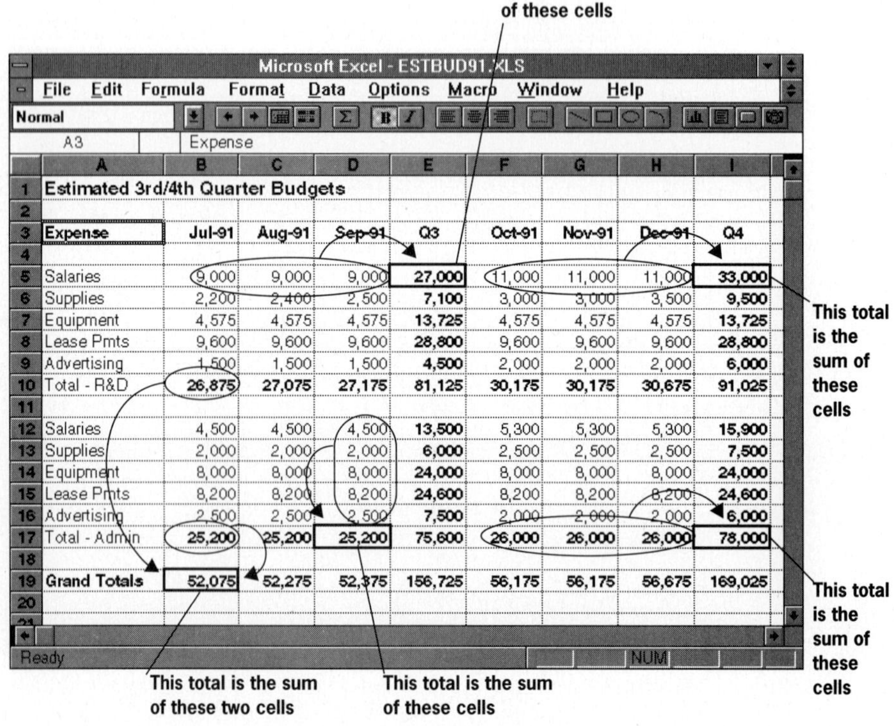

	A	B	C	D	E	F	G	H	I
1	Estimated 3rd/4th Quarter Budgets								
2									
3	Expense	Jul-91	Aug-91	Sep-91	Q3	Oct-91	Nov-91	Dec-91	Q4
4									
5	Salaries	9,000	9,000	9,000	27,000	11,000	11,000	11,000	33,000
6	Supplies	2,200	2,400	2,500	7,100	3,000	3,000	3,500	9,500
7	Equipment	4,575	4,575	4,575	13,725	4,575	4,575	4,575	13,725
8	Lease Pmts	9,600	9,600	9,600	28,800	9,600	9,600	9,600	28,800
9	Advertising	1,500	1,500	1,500	4,500	2,000	2,000	2,000	6,000
10	Total - R&D	26,875	27,075	27,175	81,125	30,175	30,175	30,675	91,025
11									
12	Salaries	4,500	4,500	4,500	13,500	5,300	5,300	5,300	15,900
13	Supplies	2,000	2,000	2,000	6,000	2,500	2,500	2,500	7,500
14	Equipment	8,000	8,000	8,000	24,000	8,000	8,000	8,000	24,000
15	Lease Pmts	8,200	8,200	8,200	24,600	8,200	8,200	8,200	24,600
16	Advertising	2,500	2,500	2,500	7,500	2,000	2,000	2,000	6,000
17	Total - Admin	25,200	25,200	25,200	75,600	26,000	26,000	26,000	78,000
18									
19	Grand Totals	52,075	52,275	52,375	156,725	56,175	56,175	56,675	169,025

2. Click on Formula, Outline. The dialog box shown below appears. Make sure that both of the selections in the Direction box are checked.
3. Click on the Create button.

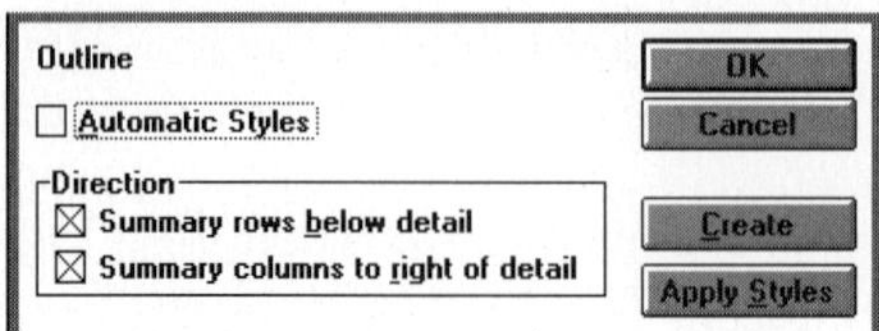

Note that the dialog box gives you the option of creating an outline for both the rows and the columns. Normally, you would let Excel create an outline in both dimensions. It will then quickly determine the relationship of the formulas present in the model and then create an outline based on its best guess of how you have set up your data. In this case, the resulting outline looks like Figure 9.3.

Figure 9.3
ESTBUD91 with outlining symbols

Microsoft Excel - ESTBUD91.XLS

File Edit Formula Format Data Options Macro Window Help

Normal

A3 Expense

	A	B	C	D	E	F	G	H
1	**Estimated 3rd/4th Quarter Budgets**							
2								
3	**Expense**	**Jul-91**	**Aug-91**	**Sep-91**	**Q3**	**Oct-91**	**Nov-91**	**Dec-91**
4								
5	Salaries	9,000	9,000	9,000	**27,000**	11,000	11,000	11,000
6	Supplies	2,200	2,400	2,500	**7,100**	3,000	3,000	3,500
7	Equipment	4,575	4,575	4,575	**13,725**	4,575	4,575	4,575
8	Lease Pmts	9,600	9,600	9,600	**28,800**	9,600	9,600	9,600
9	Advertising	1,500	1,500	1,500	**4,500**	2,000	2,000	2,000
10	Total - R&D	**26,875**	**27,075**	**27,175**	**81,125**	**30,175**	**30,175**	**30,675**
11								
12	Salaries	4,500	4,500	4,500	**13,500**	5,300	5,300	5,300
13	Supplies	2,000	2,000	2,000	**6,000**	2,500	2,500	2,500
14	Equipment	8,000	8,000	8,000	**24,000**	8,000	8,000	8,000
15	Lease Pmts	8,200	8,200	8,200	**24,600**	8,200	8,200	8,200
16	Advertising	2,500	2,500	2,500	**7,500**	2,000	2,000	2,000
17	Total - Admin	**25,200**	**25,200**	**25,200**	**75,600**	**26,000**	**26,000**	**26,000**
18								
19	**Grand Totals**	**52,075**	**52,275**	**52,375**	**156,725**	**56,175**	**56,175**	**56,675**
20								

Ready NUM

Excel will outline the entire sheet if you do not explicitly highlight a range. If you want to outline just a particular range of cells, you must first highlight the range you want to outline.

Description of Screen Items

There are several new screen elements you'll use in outlining a worksheet. Refer to Figure 9.4 for the following discussion of the functions of some of the toolbar buttons and other screen elements. (The following sections will show these tools in action.)

Promote and Demote Buttons These buttons respectively raise and lower selected rows or columns in the hierarchy of the outline. Use these buttons when you are manually creating an outline or modifying an outline that Excel automatically created for you.

Show Outline Symbols Button With this button, you can enable or disable the presentation of the special outline symbols and controls. This feature is

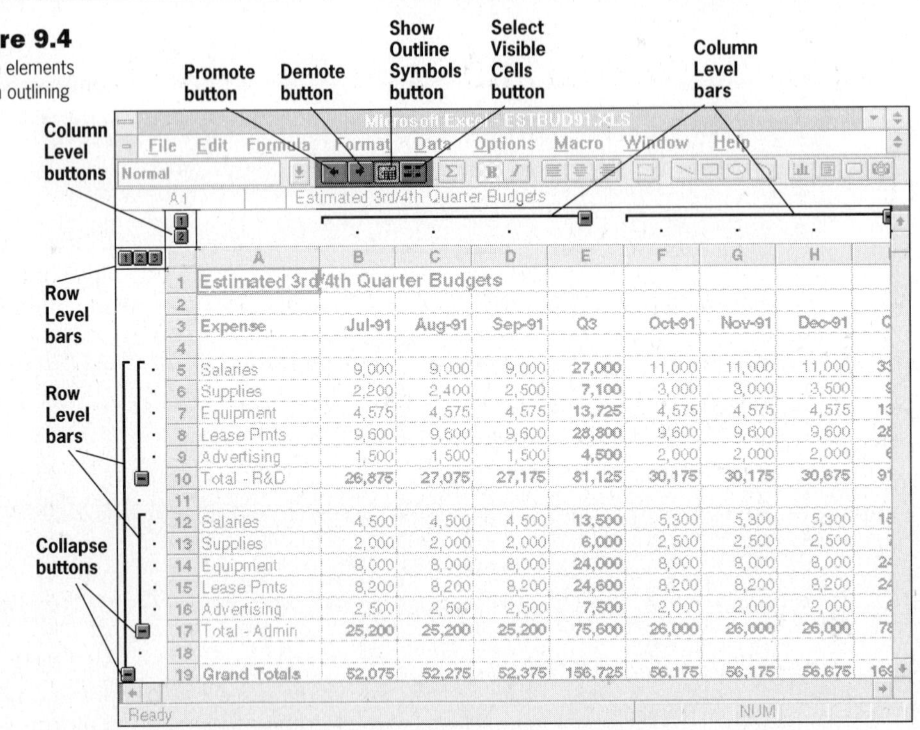

Figure 9.4
Screen elements used in outlining

very useful after you have configured the outline—collapsing or expanding various sections—to your liking. Then, you can just click on the Show Outline Symbols button to make the special symbols and outlining characters go away for a cleaner presentation. The structure of the outline does not change, just the appearance of the screen.

Select Visible Cells Button This is another tool to help you better present the information contained in your outline. As previously mentioned, even though you might see only some of the cells, all the data and cells are still live "beneath" the outline. But what if you only want to work with a subset of your data—perhaps just those data elements that are visible on your screen? If you simply selected a range and then charted it, you would get a chart depicting all the data within that range, even though the outline is only showing a few cells. The Select Visible Cells button is designed for this purpose. Once you have configured your outline to only show a certain level of information, you can choose to select only the visible cells for charting or data presentation.

Column and Row Level Bars These bars indicate the detail items that go into making up one level of the outline. It's a rather hard topic to describe—you'll see it in action in a moment. Note how the level bars bracket the data they control.

Expand and Collapse Buttons At the end of each of the row and column level bars are small buttons with a minus sign. They are the Collapse buttons and, coupled with the level bars, indicate that you are seeing as much data as is possible at that level.

Conversely, the other small buttons with a plus sign—not visible in Figure 9.4—are called Expand buttons. They signify there is data underneath them that can be expanded.

As you might guess, clicking on a Collapse button will collapse the data contained within the bracket of the level bar, and clicking on an Expand button will open up a new level of data.

Note. You can create outlines with up to eight levels of detail. Although that might prove to be a bit unwieldy, it might also be the only way to efficiently present your data.

Column and Row Level Buttons These buttons—both in the row and the column context—quickly control how much of the outline you will see. For example, although you can manually click on all the Expand buttons until you have revealed all of the detail and there is nothing left to expand, it's much quicker to simply click once on the highest-numbered level button available. In the case of Figure 9.4, clicking on level 3 for the rows and level 2 for the columns quickly displays all the detail available in this worksheet.

Using the Outline

In order to get an idea of the usefulness of the outline feature and how to work with it, pretend that you have prepared the ESTBUD91 worksheet for a number of different people. They have since asked you to print it out with only the information relevant to each of them showing.

Displaying/Hiding Outline Symbols

Before you can go too far, you need to know how to turn on or off the outline symbols. Obviously, the presence of the outline symbols would make the worksheet look inelegant when it came time to present it to someone else.

Excel provides two ways to enable and disable the outline symbols. You'll use one method to first turn them off and then the other to turn them back on as you work with the outline.

1. Click on Options, Display. The dialog box shown in Figure 9.5 will appear.
2. Click on the box marked "Outline Symbols" until the X disappears.
3. Click on OK to carry out the command.

Figure 9.5
Options Display dialog box

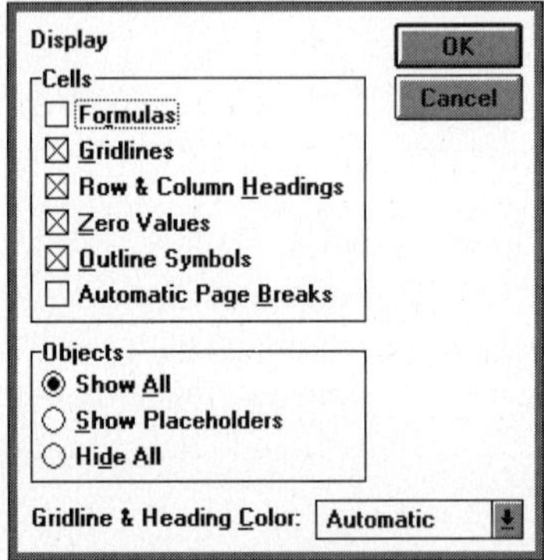

You can see that even though Excel has stopped displaying the outline symbols, the structure of the outline remains intact. As soon as you turn on the outline symbols again, you'll be able to work with the outline.

Turning them back on is very simple: Just click once on the Show Outline Symbols button in the toolbar—it's the one that looks like the corner of a worksheet. When you finish, your worksheet should again look like Figure 9.3.

Displaying the Outline

Now that you can change the worksheet's appearance by turning the outline symbols on and off, it's time to look at some of the permutations of this worksheet that you can create . You'll work from the most data visible to the least as you present this worksheet to the higher levels within your fictitious company.

First, the divisional director in charge of both the R&D and Administration departments wants a report showing each department's total estimated budget—she doesn't want to be bothered with all of the detail that goes into making up each department's budget.

To create an outline for her, click on the Level 2 Row button. It's the one that controls the level of detail displayed in the rows. The report you would print out for the divisional director looks like Figure 9.6.

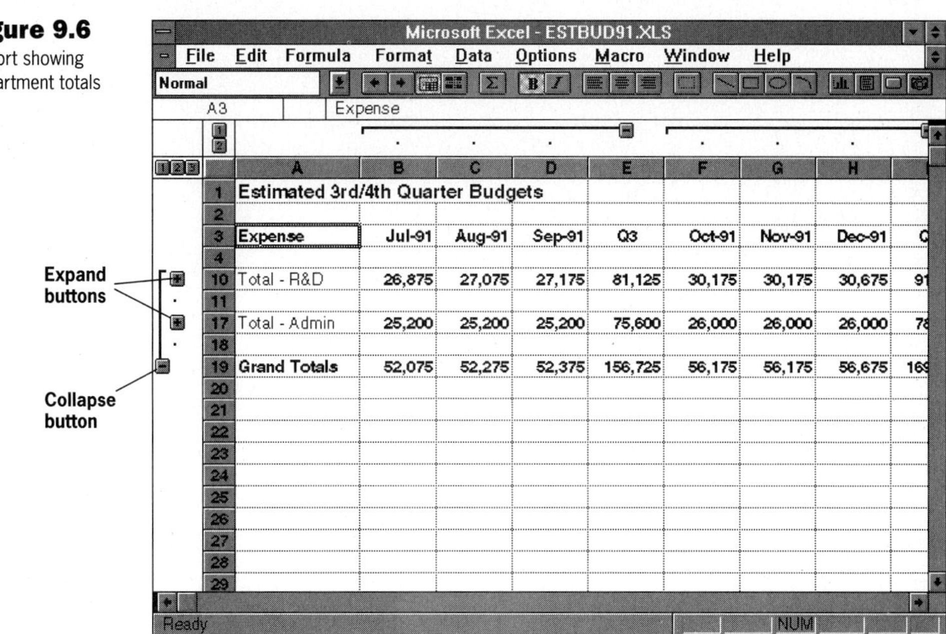

Figure 9.6 Report showing department totals

Now the same director calls back and says that she would also like to see the report with just the overall figures for both the third and fourth quarters. Changing the report is pretty easy: Click on the Level 1 Column button. The resulting worksheet looks like Figure 9.7.

Finally, your boss calls and says that you need to format a brief report for the CFO to use at a meeting that shows only the bottom line: just the Q3 and Q4 totals for both departments. Here's how to do it:

1. Click on the Level 1 Row button.
2. Click on the Level 1 Column button. The worksheet should look like Figure 9.8 when you finish.

At this point, you should experiment a bit with the way that the various buttons on the worksheet work in combination. Try clicking on the Level buttons in both the row and the column dimension. You can also try clicking on the individual Expand and Collapse buttons to see how they react.

Enabling/Disabling Visible Cells

There is one more option that you need to explore before moving on. Remember that even though you might be displaying only a small subset of

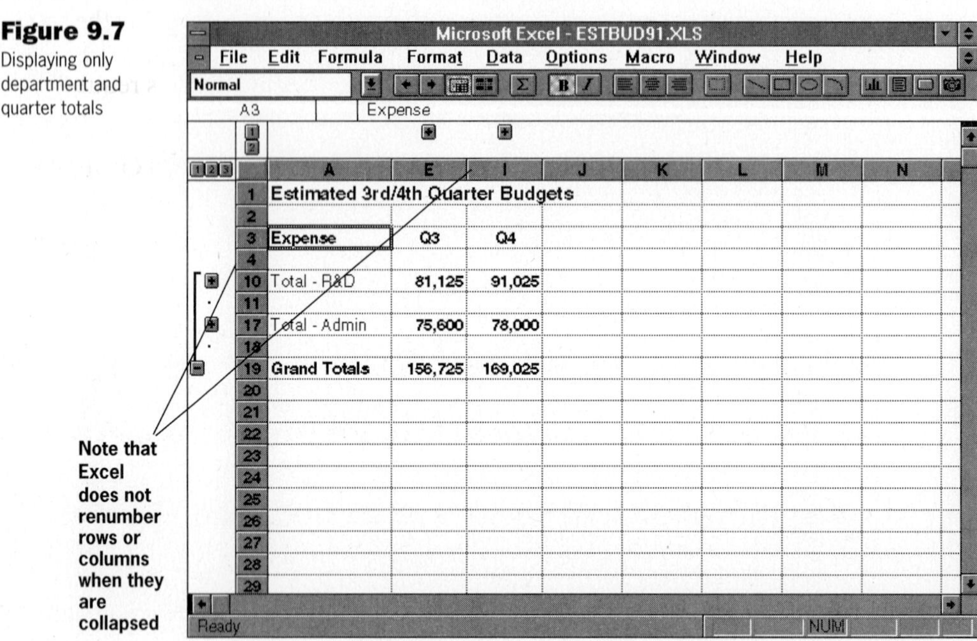

Figure 9.7 Displaying only department and quarter totals

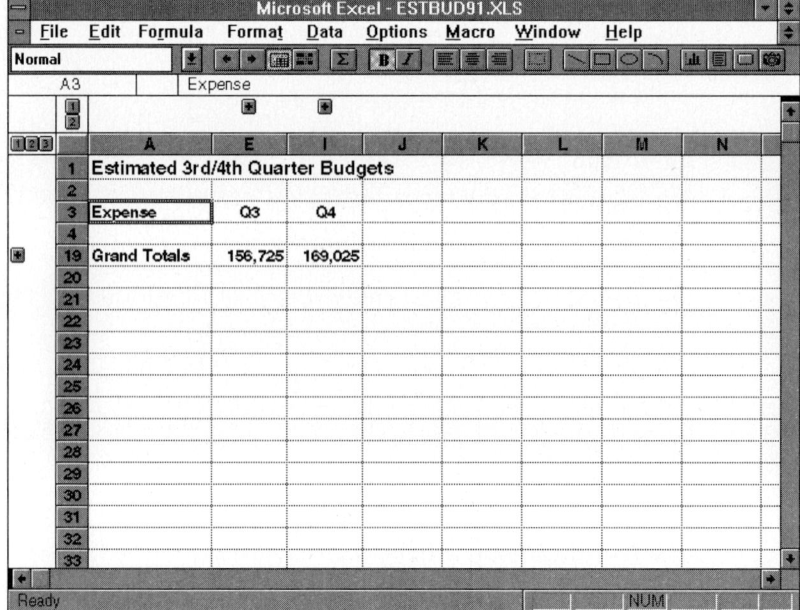

Figure 9.8 Level 1 totals for both rows and columns

data (as in Figure 9.8), all the detail beneath what you see is still live and accessible. To demonstrate this, consider the following scenario: Say the R&D department manager wants a simple graph that shows the overall change in the budget figures from Q3 to Q4. To accommodate his request, perform the following steps:

1. Click on the Level 2 Row button. You should see the Q3 and Q4 totals along with the totals for the R&D and Administration departments.
2. Highlight the range E10:I10. There should only be two cells highlighted. Your worksheet should look like Figure 9.9.
3. Click on File, New to bring up the corresponding dialog box.
4. Click on Chart.
5. Click on OK to create the default chart. When you do so, your chart should look like Figure 9.10.

What's the problem with this chart? It contains more than just two series. How can that be the case if you only selected two cells? It's because Excel created the chart based on the invisible as well as the visible data in the range you selected. Series 1 and 5 are the data you are looking for, and series 2, 3, and 4 are figures from the Q4 detail. If you're not sure, compare the data values. The range you specified should help clarify this as well. You selected the range of cells from E10 to I10—that's columns E, F, G, H, and I—five data series in all. (On a collapsed outline, the row and column numbers will not be sequential.)

What you really wanted to do was to create a chart that just depicted the two quarter totals. How do you do this? The answer is to select only the visible cells. Here's how Excel lets you do that:

1. If you have not done so yet, close the chart by clicking on File, Close and answering No to the prompt about saving the chart—it wasn't what you wanted anyway.
2. Highlight the range E10:I10 again.
3. Click on the Select Visible Cells button (see Figure 9.4) in the toolbar. Excel now only considers the two highlighted numbers to be in the selection. When you create your chart, it will then reflect the correct number of data series.
4. Click on File, New and select Chart.
5. Click on OK to create a new chart.

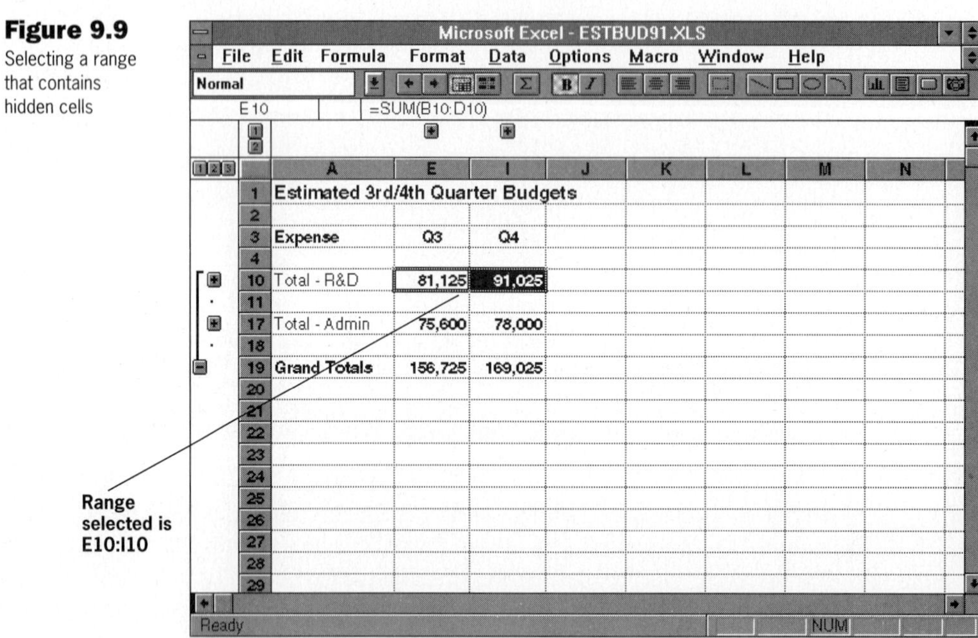

Figure 9.9 Selecting a range that contains hidden cells

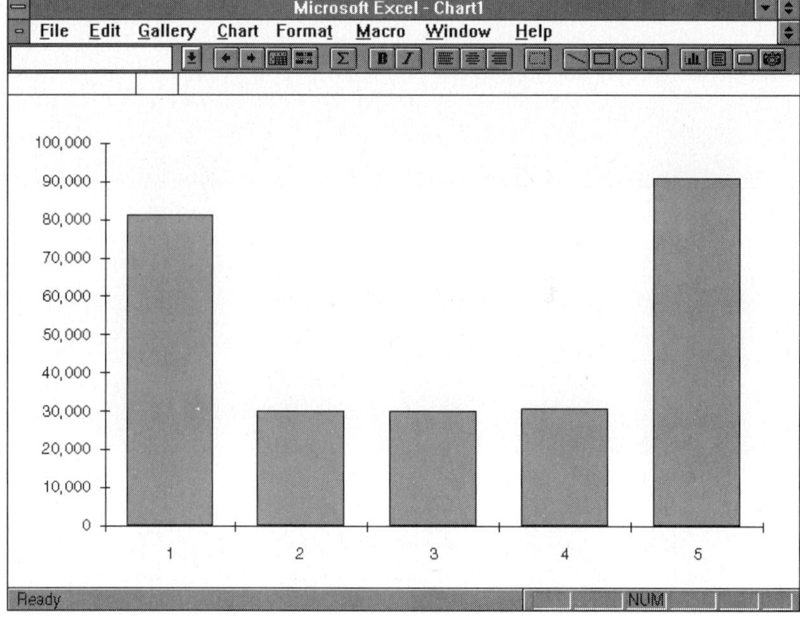

Figure 9.10 Chart with incorrect data series

When Excel creates the new chart (see Figure 9.11), it is based on only those cells that were visible at that level of the outline. It isn't pretty, but you know how to fix that. At least it has the data that you wanted to graph.

This feature is also useful for applying a format to a certain group of numbers or text labels. Say you wanted the level 1 items to be blue instead of black. You could simply configure the outline as you wanted it to be, highlight the range of (visible) cells that you wanted to format, click on the Select Visible Cells button, and then apply the desired formatting.

Figure 9.11
Chart created with visible cells only

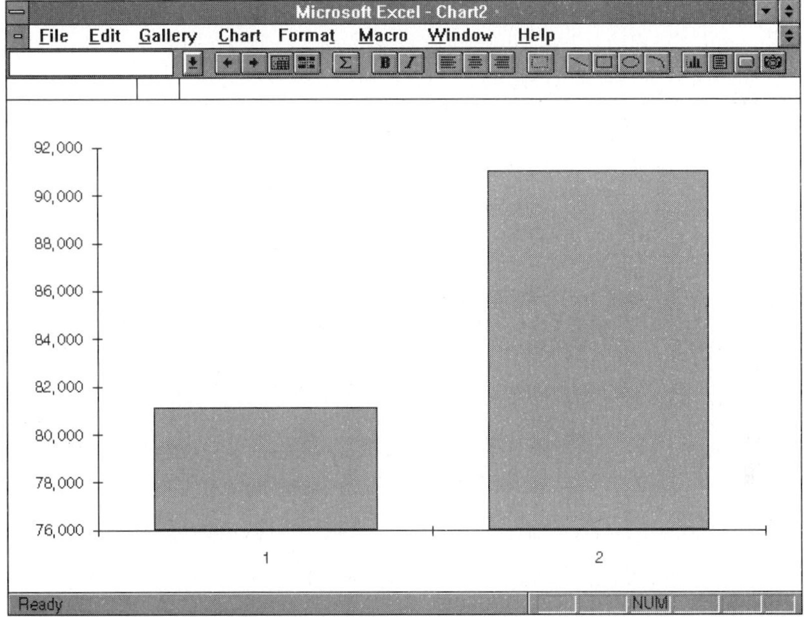

Applying Automatic Styles

To backtrack a little, now that you've seen some of the potential of outlining, you might want to add some formatting commands to differentiate the summary rows and columns from the detail items (if you haven't already done so, since Figure 9.1 is formatted).

Excel can add formatting information to your worksheet outline either when you create it for the first time or at any time later on. With Automatic Styles, Excel will simply format the row and column totals in bold for emphasis. To have Excel automatically add styles to your outline when you create it, check the box marked "Automatic Styles" in the Formula Outline dialog box. Then, when Excel creates the outline, it also applies the automatic styles to the worksheet. You can always manually change the styles later, to suit your taste.

Since you probably did not have Automatic Styles enabled when you created the outline, let's apply styles now. To return to the full outline where you can see all the elements, just click on the Column Outline Level 2 button and Row Outline Level 3 button. (If you don't remember where these are, refer back to Figure 9.4.) This will show all levels of both the row and column outlines.

Now, use the following steps to apply Automatic Styles to your worksheet:

1. Open the Formula Outline dialog box.
2. Click on the Apply Styles button.
3. Click on OK to carry out the command and close the dialog box.

Note that if you turn on Automatic Styles, Excel will apply boldfacing to the entire row or column that it deems to be a summary row or column. It's not a problem most of the time, but remember that any data outside the outline, but within a row or column that Excel believes to be a summary row or column, will also have the style applied to it automatically.

This is important because you might have some data outside the outline range that would be reformatted if you ask Excel to apply automatic styles. Depending on how your worksheet is designed, it might be better to simply format the row and column totals by hand and not have to worry about where Excel is applying styles on your behalf.

Removing an Outline from a Worksheet

Suppose you decide you don't want your data to be outlined anymore. What do you do if you want to remove the outlining structure but preserve the data that made up the outline? Excel provides a simple way to remove an outline from a worksheet. Use the following instructions to do so:

1. Select the entire outline. In this case, it means selecting the entire worksheet.
2. Click once on the Promote button—it's the second button in the toolbar, the arrow that points to the left. Excel will display the following dialog box asking if you want to promote a row or a column:

3. Select Rows.
4. Click on OK to promote the row.
5. Follow steps 2 through 4 again until you can no longer see any outlining symbols (level bars, Expand and Collapse buttons, and so on) to the left of the rows.
6. Follow steps 2 through 5, this time substituting columns for rows to remove the column outlining symbols.

Creating the Outline Manually

Sometimes Excel may not be able to set up the outline exactly as you require. In these cases, it's up to you to manually create an outline. Since you just removed the automatic outline from your worksheet, it's a good time to re-create the outline manually. Use the following steps to create an outline with the ESTBUD91.XLS worksheet:

1. Highlight rows 5 through 9. These are the rows you want to collapse under Total — R&D.
2. Click on the Demote button in the toolbar (the arrow that points to the right). Note that Excel shows a Row Level bar and Collapse button automatically, based on the range of rows you specified. Verify that the rows collapse and expand correctly by clicking once on the Collapse button to collapse them. Then click on the Expand button to expand the rows out again.
3. Highlight rows 12 through 16. These are the rows that will collapse under Total —Admin.
4. Click again on the Demote button in the toolbar.
5. Finally, highlight rows 5 through 18.
6. Click on the Demote button in the toolbar. This will create a level bar that encompasses both the R&D and Admin subcategories.

After you finish setting up these categories and subcategories, your worksheet should look like the one in Figure 9.12.

Outlining Columns

So far, you have only manually assigned outline levels to the rows, which is analogous to creating an outline with a word processor. However, Excel adds another dimension to the power of outlining. You still need to create

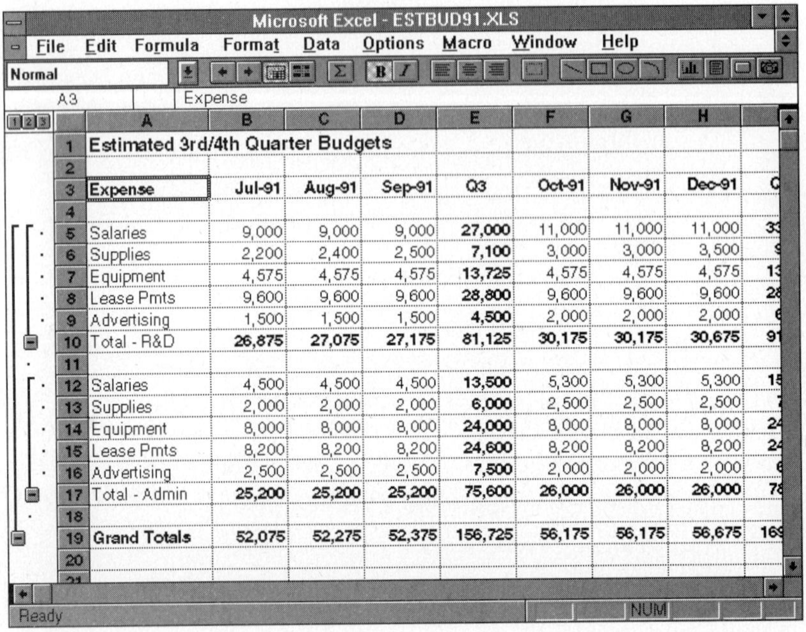

Figure 9.12 Outline after selecting and demoting three levels of data

Microsoft Excel - ESTBUD91.XLS

File Edit Formula Format Data Options Macro Window Help

Normal

A3 Expense

	A	B	C	D	E	F	G	H	
1	Estimated 3rd/4th Quarter Budgets								
2									
3	Expense	Jul-91	Aug-91	Sep-91	Q3	Oct-91	Nov-91	Dec-91	C
4									
5	Salaries	9,000	9,000	9,000	27,000	11,000	11,000	11,000	33
6	Supplies	2,200	2,400	2,500	7,100	3,000	3,000	3,500	9
7	Equipment	4,575	4,575	4,575	13,725	4,575	4,575	4,575	13
8	Lease Pmts	9,600	9,600	9,600	28,800	9,600	9,600	9,600	28
9	Advertising	1,500	1,500	1,500	4,500	2,000	2,000	2,000	6
10	Total - R&D	26,875	27,075	27,175	81,125	30,175	30,175	30,675	91
11									
12	Salaries	4,500	4,500	4,500	13,500	5,300	5,300	5,300	15
13	Supplies	2,000	2,000	2,000	6,000	2,500	2,500	2,500	7
14	Equipment	8,000	8,000	8,000	24,000	8,000	8,000	8,000	24
15	Lease Pmts	8,200	8,200	8,200	24,600	8,200	8,200	8,200	24
16	Advertising	2,500	2,500	2,500	7,500	2,000	2,000	2,000	6
17	Total - Admin	25,200	25,200	25,200	75,600	26,000	26,000	26,000	78
18									
19	Grand Totals	52,075	52,275	52,375	156,725	56,175	56,175	56,675	169
20									

Ready NUM

the outline levels that let you summarize columnar data—that is, the two groups of detail that make up the Q3 and Q4 totals. Follow these steps to complete the outline of the columnar data:

1. Highlight columns B, C, and D. These columns are the subcategory for Q3.
2. Click on the Demote button in the toolbar.
3. Highlight columns F, G, and H. These relate to Q4.
4. Click on the Demote button.

When you finish, your completed worksheet outline is ready to use and should look like the one in Figure 9.13.

Finally, as you have been asked to do at the end of each chapter, save your work. If you have not already done so, title your worksheet EST-BUD91.XLS and save it. If you followed the instructions earlier in this chapter and have already titled the worksheet, simply click on File, Save to save the file.

Figure 9.13
Completed outline for ESTBUD91.XLS

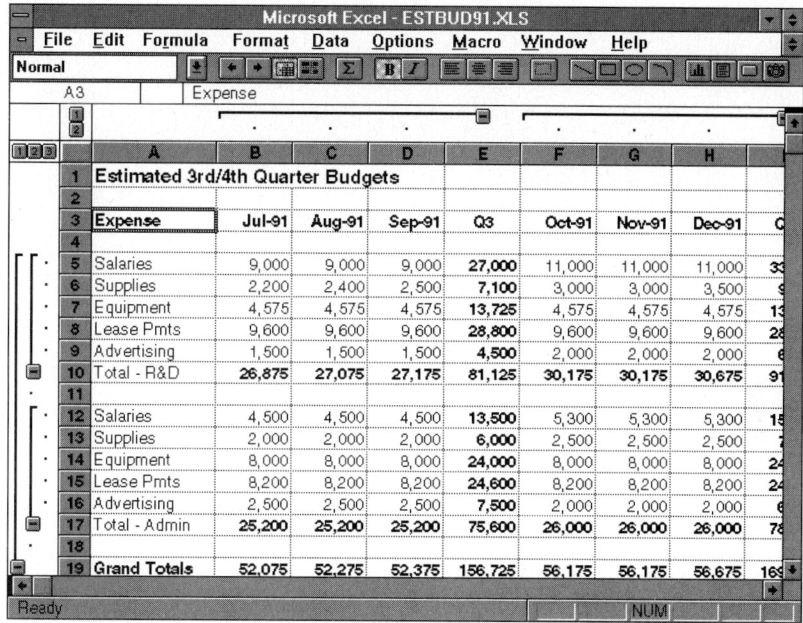

Microsoft Excel - ESTBUD91.XLS

File Edit Formula Format Data Options Macro Window Help

A3 Expense

	A	B	C	D	E	F	G	H
1	**Estimated 3rd/4th Quarter Budgets**							
2								
3	**Expense**	**Jul-91**	**Aug-91**	**Sep-91**	**Q3**	**Oct-91**	**Nov-91**	**Dec-91**
4								
5	Salaries	9,000	9,000	9,000	**27,000**	11,000	11,000	11,000
6	Supplies	2,200	2,400	2,500	**7,100**	3,000	3,000	3,500
7	Equipment	4,575	4,575	4,575	**13,725**	4,575	4,575	4,575
8	Lease Pmts	9,600	9,600	9,600	**28,800**	9,600	9,600	9,600
9	Advertising	1,500	1,500	1,500	**4,500**	2,000	2,000	2,000
10	Total - R&D	**26,875**	**27,075**	**27,175**	**81,125**	**30,175**	**30,175**	**30,675**
11								
12	Salaries	4,500	4,500	4,500	**13,500**	5,300	5,300	5,300
13	Supplies	2,000	2,000	2,000	**6,000**	2,500	2,500	2,500
14	Equipment	8,000	8,000	8,000	**24,000**	8,000	8,000	8,000
15	Lease Pmts	8,200	8,200	8,200	**24,600**	8,200	8,200	8,200
16	Advertising	2,500	2,500	2,500	**7,500**	2,000	2,000	2,000
17	Total - Admin	**25,200**	**25,200**	**25,200**	**75,600**	**26,000**	**26,000**	**26,000**
18								
19	**Grand Totals**	**52,075**	**52,275**	**52,375**	**156,725**	**56,175**	**56,175**	**56,675**

Ready NUM

Working with Multiple Files and File Protection

Data Consolidation and Linking

Worksheet Analysis Tools

Programming Excel

PART 3

Increasing Your Productivity

CHAPTER

10

Working with Multiple Files and File Protection

Working with Workspaces

Workgroup Editing Mode

Protection for Worksheets

ALL THE WORK YOU'VE DONE TO DATE WITH THIS BOOK IS PREDICATED on the notion that you would be the only one working with your own files. In that scenario, you wouldn't have to worry about security since no one else would have any contact with your data. Normally, however, your data will be shared with others. Data is an investment in time and effort that is meant to be shared, but destined to be protected.

This chapter will discuss the various ways you can protect your documents. There are two levels of protection you can use: *cell level*, where selected data can be protected from change or hidden from view, and *file level,* where no one can look at any part of a file without knowing the password. As with other facets of the program that you have already seen, Excel is very flexible about showing just what you want it to show and hiding those things you do not want to reveal.

In addition, you'll learn how to use the *workspace*—collections of worksheets and charts you can save and recall as a single unit. If you routinely work with the same group of worksheet files, you should consider using a workspace.

Working with Workspaces

Along the way to becoming more proficient with Excel, you will learn to use the workspace, which is simply the place where you interact with Excel. Within the workspace, you can have several worksheets, charts, or even macro sheets open at one time. Each sheet or chart fits within its own window, and the collection of windows makes up the workspace. Figure 10.1 shows an example of a busy workspace. Note that there are several worksheets and a chart open at one time.

The beauty of the workspace concept is that you can save all those sheets and charts in a single file by giving just one command. Then, when you return to your computer and want to begin where you left off, you simply retrieve that file just as you have retrieved the BUDGET1.XLS file, and all the charts and worksheets you saved before will reopen exactly as you left them. This feature is perfect for work in progress—when you want to save everything you're doing and then return to it later. All workspace files are saved with the extension .XLW to identify them as workspace files.

There is one important thing to remember about the workspace. When you save a workspace file to disk, all you are saving is a *list* of files, along with some information about their window position on-screen, whether the window was hidden or not, and so on. Thus, you must make sure that you save each individual file before you close it. Simply saving a workspace file will not ensure that the worksheet data will be retained if you close a file without saving it. As always, Excel will prompt you if you are about to close a file without saving it.

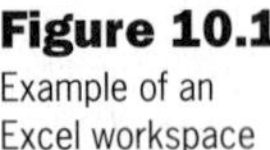

Figure 10.1
Example of an Excel workspace

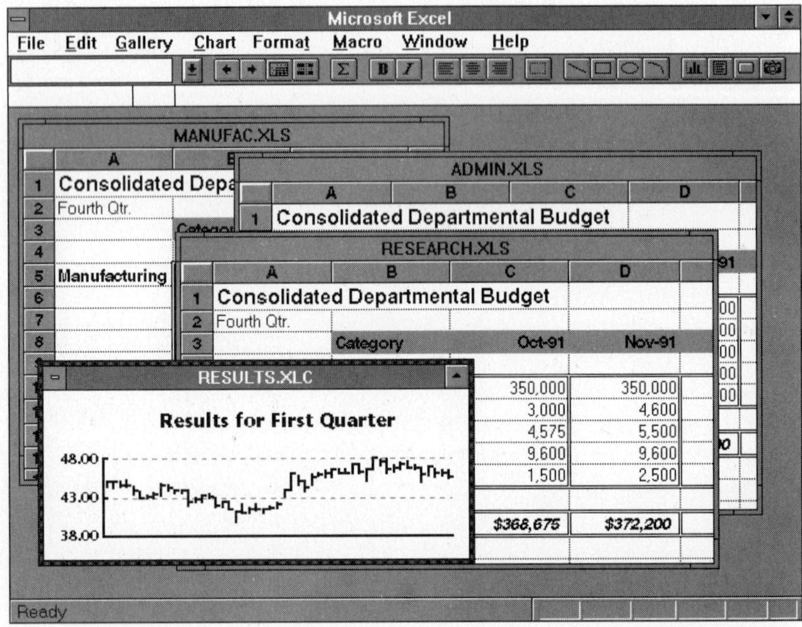

Creating New Worksheets

In order to start working with workspace files, you will need to create a few more worksheets. You will use these files later for some exercises in data consolidation. Meanwhile, they will form your work in progress as you learn more about the workspace.

Consider the following scenario: You are a divisional manager with responsibility for three departments: Research, Administration, and Manufacturing. Assume that each of your department managers has prepared a departmental budget summation, and you want to work with these reports so that you can present the division's situation to your boss. Apply the following steps to create two more files that represent the Administration and Manufacturing departments:

1. Bring up the BUDGET1.XLS file (from Chapter 6) on your screen.
2. Change the department name from Research to **Administration**.
3. Change each Salary figure to 100,000. Either type **100,000** into each of the three cells, or type it just once and copy it to the other cells.
4. Reduce each value in the Office Supplies row by $1,000.

5. Click on File, Save As. (Do not use File Save here since you want to create a duplicate file.)
6. Type the name of the new file as **BUDGET2.XLS**.
7. Click on OK to complete the command.
8. Change the department name from Administration to **Manufacturing.**
9. Increase the salary levels to $500,000 across the board.
10. Click on File, Save As.
11. Type the name of the new file as **BUDGET3.XLS**.
12. Reopen the two files you saved previously: Click on File, Open and then open both BUDGET1.XLS and BUDGET2.XLS by clicking on their names at the bottom of the menu.
13. Make BUDGET2.XLS the active window by clicking anywhere in that worksheet.
14. Highlight the range C6:C9.
15. Click on File, New and then click on Chart.

When you finish, you can move the windows around or resize them to your satisfaction. Figure 10.2 shows an example of what your screen might look like.

Setting up the Workspace

Note. You might begin to feel that the size of your standard VGA screen prevents you from taking full advantage of the Windows operating environment. Many users have upgraded to 16-inch or 20-inch monitors in search of more "real estate" for their programs and utilities.

With several Excel files (and therefore windows) open, you can manipulate them just as you do any other windows in the Windows environment (see Appendix A). There are also some useful Excel commands for you to know about at this point. For example, Excel has a feature that can quickly size the windows so that you can see all of them at once. This process is called *tiling,* and refers to the way Excel can make the windows fit within the workspace the same way tiles fit together on a floor.

To see this, just click on Window, Arrange All and watch as Excel arranges all the windows to fit on the screen. Admittedly, you aren't seeing much of each window, but you can see which file is which and get a general idea of the contents of each sheet or chart. After you issue the Window, Arrange All command, your worksheet will look more or less like the one in Figure 10.3.

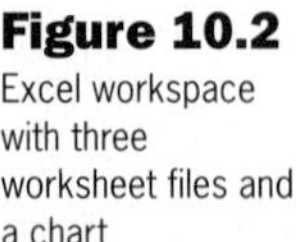

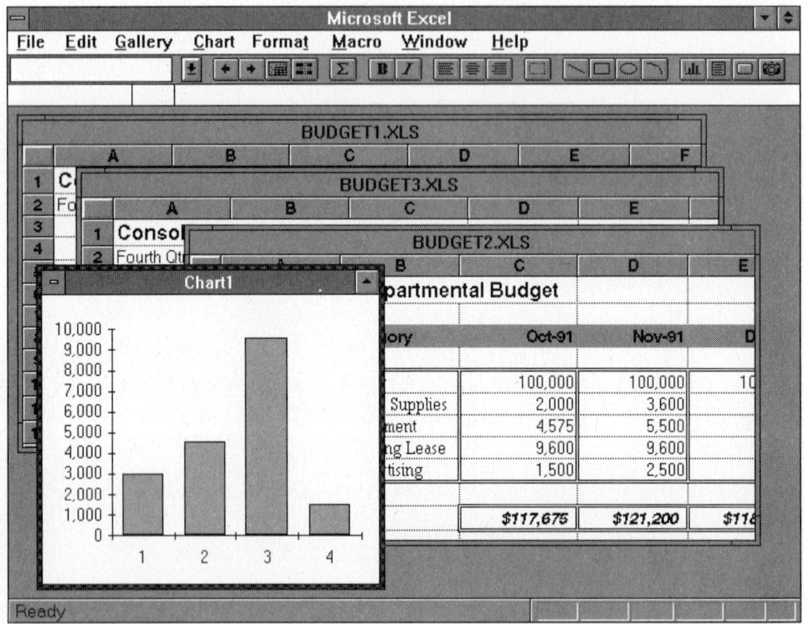

Figure 10.2
Excel workspace with three worksheet files and a chart

Changing the Worksheet Settings

Another useful way you can customize your workspace is to enable and disable certain window features of the worksheet. This feature—coupled with password protection—is useful if you want to control access to how much of a worksheet's data someone sees. For example, you can disable the scroll bars along the right side and the bottom of the window so that it's impossible to scroll the worksheet and see other parts of it. Or you can disable the formula bar so that when the cell pointer is moved to a cell, the underlying formula in the cell would not be visible—only the results of the computation could be seen. If you then lock out the user's ability to modify the worksheet (with Excel's built-in password protection), you have effectively limited what parts of the worksheet someone can see.

In this exercise, you will learn about some of the display options available to you:

1. Select any one of the worksheet windows visible on the screen. If you still have the windows tiled, the active window is the one with a different color on the title bar.

2. Click on Options, Workspace. The dialog box shown in Figure 10.4 appears.

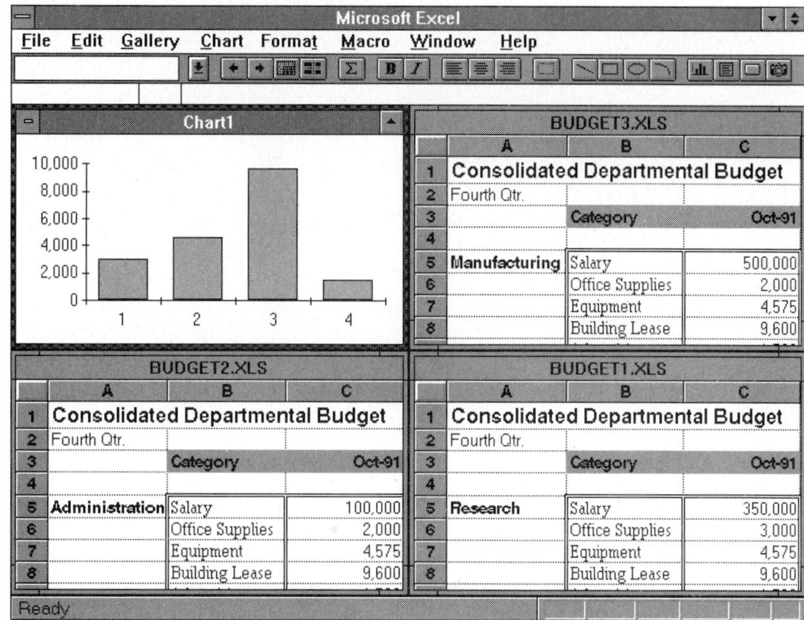

Figure 10.3 Workspace after the Window, Arrange All command

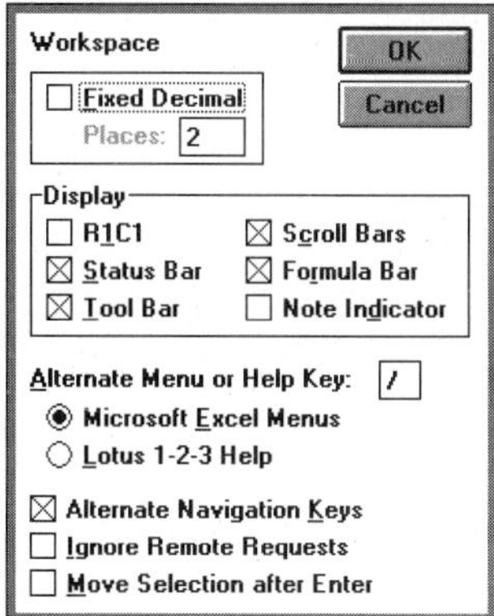

Figure 10.4 Options Workspace dialog box

3. Disable the scroll bars, the formula bar, the status bar, and the toolbar (that is, remove the check marks from those options).

4. Click OK to carry out the command.

As soon as you click on the OK command button, Excel redisplays all the windows on screen using the changes you have made. Because you turned off the toolbar, scroll bars, and formula bar, there is now extra space on the screen. Note that the windows show only the data so that you are somewhat limited in the ways you can alter the data. If you want the tiled windows to again fill the screen, you can issue the Window, Arrange All command. If you do so, your workspace will look like Figure 10.5.

Figure 10.5
Screen with scroll bars, formula bar, tool bar, and status line disabled

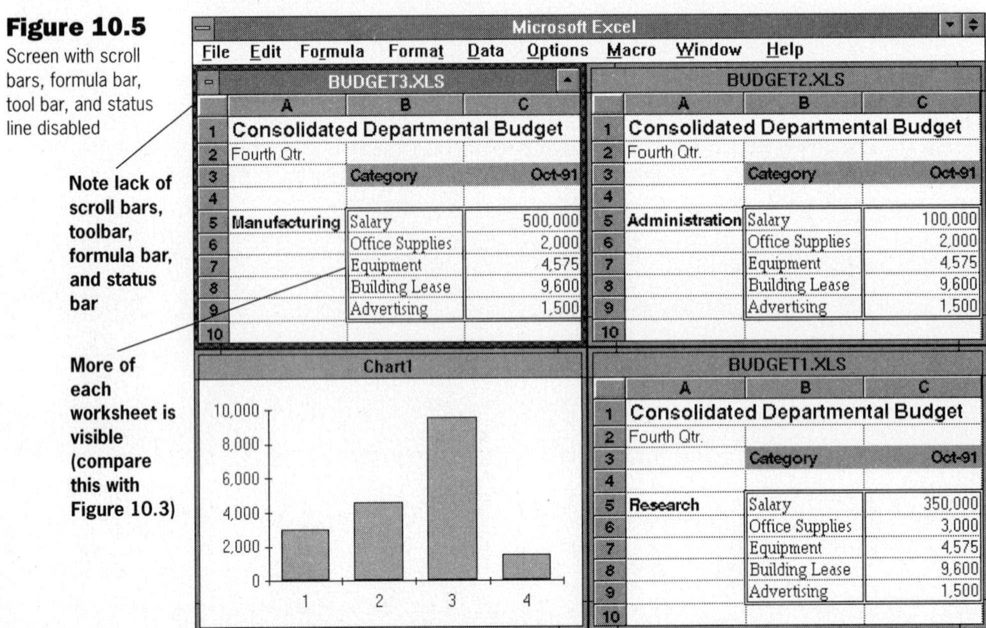

Hiding/Showing a Worksheet

What if you wanted to hide one of the worksheets from view? Suppose, for example, that data from one worksheet was linked to another (you'll learn more about linking in Chapter 11) and you only wanted to show the worksheet that summarized the data. With Excel, you could easily hide the worksheet containing supporting data and only display the one that provided the summary. Use the following instructions to first hide a window and then redisplay it later.

1. Select the window that you want to hide. For this exercise, choose BUDGET3.XLS. Remember that the active window is the one that has a different color on the window title bar.

2. Click on Window, Hide.

Excel immediately removes the window from your view. Although the window is still part of the workspace, it is now hidden. Excel will not make any attempt to resize the remaining windows, but if you issue another Window, Arrange All command, Excel will rearrange the three visible windows as if the fourth window was not there.

Now it's time to reinstate the hidden window:

1. Click on Window, Unhide.

2. Click on the window that you want to reinstate. In this case, there is only one, but there could be more than one hidden window. This is the point where you would choose which window to bring back.

3. Click on OK to carry out the command.

Excel will redisplay the workspace with all windows displayed as they were before you hid the worksheet. When Excel *unhides* a window, it is restored to the position it occupied before being hidden.

Saving the Position and Status of Files

So far, you have only worked with multiple files in a workspace. But say you've been working on these files for several hours and now it's time to close everything down for the day. Use the following set of instructions to create a workspace file that will save the positions and status of all of the worksheet and chart files:

1. Click on File, Save Workspace.

2. Excel brings up a dialog box that looks very much like the File Open/-Save dialog box. This box prompts you for the name of the workspace file.

3. Type **MY_SAVE** in the file name box.

4. Click on OK to complete the command.

Excel will save the positions of the files into a file called MY_SAVE.XLW. Remember that the Excel data files are usually identified by their file extension—.XLW for workspace files, .XLC for chart files, and .XLS for worksheets.

Excel will then ask you if you want to save each file that has been in the workspace. Just as you have found when closing a file, you can choose to save or to ignore the save process for each individual file. For this exercise, choose Yes to save the files when prompted. When Excel gets to the chart, choose a name like **BUDGET** and click on OK.

After you have responded to the save prompt on each file, you can continue to work on each file if you choose. Even if you close all the files and then return to work on just one of them, any changes you make to that file will be reflected when you retrieve the workspace file.

Retrieving the Workspace File

Retrieving a workspace file is just like retrieving a normal worksheet file, except that the worksheet file has a file extension of .XLW. Excel treats a workspace file just like a worksheet file, so you will find it on the list of the four most recently used files at the bottom of the File menu.

To load a workspace file, including all the files that were saved with it, just click on File, Open and select the name of the workspace file that you want to open. Then click on OK to carry out the command.

Deleting Workspace (and Other) Files

There will be times when you want to erase a file from disk, and Excel gives you the ability to do so without exiting the program. Use the following steps to delete a file (you'll stop one step short of doing so, however):

1. Click on File, Delete.
2. Scroll through the list box of file names until you find the one that you want to delete. Select MY_SAVE.XLW.
3. To delete the file, you would click on OK to carry out the command. Then Excel would prompt you "Delete this file?" In this case, answer No if you've gone this far. If you actually wanted to delete a file, you would, of course, answer Yes.
4. Click on Close to close the dialog box and return to Excel.

Note that if you had deleted MY_SAVE.XLW, only the workspace file would have disappeared. The files it references would remain intact.

Workgroup Editing Mode

With the ability to have several files in memory at once, there should be a way to issue commands that will affect all the worksheets at once—and in Excel there is. The function that does this is called a *workgroup*. The way to remember workgroup is to remember that you are editing *work*sheets as a *group*. When worksheets are combined into a workgroup, almost any change to the active worksheet is reflected across the whole group. This feature not only applies to formatting and data entry, but also to printing. If you define a workgroup before you print one of the worksheets, all the worksheets defined in that workgroup will print out together.

Creating a Workgroup

To create a workgroup, first make sure that the sheets that you want to be a part of that workgroup are open—in this case, BUDGET1.XLS, BUDGET2.XLS, and BUDGET3.XLS. Although you can have more files open than you will put into the workgroup, all the files you put into the workgroup must be open. By definition, charts aren't part of a workgroup—only worksheets and macro sheets are. (Macro sheets are discussed in Chapter 13.)

Follow these instructions to create a workgroup:

1. Click within the window of BUDGET1.XLS. This activates the worksheet that you want to use as the "master" when entering changes.
2. Click on Window, Workgroup.
3. If they are not already selected, highlight all the worksheet files listed in the dialog box. You can choose any or all of the files here by holding down the Shift key and clicking on each file name.
4. Click on OK to carry out the command.

Figure 10.6 shows what the worksheets look like after they have been added to the workgroup. You will notice that any worksheet that is part of the workgroup will have "[Workgroup]" in its title bar.

After you have created the workgroup, you can make a change in any of the worksheets and have that command carried out on all of the worksheets within the workgroup. As an example, use the following instructions to remove the bold attribute from the title of all three worksheets:

1. Highlight the cell you want to change throughout the workgroup. For this exercise, highlight cell A1.
2. Click on Window, Arrange Workgroup to show and arrange all the sheets that make up the workgroup on the screen at one time.
3. Click on Format, Font and remove the bold attribute from the text (or click on the B in the toolbar if it is displayed). As soon as you remove the bold attribute from the cell, all the worksheets redisplay the title in a normal typeface. When you finish this command, your screen should look more or less like Figure 10.7.

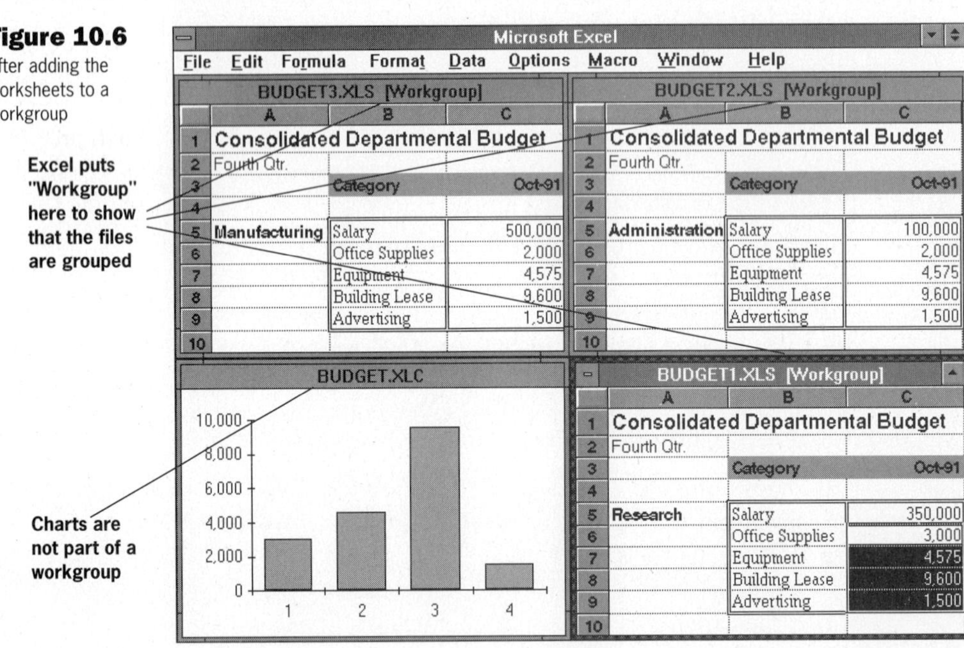

Figure 10.6
After adding the worksheets to a workgroup

Figure 10.7
After removing the bold attribute in all three worksheets

Changes in this cell affected the other worksheets in the workgroup

Protection for Worksheets

Excel offers a wide range of options when it comes to protecting your documents and data. This is especially important if you plan to share worksheets with others or if your worksheets contain sensitive data.

Excel provides security for worksheets at two general levels. First, protection is available while the data is stored in a worksheet on disk. This is how data is saved when you are not working on it and you have saved the file to disk (file level). The second level of protection occurs while the file is open and you or someone else is working with the worksheet interactively (cell level).

Locking the Worksheet with a Password

When you are ready to save data to disk, you can tell Excel that you would like to use a password. This password can be up to 16 characters in length and can be made up of any combination of letters, numbers, and symbols. Furthermore, Excel's password is case-sensitive: "hide*me" is not the same as "Hide*ME".

In the following exercise, you will learn how to prevent someone from opening the worksheet unless they know the password:

1. Close down and save all the files except for BUDGET1.XLS by activating them one at a time and clicking on File, Close. Remember to save your work when Excel prompts you to do so. Because Excel will leave BUDGET1.XLS exactly where it was, you might want to resize the window a bit to better see it.
2. Click on File, Save As.
3. Click on the Options command button.
4. In the resulting dialog box (shown in Figure 10.8) type a password of your own choosing in the Protection Password box. Watch as Excel types an asterisk for each character that you type—it's considered bad for security if someone can read the password you type.

Figure 10.8
File Save As Options dialog box

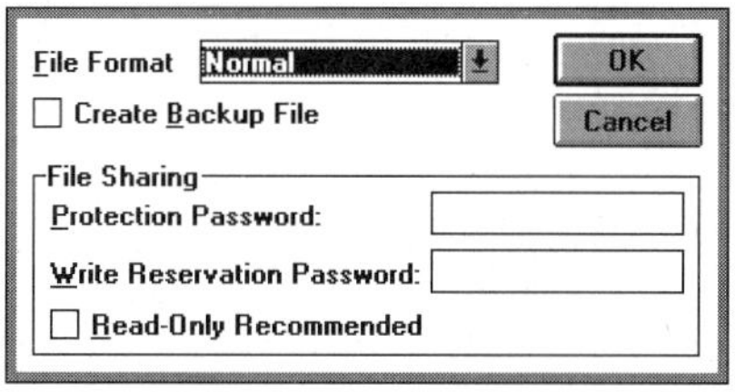

File Format Normal
OK
Create Backup File
Cancel
File Sharing
Protection Password:
Write Reservation Password:
Read-Only Recommended

5. Click on OK to accept the password.
6. Excel will prompt you to retype the password to verify that you typed it correctly the first time.
7. Click on OK to accept the verification password.
8. Save the file as you would normally. If Excel prompts you to replace an existing file, do so.
9. Finally, close the file by clicking on File, Close.

Opening a Password-Protected File

Now, when you come back to open this file, Excel will prompt you for a password before you can see any of its contents. The following steps illustrate how to open a worksheet that has been password protected:

1. From the File menu, choose the file that you just saved from the list of the last four files opened.
2. Excel will present a dialog box (see Figure 10.9) asking for your password. Enter your password now.
3. Click on OK to complete the command.

Figure 10.9
Excel's dialog box for password-protected files

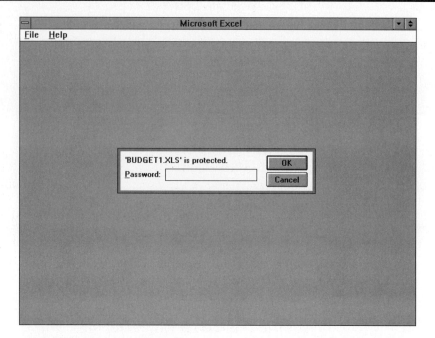

CAUTION! *Excel's password-protection scheme is very effective. If you lose or forget the password, the file is not usable anymore. Don't bother calling Microsoft to help you. The staff there can't unlock your password-locked file either. This is for your protection, but it means that you need to be very careful when you work with passwords.*

Removing Password Protection from Worksheets

When adding passwords to worksheets, it's nice to know that there are ways to remove them as well. First you must have the file open on your screen. Then, use the following steps to remove a password from a worksheet:

1. Click on File, Save As.
2. Click on the Options command button.
3. Highlight the asterisks that represent the password in the Protection Password box.
4. Press the Del key.
5. Click on OK to close the dialog box.
6. Click on OK again to save the file to disk without the password.

Hiding and Locking Worksheet Cells

One of the ways you can protect cells on the worksheet is to hide them. Hiding cells is not like hiding a worksheet within the workspace—the cell does not disappear. Instead, hiding a cell means that the contents of the cell—formula or value—do not appear in the formula bar. This lets you create models where the user cannot see the calculations or the base values used to derive the result of a model. When you *hide* a cell, only the current value of that cell is visible.

In contrast, *locking* cells means that you cannot make any changes to the cells. You can see the actual contents of the cells in the formula bar—you just can't modify the contents of the cells. Between locking a cell and hiding it, you have a good deal of flexibility in the way that you secure your worksheet.

Conceptually, setting up document protection is slightly different from, say, making a range of cells bold. When you format cells, you first select a range of text and then command Excel to apply the bold attribute to each cell in that range.

Hiding and locking cells is similar, but goes one step further. First you select the range that you want to be locked or hidden or both. Then you apply the attributes to that range. Finally, and this is what the boldfacing example didn't do, you must turn on the global cell protection from a menu. Only then will the protection settings take effect.

Locking All the Cells in a Worksheet

By default, cells on a new worksheet are formatted to be locked, but not hidden. But because the global protection has not yet been enabled (it will be shortly), you are still able to enter new data into the cells and edit existing data already in the worksheet. However, the moment that you turn on *global* (meaning the whole worksheet) cell protection, all the cells will be locked, and you will not be able to modify their contents. Let's do a few exercises to better illustrate this concept:

1. Click on Options, Protect Document. The following dialog box appears:

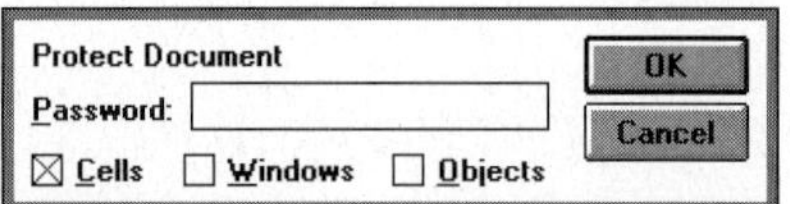

2. Make sure that the box next to Cells is checked and that the box next to Windows is not checked.
3. Click on OK to complete the command.
4. Now highlight any cell on your worksheet.
5. Attempt to change the contents of the cell by typing a new label. You should see the dialog box shown in Figure 10.10.

Since each cell, by default, has cell protection enabled, the cell becomes locked when you turn on global protection. Remember that cell protection is an attribute you can assign to a cell and that making a cell unavailable is a two-step process. First you must ensure that cell protection is set for a given cell (as it is by default), then you must turn on global protection.

To illustrate, imagine two ranges of cells: range A and range B. You want to make the cells in range B locked so that nobody can tamper with the data there, but you don't mind if others make changes to range A. Since all the cells have protection set by default, you must first format range A to *not have* the protection attribute set. Then, when you turn on global protection, range B will be locked (because its cell protection was enabled by default), and people will be free to make changes to range A.

Conversely, if you did nothing to the worksheet except turn on global protection (Options, Protect Document), all the cells in the worksheet would be locked, and you would be unable to enter new data or edit existing data until you turned off global protection.

You can also apply protection to the graphical elements and windows within the workspace. By applying protection to windows, you lock the window into place so that it cannot be moved, resized, opened, or closed. You can also apply a password to the global cell protection function so that you can control who determines the protection of the worksheet. Entering a password in the dialog box prevents others from turning off the protection you enabled.

Figure 10.10
After turning on worksheet protection

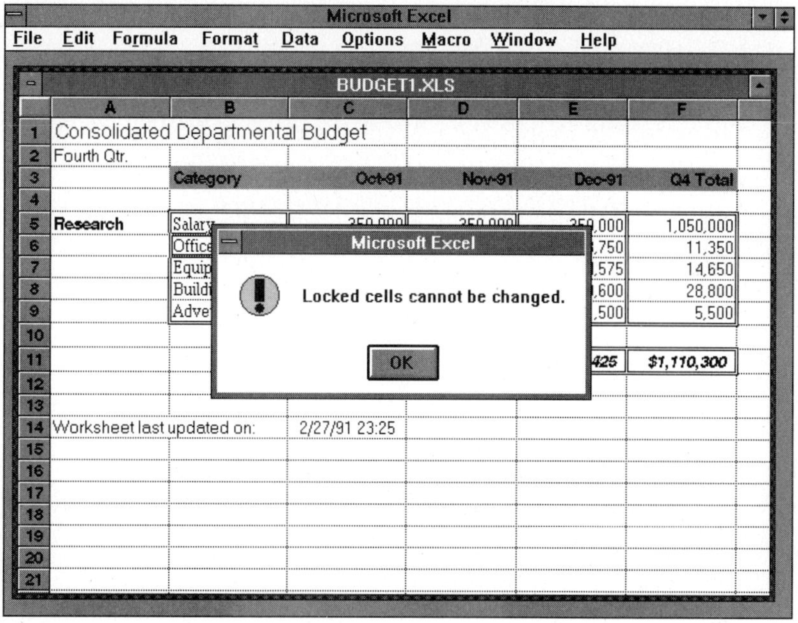

Locking Selected Cells

Consider the following scenario: What if you wanted to allow someone to change just a few cells in this model? Furthermore, you did not want them to see the way you calculated the totals for each of the years in the BUDGET1.XLS worksheet. Perhaps you plan to distribute this worksheet to your department managers, each of whom will modify only his or her department's figures. Conceptually, you would simply turn off the global protection and then manually change the attributes for each cell according to the kind of protection you want. The following steps detail the process:

1. Click on Options, Unprotect Document. You can now freely make changes to any cell within the worksheet.

2. Highlight the range C6:E9. This is the range you want to modify so that someone can make changes to the numbers.

3. Click on Format, Cell Protection. The following dialog box appears:

4. Remove the X that appears next to Locked.
5. Click on OK to complete the command.

Although the worksheet will not look different, the cells you just unlocked will now be free to change, even when you reenable the global cell protection.

Hiding Selected Cells

Suppose that in addition to locking certain cells, you also want to hide the calculations that make the totals at the bottom of each column. In this example, you probably don't care too much if people know that you simply added up all the numbers. In your real model, however, you might be calculating prices based on a certain percentage of profit, and you might not want your sales prospect to see those calculations or percentage figures. The following steps will format the cells as hidden:

1. Highlight the range C11:F11.
2. Click on Format, Cell Protection.
3. Place an X next to Hidden.
4. Make sure that there is also an X next to Locked.
5. Click on OK to complete the command.

Again, the worksheet does not appear to change. The only way to ensure that this worked correctly is to try it. Before you see if the commands worked, however, you'll need to turn on some of the options you turned off earlier. Click on Options, Workspace and enable the status bar, scroll bars, formula bar, and the toolbar. Then, click on OK to complete the command. Once you have the turned the indicators back on, follow along with these instructions to see if the cell protection is now the way you want it to be:

1. Click on Options, Protect Document.
2. Make sure that the Cells box has an X in it.
3. Click on OK to complete the command.
4. Highlight cell B7 and attempt to change it. That cell is locked.

5. Highlight cell C7 and attempt to change the value. Because this cell was formatted to be unlocked when you applied the global protection, this cell remains unprotected. (Be sure to reverse any changes you make.)

6. Now, highlight cell C11. Look in the formula bar to see if you can find the formula that comprises the actual contents of the cell. With that cell formatted as hidden, only the result of whatever is in that cell shows on the worksheet (see Figure 10.11).

7. Finally, as you conclude this chapter, save your files again.

Figure 10.11
Cell C11 is hidden

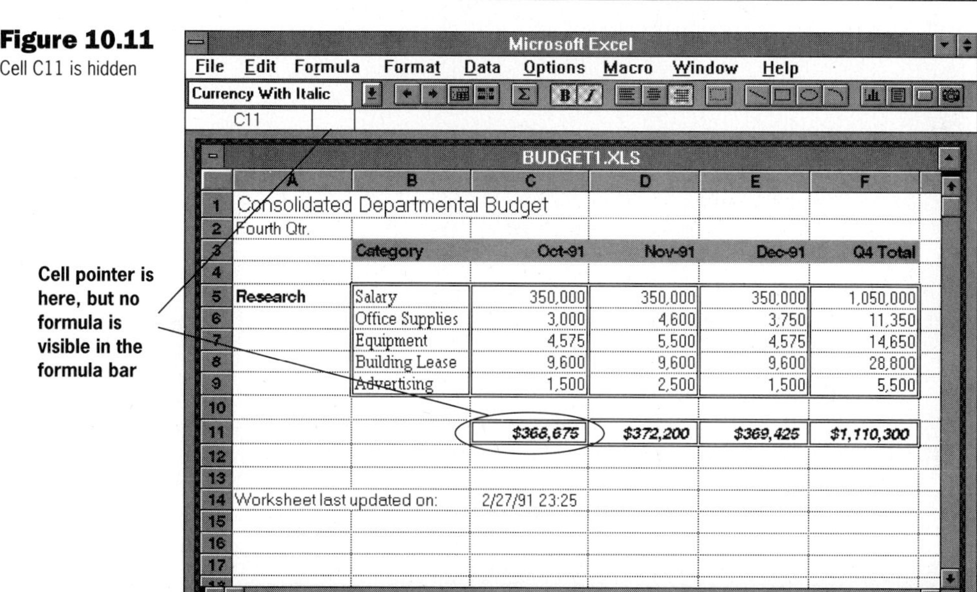

CHAPTER

11

Data Consolidation and Linking

AS MENTIONED IN EARLIER CHAPTERS, IT'S BETTER TO BREAK UP COMplicated models and create a number of smaller worksheets than it is to maintain one large, cumbersome sheet. Trying to do everything in one worksheet poses several problems. First, it's easy to lose sight of your project—both literally and metaphorically. As the worksheet grows, you begin to forget where your data is in relation to where you are working. The situation is even worse if you aren't using named ranges.

Fortunately, the Excel environment offers several different ways to deal with problems of worksheet sprawl and help you keep a handle on all the parts of your worksheet model.

Excel's flexible *consolidation* feature lets you bring together data that is stored in separate worksheets using a relatively simple set of commands. When you perform a consolidation with Excel, you normally need to do so only once. Then later you simply update the data when you need to.

Worksheet *linking*, on the other hand, is a more generic feature and is useful in more cases than consolidation. By allowing you to create links between cells on a single worksheet, between cells on different worksheets, and even between locations in different Windows applications, linking gives you a great deal of flexibility about where you store data.

Benefits of Consolidation

Excel 3.0's consolidation feature is greatly improved over earlier Excel 2.x versions. Data consolidation techniques are used to help you bring data in from other worksheets and summarize that data in one main worksheet.

Like other Excel operations, data consolidation is accomplished by constructing a formula consisting of functions and addresses. In addition, since you're working with more than one file, the names of the worksheets must also be included in the formula. As with other Excel formulas, there is more than one way to enter the data consolidation formula: by typing and by means of a dialog box.

To see data consolidation's usefulness, consider the following scenario: You are the financial controller for a medium-sized company. You have been receiving quarterly budget information from each departmental manager on printouts, and each manager has been using his or her spreadsheet product of choice. Not only is this confusing because each report is different, but you don't have an easy way to manipulate the data or perform any sort of analysis yourself unless you choose to manually enter the data into your own spreadsheet.

In order to make this process easier, you design a template (see Chapter 5) that contains all the requisite calculations and labels. The managers simply need to fill in the corresponding budget information for their department. In fact, the template you design looks very much like the worksheets you've been working with since the start of the book.

When you finish with the template, you send it out to each department and instruct your managers to complete the monthly budget using that worksheet. They then send the completed worksheets to you.

At the end of each quarterly budgeting cycle, you thus have a dozen or so worksheets on your hard disk with identical structures. In other words, each *supporting* or *source worksheet* has the same information at the same place on each worksheet. That is, the salary information is always in the same range on each worksheet, as is the building lease information, and so on.

But once you have this information in a format you can use, how do you consolidate all the information into your master budget worksheet (also called the *destination worksheet*)? Here's where Excel's data consolidation functions shine. With a little practice and a couple of concepts behind you, you'll be able to summarize all the information and produce graphs and reports based on that information.

Methods of Consolidation

Excel's consolidation features are quite flexible and can be very powerful, depending on what you're trying to accomplish. Both its power and its flexibility derive from an important concept you should understand before you get too far into consolidation. This concept is the distinction between the two ways that Excel handles consolidation.

Consolidation by Location

The kind of consolidation easiest to understand is *consolidation by location*. This situation is very similar to the hypothetical scenario described above, in which you have two or more supporting worksheets that are structured identically. When you receive these worksheets, you can expect that the number that appears in cell D5, for instance, of each worksheet will be the November figure for salaries.

As you have already seen, you can have multiple worksheets on the screen at one time. Imagine picking up each worksheet from the computer screen and then stacking the sheets as you would loose pieces of paper on a desktop. If you could do that, each worksheet's data would line up in the exact same position under the top (master) sheet's corresponding cells.

At this point, data consolidation is simply a matter of telling Excel that you want to sum up all the cells of the sheets behind the master, and then to put that sum into the master worksheet. Thus the master worksheet's cell D5 would have the grand total of salary payments for November. If this seems confusing, have patience. It will get clearer shortly.

Consider the situation in Figure 11.1. This hypothetical company has manufacturing facilities in Denver and Chicago. Each plant makes pens and pencils. You could do a consolidation by location on cells C3 and C4 because they contain the same information about each facility—in this case, the number of pens and pencils manufactured. Adding these numbers together for each plant is an "apples-to-apples" comparison.

Figure 11.1
Worksheets before consolidation by location

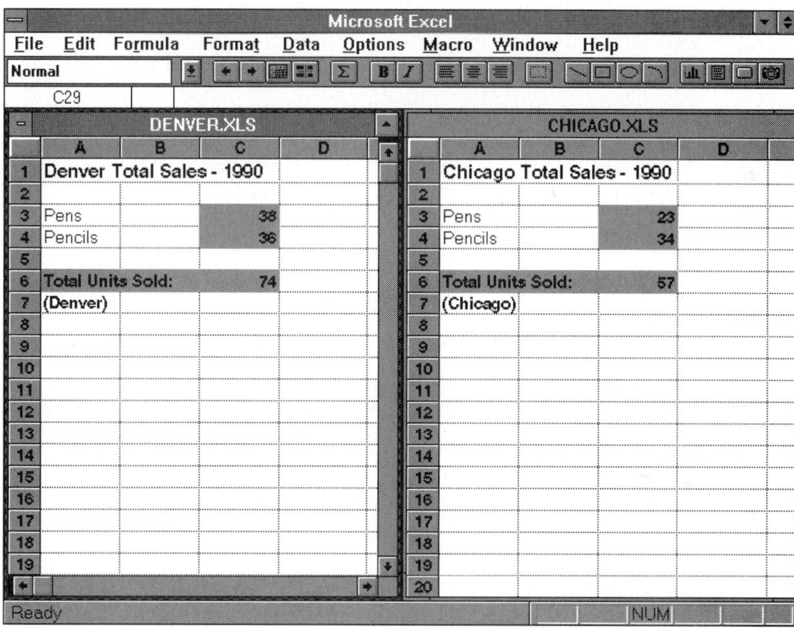

After you perform the consolidation, the master worksheet looks like Figure 11.2. Note that the totals make sense in light of the data you consolidated.

By the way, you don't have to just sum the numbers in the source worksheets. You can perform several other operations on the range(s) of cells you want to consolidate—averaging and multiplying, for example. So if you wanted to compute the average salary from the worksheets sent to you by the departmental managers, you would use the AVERAGE() function for the consolidation formula. Table 11.1 shows the functions you can use with consolidation.

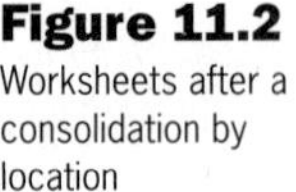

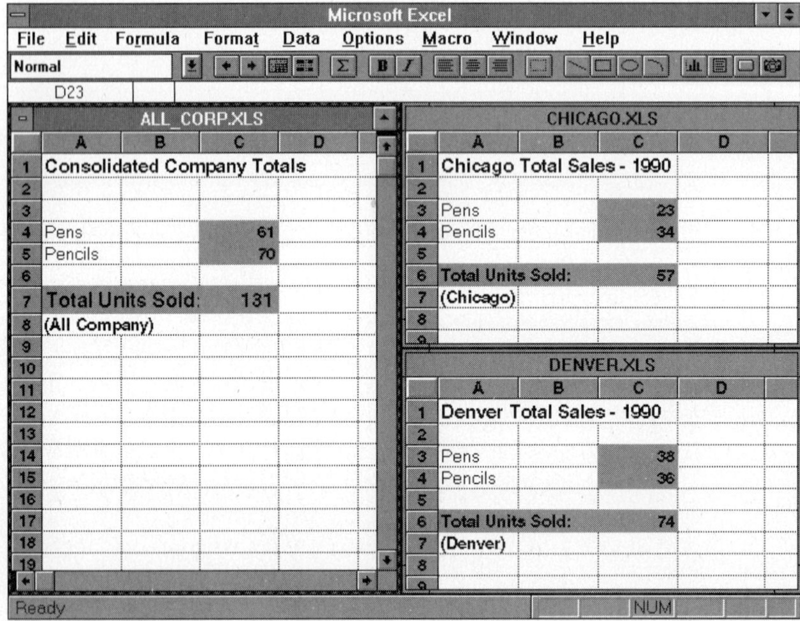

Figure 11.2 Worksheets after a consolidation by location

Consolidation by Category

Consolidation by category is a bit more complicated than consolidation by location, but it is potentially much more powerful. With consolidation by location, each of the worksheets you want to consolidate must be identical in structure so that Excel can find the same information on each worksheet you ask it to consolidate. (Remember that in Figure 11.2 portions of the worksheets were identical so that Excel was able to find both Chicago's and Denver's pencil and pen figures in the same cells.)

The problem with consolidation by location is handling those situations in which the worksheets don't share exactly the same structure. For example, what do you do in the case of the Chicago facility, which makes products A, B, and C, whereas the Denver factory makes products A, B, and D? Consolidation by category avoids this problem by using row and column headings (rather than location) to identify the information you want to consolidate.

Tip. To avoid logical errors, wherever possible check your work to see if the results you get are reasonable. Excel will do exactly (and only) what you tell it to do. Make sure you're telling it to do the right things!

Consider the situation in Figure 11.3. Here are two worksheets that are similar in structure (that is, all the data is in the range C3:C5 on both worksheets) but the factories have different product mixes. If you performed a consolidation by location, you would end up with the correct totals for pens and pencils, but Excel would add together the figures for notepads and rulers to

Table 11.1 Functions Available with Consolidation

Function	Purpose of Function
AVERAGE()	Computes the average of a consolidated range within the source worksheets
COUNT()	Computes the number of items in a consolidated range
COUNTA()	Counts the number of nonblank items in a consolidated range
MAX()	Determines the largest value within a consolidated range among the source worksheets
MIN()	Determines the smallest value within a consolidated range among the source worksheets
PRODUCT()	Multiplies the values of a consolidated range
STDEV()	Computes the sample standard deviation of a consolidated range among the source worksheets
STDEVP()	Computes the population standard deviation of a consolidated range among the source worksheets
SUM()	Computes the total of a consolidated range among the source worksheets (this is Excel's default function)
VAR()	Computes the sample variance of a consolidated range among the source worksheets
VARP()	Computes the population variance of a consolidated range among the source worksheets

create one total that is both incorrect and very misleading—a classic example of a logical error.

However, when Excel computes the consolidation by category and realizes that there are really four distinct products in question, the resulting consolidation (Figure 11.4) correctly identifies the distinct products and produces a correct answer.

Using Consolidation

Let's get into doing a consolidation. First, you will need a master worksheet to hold the results of the consolidation. Remember that you are in the role of the company financial officer and you want to consolidate data from the three departments you oversee: Administration, Manufacturing, and Research. You'll also remember that you had created worksheet templates

Figure 11.3
Example with same companies, different product mix

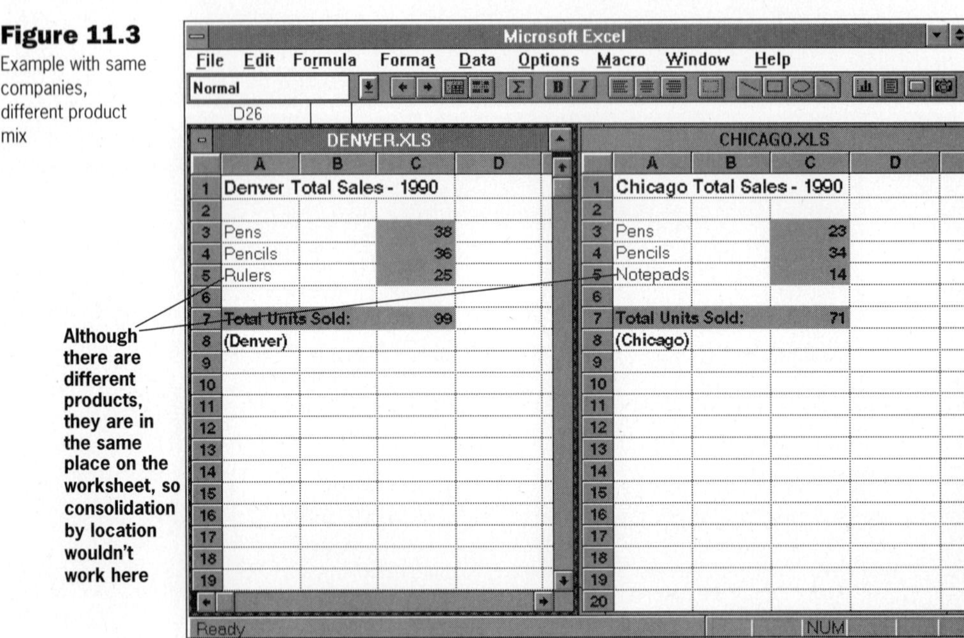

Figure 11.4
Worksheets after a consolidation by category

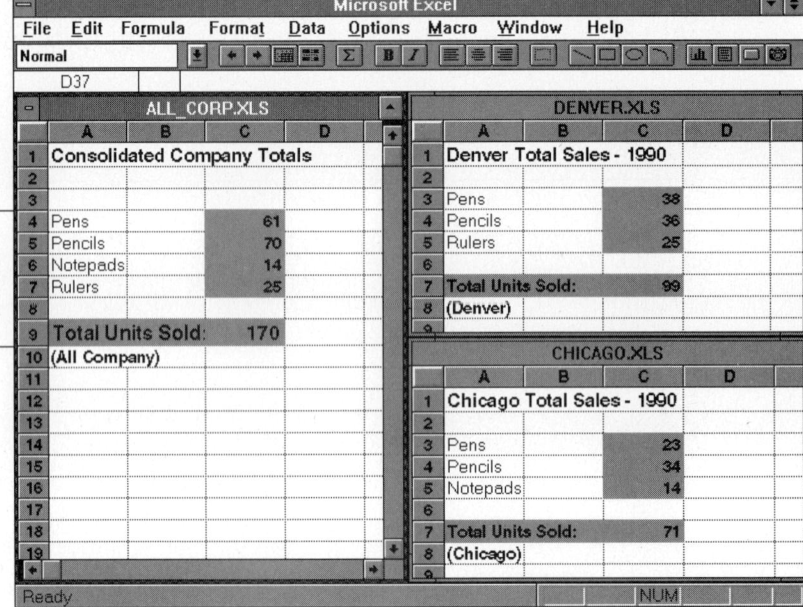

which you distributed to each department. So now you need to have your own worksheet that will serve as the repository of the consolidation. Follow these steps to create a worksheet you can use for subsequent exercises:

1. Open up the BUDGET3.XLS file you created in Chapter 10—it's the one that contains the information for the Manufacturing department. See Figure 11.5.
2. Change the name of the department from Manufacturing to **ALL DEPTS.**
3. Highlight the range C5:F9.
4. Click on Edit, Clear. Make sure that the Formulas button is checked, and then click on OK to clear the data from the range.
5. Click on File, Save As and name this new worksheet **ALL_BUD.XLS**. When you finish, your worksheet should look like Figure 11.6.

At this point, you have created a worksheet that mirrors the structure of the worksheets you distributed to your departmental managers.

Figure 11.5
BUDGET3.XLS worksheet

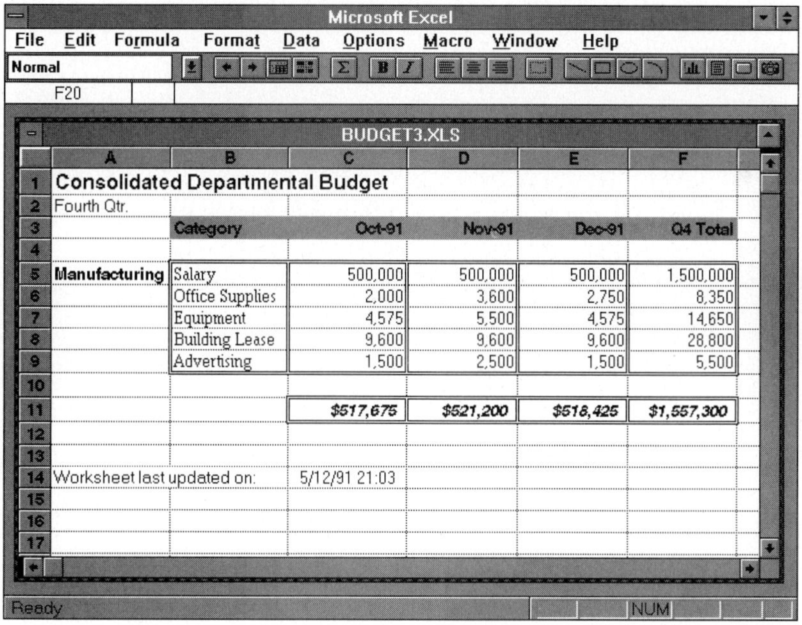

Microsoft Excel

File Edit Formula Format Data Options Macro Window Help

Normal

F20

BUDGET3.XLS

	A	B	C	D	E	F
1	Consolidated Departmental Budget					
2	Fourth Qtr.					
3		Category	Oct-91	Nov-91	Dec-91	Q4 Total
4						
5	Manufacturing	Salary	500,000	500,000	500,000	1,500,000
6		Office Supplies	2,000	3,600	2,750	8,350
7		Equipment	4,575	5,500	4,575	14,650
8		Building Lease	9,600	9,600	9,600	28,800
9		Advertising	1,500	2,500	1,500	5,500
10						
11			$517,675	$521,200	$518,425	$1,557,300
12						
13						
14	Worksheet last updated on:		5/12/91 21:03			
15						
16						
17						

Ready NUM

Figure 11.6
New master worksheet

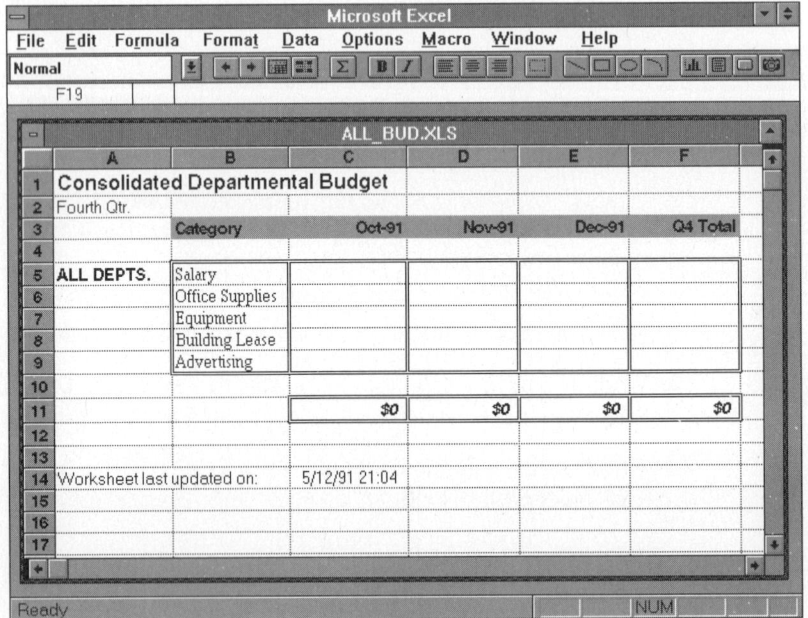

Performing the Consolidation

Tip. Since Excel can read and write most Lotus 1-2-3 file formats, you can also tell Excel to consolidate data from 1-2-3 worksheets. The syntax is the same—just remember to use the full name of the Lotus file (the file name and the .WK1 or .WK3 extension) when you perform the consolidation. See Chapter 15 for more information on using Lotus 1-2-3 files.

Now that you have created the master worksheet (ALL_BUD.XLS, in this case), you are ready to perform a consolidation. Note that the worksheets you want to consolidate do not have to be open in order for Excel to perform the consolidation correctly (although consolidation will also work fine if the worksheets are open). In this case, you won't open the other three worksheets. Try the consolidation now:

1. Highlight the range C5:F9. This is called the *destination range* and refers to the range that will receive the consolidated data.
2. Click on Data, Consolidate. The dialog box that appears is shown in Figure 11.7.
3. Verify that the function selected is SUM. This is the default selection; Excel will highlight it unless you explicitly change the function.
4. Next, type in the references to the worksheets you want to consolidate. In the Reference field, type **BUDGET*.XLS!C5:F9** and then click on the Add button (more on this syntax in a moment). If you want to add other references to other worksheets you could do so at this point.

5. Click on OK to perform the consolidation. Excel immediately goes to the worksheets you've defined as having the data you need for this consolidation and then performs the requested operation (a SUM() in this case, but you could have chosen AVERAGE(), STDEV(), and so on) and then places the results in the specified destination range. When you finish, your worksheet should look like Figure 11.8. (You might have to widen some columns on your worksheet.)

Figure 11.7
Data Consolidate dialog box

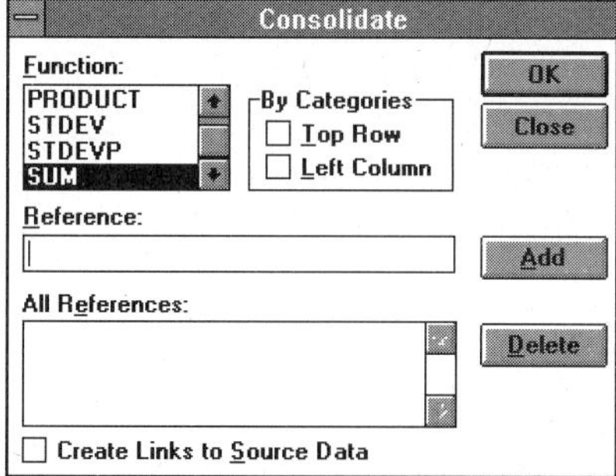

Figure 11.8
Worksheet after a data consolidation by location

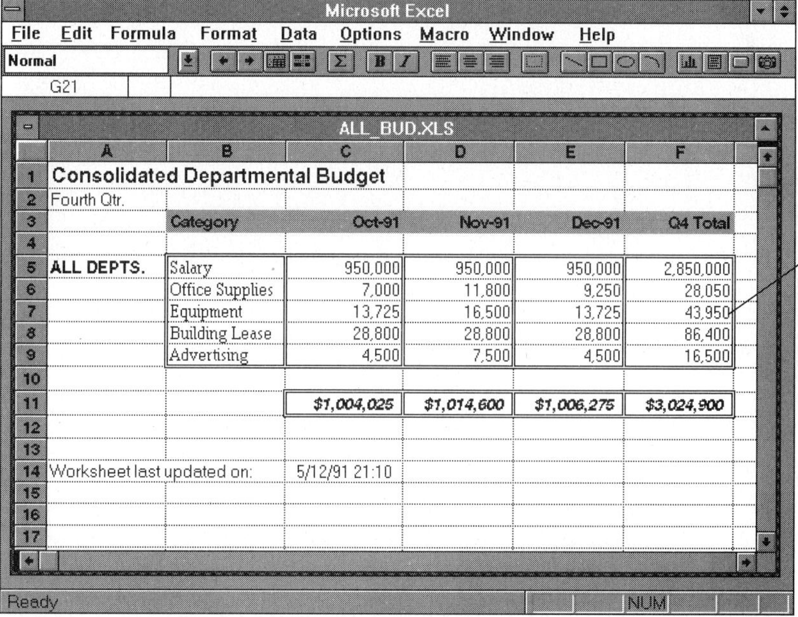

Consolidation Syntax

In the preceding example, you had to enter the source reference by typing a particular syntax that tells Excel where to find the data you want to consolidate. Here is the source reference you used:

```
BUDGET*.XLS!C5:F9
```

The first part of this reference (BUDGET*.XLS) stands for the names of the worksheets that you want to consolidate. Whenever the data is on separate worksheets, you must enter the name of the sheets here. Note that you can enter either the name of a single sheet, or, as you have done here, enter a reference to a group of worksheets.

Note the * character immediately following the BUDGET file name. The asterisk character is called a *wildcard* and is a character that can take the place of any number of others. Thus, in the current example, the file name BUDGET*.XLS will match on the names BUDGET1.XLS, BUDGET2.XLS, and BUDGET3.XLS, which is what you wanted to accomplish. Note, however, that if you had another file that was called BUDGET91.XLS, the wildcard character would have matched on it (another potential logical error).

Another wildcard character is the ? character. Unlike the asterisk, which matches any number of characters, the question mark matches only one character. So you could have written the above file reference as BUDGET?.XLS because you only wanted files in which one character changes (BUDGET1, BUDGET2, and so on).

Wildcard characters can be used in the file name extension as well—even when they're also used in the file name. For example, you could have a source reference like this:

```
BUDGET?.W*
```

This file reference would match on BUDGET1.WK1, BUDGET3.WKS, and BUDGET8.WK3, but it would not match on BUDGET12.XLS.

The preceding are examples of how you can refer to multiple sheets with similar names using a single reference (called a *source* in the Excel documentation). However, you can use up to 256 different consolidation references. If your consolidation needs to get data from BUDGET1.XLS, SALESCST-.WK1, and FOREIGN.XLS, you would add three different source references to the formula you build in the Data Consolidate dialog box (Figure 11.7). As you add source references, they appear in the All References box of the Data Consolidate dialog box.

Also note the exclamation point (!) character in the examples. Its purpose is simply to separate file and sheet names from range names. In the preceding example, the file name is BUDGET*.XLS and the range reference is C5:F9. Excel always uses the ! symbol when you construct range references that refer to other sheets. So, to refer to a range on another worksheet, you just give the sheet name, an exclamation point, and the reference. For example, the named range called TOT_SALES on a worksheet called YTD_91 would be referenced from the current sheet by typing YTD_91!TOT_SALES. This is called a *remote reference* and its syntax is quite common in consolidation and linking formulas.

The second part of the source reference (!C5:F9 in the example) can also be quite flexible. First, you may use relative or absolute cell addressing (see Chapter 4 for more information) as you define where the data will be coming from.

Alternatively, you can use named ranges to define the source range. In fact, this is always a good idea since it eliminates yet another chance for logical errors to occur.

So far, you have only performed a consolidation by location. But in practice, doing a consolidation by category is almost identical to consolidation by location. You might want to refer back to the example of the Denver and Chicago factory (Figures 11.3 and 11.4) while you learn about the differences.

In a consolidation by category, when you define the source ranges in the Data Consolidate dialog box (Figure 11.7), you must include the row and column names in the range. In the case of the Chicago and Denver example, the source range for each worksheet was C3:C4.

In addition, you must turn on either the Top Row or Left Column check box if the data you want to consolidate is located in different places on the worksheets. For example, if in the Denver and Chicago worksheets (Figure 11.3) the corresponding columns had been in different locations on the worksheets, Excel would still have consolidated the data correctly, provided that Top Row was selected.

However, since it was the data in the rows that differed, you must turn on the Left Column option so that Excel will correctly consolidate the differing product mix at the two plants. Note that even though both supporting worksheets had only three rows of data, the consolidation created a range with four rows because there were really four products manufactured between the facilities, not just three.

The Top Row and Left Column choices demand some explanation. You choose one or the other (or both) depending on how you want Excel to consolidate the worksheets. For example, if you have a set of worksheets you want to consolidate that have expenses for the month of November at the top of the sheet, but in each sheet the data might be in column A, B, or C, you would want to use the Top Row option. That way, the master worksheet will consolidate the data correctly based on the category of the data (its column heading of "November") rather than its relative position on each worksheet.

Conversely, suppose you have several worksheets that have data organized in rows, much like the Denver and Chicago example. In that case, the category titles were in the left column of the source range. Excel correctly consolidated that data because you selected the Left Column option in the Data Consolidate dialog box. Excel recognized that data in both worksheets that had the category titles Pens and Pencils should be summed. But it also recognized that you wanted to keep Rulers (from Denver) and Notepads (from Chicago) as separate items.

If you only select one of the two checkboxes, Excel will do a consolidation by category for the option that you have enabled and will do a consolidation by position on the other one. In the Chicago and Denver example, it was only important to have the Left Column option enabled since the columnar data was in the same place (column C) on both worksheets.

Worksheet Data Links

Linking and data consolidation are conceptually similar, but they have several differences in implementation that you should be aware of. Linking gives you a great deal of flexibility as you begin to work with models that include data stored in more than one worksheet.

What Is Linking?

Linking is the method by which you create dynamic links between different parts of a worksheet, cells in different worksheets, or even to locations in other applications. These dynamic links are sometimes referred to as "hot links" because every time the data changes in one worksheet, the data will change in the other worksheet as well.

In fact, you have already seen linking at work, even if you didn't recognize it. Back in Chapters 7 and 8, you created charts that would change automatically if the data they were based on changed. This was simply a case of Excel automatically creating a link from the cells of the worksheet to the chart. When the supporting data changed, so did the chart value.

Linking Options

One of the principal differences between linking and consolidation is the wide variety of situations in which you can use links to other worksheets. Here are some of the ways you can use linking:

Consolidation of Data Consolidating data by linking looks very much like data consolidation and is also conceptually similar. One benefit of breaking up data onto several worksheets—aside from making your model easier to understand—is that other users can access the supporting worksheets and make any necessary changes before you perform a consolidation or update a link.

Accessing Data from Other Programs Linking is the process you use to access data in other Windows applications. Microsoft Windows supports a data transfer *protocol* (set of rules) called *Dynamic Data Exchange* (DDE). Through DDE, Excel can communicate with other Windows-based applications, such as Word for Windows, and transfer data back and forth. More importantly, the link can be dynamic—if you change some data in Excel, your Word for Windows document will reflect the changes. You'll learn more about DDE and basic application integration later, in Chapter 16.

Compartmentalizing and Streamlining Your Data Dividing your data among smaller worksheets makes more efficient use of your computer's resources. Smaller worksheets load and save faster and can recalculate much more rapidly.

Creating Links

Excel gives you two ways to create links between worksheets. As with consolidation, you can simply type the linking syntax into the cell where you want the link to be, or you can point to the data you want to link and Excel will build the syntax for you automatically.

Copy/Paste Link Method

Using the Copy and Paste features is probably the easiest way to link cells since Excel builds all the links for you automatically. Before you proceed, you'll need to prepare the ALL_BUD.XLS worksheet so that you can come back to it later. First, make sure it looks like Figure 11.8. Then save the worksheet file.

Next, delete the line on the worksheet that shows the last time and date that the worksheet was updated: Highlight row 14 and click on Edit, Delete. Now, follow these steps to create some links from one worksheet to another:

1. Open up the BUDGET3.XLS worksheet. This worksheet is called the *supporting worksheet* in this case because it is the one that has the information you want. The ALL_BUD.XLS worksheet is the *dependent spreadsheet* since it is the one that receives the data. Under most circumstances, the linking formula is in the dependent worksheet.

2. Click on Window, Arrange All so that both worksheets appear side by side on your monitor. Depending on the size of your monitor and how you have Windows configured, your screen will look more or less like Figure 11.9.

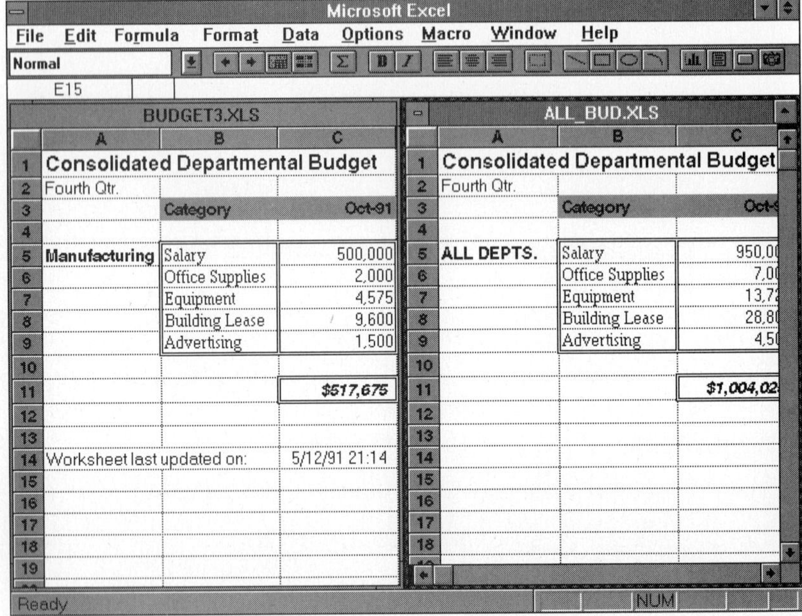

Figure 11.9
ALL_BUD and BUDGET3 worksheets

3. Make sure BUDGET3 is active. If it isn't, click anywhere within its window. Remember that BUDGET3 is the supporting worksheet.

4. Choose the cell you want to link to. In this case, highlight C5. (Remember Excel's very important location-action principle—you first select the object or range that you want to work with, *then* you select the action you want to perform.)

5. Click on Edit, Copy. This copies the contents of the cell onto the clipboard. Also notice the marquee that appears in the supporting worksheet to remind you what range you have selected for the link.

6. Activate the dependent worksheet, ALL_BUD.XLS, by clicking anywhere within its window.

7. Select the cell that you want to hold the link. Highlight cell A12.

8. Click on Edit, Paste Link. Watch as Excel immediately builds the link and displays the data. You can verify that the link is active by activating BUDGET3 again and changing the number in cell C5. Then watch the number change in the ALL_BUD worksheet as well.

Linking a Range of Cells

It's also easy to create links to an entire range in the supporting worksheet. The following steps create a link to a range of cells in BUDGET3.

1. Activate BUDGET3 as the supporting worksheet.
2. Highlight the range of cells that you want to link to. For this exercise, highlight the range C5:C9.
3. Click on Edit, Copy to copy the contents of that range to the Windows clipboard.
4. Activate the dependent worksheet, ALL_BUD.XLS.
5. Highlight the cell that will be the upper-left corner of the range you plan to link to. In this case, highlight cell A12—you will paste the range over the link you created in the last exercise.
6. Click on Edit, Paste Link. After Excel creates the link, your worksheets should look similar to Figure 11.10.

Figure 11.10 Worksheets after linking to a range of cells

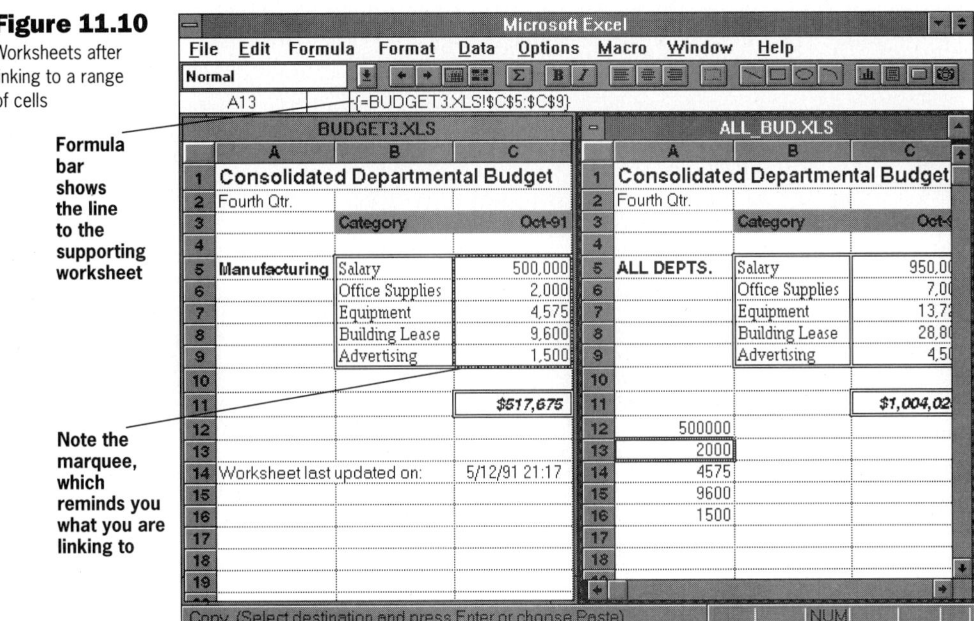

If you move the cell pointer to one of the cells on the dependent worksheet, the formula bar shows the links Excel automatically set up for you

when you told it to make the link. Note how the syntax looks very similar to what you used when selecting sources of data for subsequent consolidation.

Creating a Link with Formulas

Up to now, the links you have created only duplicate, cell by cell, ranges that exist in other spreadsheets. In many cases, however, you won't want to see detailed pieces of data, but instead you need the results of a calculation based on information in other spreadsheets. In other words, there are times when you would rather just see the results, not the method of calculation.

Using the two worksheets you have been working with, follow the steps below to perform a few calculations on data stored in another worksheet. This exercise will also show you how to enter a link from the keyboard rather than with the Copy/Paste Link procedure. Remember, too, that the supporting worksheets do not have to be open and in memory—you can also link to worksheets that are currently stored on your hard disk.

1. Make sure that both the supporting worksheet (BUDGET3.XLS) and the dependent worksheet (ALL_BUD.XLS) are open and arranged side by side on your screen. Refer to Figure 11.10 if you need to get back in sync.
2. Activate the dependent worksheet by clicking anywhere within its window. (Remember that most links originate with the dependent worksheet.)
3. Erase the range A12:A16: Highlight the range, click on Edit, Clear, then click on OK. (This is the link you created earlier.)
4. Position the cell pointer in cell A12.
5. Enter the following formula into cell A12 as you would any other formula or number:

```
=SUM(BUDGET3.XLS!$C$5:$C$9)
```

When you complete the formula (by pressing the Enter key or by clicking on the check box), Excel creates the link to the supporting worksheet and then performs the requested calculation.

6. Move the mouse pointer down one cell, to cell A13, and enter the same formula as before but substitute the AVERAGE() function this time:

```
=AVERAGE(BUDGET3.XLS!$C$5:$C$9)
```

When you finish entering this formula, your worksheet should look like the one in Figure 11.11.

You might have noticed that the formulas you typed in used absolute references. Why? If you had used relative references and had subsequently copied the formula to another place on the dependent worksheet, Excel would

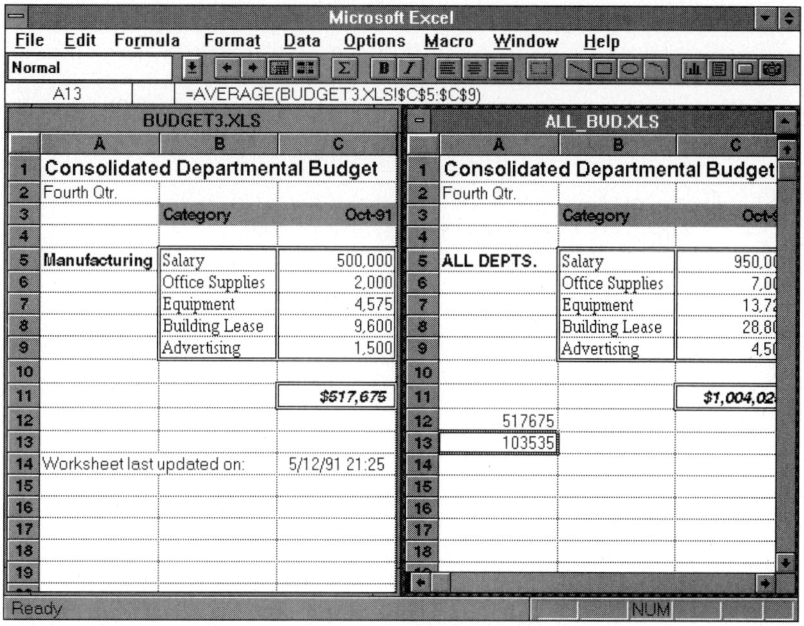

Figure 11.11 Worksheets after creating two links

have tried to adjust the range references according to its rules. In this case, it's pretty clear that you want the formula to always return the value of the sum (or average) of the range C5:C9.

Creating a Link with Named Ranges

The safest way to create links is to use named ranges for your linking formulas. In this last exercise you will see how easy it is to use named ranges in a linking formula.

Just as in most other cases, a named range can take the place of a regular range reference. Way back in Chapter 3 you assigned a series of range names to the original BUDGET worksheet. When you copied and modified that file in Chapter 10 to create two new files, the defined range names stuck. Thus, the BUDGET3.XLS worksheet has a named range called Q4_Totals that was defined as the range F5:F9. (If you want to verify this, activate BUDGET3 and click on Formula, Define Name.)

Now, simply go to cells A12 and A13 of ALL_BUD and either reenter the formulas or edit them to use the named range Q4_Totals instead of the range C5:C9. When you finish, they should look like this:

```
=SUM(BUDGET3.XLS!Q4_Totals)

=AVERAGE(BUDGET3.XLS!Q4_Totals)
```

Avoiding Problems with Linking

Linking between worksheets is one of those areas ripe for logical errors. Linking is a useful tool that you might appreciate, but at the same time, it's possible to get into some trouble with models that rely on the concept of linking. The following is a discussion of some of the potential problems and how to avoid them when working with linking.

Saving Worksheets with Links

One potential area for conflict is the case in which you have a worksheet with a link to a worksheet with data that isn't current. In general, you should always save and close the supporting worksheets before you save and close the dependent worksheet. This ensures that the names of the supporting worksheets are current and correct in the dependent worksheet.

Although you can rename a supporting document, you must have the dependent document open in order for the link to be updated so that it refers to the new name of the supporting document.

Linked Worksheets in Different Directories

Excel uses a rigid, formulaic method to track the location of worksheets if your supporting and dependent worksheets aren't all stored in the same directory. The easiest way to ensure that worksheet links are maintained correctly is to simply keep all the worksheets in the same subdirectory.

In all cases, however, if Excel cannot find a link to a worksheet—perhaps because you moved or deleted the worksheet—the program will display a dialog box to alert you to a potential problem. Then you can track down the problem or locate the errant worksheet and put it back where it belongs.

Logical Errors

Once again, the possibility exists for logical errors to occur in your worksheet if you use data consolidation or linking. With the ability to link to files on disk and not even see where you're going, so to speak, it's easy to link to the wrong place.

Fortunately, this particular problem has a straightforward solution: You should always try to use named ranges when you perform linking. And if you are careful with your range names when creating the supporting worksheet, your dependent worksheet will be far more accurate.

Linking to Other Applications

As previously noted, Excel is one of literally hundreds of Windows applications that support thc DDE protocol, which governs how Excel can interchange data with these other applications. This final section is meant as an introduction to Dynamic Data Exchange, in the context of linking from one application to another. DDE will be covered in more detail in Chapter 16.

Because it holds the potential for letting virtually any Windows application talk to any other, DDE is a very powerful and flexible technology. It might even come to change the way we all work with applications. (That's a ways off, however.) Today, DDE is still limited to programmers and those who understand its often-cryptic syntax. However, there are still ways for you to take advantage of a DDE link between applications.

In this scenario, you are composing a document in Word for Windows, a Microsoft word processor also designed for the Windows environment. You want to create a twice-monthly report document that includes a consolidated view of the Chicago and Denver office supply factories you saw earlier in the chapter. Since the data can change frequently, and is kept up to date in an Excel worksheet, you don't want to have to type the numbers in by hand each time you prepare the report.

Figure 11.12 shows both the worksheet that contains the figures you need, as well as the Word for Windows document that is ready to go except for the figures in the worksheet. The following steps will create links between the two applications.

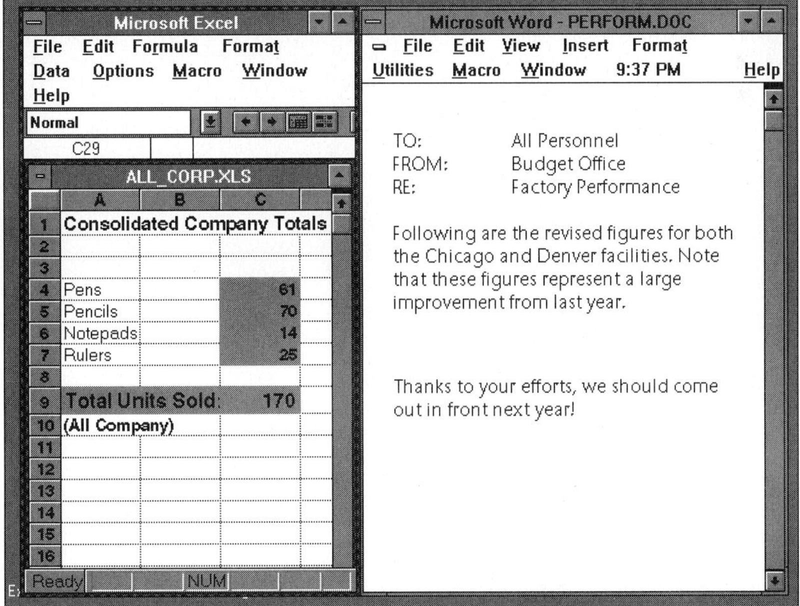

Figure 11.12
Excel worksheet and Word for Windows document

1. Activate Excel by clicking anywhere within its window.
2. Highlight the range you want to have linked to Word for Windows. The concept of support and dependency still holds here. Word for Windows will be the dependent document in this link. For this exercise, the range you want to link to is A4:C7.
3. Click on Edit, Copy to copy the contents of the range into the Windows clipboard.
4. Activate Word for Windows by clicking anywhere within its window.
5. Position the text cursor where you want the linked cells from Excel to appear.
6. In the Word for Windows menu bar, click on Edit, Paste Link. Word for Windows displays a dialog box asking if you want the link to automatically update each time the figures change in Excel. Leave the check box empty and click on OK to complete the command. Word for Windows will establish a link via DDE and then display the cells. The result looks more or less like Figure 11.13.

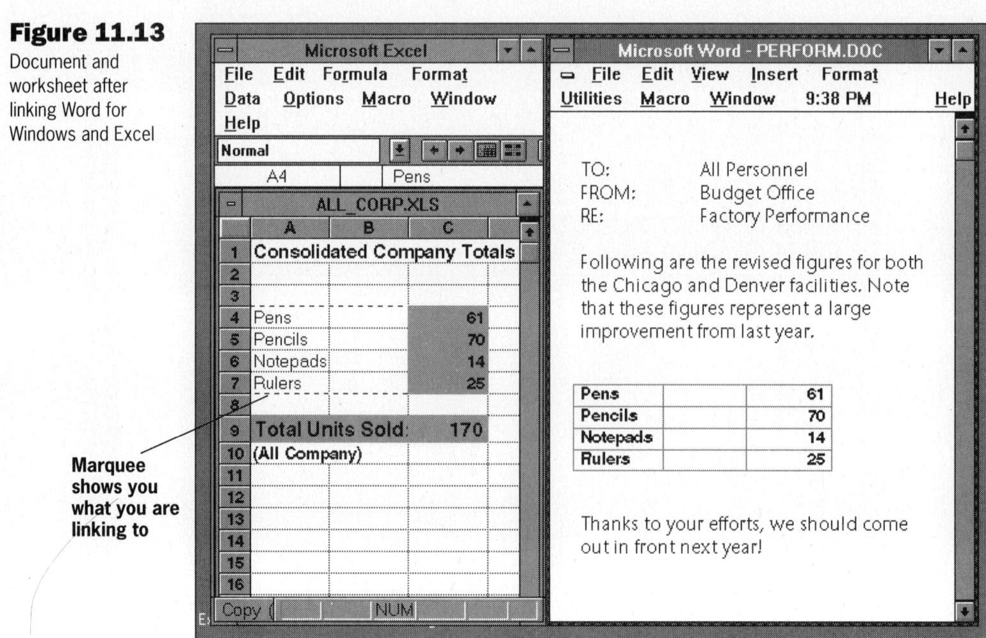

Figure 11.13 Document and worksheet after linking Word for Windows and Excel

Depending on how you have configured your Word for Windows program, you might see something other than a grid of cells with values in them. If you see something that looks like a line of codes beginning with the word "DDEAuto", then follow these steps:

1. In the Word for Windows menu (not Excel), click on View.
2. Look for the last option, View Field Codes. Click once on that option. Your linked spreadsheet should now appear instead of the DDE code that describes the link to Word for Windows.

There is more to the concepts of DDE and data transfer and integration between applications—much more than can be covered in a chapter or even in a single book. Nevertheless, you have seen a little bit of the potential for data integration between Windows applications.

Close the BUDGET3.XLS and the ALL_BUD.XLS files now. Since you made some changes to the BUDGET3 file that you don't want to keep, answer No when you are prompted to save the file contents.

CHAPTER

12

Worksheet Analysis Tools

UP TO THIS POINT, THE WORKSHEET MODELS YOU HAVE CREATED HAVE been relatively small compared to the size some models can grow to be. In addition to data consolidation and linking, which was discussed in Chapter 11, Excel provides several features that can help as you begin to create larger models. These tools and techniques control the way your models are calculated, and in so doing can save you a lot of time.

In addition to tools that help your models perform more efficiently, Microsoft has endowed Excel with the ability to calculate certain types of problems that had been heretofore either very difficult or impossible to solve with a PC-based spreadsheet program.You can now use Excel 3.0 to solve so-called linear algebra problems. This is the kind of problem in which you have a set of variables that can change in any number of combinations and permutations. How do you mix the variables so that another variable is either maximized or minimized? You'll learn later just how practical such a tool can be, even if you've never considered this type of calculation before.

Controlling Calculations

By default, every time you change a number in Excel, all values in the worksheet are recalculated so that they remain accurate. You can verify that this recalculation occurs by opening up any of the worksheets you've created during the course of this book. Move the cell pointer to any number that is part of a calculation and then change that number. Watch as Excel recalculates and redisplays the result of the calculation almost immediately.

Excel's method of recalculation is meant to minimize the time you spend waiting for the worksheet to recalculate. In fact, Excel knows how to tell if a particular formula needs to be recalculated and will ignore it if it doesn't. This way, Excel only calculates those cells whose values have changed. This is called *selective recalculation.*

You can enter commands and make changes to the worksheet while it is calculating, but you have to wait for the worksheet to finishing calculating before you can rely on the numbers in the worksheet.

Switching to Manual Calculation

There are benefits to switching from Excel's automatic recalculation to *manual recalculation*. Because the worksheet is not automatically recalculated when calculation is set to manual, you can make a lot of changes and not have to wait for the worksheet to recalculate and the charts to redraw. When you have completed the editing process, you can then recalculate the values. Of course, when you change the worksheet to manual calculation, you must manually give the command to recalculate the worksheet.

Here's how to change the worksheet from automatic to manual calculation:

1. Open a new worksheet. Click on File, New and choose Worksheet.
2. Click on Options, Calculation. The dialog box that appears looks like the one in Figure 12.1.
3. Click on Manual.
4. Click on OK to complete the command.

Figure 12.1
Options Calculation dialog box

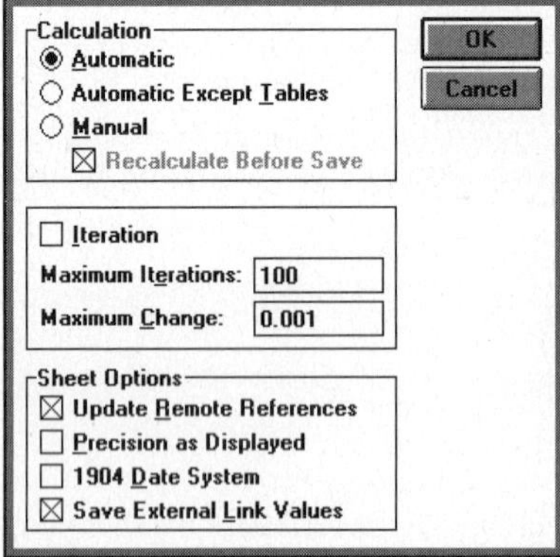

Using Manual Calculation

Now that you've set the calculation to manual, you must tell Excel whenever you want to calculate the document. Excel gives you the option of calculating only the active worksheet or calculating all open worksheets. You don't have anything to calculate yet, but when you do it's simple:

1. Activate the worksheet you want to calculate by clicking anywhere within that document.
2. Hold down the Shift key and then click on Options, Calculate Document. Note that this option only appears on the menu when you are holding down the Shift key as you click on the Options menu choice.

Tip. A shortcut for recalculating the active document is Shift-F9. To recalculate all open worksheets, press F9.

To calculate all the open worksheets, including open chart sheets, click on Options, Calculate Now.

How do you know when the worksheet needs to be calculated if you've turned off automatic recalculation? The status bar at the bottom of the Excel screen displays the word "Calculate" whenever some value has changed in the worksheet and you need to perform a calculation in order to bring everything up to date. Here's a simple demonstration:

1. Make sure the status bar appears at the bottom of your screen. If it doesn't, click on Options, Workspace and then click in the box labeled "Status Bar". Click on OK to complete the command.

2. In cell A1 enter the value **100**.

3. In cell A2 enter the value **100**.

4. Highlight cell A3. Then click twice on the Autosum tool. The resulting formula simply adds together the values in cells A1 and A2 and displays the results of the calculation: 200. Note that even though you have turned off automatic recalculation, Excel will always display the initial value of a formula, as it did here. If you go back and *change* the value in either A1 or A2, Excel will still display 200 until you manually recalculate the worksheet.

   Note that Excel also immediately displays the word "Calculate" in the status bar, like this:

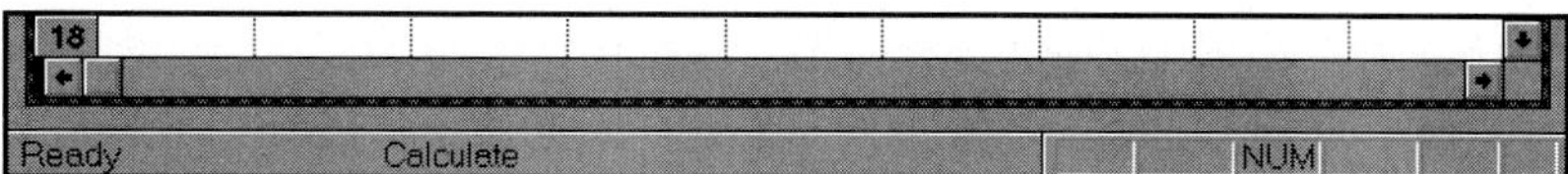

   This means you have entered a formula and that automatic calculation is turned off.

5. In cell A1, change the value from 100 to **200**. Notice that the value in cell A3 does not change—it still shows the answer to the previous calculation. Note also that Excel still displays the "Calculate" message, telling you that some value has changed somewhere on the worksheet and that you need to recalculate for the numbers to be correct.

6. Perform a recalculation now by either clicking on Options, Calculate Now or by pressing F9. As soon as you do, Excel immediately calculates the worksheet and removes the "Calculate" message from the status bar.

Saving Worksheets Without Calculating

With automatic calculation turned on (the default), every time Excel saves a file, it first performs a calculation to ensure that the values are up to date before you put the worksheet away. However, there may be times when you would rather just put away a large model and then come back to it later without recalculating. For example, if you have turned off automatic calculation, there may be a large number of cells that Excel wants to calculate before you save the worksheet, but you might want to save the file without calculating it, just to save time.

Use these steps to save the current worksheet without first calculating it:

1. Click on Options, Calculation.
2. Remove the check mark from the Recalculate Before Save check box.
3. Click on OK to complete the command.

Once you've turned off this option, you must manually calculate the worksheet before you save it if you want the values to be up to date before the file is saved to disk.

It's important to remember that even if you don't choose to recalculate before you save the worksheet, all the values you have entered or changed during your session will be saved correctly to disk. It's just that the formulas are not calculated, so the cells containing formulas will not necessarily display the correct values. In all cases, just choosing Options, Calculate Now or pressing the F9 key will force Excel to recalculate the worksheet and bring everything up to date.

Using Displayed Values

Earlier in this book, you learned that Excel actually stores numbers with up to 15 digits of precision. That is, Excel calculates numbers accurately to the 15th digit to the right of the decimal place. This level of accuracy is usually sufficient for all but the most demanding of mathematical models and worksheets. However, with certain types of models it's preferable to have Excel use less than this degree of precision.

Consequently, Excel provides a way for you to calculate the spreadsheet using the values as they are displayed. (This is different from changing a number's formatting to display fewer decimal places, since the formatting doesn't change the way Excel stores the number internally.) With Excel's Displayed Values option you can set up your worksheet to calculate results based on the displayed values instead of the actual stored values.

For example, say you wanted to keep your family's budget in an Excel worksheet. In this case, you probably don't need all of Excel's inherent accuracy. Consider this fragment of a worksheet:

	A	B
1	14.006	14.01
2	15.007	15.01
3		
4	29.013	29.01
5		
6		
7		

In both columns you are adding the same two numbers together: 14.006 and 15.007. Column A shows the numbers as you entered them. Column B has the exact same numbers, but they are formatted to two decimal places (as you would do if you were working with money). The result in column B—14.01 + 15.01 = 29.01—doesn't look right. In this case, the problem is just an anomaly caused by rounding. (You might, however, rightly suspect a problem with your logic. This is exactly the kind of result that should make you want to investigate further. It might not be quite so benign in other cases.

Turning on the Precision as Displayed option causes Excel to calculate the numbers based on the way they are formatted. In essence, you've told Excel to change the values stored internally to those values currently being displayed. And, in fact, that's exactly what Excel does. As soon as you turn on Precision as Displayed, Excel changes the numbers to the displayed values.

For example, if a number on your worksheet is stored internally as 14.24634 and you have formatted that number to two decimal places, it would be displayed as 14.25 (remember the rounding effect). If you then turn on Precision as Displayed, that number would actually be changed to 14.25, and it would retain that value forever more.

CAUTION! *Changing the precision is a one-way street: You cannot convert a number back to the way it was before. So be careful—it can have destructive consequences for your worksheet model.*

Use the following steps to change the precision status.

1. Click on Options, Calculation, and the dialog box shown in Figure 12.1 appears.
2. Turn on the Precision as Displayed check box.
3. Click on OK to complete the command. Excel will issue a warning like that shown in Figure 12.2.
4. Click on OK to acknowledge the warning.

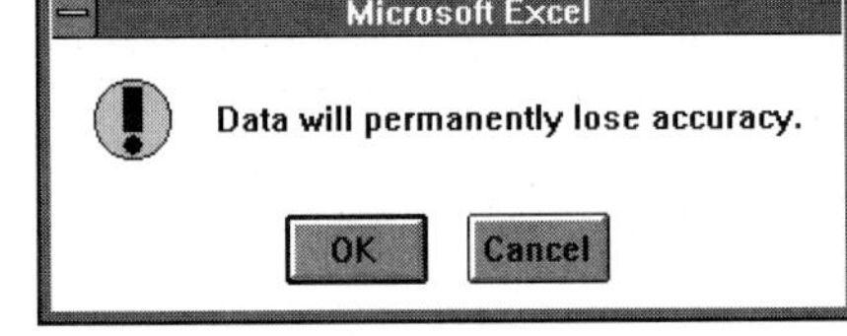

Figure 12.2 Dialog box warning that you are about to affect the contents of the worksheet

Circular References and Iterative Solutions

So far you have only dealt with worksheet formulas that do not refer back to themselves; that is, your formulas have always been the kind in which, for example, the solution in cell A3 simply adds the contents of A1 and A2. However, there are cases where you might want the formula to refer back to itself as part of the solution to the problem. Here's an example:

	A	B
1	Profit	$5,000.00
2	Net	$4,166.67
3	Employee Bonus	$833.33
4		
5		

In this example, you are trying to solve for the employee bonus amount, which is based on net profit, but the net profit is determined by the amount of the bonus. (The company's overall profit is $5,000.) Clearly, the formulas here would have to refer to each other. This is called a *circular reference* and requires a different kind of calculation, called *iteration*, to reach the appropriate solution.

Solving this problem requires that Excel perform the calculation a certain number of times, each time using the solution to the previous iteration as a basis for the correct answer. You can control the number of times Excel performs the calculation by modifying the Options Calculation dialog box (Figure 12.1).

Follow these steps if you need to perform iterative calculations:

1. Click on Options, Calculation. The dialog box will appear.
2. Turn on the check box marked "Iteration".
3. In the Maximum Iterations box, specify the maximum number of iterations that you want Excel to perform. For most worksheet models, the default of 100 is an appropriate number.
4. In the Maximum Change box, type the maximum amount that you want the result to vary each time. If you specify a smaller number than the default, Excel will take longer to calculate the result but will also return a more accurate result. Again, the defaults are usually fine.
5. Click on OK to complete the command.

Excel will display a warning dialog box when you enter a circular reference that it cannot solve. Figure 12.3 shows what the message looks like when you try to resolve a circular reference without turning on iteration.

Figure 12.3
Message identifying circular references

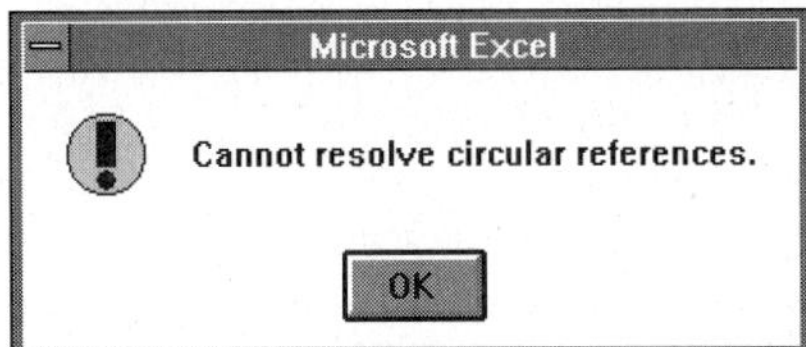

In addition to the message stating that there are circular references in the worksheet, Excel will also display a message on the status bar that notes the circular reference and identifies the cell that contains the reference, as shown here:

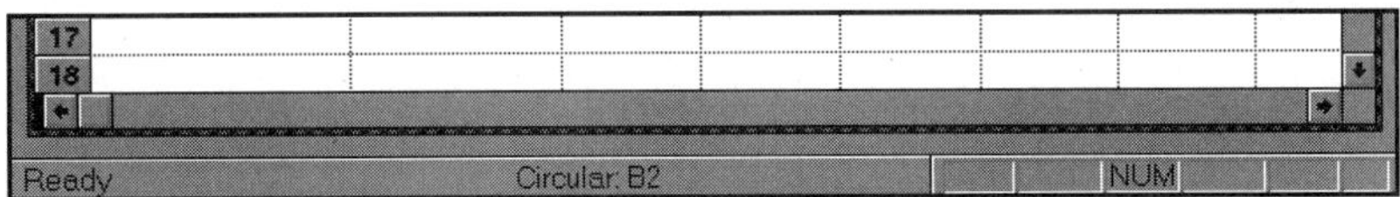

Two Kinds of Solver Tools

Spreadsheet products have always been excellent tools for playing "what-if" games: "What if I adjusted the value by 2 percent?" "What if I was able to cut costs just a little more in this department?" With a worksheet model, you can try some figures, and then try some others, to see how different numbers affect the rest of your model. And because the worksheet provides such rapid recalculations, it's very easy to try something and see if it works.

As a second-generation worksheet product, Excel offers two tools that let you more easily perform variations on the "what-if" scenario. Excel contains two *goal-seeking tools* that help you identify correct values in order to achieve a preset result: "What would have to happen to accomplish X?" Although these tools are easy to use, they are also easy to misunderstand, which could lead to certain types of logical errors.

Goal Seeking

Once you've set up the calculations in a model and have stated all the relationships in the form of formulas, Excel's Goal Seek feature can quickly solve for a single variable—saving you the trouble of constructing a complex formula. Here's an example: Say you have a salesperson in your office who is currently making $48,000 per year in base salary and earning 9 percent commission on total annual sales. Her combined income for this year, then, is simply the sum of the base salary plus 9 percent of sales—in this case a total earnings of $69,420.

Consider the model shown in Figure 12.4. The goal of this exercise is to increase this salesperson's percentage of commission by whatever amount it would take to make her income $75,000.

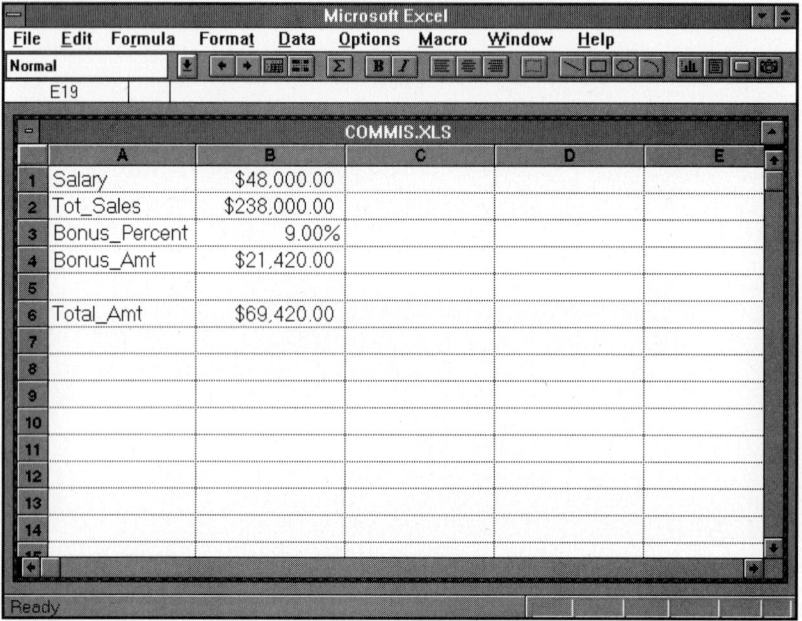

Figure 12.4 Salesperson commission model

Using Goal Seek, you simply fill in two fields and then let Excel calculate the variable (percentage, in this case) and report when it has an answer. Use these steps to try the Goal Seek feature:

1. Erase the contents of cells A1:A3.
2. Create a model that looks exactly like the one shown in Figure 12.4. Cells B1, B2, and B3 are constants—just enter the values you see. Cell B4 is cell B2 multiplied by cell B3. Finally, cell B5 is the sum of B1 and B4. If you like, you can format cells B1, B2, B4, and B6 to some kind of numeric format and cell B3 to a percentage format.
3. Highlight cell B6. This is the formula whose result you want to change by manipulating some other cell.

4. Click on Formula, Goal Seek. The dialog box that appears looks like this:

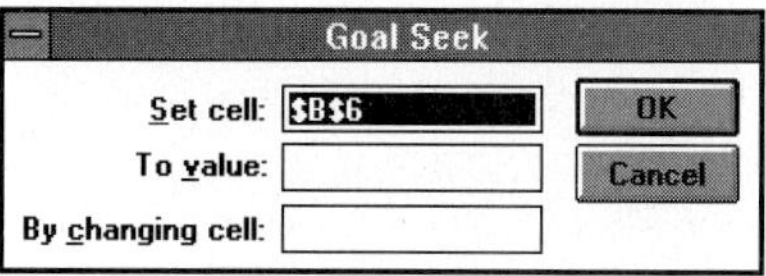

(You might have to move the box around a bit so that you can see all of your model beneath it.) Note that Excel has already entered cell B6 in the dialog box. This is simply a nice gesture on the part of Excel; you could still enter another cell if you preferred.

5. Set the new value that you want cell B6 to have. In this case, you want to increase the total salary to $75,000, so enter this amount in the field labeled "To value:".

6. Finally, tell Excel what cell it should vary as it solves for the number that will yield $75,000 in cell B6. For this example, type **B3** into the field. Before you click on OK to carry out the command, the Formula Goal Seek dialog box should look like this:

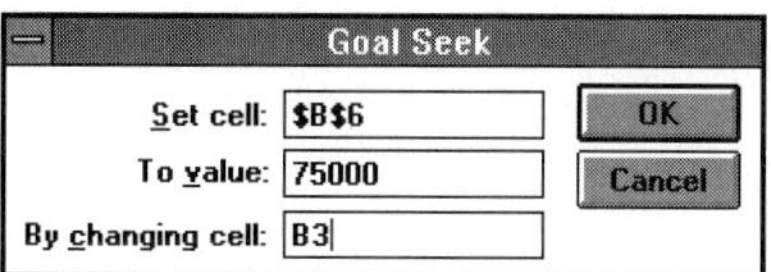

7. Now just click on OK to perform the calculation. When Excel is finished solving your problem, the screen should look like the one in Figure 12.5.

Note that when Excel found the solution, it displayed a dialog box and presented the solution. In addition, note that the values on the spreadsheet have been altered, perhaps on the assumption that you would want the numbers altered. If you click on OK, the changes to the worksheet are permanent, but if you click on Cancel, the original worksheet will be restored.

Excel Solver

Excel offers a more complicated version of Goal Seek for more complex models, called the Excel Solver. Although the Solver is relatively easy to use, setting up the models may not be that simple. Setting up a model is the worksheet equivalent of solving the word problems in your high-school math

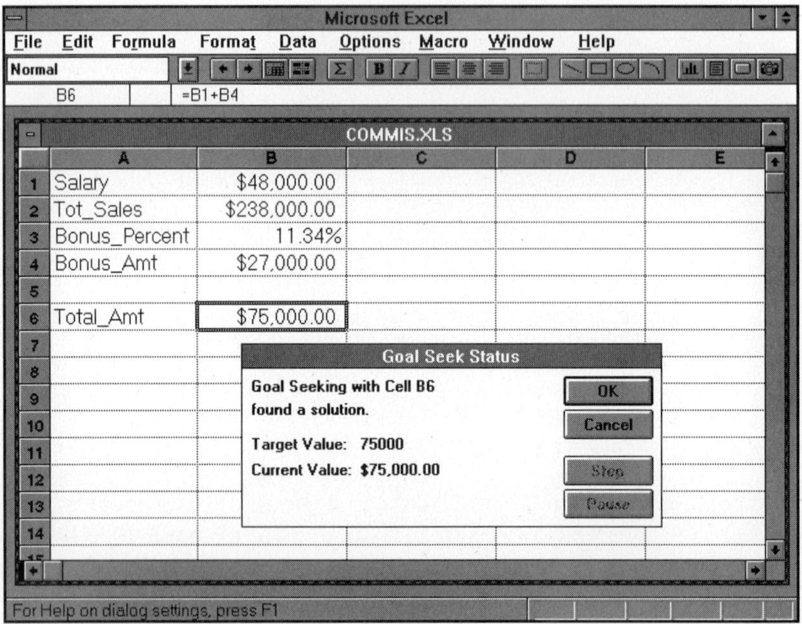

Figure 12.5
Results of a Formula Goal Seek calculation

class. It takes a lot of practice to be able to set up your models to work correctly and return accurate results.

Instructions in the use of the Solver are beyond the scope of this book, but you should know what it's capable of and simply know it's there in case you want to explore further in the Excel documentation.

The Microsoft Excel Solver is based on sound, well-tested mathematical concepts called linear algebra. These techniques let you construct models that will solve for a number of variables in order to maximize or minimize another variable.

Say you are the plant manager of a factory that produces a variety of furniture pieces from a common inventory of parts. You always know exactly how many parts are in your inventory and you want to produce the number of products that will maximize your profit. You also know how much you can sell a table for, as compared to a chair, but how many tables and chairs must you make in order to make the most money in the end? The answer isn't always to make as many as you can of the more expensive product. That particular product mix doesn't leave any parts left over for the less expensive product, the construction of which may well increase profit when constructed in the right proportion.

The way to solve this in Excel is to first create your worksheet models as you always have. You then identify three key pieces of information that Excel will need to proceed with the solution:

- First you must set the *adjustable cells*. These are the cells that Excel will adjust until the appropriate solution is found. In the furniture product-mix example, the adjustable cells are the final quantities of tables and chairs. Excel will vary these cells in many different combinations until the best mix is found for your goal—maximizing profit.
- Next, identify the *constraint cells*, those cells that establish the boundaries of a model. In the furniture example, the constraint cells are those that place constraints on the solution, such as the actual inventory levels and pieces required to construct a unit. After all, you can't create a chair with only two legs.
- Then you can optionally select a cell whose value you want to be maximized, minimized, or even set to a certain value.

After you have identified these important ranges, Excel will calculate the worksheet iteratively. Because of the mathematics involved, Excel knows that it is getting close to a solution and when it must adjust the appropriate cells to get even closer to its final results.

In some ways, the Solver box looks like the Goal Seek dialog box that you saw earlier. It's a bit more complicated, but it's also fairly self-explanatory. Take a look at Figure 12.6 to see what the Solver dialog box looks like and how straightforward the Solver is.

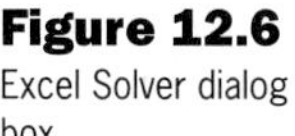

Figure 12.6
Excel Solver dialog box

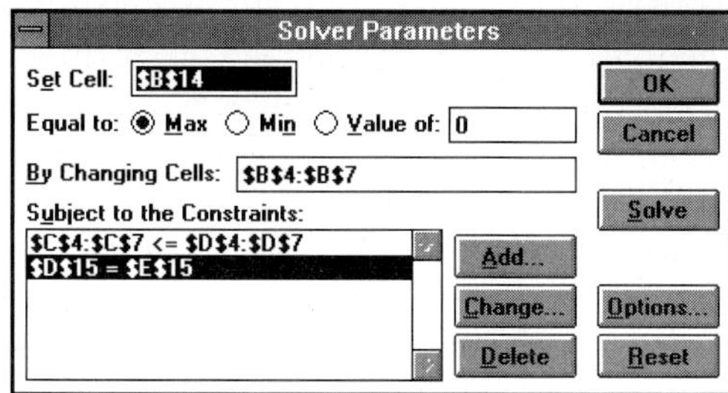

Some Examples Using the Solver

There is a seemingly endless list of things you can use the Solver for—if you are able to construct a model to do it. Here are just a few examples of its usage:

Product Mix You've already seen an example in which you might want to determine the appropriate numbers of products to create in order to maximize profits, minimize shop-floor downtime, or minimize inventory if storage costs are expensive for you.

Note that the concept of product mix does not have to refer only to physical products. You can use this feature to determine the best variety of investment vehicles to have in order to maximize your return on an investment. In this case, your constraint cells might be your personal risk assessment: "I don't want to incur a liability of more than X dollars," or "I don't want the interest rate to drop below X percent."

Route and Personnel Scheduling The Solver is helpful for this type of category as well. Here, you might use the Solver to help you solve the problem of shipping any one of several products to any one of several locations throughout the country. To a large extent, these mathematical principles are used by airlines as they try to find the best mix of planes to fly along what routes in order to maximize profit, minimize downtime, minimize costs of fuel, and so on.

Another example of this is staff scheduling, where your goal is to make sure that all the shifts are covered, but that you do so with the least expense.

All in all, Excel offers a very powerful environment for the analysis and solution of problems that require not only brute force to solve, such as the best mix of products to maximize profit, but also those that require a bit of finesse and preparation. The time you spend preparing to work within the mathematical environment of Excel will be rewarded by intelligent solutions and the ability to model things that would have been difficult or impossible before.

CHAPTER

13

Programming Excel

Command Macro Basics

Creating Macros by Recording

Viewing the Macro Sheet

Building an Application—The Basics

Setting the Start-up Directory

Programming Macros on a Worksheet

"WAIT A MINUTE," YOU SAY, "I'M NOT A PROGRAMMER AND I don't want to be one!" "True enough," I say, "but you already have become one." How so? When you started out at the beginning of this book, Excel greeted you with a blank screen—a sheet waiting for you to instill some order and logic to it. Now, several chapters later, you've added text labels, numeric values, and even calculations. In short, you've programmed Excel to do what you want it to do.

So far, however, you've only worked with Excel in an *interactive* fashion: You have performed some action, waited for a result, and then performed another action, depending on the results of the first. But Excel can also perform a number of actions on your behalf without your intervention. It can, for example, be told that you want it to perform a series of actions you might normally do at the keyboard. This *programmatic* way of doing things is one of Excel's strongest features, and it can help you to work more quickly and efficiently.

Command Macro Basics

The programming you do in Excel is accomplished by means of *command macros*. These command macros are sequences of Excel commands that you record and can then play back to accomplish a set of actions. Command macros are especially useful when you want to automate a routine, but tedious, task: You just record the usual steps and then play it back when you want to perform the action. Once you have recorded a macro, you can play it back from a menu selection or by assigning a shortcut key to it.

However, recording command macros is only one way to program the Excel spreadsheet to perform repetitive or complicated tasks. You can also just type the macros in by hand. Once you have some experience in recording command macros, you can begin to directly program Excel by just opening a new macro sheet and typing the commands into it.

Perhaps the best compromise is to record the majority of your command macros and then know how to edit the resulting macro by hand to achieve the exact effect you are looking for. However, programming the Excel worksheet by hand and constructing entire applications by programming is well outside the scope of this book. Other books are available that cover the topic in depth.

Excel stores command macros on *macro sheets* just as it stores your models on regular worksheets. In fact, in all but a few details an Excel macro sheet is exactly the same as a regular worksheet. All the formatting, navigational, printing, and editing commands work the same way on a macro sheet as they do on a regular worksheet.

Excel uses a separate sheet (sometimes called a document) for your macro so that you can use the same command macro with any number of worksheets. That way, if you have automated some task for one worksheet, you are able to use that same recorded task with any other worksheet you open. For example, say you create a command macro that formats a cell in a particular way. Once you have created this macro and you have the macro sheet that contains it open, you can use that macro on any other worksheet you open.

Furthermore, the fact that Excel uses separate macro sheets for command macros means that you have a lot of flexibility about the way you group and store your macros. Since you can have multiple macro sheets open at any given time, you can use a single sheet that only contains a few of your macros, or you can open a set of sheets containing all your macros. The way you organize your macros is completely up to you.

What Can Macros Do?

Command macros can do virtually anything you can do at the keyboard, and more. In fact—depending on how much effort you want to expend—you can create an entire application and construct it in such a way that users will never know they are in Excel, so powerful is the language. The following sections list some of the things that you can do with Excel's macro language.

Getting Information into the Worksheet

You're already familiar with the way Excel uses dialog boxes to interact with the user. The Excel macro language has a complete set of instructions for creating and using *custom* dialog boxes. You can create dialog boxes both to get input from the user and as a way to warn users if something is wrong with the worksheet. These dialog boxes can be very simple, asking the user for a single value, for example, or they can be very complex with radio buttons, check boxes, and multiple input fields.

Not all input into a program, however, comes from the user typing at a dialog box. Sometimes an Excel application will need input from some other source such as another Excel worksheet or a disk file in a completely different format. Not only can you use the macro language to get input from the user, but you can also use it to work with files on disk. For example, you might have data stored in the dBASE database file format that you want to use as part of an analysis. Using command macros, you can create applications that write to and read from the dBASE-format disk files.

Branching and Looping Structures

One of the measures of the completeness of a programming language is its ability to alter its flow based on certain conditions. The availability of these programming structures means that you can perform *loops* (repetitions) and *branching* (conditional actions).

Although it's beyond the scope of this book, an example of this is a macro that loops a specified number of times or loops until a certain condition is met. In contrast, conditional branching enables you to create a macro that takes different paths through the program depending on the results of a calculation. An example of this is a programming construct that says "Jump to this part of the program if Day=Monday, but go to another section of the program if Day=Thursday."

Custom Menus

Finally, Excel's macros let you do some fancy customization of the standard Excel menus. For example, with the macro language, you can change the menu choices—eliminating some and adding others. This ability is helpful in those cases where you want certain users to have access to only some—not all—of the standard Excel menus.

In addition, by associating a new macro with the menu entry, you can change the function of the current menu commands. For example, suppose you wanted to offer additional functionality for the File, Open command. You would write new File, Open commands that add the functionality you want. Then you simply tell Excel to use the new definition rather than the older, default definition.

Creating Macros by Recording

There are two ways to create a command macro with Excel. The first, and by all measures the easiest, is to *record* the macro as you perform the steps manually. You can then play it back later. Excel's macro recorder is analogous to a tape recorder. When you tell Excel to begin recording a macro, it appears as if everything is recorded until you tell Excel either to stop or to pause briefly.

In fact, however, not everything is recorded. The *result* of the action is what Excel keeps track of, not necessarily the steps leading up to the event. So, for example, if you wanted Excel to record an action, Excel would record the final result of that action, not the mouse moves and clicks you made until you achieved the desired action.

Starting the Recorder

In the following exercise, you will record a command macro and then learn how to play it back. You'll also have the chance to see what the command macro looks like and get an explanation of what's happening when you run this macro.

Use these steps to create a simple command macro:

1. Make sure Excel is running and you have a blank worksheet on the screen. If you just started Excel, you will have a blank worksheet on the screen. Otherwise, click on File, New and select Worksheet. Then click on OK.

2. Position the cell pointer in cell B3 of the worksheet.

3. Click on Macro, Record. The following dialog box appears:

4. Enter a name for the macro you are about to record. In this case, type **Add_Now_Function.** Note the underscore characters. Since Excel won't let you enter a name that contains spaces, the underscore characters let you create a more readable name. If you don't name a macro, Excel will use a default name such as Record1, Record2, and so on.

5. Now use the Tab key to move to the next box and enter the key that you want to use as the shortcut key for this macro. This is what you will press in conjunction with the Ctrl key to run this macro. For now, just accept Excel's default of the lowercase "a."

Note. You have 52 choices of shortcut key: lowercase "a" through "z" and uppercase "A" through "Z." If you accept the default choice, Excel will begin with the lowercase "a" and work through the alphabet. When it reaches "z" it will start over with the uppercase alphabet.

6. Click on OK to complete the dialog box and start the macro recorder. Note how the status line changes to show that the recorder is running.

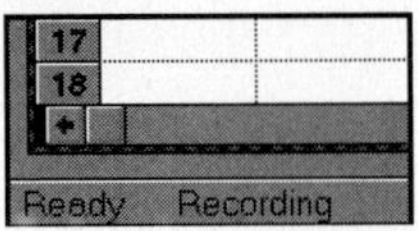

Everything you now do (though not necessarily what you do to achieve it) will be recorded by Excel until you stop the recorder.

7. Click on Formula, Paste Function. Then click on the down arrow on the vertical scroll bar to locate the NOW() function and highlight it.

8. Click on the OK button to complete the command.

9. Click on the check box to the left of the formula bar or press Enter to accept the NOW() function.

10. Click on Format, Number. Click on the down arrow key in the scroll bar until you get to the date and time format—it's the last one. Select that format.

11. Click on the OK button to complete the command. (Remember that you're still recording—look at the status line.)

12. Click on Format, Column Width. When the dialog box appears, click on Best Fit.

13. Click on Macro, Stop Recorder. When you finish, cell B3 should look more or less like this (with a different date and time):

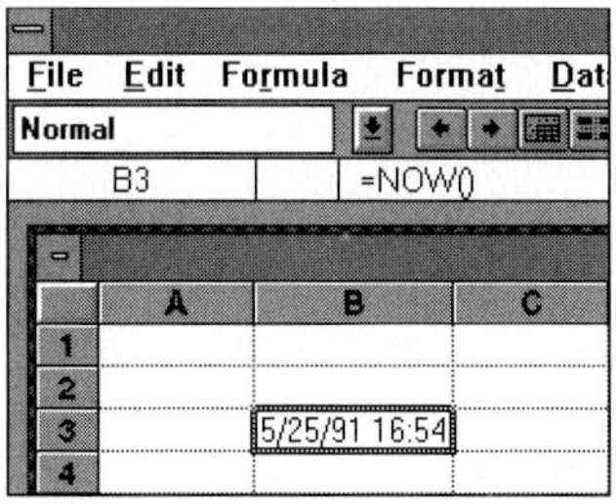

Notice also that "Recording" has disappeared from the status line.

There, you've just programmed your first macro. That wasn't so bad, was it? Admittedly, this example isn't something that is going to save you a lot of time, but it illustrates how easy it is to record a macro for something you do over and over.

Want to see it work? Make sure you watch the screen closely because Excel is going to accomplish in less than a second what took you at least 30 seconds to do before. Try this:

1. Move the cell pointer to any other cell, preferably one in a different column, say cell C5.

2. Hold down the Ctrl key and then press the "a" key. Try using this macro in other places on the worksheet, as well, if you like.

Pausing During Recording

It's possible to halt the macro recorder if there is something that you want to do but not record. One example might occur when you are recording a long, complicated macro and halfway through you want to check something in some other area of a worksheet.

To pause the macro recorder, just click on Macro, Stop Recorder. When you are ready to proceed, click on Macro, Start Recorder. This will pick up the recording from the point where you left off. Note that Macro, Stop Recorder is used both to pause the recorder and to end a macro. If you subsequently want to record a new macro, be sure to use the Macro, Record command. This will prompt you for a name for the new macro and an associated shortcut key.

"Keyless" Command Macros

As you've long ago discovered, Excel has several ways to do the same thing. Before you see another way to run macros, try recording one more to illustrate one other point:

1. Put the cell pointer in cell B6 and type the word **BOLD**. Then press Enter or click on the check box to the left of the formula bar.
2. Click on Macro, Record.
3. When the dialog box appears, type in a new name such as **Make_it_Bold**.
4. Use the Tab key to move to the shortcut key section of the dialog box. Instead of accepting the default of "b", use the Del key to erase what is there. Make sure your dialog box looks like this before you proceed:

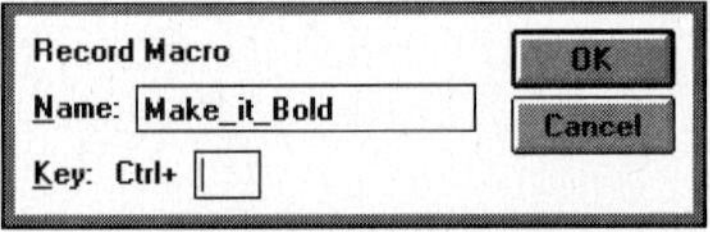

5. Click on OK to complete the command. Note in the status line that the recorder is now on.
6. Click on Format, Font. Then click on the check box next to the Bold attribute so that an X appears there. Verify that the text is bold by looking in the Samples box.
7. Click on OK to complete the command.
8. Click on Macro, Stop Recorder.

You've just created a macro that applies the bold attribute to the text in any cell where you execute the macro. As macros go, this is a pretty simplistic example. You could have instead made this a named style or even just moved to the cell and clicked on the Bold button in the toolbar. The exercise, however, demonstrates another way to *run* macros.

Recall that you have 52 choices of shortcut keys that you can use before you run out. Admittedly, you probably won't run out of shortcut keys right away. But there are circumstances where you want to have macros that don't have shortcut keys. (More on this appears later in this chapter.)

Here's how to play back a macro that you've recorded without a shortcut key:

1. Move the cell pointer over to cell C2 and enter one or two words of text—it doesn't matter what.
2. Click on Macro, Run. The dialog box that appears looks like the one in Figure 13.1. This is where Excel lists all the active macros. Note that one of the macros has a shortcut command associated with it (the "a" assigned to your earlier macro), and the other does not.
3. Highlight "Make_it_Bold" and then click on OK. Or you can just double-click on the name to run the macro. The dialog box will go away and you will see that Excel has made bold the contents of the cell that was highlighted.

Figure 13.1
Macro Run dialog box

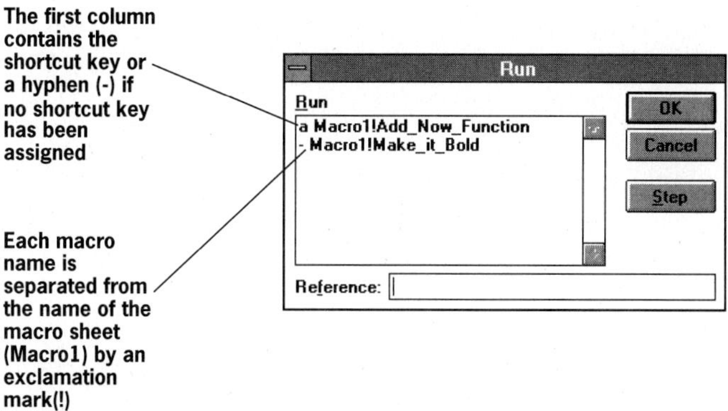
The first column contains the shortcut key or a hyphen (-) if no shortcut key has been assigned
Each macro name is separated from the name of the macro sheet (Macro1) by an exclamation mark(!)
Run
Run
a Macro1!Add_Now_Function
- Macro1!Make_it_Bold
OK
Cancel
Step
Reference:

Viewing the Macro Sheet

Let's take a look at how Excel manages the macros that you record. You'll recall that Excel stores your macros in a special place called a macro sheet. But where does it come from? You haven't asked Excel to create one for you. The answer to this puzzle is that Excel automatically creates a macro sheet when you tell it you want to record a macro.

However, you can also explicitly tell Excel to create a new macro sheet. Usually you'll do this when you're creating a macro from scratch. As you get more comfortable with Excel you might want to do that, but for the most part you will probably be happy with the work you can do with the macro recorder.

To look at the macro sheet that Excel has created for you, use these steps:

1. Click on Window and look at the selections. Your Window menu should look like this:

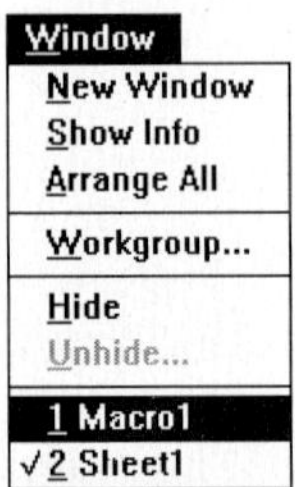

2. Click on the selection marked "Macro1." If you've been playing around with macro sheets during the current Excel session, the macro sheet containing the chapter examples might be named Macro2 or Macro3, but since you haven't saved it yet, its name will begin with "Macro." Excel will bring the macro sheet to the foreground. Your worksheet is still there, but is probably not visible behind the macro sheet (depending on your computer and monitor).

3. Highlight columns A and B and format the columns so that you can see the contents of both macros. You also might have to maximize the macro sheet window to get everything in. (Click on the up arrow in the upper-right corner of the macro sheet window to maximize the window.) When you finish, your macro sheet should look like Figure 13.2.

Dissecting the Command Macro

Let's take a look at each of the macros on this macro sheet. When you told Excel to begin recording a macro for you, recall that Excel automatically created a new macro sheet and then began recording commands in the first column it found empty (column A). It then proceeded to record commands down the column. Here are the commands it recorded in column A:

```
Add_Now_Function (a)
=FORMULA("=NOW()")
=FORMAT.NUMBER("m/d/yy h:mm")
=COLUMN.WIDTH(,,,3)
=RETURN()
```

Figure 13.2
Contents of a macro sheet

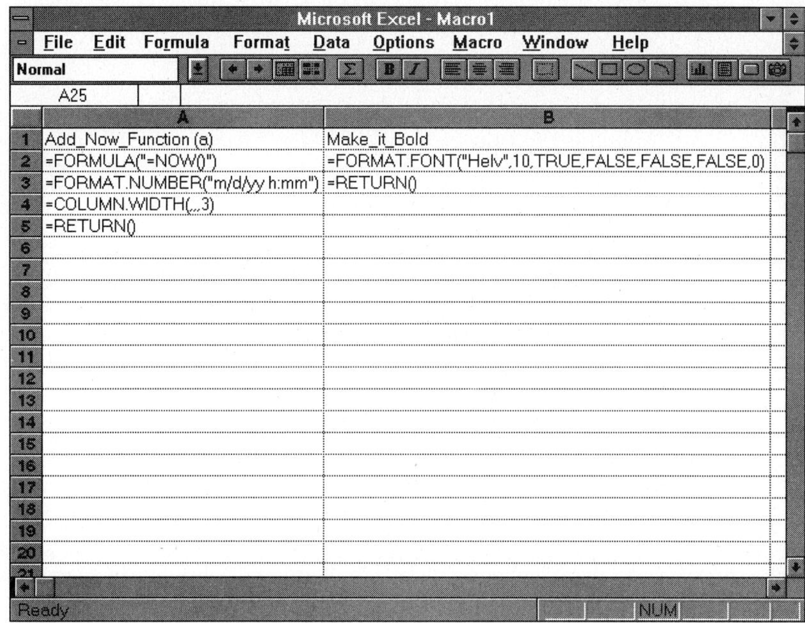

The first line of this macro identifies the macro to Excel. Remember that you called this first macro Add_Now_Function, and you let Excel give it a lowercase "a" as the shortcut key.

The second line, which contains the =FORMULA() macro function, is used to add text, formulas, or functions to the active cell. (Remember that the cursor was already over the cell you wanted to add this function to.) Note that the actual function that you wanted to appear in the cell—the NOW() function—appears here in the command macro as a quoted text string.

The third line simply formats the active cell with any valid Excel numerical format. The format is also expressed as a quoted text string.

The fourth line contains the command to format the active column with the Best Fit option. You can see that this function actually takes four arguments, but that the first three are *null*; that is, they contain nothing. In this case, Excel uses the defaults for those arguments. The last argument, the 3, means to use Best Fit to size the columns. (A 1 here would mean to hide the column by setting its width to zero. A 2 as the fourth parameter would unhide the column by setting it to the width it had before being hidden.)

The fifth line contains the =RETURN() macro function. This function is required at the end of every macro so that Excel knows when the macro has terminated.

Now, take a look at the contents of column B—the second short macro you had Excel record for you:

```
Make_it_Bold
=FORMAT.FONT("Helv",10,TRUE,FALSE,FALSE,FALSE,0)
=RETURN()
```

Note that the first command Excel recorded in Column B is just a little bit different from the one in Column A. In this example, you had named the macro Make_it_Bold, and that's the name that Excel uses to refer to this macro. Remember also that you didn't give it a shortcut key. Compare this cell with the first cell of the other macro (A1) and note that this one doesn't show a shortcut key. This means that the only way you can run this macro is to execute it from the Macro Run dialog box.

This macro is even simpler than the first one. The second line of this macro formats the current cell to be bold. The =FORMAT.FONT macro function takes seven arguments, in order from left to right: "Helv" is a quoted text string for the font name, 10 is the font size, TRUE means bold on, FALSE means italic off, FALSE means underline off, FALSE means strikeout off, 0 corresponds to the Automatic (default) color option.

Finally, the last line contains the RETURN() command to signal the end of the macro.

Saving Macro Sheets

When you are finished recording your macros and you want to save the work you've done, you need to save your macros the same way you normally save your worksheets. Macros only differ in the file name extension that they use: .XLM instead of .XLS.

At this point, let's save the macro sheet you've been working on:

1. Make sure the macro sheet is the active sheet on your screen. If it is not, you can either click anywhere in the macro sheet or you can click on the Window menu and then select the macro sheet from the list of open files.
2. Click on File, Save. Since you haven't yet saved this macro sheet, Excel will pop up a File, Save As dialog box like the one in Figure 13.3.
3. Give your macro file a name such as **MY_MACRO** and then click on OK to save your file. Excel will save the macro sheet in the current directory with an extension of .XLM.

It's important to remember that the macros you just recorded won't work if the macro sheet is not open. Use the following steps to close the macro sheet and then see if the macros work:

1. Close the macro sheet by clicking on File, Close.

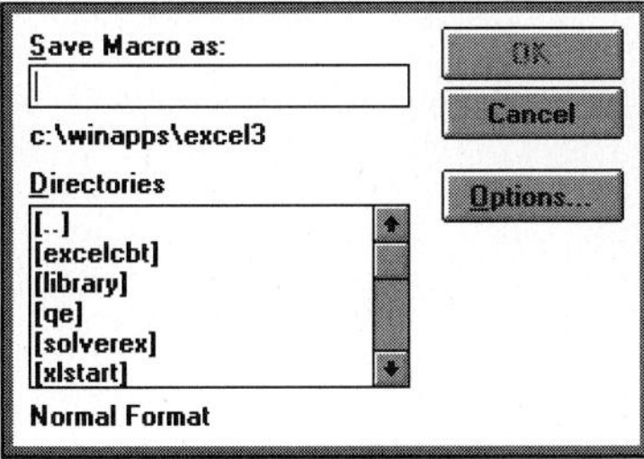

Figure 13.3
File Save As dialog box

2. Once the macro sheet is closed, the only sheet that you'll have left is the original worksheet. To verify that the macros don't work, try holding down the Ctrl key while you press the lowercase "a" key—which worked before to insert a =NOW() function and format the current cell.

With the macro sheet closed, the only thing that happens when you hit Ctrl-a is that Excel beeps.

Now that you've seen the relationship between macros and worksheets, it's time to open the macro sheet again and see how flexible macros can be.

Building an Application—The Basics

It was hinted at earlier that macros can be assigned to graphical objects such as circles and buttons. This ability lets you make very easy-to-use worksheets (applications) for people who might not be acquainted with the ins and outs of running an Excel worksheet.

A good example of the use of a button is in a complex worksheet that includes a large number of calculations. Suppose you have set Calculation to Manual so that your worksheet doesn't recalculate every time a number is changed or added. In this case, you could create a command macro that contains the macro function CALCULATE.NOW() and assign it to a button labeled "Calculate Now". Then, when all the data entry and editing has been completed, the user simply clicks once on the button and the worksheet is recalculated.

Adding a Button

This exercise shows how easy it is to assign a macro to a button. Use the following instructions to create some buttons and then associate them with command macros.

1. First make sure you have reloaded the macro sheet you saved previously. Use the File, Open dialog box to open the MY_MACRO macro sheet.
2. Make sure the worksheet is the active one by clicking anywhere on the worksheet or by selecting the worksheet from the Window menu.
3. Erase the contents of all the cells you used in the previous exercises: Highlight the range B2:C5; click on Edit, Clear; and then click on OK to complete the command.
4. Click on the Button tool in the toolbar—the second one from the right (see below). Note that the mouse pointer changes from its normal shape to a small cross to help you place the buttons more accurately.

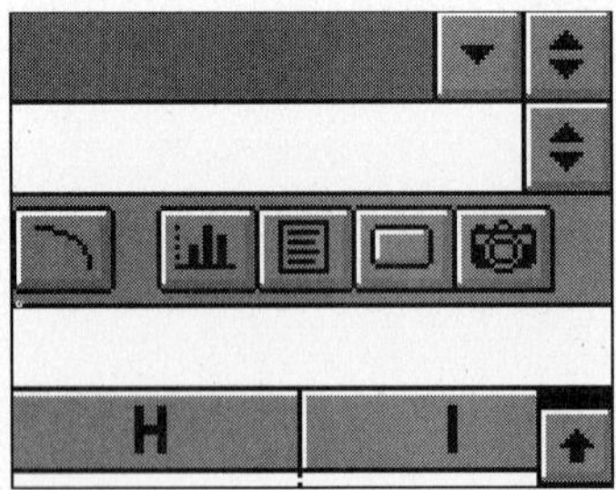

5. Place the mouse pointer in the upper-left corner of cell F4, hold down the Ctrl key to constrain the button to the cell boundaries, then click and drag with the mouse down and to the right to the lower-right corner of cell G5. Then release the mouse button and the Ctrl key.

The dialog box shown in Figure 13.4 should appear. This box lets you assign a recorded command macro to a graphical object or button so that clicking on the button or object will cause the macro to execute.

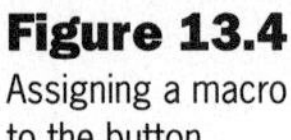

Figure 13.4
Assigning a macro to the button

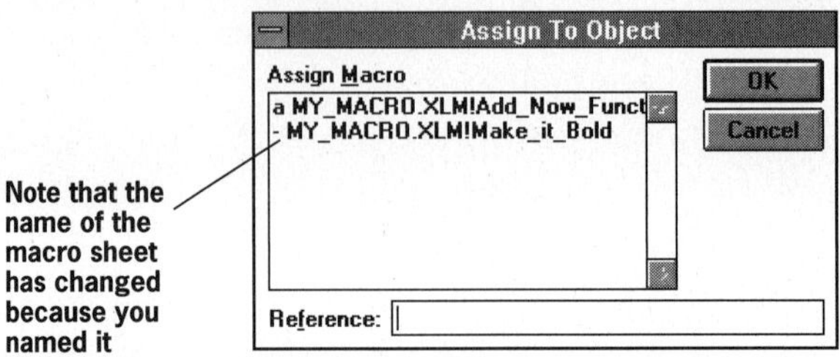

6. Highlight the Add_Now_Function macro and click on OK. Figure 13.5 shows what the button should look like at this stage. Note that the button is highlighted and still has handles around it. This is the appropriate time to resize the button or move it around if you like.

Figure 13.5
Worksheet after placing the first button

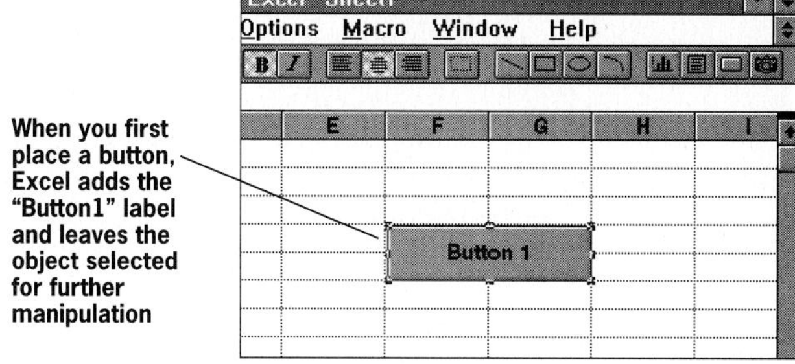
When you first place a button, Excel adds the "Button1" label and leaves the object selected for further manipulation
Excel - Sheet1
Options Macro Window Help
E F G H I
Button 1

Excel names the buttons sequentially as you place them—Button 1, Button 2, and so on. You probably want your button names to be a little more descriptive, however. Here's how to change the text of the buttons:

1. While the button is still highlighted, move the mouse cursor into the button. Notice that the cursor changes shape once again, this time to an I-bar.
2. Click once within the text and then use the Delete and Backspace keys to erase the existing text and add something new. Call this button **Add Current Date**. Then hit the Escape key to signal to Excel that you have finished with the editing, or simply click somewhere outside the button. When you have finished with these steps the macro button should look like the one in Figure 13.6.

Figure 13.6
Completed button

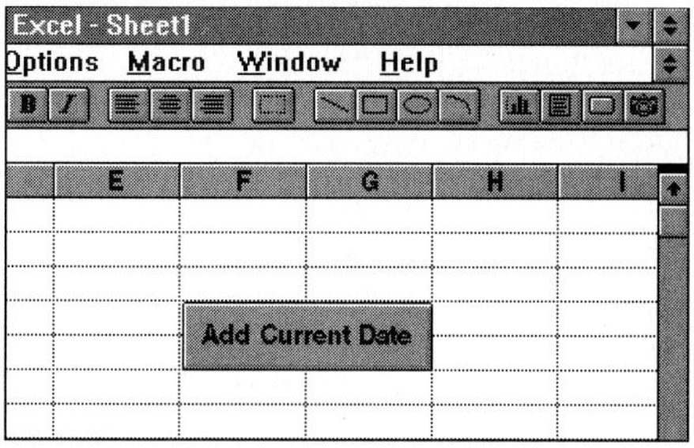

Now, to verify that everything works correctly, just highlight any empty cell, perhaps B6, and click once on the Add Current Date button. Then watch as Excel runs the macro associated with the button. Note also that the mouse pointer changes from its normal shape to a small hand when you move the mouse pointer over the button—or any other object that has a macro associated with it.

Adding Other Objects

Now that you've seen how to add a button and associate a macro with it, you can just as easily add any other type of graphical object and assign a macro to that object:

1. Somewhere in the lower-middle area of the worksheet screen, add a small circle. Remember to first pick the oval tool from the toolbar, hold down the Shift key to constrain the object to a circle, and then click and drag a small circle.
2. Note that when you have finished placing the circle, it remains selected for further manipulation—if you like. Click on Macro in the menu bar and note that Assign to Object is available. This menu choice is only active if you have selected an object or group of objects.

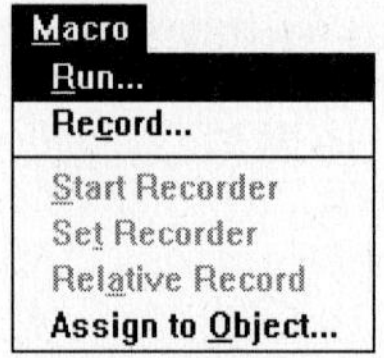

3. Click on Assign to Object. The dialog box that lets you assign a macro to an object appears (Figure 13.4).
4. Highlight the macro you want associated with this graphical object. In this case, highlight "Make_it_Bold" and then click on OK to complete the command.
5. Test the macro assignment by putting some text in one of the empty cells and then clicking once on the circle. Watch as Excel makes the text bold.

Working with Assigned Objects

One final point about using buttons and graphical objects is important. You might recall from Chapter 8 that if you wanted to modify the characteristics of a graphical object, you could just double-click on the object and Excel would pop up a dialog box containing options about what you could do with the object.

Once you've assigned a macro to a button or an object, clicking on it causes a minor problem—it runs the macro assigned to it instead of popping up the dialog box with your options! Never fear, Excel has a solution for you.

Once you have assigned a macro to an object, one way to select the object is to use the selection tool on the toolbar.

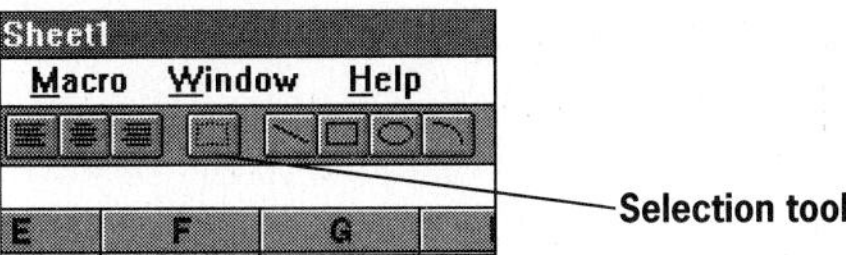

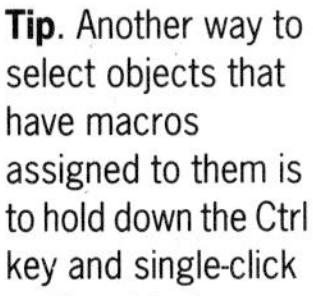

Tip. Another way to select objects that have macros assigned to them is to hold down the Ctrl key and single-click on the object.

Simply click on the selection tool and then drag the dotted line around the objects you want to select. Those objects completely surrounded by the bounding box will be selected. For example, in Figure 13.7, only the command button will be selected when you release the mouse button because the circle is not completely inside the dotted bounding box.

Figure 13.7
Using the selection tool to select graphical objects

Anything completely enclosed in this dotted bounding box will be selected

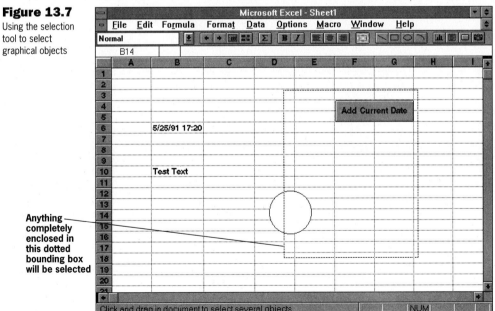

Now that you've seen how to implement command macro buttons, your imagination and time will be the only limit to how you design your worksheets. These objects add a great deal of functionality and flexibility to the way others interact with the worksheet.

Setting the Start-up Directory

As you have learned, if you want to have macros available when you are working with other worksheets, you must remember to open the macro sheet or sheets as well as the worksheet file. Fortunately, Microsoft engineers thought of this eventuality and provided an Excel feature to circumvent the problem.

When you installed Excel, the Excel setup program created several subdirectories below the main Excel directory. One of these subdirectories is called XLSTART. Any file placed in this directory—worksheets, charts, macro sheets, and workspace files—will automatically be loaded when you start Excel. This means you can keep your macro file there and it will load automatically each time Excel starts.

Programming Macros on a Worksheet

So far, you've only created command macros by using the macro recorder, but even so it should be apparent that Excel's command language is a very powerful and flexible way to create applications for yourself and for others. Discussing all the issues involved in writing command macros by hand (as opposed to recording the steps) could fill two more volumes and would greatly exceed the scope of this book.

However, it's important to realize that Excel's command language can do literally everything in a command macro that you can do by hand at the keyboard. In fact, one might argue that the command macro language is even more powerful than that because it allows you to create custom dialog boxes that prompt others for information. It might be impossible to get that information into a worksheet without this ability.

Using Excel as a Database

Using Excel with External Files

Data Exchange with the Clipboard and DDE

PART

4

Integrating and Sharing Data

CHAPTER

14

Using Excel as a Database

YOU MAY HAVE SEEN REFERENCES TO EXCEL'S DATABASE CAPABILITIES ties several times by now. Any data that you want to store can be maintained, manipulated, sorted, and extracted using Excel's built-in tools. This chapter will give you a taste of some of the database features available to you from within Excel.

Database Basics

Before you begin the exercises, you'll need to create one more worksheet, which you'll use for the rest of the book.

Use Excel's File, New Worksheet command to create a new worksheet and then enter the information shown in Figure 14.1. The labels in row 1 are only in bold to set them off from the rest of the worksheet—you needn't make them bold if you don't want to. However, they must be in the worksheet at the very top of each column, for reasons you'll see shortly.

Once you have finished entering the data, save the worksheet with the name **NAMELIST.XLS**.

Figure 14.1
NAMELIST.XLS database worksheet

NAMELIST.XLS

	A	B	C	D	E	F	G
1	**SAL**	**L_NAME**	**F_NAME**	**ADDR**	**CITY**	**STATE**	**YEARS**
2	Mr.	Smith	Dale	13 Main Street	Acton	MA	12
3	Ms.	Sullivan	Samantha	Rt. 1, Box 12	Boston	MA	5
4	Mr.	Charles	Winston	234 Shaffer Road	Chino	CA	4
5	Ms.	Simpson	Suzanne	24922 Muirlands	Boise	ID	15
6	Ms.	Silverburg	Linda	2403 Salem Street	Bozeman	MT	23
7	Mr.	Starkowski	George	9 Savoy Road	Encino	CA	4
8	Mr.	Salesman	John	884 Las Vegas Blvd.	Las Vegas	NV	3
9	Mr.	Billitson	Michael	3993 Congress Ave.	Boca Raton	FL	13
10	Ms.	Phillips	Amanda	19 Snake Gulch Rd.	Henderson	NV	6
11	Ms.	Zemonson	Claudette	22 Orange Ave.	Miami	FL	6
12	Mr.	Archuleta	Hector	2606 Swan Drive	Yonkers	NY	15
13	Mr.	Sullivan	Thor	35 Lower Keys Road	Tampa	FL	22
14							
15							

Field names

Records

Fields

This worksheet illustrates the parts of a database that you will need to understand before working with the database. In Excel, a database is simply a defined set of columns and rows. Each column contains a *field* and each row contains a *record*.

Each column has the same type of data for each record. For example, the AGE field in a database would contain the age data for each record. On the other hand, each record contains the same types of information as every other record in the database, organized in the same order as in the other records. So, if one record contained NAME, AGE, and HEIGHT fields, in that order, so would every other record.

At the top of each column is a *field name*. The field name is required and each must be different from the other field names. The top row of the database must contain a row of field names—this is the only way Excel can locate and identify the contents of the records.

Finally, the entire database is defined by a named range called, not surprisingly, Database. This is how Excel knows where to find the data. You'll see shortly that you can either assign this name manually or let Excel do it for you.

Building a Database

Building a database is fairly straightforward, if you follow a few simple rules. You've already completed the data entry portion of this exercise, but one thing remains: You must create a named range that identifies the database to Excel. Failure to do so will cause Excel to beep loudly.

Identifying Database Ranges

As previously mentioned, there are two ways to identify the database range for Excel: You can enter it yourself by using the Formula, Define Name command, or you can tell Excel to create the necessary range names. The latter is the easier method and that's what you'll do here. Use the following steps to name the database range:

1. Make sure the NAMELIST.XLS file is open. You might want to fiddle with the fonts or the window positions to get it to look more or less like Figure 14.1.
2. Highlight the range that comprises the database. Remember that you must include the field names at the top of each column. For this exercise, the range you should highlight is A1:G13.
3. Click on Data, Set Database. It's a pretty boring command since nothing appears to happen on the screen, but the range name Database has been correctly assigned to the range.
4. Verify this by clicking on Formula, Define Name. Note that there is a range named Database. If you highlight that range name (single click on it), you can see that the database has been defined correctly.

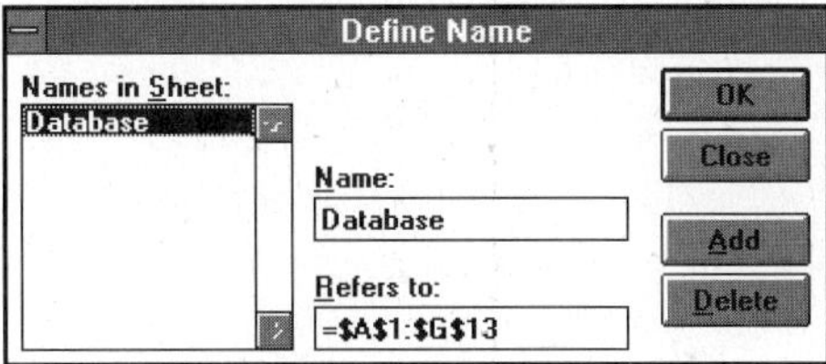

The other way to name this database would have been to highlight it as you did, then click on Formula, Define Name, enter the name **Database**, and click on OK. Both methods work to name the database, but the first one is a bit easier.

Using Data Forms

At this point, the database is just a collection of labels that happens to be arranged to look like a database. There isn't much difference between a database and other data, except for the way it's laid out. That is, the term *database* doesn't mean that data is stored any differently from the data in a regular worksheet, just that the data itself has some special characteristics.

Thus, if you wanted to add some data to this database, you could add more rows—either in the middle of the database, if the order of the data wasn't important, or to the end of database. A better way to do so, however, is with a Data Form.

A Data Form is a feature that Excel provides to help you work with databases, especially when you are just starting out. The Data Form takes care of most of the housekeeping chores associated with database maintenance, and it gives you a quick and easy way to work with data—albeit one record at a time.

Now that you've identified your database range to Excel, creating a Data Form is a snap: Click on Data, Form and watch as Excel pops up a dialog box containing your data, as illustrated in Figure 14.2

There are several things to notice about the Data Form. First, it only displays your data one record at a time. Still, that's not too bad for one mouse click. The field names are displayed on the left side of the Data Form, and the corresponding field values are displayed to the right.

Excel gives you a scroll bar for you to move around within the database. Note that your position in the database is displayed with a position indicator above the command buttons ("1 of 12" in Figure 14.2). Moving up or down through the database is simple: Just click on the up or down arrows in the scroll bar to move forward or back one record.

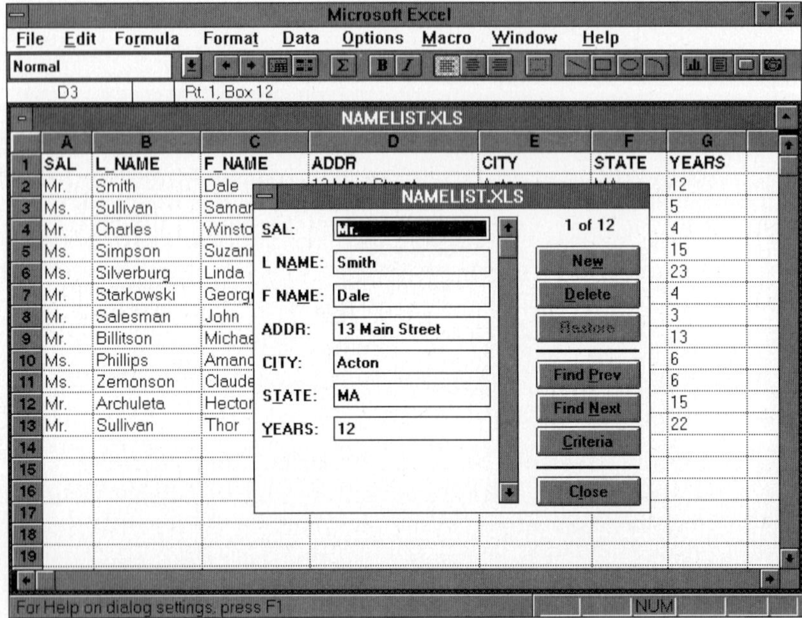

Figure 14.2
Excel's Data Form

Adding New Records

Take a look at the command buttons on the Data Form. As shipped from Excel, the Data Form is a very powerful tool which makes it easy for you to add, modify, or delete records from the database. Let's try to add a couple of records using the Data Form:

1. With the Data Form still on the screen, click on the New command button. Watch as Excel clears the Data Form and waits for you to start entering data.

2. Type in the following information for the new record, using the Tab key to move from field to field:

   For SAL, type **Ms.**

   For L_NAME, type **Jenkins**

   For F_NAME, type **Susan**

   For ADDR, type **123 Main Street**

   For CITY, type **Buffalo**

   For STATE, type **NY**

   For YEARS, type **5**

3. When you are finished entering data into the fields, hit the Enter key. You will then be given another blank form. If you had more records to add you could now do so. For now, just click on Close to return to the main worksheet. If all went well, it should now look like the one in Figure 14.3.

Figure 14.3
NAMELIST after adding a record

Microsoft Excel

File Edit Formula Format Data Options Macro Window Help

Normal

H24

NAMELIST.XLS

	A	B	C	D	E	F	G
1	SAL	L_NAME	F_NAME	ADDR	CITY	STATE	YEARS
2	Mr.	Smith	Dale	13 Main Street	Acton	MA	12
3	Ms.	Sullivan	Samantha	Rt. 1, Box 12	Boston	MA	5
4	Mr.	Charles	Winston	234 Shaffer Road	Chino	CA	4
5	Ms.	Simpson	Suzanne	24922 Muirlands	Boise	ID	15
6	Ms.	Silverburg	Linda	2403 Salem Street	Bozeman	MT	23
7	Mr.	Starkowski	George	9 Savoy Road	Encino	CA	4
8	Mr.	Salesman	John	884 Las Vegas Blvd.	Las Vegas	NV	3
9	Mr.	Billitson	Michael	3993 Congress Ave.	Boca Raton	FL	13
10	Ms.	Phillips	Amanda	19 Snake Gulch Rd.	Henderson	NV	6
11	Ms.	Zemonson	Claudette	22 Orange Ave.	Miami	FL	6
12	Mr.	Archuleta	Hector	2606 Swan Drive	Yonkers	NY	15
13	Mr.	Sullivan	Thor	35 Lower Keys Road	Tampa	FL	22
14	Ms.	Jenkins	Susan	123 Main Street	Buffalo	NY	5
15							
16							
17							
18							
19							

Ready NUM

Deleting a Record

The Data Form can also be used to delete records from the database. If you want to delete a record, simply find the record that you want to remove and click on the Delete button. After you answer a warning about removing the data, Excel will delete the record and move the remaining data up from beneath to fill in the spot just vacated.

CAUTION! *You may remember that in most cases you can undo whatever you have last done in Excel by selecting Edit, Undo. This is one of the few places where that will not work! Be sure you are ready to delete that data when Excel pops up the dialog box and asks if you really want to delete the record.*

Editing the Data

Editing data from within the Data Form is also easy. Excel lets you edit the data in a record and then saves the new record as soon as you move to another one. It's important to verify your changes before you move on to another record because the change is permanent—until you change it again, of course.

If you are in the middle of editing a record and you decide that you want to have the original record back—that is, you don't want to "commit" your changes—you can click on the Restore command button, and your original record will be restored without saving your changes.

Editing the Database Without Data Forms

The preceding sections assume you're working from within the Data Form. However, as long as you are willing to ensure that the Database range name is maintained (that is, that Database always accurately represents the database area along with the field names), you can do all the editing, adding, and deleting you please using the standard Excel commands to insert or delete rows and edit individual cells. The job of the Data Form is simply to make it easier for you to work with data by both presenting the data for you to edit and maintaining the Database named range, whether you make the database grow or shrink.

If you choose not to use the Data Form, remember that the data you want to include in your database must always fall within the database range. For example, if you add a record to the end of the database range, it might fall outside the database range, and thus any subsequent database operations would not be applied to the data you just added. There are two ways to avoid this problem. Either make sure that you add data to the middle of the database and then re-sort it, or define a database range that includes a blank record at the end of the database. Then, when you manually add a row for the new record, the data will remain within the database range.

Sorting a Database

One of the things you cannot do with the Data Form is sort your database. A *sort* of the database is what it sounds like: a way to rearrange the records so that they are ordered in a specific way. You use the Data Sort command to reorder your records either numerically or alphabetically and in either ascending or descending order.

Sorting requires the use of a *sort key*. The sort key specifies a particular field to use for the sort and is how Excel knows what order to place the data in the database. For example, suppose that you want to sort the NAMELIST database so that the records are arranged in alphabetical order by last name. To do this, you would select the L_NAME column as the sort key.

This selection is fine if every record in the L_NAME column is unique, but what happens when you have two or more people (records) with the same last name (duplicate keys)? In that case, you can specify a second key, say the F_NAME column. There might be several Sullivans, but there can't be too many Thor Sullivans around. Excel first sorts the records based on the primary key, then on the secondary key, and finally on the tertiary (third-level) key.

Use the following steps to sort your database first by last name and then by first name:

1. Highlight the portion of the database that you want to sort. Although there might be times when you only want to sort a subset of the database, you'll normally sort the whole thing. For this exercise, highlight the range A2:G14. Note that when you sort you must *not* include the field names. If you do, you'll end up with the field names sorted in with the main database.

2. Click on Data, Sort. The dialog box that appears is shown in Figure 14.4.

Figure 14.4
Data Sort dialog box

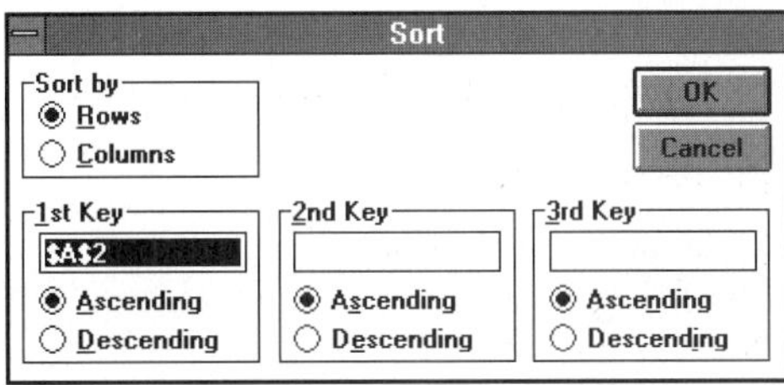

3. Select the primary key to sort on. Note how the 1st Key field is highlighted in the dialog box. If the reference in that field is for the column you want to sort on, then just leave it. However, if what's shown is the wrong column, simply click on the correct column. In this case, the sort key Excel picked for you is actually the Salutation field—column A. Since you want to sort on the last name column, just click once in column B and verify that the reference in the dialog box changed to B.

4. Now you must decide whether you want Excel to sort that column in ascending or descending order. You can choose either, but lists of names are usually sorted in ascending order. Since that's what Excel has given you as the default, just leave it.

5. Move the mouse pointer into the 2nd Key field (or press Tab twice to get there). Now pick the column that you want to be the secondary key. For this exercise, click once with the mouse in column C, the column that contains the first names.

6. Make your choice of either ascending or descending sort order. Again, for now accept the default of Ascending.

7. Once you've looked over your selections and made sure you have everything set up correctly, click on OK to begin the sort. Depending on the size of your file, the sort might take several seconds or it might happen virtually instantly.

If all went well, your database now looks like Figure 14.5. Note how the records are now in the correct order—look at the Sullivans to see how Excel correctly handled the two records with identical last names and different first names.

Figure 14.5
Database after the sort

	A	B	C	D	E	F	G
1	SAL	L_NAME	F_NAME	ADDR	CITY	STATE	YEARS
2	Mr.	Archuleta	Hector	2606 Swan Drive	Yonkers	NY	15
3	Mr.	Billitson	Michael	3993 Congress Ave.	Boca Raton	FL	13
4	Mr.	Charles	Winston	234 Shaffer Road	Chino	CA	4
5	Ms.	Jenkins	Susan	123 Main Street	Buffalo	NY	5
6	Ms.	Phillips	Amanda	19 Snake Gulch Rd.	Henderson	NV	6
7	Mr.	Salesman	John	884 Las Vegas Blvd.	Las Vegas	NV	3
8	Ms.	Silverburg	Linda	2403 Salem Street	Bozeman	MT	23
9	Ms.	Simpson	Suzanne	24922 Muirlands	Boise	ID	15
10	Mr.	Smith	Dale	13 Main Street	Acton	MA	12
11	Mr.	Starkowski	George	9 Savoy Road	Encino	CA	4
12	Ms.	Sullivan	Samantha	Rt. 1, Box 12	Boston	MA	5
13	Mr.	Sullivan	Thor	35 Lower Keys Road	Tampa	FL	22
14	Ms.	Zemonson	Claudette	22 Orange Ave.	Miami	FL	6

Undoing the Sort

If there is a problem with the sort—perhaps you specified the sort keys incorrectly or you didn't get all of the database when you highlighted the range to sort—you can immediately click on Edit, Undo Sort to set the database back to where it was before the sort.

Remember that you have to choose Undo before you do anything else to the worksheet. You can use the navigation keys or the mouse to cruise around and see if the sort worked correctly, but as soon as you issue a command or format a cell, you will be unable to recover from the sort.

Excel's Sort Order

Much like the order of mathematical operator precedence that Excel follows, there is also a predefined sort order that Excel uses, as follows:

1. Numbers
2. Text
3. Logical values
4. Error values
5. Blanks

This means that, within a single column, Excel will first sort on the numbers—from lowest to highest or vice versa, depending on whether you choose ascending or descending order. Then it will sort textual values. Next, it will sort by a logical value (TRUE or FALSE), then by an error value, and finally on blank records.

Knowing this, you know that any blank fields will always be sorted to the end of the database. This can be quite helpful if you think that there are some records in your database that have a particular field that is blank, but the database is so large that you don't want to have to search through it. Knowing what you do about sorting, just specify that column as the primary key and tell Excel to sort the database. Any fields that are blank will emerge at the end.

Querying the Database

After you have created a database and identified it to Excel, you still need some way to *query* the database—a way to tell Excel what records you want to work with. And once you have identified a certain set of records, you want to be able to delete those records, extract them to another part of the worksheet, or just format them. The way Excel is told to select subsets of data from your overall database involves the concept of criteria.

Specifying the Criteria

Criteria are the instructions Excel uses to test each record in the database for a match. You enter criteria into a special range called the *criteria range* and then identify that range to Excel much as you created the Database range earlier in the chapter. The criteria range, like the database range, must have as its first row the names of the fields in the database.

Unlike the database range, however, the criteria range does not have to include all of the names of the fields—only those you want to test. So, to use the NAMELIST example, your criteria range might only have

L_NAME, F_NAME, and YEARS if you only want to select records based on those fields.

In practice, the best way to ensure that the criteria names are *identical* to the field names is to just copy the column names from the first row of the database range and paste them into the first row of the criteria range. You don't have to use them all, but they're available if you need them. And because you copied them from the database range, you know they are accurate.

Excel's criteria offer a lot of flexibility in the way that you select records. For example, using the NAMELIST example, your criteria can select people whose last name begins with "S" *or* whose time with the company is between 12 and 18 years, inclusive. Or you can set up multiple criteria so that Excel will identify the records of people whose first name starts with "F" *and* who have 12 years of service with the company *and* who live in either New York or California.

Using Criteria with the Data Form

If you are just starting out with databases in Excel, perhaps the best place to get the idea of the criteria range is in the Data Form. Here, Excel manages the concept of the criteria range for you, and all you have to do is add the actual criteria that will select the subset of records that you want. Let's try entering a couple of simple criteria and see how that works within the Data Form.

1. Make sure you are in the Data Form. If you're not, click on Data, Form and Excel will pop up the data form that you were working with earlier (Figure 14.2).

2. Click on the Criteria command button. The fields will all clear to let you enter your search criteria. Use the Tab key to move to the L_NAME field. Enter **S** in that field. (Note that this is not case sensitive—either **S** or **s** will work.)

3. Click on the Find Next command button. Excel will test the records against the criteria that you entered and display only those records in which L_NAME begins with "S," one at a time.

4. Continue to click on Find Next. Excel will display each record in turn until you come to the last one, and then it will stop. You can move in the other direction by clicking on the Find Prev command button.

What if you wanted to search for someone with a last name beginning with "S" who also lived in Massachusetts? No problem:

1. Click on the Criteria command button. Note that the "S" from the previous search is still in the L_NAME field. Now use the Tab key to move down to the STATE field and type **MA**.

2. Click on the Find Next command button.

Now Excel will find only those records that pass two tests: the last name starts with "S" and the state is MA.

Follow these next steps when you are ready to view all the records again or if you want to enter new criteria and you need to clear out the existing criteria:

1. Click on the Criteria command button.
2. Click on the Clear command button. Excel will clear all the criteria out of the Data Form.

Excel lets you use two wildcard characters when you are specifying the criteria in the criteria range. These characters are the same as those discussed in the context of consolidation syntax in Chapter 11. Their purpose is to let you create more complex selections. For example, you could enter **MI*** for the state, and it would match records in which the state was MI, Mississippi, Michigan, or Missouri.

You can also use the ? wildcard character to match any single letter in a particular spot within a word. For example, ?ATHY would match both Kathy and Cathy.

Excel also provides another kind of criteria, *comparison criteria*, listed in Table 14.1. These criteria are what you use if you want to compare the values in one field to some fixed value. For example, you might want to search the NAMELIST file for those individuals who have 12 years of service, or you might want to find those who have 12 or more years of service (YEARS >= 12), and so on.

Table 14.1 Comparison Criteria

Operator	Meaning in the Criteria Range
=	Equal to
>	Greater than
<	Less than
>=	Greater than or equal to
<=	Less than or equal to
<>	Not equal to

Let's try a few comparison criteria with the NAMELIST example:

1. If the Data Form isn't showing, click on Data, Form and then click on Criteria.
2. Click on Clear to make sure there are no criteria remaining from earlier exercises.
3. Move to the YEARS field and enter a criteria of **>12**.
4. Click on Find Next to see those records that meet the criteria of YEARS greater than 12.
5. Try some other criteria if you wish. Then when you finish experimenting with the Data Form, close the form by clicking on Close. Excel will take you back to the worksheet.

You may have noticed that one record was for a person that had been with the company for 12 years, but that the preceding query didn't turn up that record. Comparison criteria are very literal. In this case, if you had used the greater-than-or-equal-to criteria (>=), that record would have been found as well.

Identifying the Criteria Range

Now that you've seen how to use criteria on a Data Form, it's time to work a bit with criteria directly on the worksheet. This is really the preferred method since it gives you more flexibility when working with criteria than does the Data Form. As you become more advanced with Excel, you will appreciate the ability to enter multiple criteria directly on the worksheet.

Remember that the criteria range is just another range on the worksheet where you specify to Excel what records from the database range you want to work with. When you want to query a certain subset of records of the overall database, you enter into the criteria range the information necessary for Excel to find, extract, or delete those particular records from the database. Then when you perform the operation, Excel will apply these criteria to the database and perform the desired operation on that subset of data.

The following exercise shows you how to create a criteria range on the NAMELIST worksheet and then how to use that range to find data in a different manner than with the Data Form. It's possible to put the criteria range anywhere on the worksheet, but for this exercise, let's put it at the top—it's easier to illustrate these concepts if the range stays on the screen as you work. First you need to add some space to the top of the worksheet.

1. Highlight rows 1, 2, and 3. Remember to click on the row numbers, not just on some of the cells in the row.

2. Click on Edit, Insert. Excel will immediately insert three rows at the top of the worksheet. (Recall that all your ranges will be adjusted automatically by Excel as you insert rows.) If this operation was successful, your worksheet will look more or less like Figure 14.6.

Figure 14.6
NAMELIST after inserting rows

Microsoft Excel

File Edit Formula Format Data Options Macro Window Help

Normal

A1

NAMELIST.XLS

	A	B	C	D	E	F	G
1							
2							
3							
4	SAL	L_NAME	F_NAME	ADDR	CITY	STATE	YEARS
5	Mr.	Archuleta	Hector	2606 Swan Drive	Yonkers	NY	15
6	Mr.	Billitson	Michael	3993 Congress Ave.	Boca Raton	FL	13
7	Mr.	Charles	Winston	234 Shaffer Road	Chino	CA	4
8	Ms.	Jenkins	Susan	123 Main Street	Buffalo	NY	5
9	Ms.	Phillips	Amanda	19 Snake Gulch Rd.	Henderson	NV	6
10	Mr.	Salesman	John	884 Las Vegas Blvd.	Las Vegas	NV	3
11	Ms.	Silverburg	Linda	2403 Salem Street	Bozeman	MT	23
12	Ms.	Simpson	Suzanne	24922 Muirlands	Boise	ID	15
13	Mr.	Smith	Dale	13 Main Street	Acton	MA	12
14	Mr.	Starkowski	George	9 Savoy Road	Encino	CA	4
15	Ms.	Sullivan	Samantha	Rt. 1, Box 12	Boston	MA	5
16	Mr.	Sullivan	Thor	35 Lower Keys Road	Tampa	FL	22
17	Ms.	Zemonson	Claudette	22 Orange Ave.	Miami	FL	6
18							
19							

Ready NUM

A criteria range has to be a minimum of two rows deep and one column wide, and that's if you only want to compare one field. The reason for the two-row minimum is that one row holds the column (field) names, and the second row is where you enter the criteria values. If the criteria range is only one cell wide, you will only be able to specify a criterion for that field name.

For instance, in our example, your criteria range could be one cell containing the field name STATE. You would only be able to enter a criteria value for the STATE field, in that case—you could not enter a criteria for L_NAME unless that field name was in the criteria range as well. Therefore, as previously noted, the better bet is to simply copy and paste all the field names from the database range. Use the following instructions to accomplish this.

1. Highlight the range containing the database field names. Since you have moved the database range down, the range to highlight is A4:G4.

2. Click on Edit, Copy to copy the contents of that range to the Clipboard.
3. Move the cell pointer to cell A1.
4. Click on Edit, Paste to paste the field names into what will be the first row of the criteria range. When you finish this step, your worksheet should look like Figure 14.7.

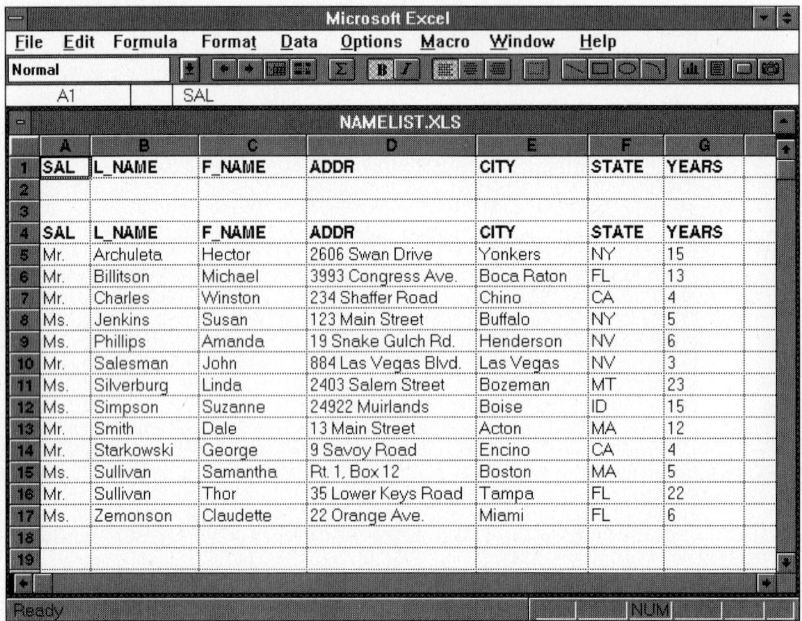

	A	B	C	D	E	F	G
1	SAL	L_NAME	F_NAME	ADDR	CITY	STATE	YEARS
2							
3							
4	SAL	L_NAME	F_NAME	ADDR	CITY	STATE	YEARS
5	Mr.	Archuleta	Hector	2606 Swan Drive	Yonkers	NY	15
6	Mr.	Billitson	Michael	3993 Congress Ave.	Boca Raton	FL	13
7	Mr.	Charles	Winston	234 Shaffer Road	Chino	CA	4
8	Ms.	Jenkins	Susan	123 Main Street	Buffalo	NY	5
9	Ms.	Phillips	Amanda	19 Snake Gulch Rd.	Henderson	NV	6
10	Mr.	Salesman	John	884 Las Vegas Blvd.	Las Vegas	NV	3
11	Ms.	Silverburg	Linda	2403 Salem Street	Bozeman	MT	23
12	Ms.	Simpson	Suzanne	24922 Muirlands	Boise	ID	15
13	Mr.	Smith	Dale	13 Main Street	Acton	MA	12
14	Mr.	Starkowski	George	9 Savoy Road	Encino	CA	4
15	Ms.	Sullivan	Samantha	Rt. 1, Box 12	Boston	MA	5
16	Mr.	Sullivan	Thor	35 Lower Keys Road	Tampa	FL	22
17	Ms.	Zemonson	Claudette	22 Orange Ave.	Miami	FL	6
18							
19							

Figure 14.7
Database after copying the field names

Now, after all that, you can create the criteria range:

1. Highlight the range that will be the criteria range. In this example, it will be two cells deep and as wide as the number of field names. Highlight the range A1:G2.
2. Click on Data, Set Criteria. Like the Data, Set Database command, this one also creates a named range—in this case, one called Criteria. You can verify this by clicking on Formula, Define Name and checking the references for both Database and Criteria. Not only is the criteria range correct, but Excel has adjusted the database range to refer to the new position it occupies since you moved it.

How to Find Data

Now that you have created the criteria range, it's time to put it to use. Excel has a command called Data Find that will test all the records defined by the database range and selected by the criteria in the criteria range and will let you scroll to only those records. This is helpful if you want to browse through a bunch of records—you have Excel show you only the ones you want to see.

However, you still have to enter a criteria before Excel can do a Data Find. With the criteria range defined but no criteria entered there, Data Find would match all records. For this exercise, we'll use a criteria similar to that used in the last exercise:

1. Highlight cell G2. Type the criteria **>=12** into the cell and press Enter. Here's what the criteria range should look like:

2. Click on Data, Find. Your worksheet will then immediately go into a special mode in which the arrow keys and up and down arrows of the scroll bar function to move from one record that matches the criteria to the next.

It's easy to see that you're in Find mode. Figure 14.8 shows what Find mode looks like: An entire record is highlighted instead of just one cell, the status bar notes that you're in Find mode, and the scroll bars show a different background.

When you are ready to leave Find mode you can either press the Esc key once or you can click on Data, Exit Find to return control of your worksheet to you.

Extracting Information

There will be times when you want to print a report or create a chart based on a subset of the database, and you will need some way to pick out those records that meet a certain set of conditions. So what do you do when you actually want to extract some of the data from the database range and put it somewhere else?

This is where the third, and final, range comes in—the *extract range*. To *extract* records simply means that Excel will take a group of records (those that match the criteria range) and copy (not move) them to another place on your worksheet. From there you can use the records in a report, for a chart, or what have you.

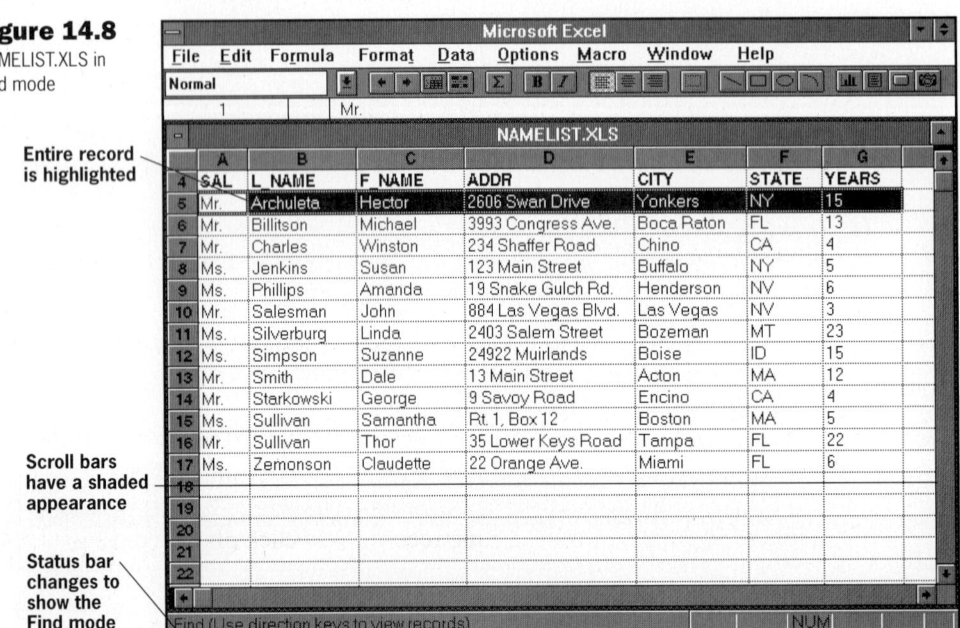

	A	B	C	D	E	F	G
4	SAL	L_NAME	F_NAME	ADDR	CITY	STATE	YEARS
5	Mr.	Archuleta	Hector	2606 Swan Drive	Yonkers	NY	15
6	Mr.	Billitson	Michael	3993 Congress Ave.	Boca Raton	FL	13
7	Mr.	Charles	Winston	234 Shaffer Road	Chino	CA	4
8	Ms.	Jenkins	Susan	123 Main Street	Buffalo	NY	5
9	Ms.	Phillips	Amanda	19 Snake Gulch Rd.	Henderson	NV	6
10	Mr.	Salesman	John	884 Las Vegas Blvd.	Las Vegas	NV	3
11	Ms.	Silverburg	Linda	2403 Salem Street	Bozeman	MT	23
12	Ms.	Simpson	Suzanne	24922 Muirlands	Boise	ID	15
13	Mr.	Smith	Dale	13 Main Street	Acton	MA	12
14	Mr.	Starkowski	George	9 Savoy Road	Encino	CA	4
15	Ms.	Sullivan	Samantha	Rt. 1, Box 12	Boston	MA	5
16	Mr.	Sullivan	Thor	35 Lower Keys Road	Tampa	FL	22
17	Ms.	Zemonson	Claudette	22 Orange Ave.	Miami	FL	6
18							
19							
20							
21							
22							

Figure 14.8 NAMELIST.XLS in Find mode

Creating the Extract Range

Creating an extract range is very similar to identifying the database and criteria ranges. For this next exercise, you'll create the extract range below the database range. Normally, however, you would want the extract range to be to one side of the database range because the database range will likely grow over time as you add records to the database.

You also need to observe caution when placing the extract range. When Excel shoots a bunch of records into the extract range, it will overwrite any data it encounters inside the extract range. Thus, you can easily lose data if you're not careful how you place the extract range.

The extract range is like the criteria range in that the extract names must exactly match the field names of the database. However (again like the criteria range but unlike the database range), you don't have to put all the field names in the extract range. This is a nice feature since it means you can extract less than the whole record if you want. Using the NAMELIST example, if you only wanted to extract the first name and state of those records that match the criteria, you could do that. In fact, the extract names don't even have to be in the same order as the database field names. You'll see it work both ways.

Follow these instructions to create the extract range. You'll use the criteria range and criteria values already in place from the last exercise (YEARS >= 12).

1. Highlight the database field names again. The range is A4:G4.
2. Click on Edit, Copy.
3. Move the mouse pointer down to cell A19.
4. Click on Edit, Paste to paste the field names to the first row of the Extract range.
5. The range A19:G19 (with the field names) should still be highlighted. If it isn't, highlight it now.
6. Click on Data, Set Extract to specify where the extract range should be.
7. Finally, click on Data, Extract. If you've set everything up correctly, Excel will first pop up a small dialog box (shown below) giving you the option of extracting only unique records. Just click on OK for now.

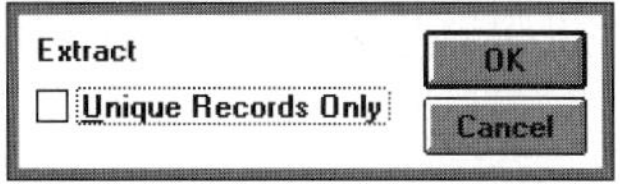

Excel will immediately perform the extract and copy all records that have 12 or a higher number in the YEARS field. Figure 14.9 shows the result of the extraction. You might have to scroll down a bit to see all the extracted data.

The little dialog box that popped up was asking what to do about duplicate records that matched the criteria. If there were duplicate records (there weren't in this database), you could choose to see all the records (the default) or just one from each group of matching records.

Extracting Specified Fields

Now try one more exercise to see how extraction works with only certain fields selected:

1. Carefully clear the data from cells A20:G25. Highlight that range and click on Edit, Clear. Then click on OK to remove the data from the range.
2. Highlight the range C19:G19 and clear the field names that are still there. Your worksheet should look like Figure 14.10, with just the SAL and L_NAME field names in row 19.

Figure 14.9
Database after the data extraction

	A	B	C	D	E	F	G
11	Ms.	Silverburg	Linda	2403 Salem Street	Bozeman	MT	23
12	Ms.	Simpson	Suzanne	24922 Muirlands	Boise	ID	15
13	Mr.	Smith	Dale	13 Main Street	Acton	MA	12
14	Mr.	Starkowski	George	9 Savoy Road	Encino	CA	4
15	Ms.	Sullivan	Samantha	Rt. 1, Box 12	Boston	MA	5
16	Mr.	Sullivan	Thor	35 Lower Keys Road	Tampa	FL	22
17	Ms.	Zemonson	Claudette	22 Orange Ave.	Miami	FL	6
18							
19	SAL	L_NAME	F_NAME	ADDR	CITY	STATE	YEARS
20	Mr.	Archuleta	Hector	2606 Swan Drive	Yonkers	NY	15
21	Mr.	Billitson	Michael	3993 Congress Ave.	Boca Raton	FL	13
22	Ms.	Silverburg	Linda	2403 Salem Street	Bozeman	MT	23
23	Ms.	Simpson	Suzanne	24922 Muirlands	Boise	ID	15
24	Mr.	Smith	Dale	13 Main Street	Acton	MA	12
25	Mr.	Sullivan	Thor	35 Lower Keys Road	Tampa	FL	22
26							
27							
28							
29							

Excel extracted only those records from the database that matched the criteria (YEARS >= 12)

Figure 14.10
Database after clearing some data from NAMELIST

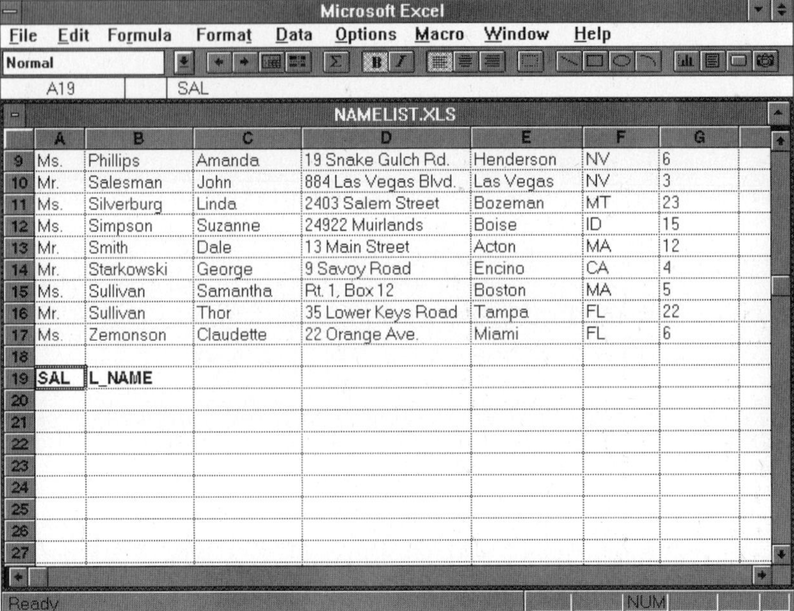

	A	B	C	D	E	F	G
9	Ms.	Phillips	Amanda	19 Snake Gulch Rd.	Henderson	NV	6
10	Mr.	Salesman	John	884 Las Vegas Blvd.	Las Vegas	NV	3
11	Ms.	Silverburg	Linda	2403 Salem Street	Bozeman	MT	23
12	Ms.	Simpson	Suzanne	24922 Muirlands	Boise	ID	15
13	Mr.	Smith	Dale	13 Main Street	Acton	MA	12
14	Mr.	Starkowski	George	9 Savoy Road	Encino	CA	4
15	Ms.	Sullivan	Samantha	Rt. 1, Box 12	Boston	MA	5
16	Mr.	Sullivan	Thor	35 Lower Keys Road	Tampa	FL	22
17	Ms.	Zemonson	Claudette	22 Orange Ave.	Miami	FL	6
18							
19	SAL	L_NAME					
20							
21							
22							
23							
24							
25							
26							
27							

3. Highlight the two field names: A19:B19.

4. Click on Data, Set Extract to identify the new extract range to Excel.

5. Click on Data, Extract and click on OK in the Unique Records Only dialog box. Watch as Excel extracts the same records as before—because they still match the original criteria of 12 or more years of service—but only those parts of the record that you asked for (the salutation and last name).

Deleting Records

Now, the fun part. You've spent all this time creating data—now it's time to destroy it. There will be times when you need to eliminate outdated records, such as closed accounts or items you no longer carry. This exercise will show you how to delete records that match your specified criteria.

Deleting records is even easier than extracting—and therein lies its danger. Since it's so easy to remove data, you might make a mistake, and there's no way to undo a Data, Delete command.

For this exercise, let's remove the records of individuals who live in Florida.

1. Move up to the criteria range and remove >=12 from cell G2. If you leave it there when you enter the criteria STATE=FL, you'll create a condition in which Excel will try to delete records that match STATE=FL AND YEARS>=12. This is called a *logical AND*, and although it is a valid construction, it's not what you want to accomplish here.

2. Highlight cell F2 in the criteria range and enter the new criteria: Type **FL** and then press Enter.

3. Double-check your work, and then if all is correct, click on Data, Delete. Figure 14.11 shows Excel giving you one more chance to change your mind before it permanently deletes those records.

4. Click on OK since you want them to go. Note how Excel automatically removes the records that met your criteria of STATE=FL and then moved all the other records up to fill in the gaps. When finished, the worksheet looks like Figure 14.12.

Database Analysis Tools

Excel provides 12 functions designed to work specifically with database ranges. These *database functions* are listed in Table 14.2. (Refer to Appendix C for further details on these functions.)

Figure 14.11
Last warning before losing records

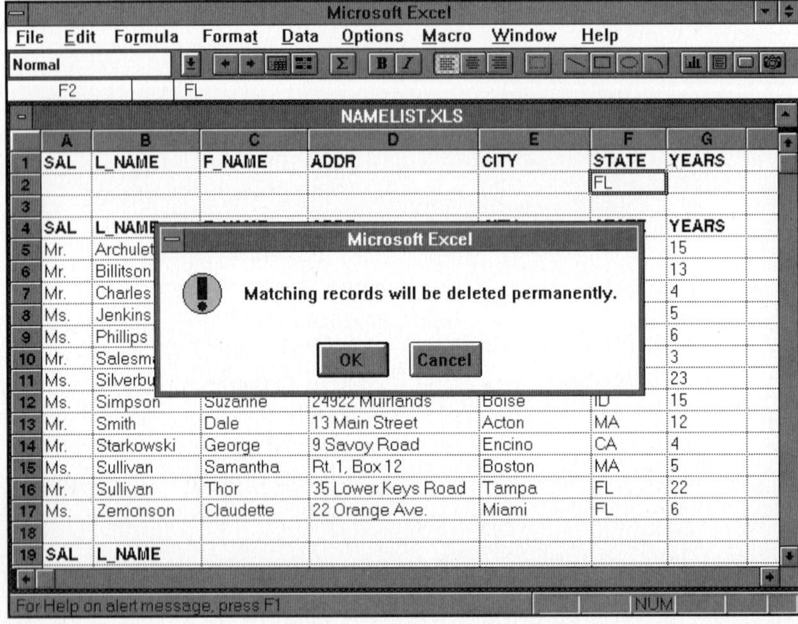

Figure 14.12
Database after deleting records

Microsoft Excel
File Edit Formula Format Data Options Macro Window Help
Normal
F2 FL
NAMELIST.XLS

	A	B	C	D	E	F	G
1	SAL	L_NAME	F_NAME	ADDR	CITY	STATE	YEARS
2						FL	
3							
4	SAL	L_NAME	F_NAME	ADDR	CITY	STATE	YEARS
5	Mr.	Archuleta	Hector	2606 Swan Drive	Yonkers	NY	15
6	Mr.	Charles	Winston	234 Shaffer Road	Chino	CA	4
7	Ms.	Jenkins	Susan	123 Main Street	Buffalo	NY	5
8	Ms.	Phillips	Amanda	19 Snake Gulch Rd.	Henderson	NV	6
9	Mr.	Salesman	John	884 Las Vegas Blvd.	Las Vegas	NV	3
10	Ms.	Silverburg	Linda	2403 Salem Street	Bozeman	MT	23
11	Ms.	Simpson	Suzanne	24922 Muirlands	Boise	ID	15
12	Mr.	Smith	Dale	13 Main Street	Acton	MA	12
13	Mr.	Starkowski	George	9 Savoy Road	Encino	CA	4
14	Ms.	Sullivan	Samantha	Rt. 1, Box 12	Boston	MA	5
15							
16							
17							
18							
19	SAL	L_NAME					

Ready NUM

Table 14.2 Database Functions

Function	Use
DAVERAGE()	Averages numbers
DCOUNT()	Counts the records
DCOUNTA()	Counts the nonblank records
DGET()	Extracts a single value
DMAX()	Finds a maximum value
DMIN()	Finds a minimum value
DPRODUCT()	Multiplies numbers
DSTDEV()	Calculates the standard deviation
DSTDEVP()	Calculates the standard deviation of a population
DSUM()	Sums numbers
DVAR()	Calculates the variance
DVARP()	Calculates the variance of a population

Each of these functions takes three arguments: the database, field name, and criteria. Now that you have worked with Excel's database features, these arguments should make sense. You might want to experiment with these functions on the NAMELIST. One exercise might be to determine the sum total of years with the company for those individuals whose last name begins with "S."

In the next chapter you'll be using the original version of NAMELIST-.XLS, so be sure *not* to save any of the changes (including the additions, deletions, and ranges) you've made in this chapter. Alternatively, if you're very attached to your work, save the worksheet under a different name.

Choose the Right Tools

One final note before closing this chapter. Although Excel all by itself is a very powerful and capable product, it is not meant to be a complete solution for everybody. Carefully consider your needs as you learn about both the power and the limitations of Excel, and think about what tools you will eventually need to accomplish a task.

For example, you might find yourself with a need to do some industrial-strength database work. Excel's features may or may not do the trick, but you should consider other products if it seems like Excel is beginning to run out of steam—either because of program limitations or limitations inherent in your system. In short, no single product is right for every job.

CHAPTER

15

Using Excel with External Files

Lotus 1-2-3 Files

dBASE III and IV Files

Other File Formats

Help for the Lotus 1-2-3 User

THE CORNERSTONE OF ANY SUCCESSFUL WINDOWS-BASED APPLICATION IS its ability to share information with other applications at all levels. This includes the ability to share screen data with other applications via the Windows Clipboard (more on this in Chapter 16) and via file format compatibility. Excel 3.0 can do both quite well.

Since it was first shipped back in 1987, Excel has been trying to catch up with another popular spreadsheet product—Lotus 1-2-3. In order to be more attractive to people who wanted to switch over from Lotus to Excel, the folks at Microsoft had to imbue Excel with multilingual capabilities—primarily the ability to bring in data (*import*) and write out data (*export*) in the Lotus 1-2-3 file format.

Although Excel is still catching up with Lotus 1-2-3 in terms of the current number of users, it is gaining in popularity. Therein lies another reason for the importance of compatibility. As time goes on, it becomes likely that more people will be exchanging data in dissimilar file formats (he has Lotus 1-2-3, but she has Excel).

Excel's already impressive file-translation features have been improved in 3.0 to include the ability to import and export many other file formats. This chapter describes some of the ways you can get information into and out of Excel worksheets.

Lotus 1-2-3 Files

Excel 3.0 is compatible with Lotus files that have a file extension of .WKS, .WK1, and .WK3, and it supports files created in Lotus 1-2-3 releases 1A, 2.x, 3.0, and 3.1. In addition, Excel 3.0 supports files created by Lotus Symphony.

In general, Excel will do the best job it can when it tries to bring in files from Lotus 1-2-3 and export files in 1-2-3 file format. However, there are some differences between Excel and Lotus in general, and between Excel and specific versions of Lotus, that hamper complete and total data interchangeability.

For example, because Lotus 1-2-3 releases 3.0 and 3.1 both support a true three-dimensional worksheet model, and Excel does not, Excel will export data to those versions of Lotus 1-2-3 as a series of linked worksheets that 1-2-3 can support. Similarly, when Excel tries to import a Lotus 1-2-3 3.0 or 3.1 file, because Excel does not support a three-dimensional worksheet model, it will import data as a series of individual linked worksheets.

For a complete rundown on the specific items—mostly minor—that are not supported when moving from one file format to another, consult the Excel 3.0 documentation.

Exporting to Lotus 1-2-3

In the following exercise, you will save a file in Lotus 1-2-3 file format and then bring it back into Excel. Since you may not have Lotus 1-2-3 on your machine, a figure shows what the file looks like in Lotus 1-2-3 before you save it. When you import the file back into Excel, you will see the sorts of things, such as character and cell formatting, that don't survive the transfer very well.

Although the version of Lotus that you'll save the file in is 2.2, the following instructions hold true for any version of Lotus 1-2-3 that Excel supports:

1. Open the BUDGET1.XLS file that you've used in previous chapters. For the purposes of comparison, it's reproduced here in Figure 15.1.

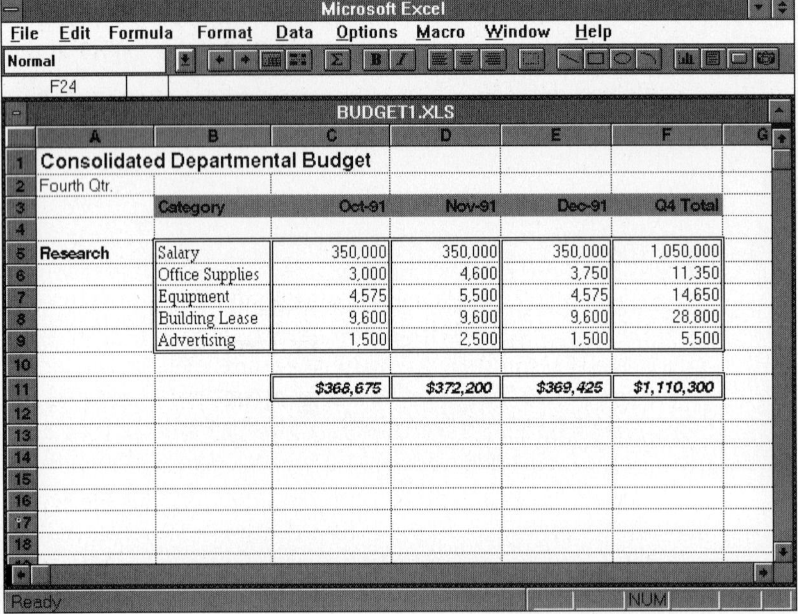

Figure 15.1 BUDGET1.XLS before exporting to 1-2-3

2. Click on File, Save As.
3. Click on the Options command button in the File Save As dialog box. The dialog box shown in Figure 15.2 appears.
4. Note that the File Format field is highlighted and is showing the Normal (Excel's default) file format. Click on the arrow to the right of the File Format field.

Figure 15.2
File Save As Options dialog box

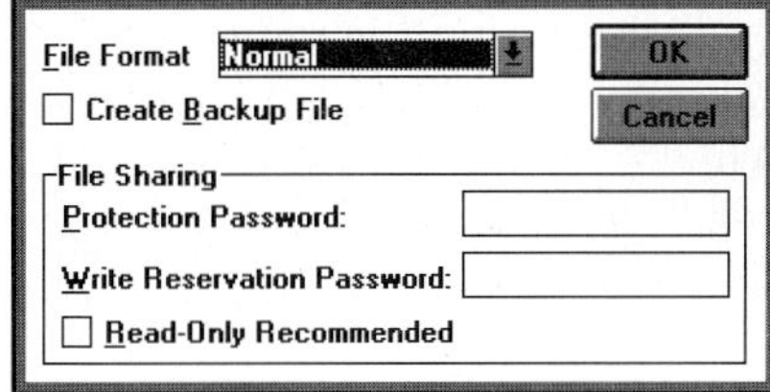

Tip. The File Format field is called a *combo box*—you've seen these before in other dialog boxes. Instead of clicking on the down arrow to the right of the field, you can simply press the Down Arrow key on the keyboard repeatedly until the choice you want appears in the combo box.

5. Scroll through that list until you see a choice marked "WK1." This is the format for Lotus 1-2-3 release 2.2. Highlight it now.
6. Click on OK to complete your choice. Note how Excel leaves the name of the file as is in the File Save As box ("BUDGET1") and simply changes the file extension to .WK1 (see Figure 15.3). Alternatively, you could have just typed the name **BUDGET1.WK1** at the file name prompt if you wanted to.
7. Click on OK to save the file in Lotus 1-2-3 2.2 format. When you finish, the only thing visibly different is the title bar of the window. Instead of reporting the name of the file as BUDGET1.XLS, it will be BUDGET1.WK1, like this:

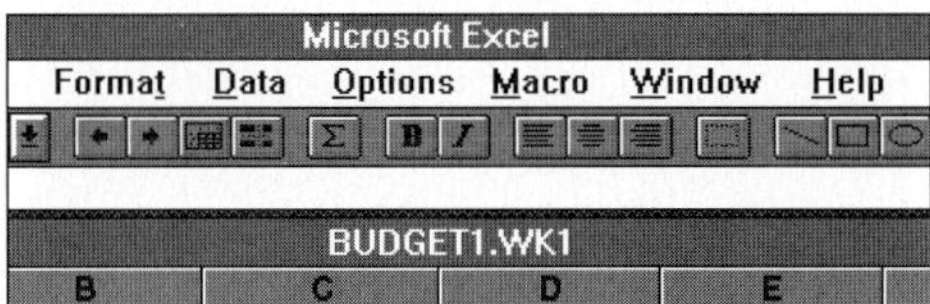

If at this point you do any more work with this file and then save it again, it will be saved as BUDGET1.WK1. The original file, BUDGET1.XLS, is still on disk and has not been modified. When you use File, Save As to save a file to another name, the data is immediately stored to the new file name and any subsequent changes that you make to the file are stored under the new name. You can always see the name of the file you're working on by looking at the Window title.

Importing from Lotus 1-2-3

Now that you've saved the file "out" to the Lotus 1-2-3 file format, it's time to bring it back into Excel. If you have a version of Lotus 1-2-3, you can look at the file to see what survived the translation. If not, Figure 15.4 shows what the file looks like as soon as you open it in Lotus 1-2-3.

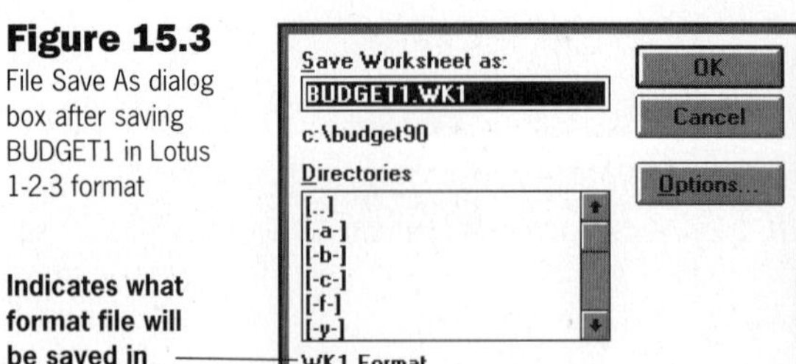

Figure 15.3
File Save As dialog box after saving BUDGET1 in Lotus 1-2-3 format

Indicates what format file will be saved in

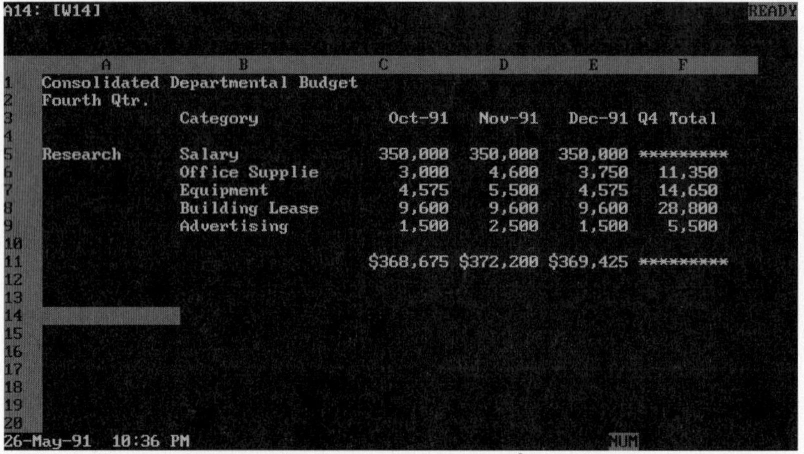

Figure 15.4
BUDGET1.WK1 in Lotus 1-2-3

Importing a file from a "foreign" file format such as Lotus 1-2-3 is usually as simple as opening that file with Excel's normal File, Open menu procedure. Here are the steps:

1. Make sure you've closed the Lotus 1-2-3 file format version of BUDGET1 (in Excel) that you were working with.

2. Click on File, Open to open the file. You can either pick the file name from the list box of files, or just go to the end of the File menu and look at the list of the last four files you have saved. Since you just saved the BUDGET1.WK1 file, it will be number 1 on the list. Figure 15.5 shows the resulting file that opens up for you.

Figure 15.5
BUDGET1.WK1 imported into Excel

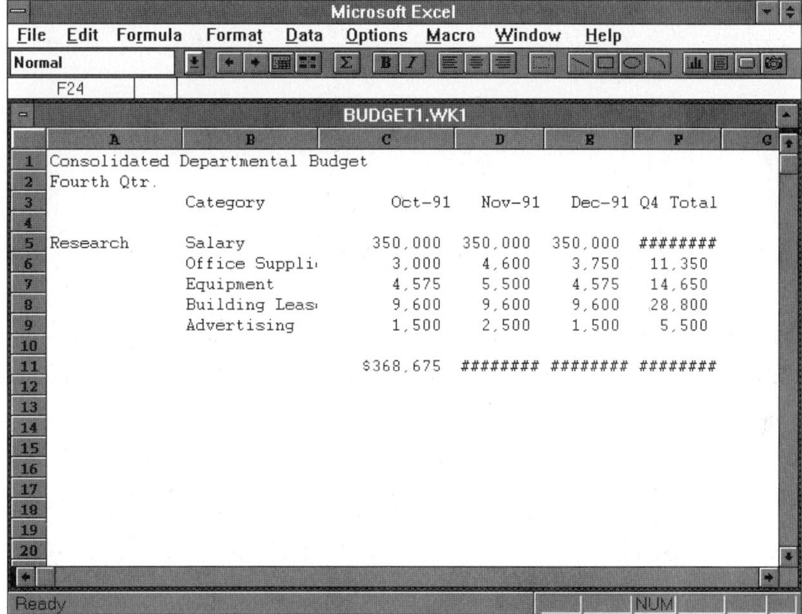

It sure looks different than the original worksheet (Figure 15.1), doesn't it? You can immediately see that any font information is lost in the translation from one file format to the other—all of the text on the worksheet is now in Courier type. In addition, some of the columns aren't wide enough to display the numbers in them. These display a string of pound signs (#####).

Note, however, that all the text and numeric data and the formulas and functions translated correctly. It will not always work out that way, however, due to some differences in the way that Excel and Lotus (or other spreadsheet programs for that matter) perform calculations.

One more important point to remember: Now that you've imported the Lotus file, any changes that you make to it will be saved back out in Lotus 1-2-3 format. This means that if you make any changes to the appearance of the file, save it, then reload it without remembering that it's a Lotus 1-2-3 file, all your pretty cell formatting will be lost. If you want to import a Lotus 1-2-3 file and intend for it to be a file used in Excel, you must save it with the File, Save As, Normal option.

dBASE III and IV Files

Do you know what the most popular database product for the PC has ever been? It's probably not your first guess, but Lotus 1-2-3 takes the top spot.

However, somewhere pretty close to the top of that list you'll find Ashton-Tate's dBASE II, III, and IV. In addition to dBASE products, there are also mountains of data stored in the file format used by myriad dBASE-compatible products such as Clipper and FoxPro. The file format and command structure of dBASE have become so ubiquitous that the term "xBASE" has been coined to refer to not only Ashton-Tate's dBASE products, but to all programs that store data in the dBASE file format and use commands that mimic those used by the dBASE database management program.

Note that many other database management products exist that do not use as their normal storage method the dBASE-compatible file format. However, products such as Borland's Paradox, Symantec's Q&A, and Alpha Software's Alpha Four can all read and write dBASE files and so can share data with Excel.

Exporting to dBASE Files

Exporting to a dBASE file format is virtually identical to exporting data to a Lotus 1-2-3 file format—with one important exception. Before Excel will save a file in any of the dBASE file formats—dBASE II (DBF 2), dBASE III (DBF 3), or dBASE IV (DBF 4)—there must be a range named in your worksheet called Database, just as you must have when using Excel as a database (see Chapter 14). This range is a special range, and it must contain field names in its first row.

Follow these steps to open the file and name the appropriate range in the file:

1. Close any open files that you've been using in previous exercises.
2. Use the File, Open command to open the NAMELIST.XLS file from Chapter 14—see Figure 15.6. The first row of the worksheet file holds what will be the field names: SAL, L_NAME, F_NAME, ADDR, and so on.
3. Highlight the range that encompasses the entire data file, including the field names. In this case, the range you should highlight is A1:G13.
4. Click on Formula, Define Name.
5. In the highlighted field of the dialog box, type **Database** as the name for this range, as shown here:

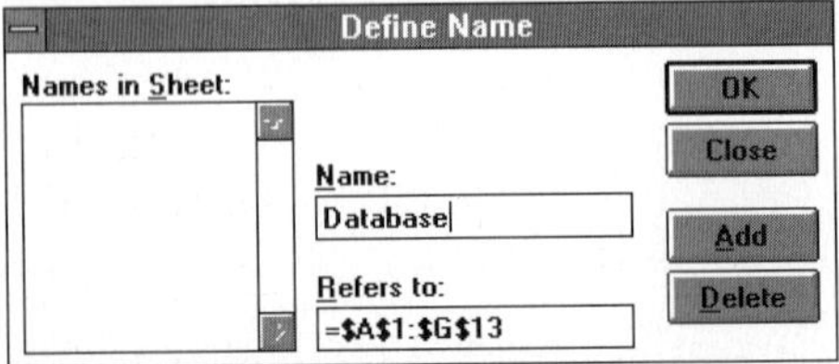

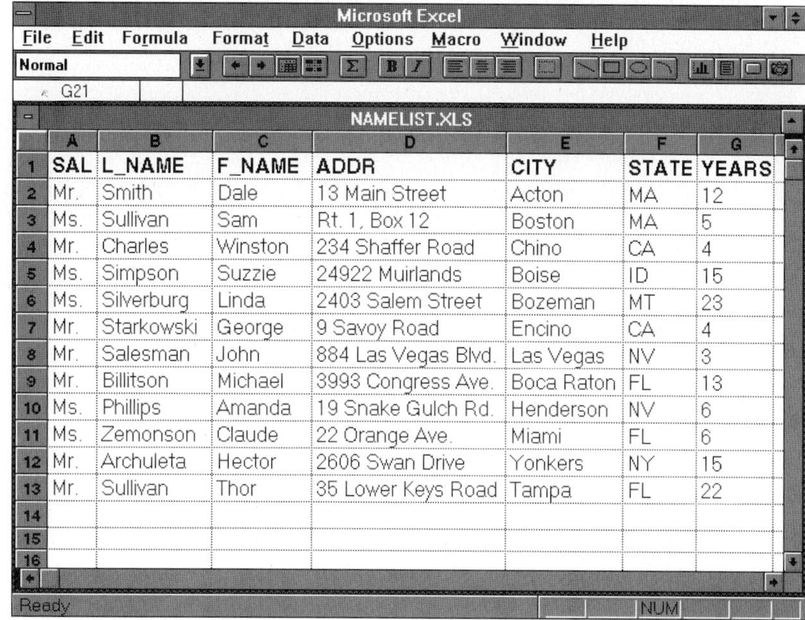

	A	B	C	D	E	F	G
1	SAL	L_NAME	F_NAME	ADDR	CITY	STATE	YEARS
2	Mr.	Smith	Dale	13 Main Street	Acton	MA	12
3	Ms.	Sullivan	Sam	Rt. 1, Box 12	Boston	MA	5
4	Mr.	Charles	Winston	234 Shaffer Road	Chino	CA	4
5	Ms.	Simpson	Suzzie	24922 Muirlands	Boise	ID	15
6	Ms.	Silverburg	Linda	2403 Salem Street	Bozeman	MT	23
7	Mr.	Starkowski	George	9 Savoy Road	Encino	CA	4
8	Mr.	Salesman	John	884 Las Vegas Blvd.	Las Vegas	NV	3
9	Mr.	Billitson	Michael	3993 Congress Ave.	Boca Raton	FL	13
10	Ms.	Phillips	Amanda	19 Snake Gulch Rd.	Henderson	NV	6
11	Ms.	Zemonson	Claude	22 Orange Ave.	Miami	FL	6
12	Mr.	Archuleta	Hector	2606 Swan Drive	Yonkers	NY	15
13	Mr.	Sullivan	Thor	35 Lower Keys Road	Tampa	FL	22
14							
15							
16							

Figure 15.6 NAMELIST.XLS worksheet

6. Click on OK to complete the command and assign the name to the range.

Now that you have completed the steps Excel requires before it can export the data to a dBASE file, you can perform the operation. Even though you highlighted the whole worksheet in this case, this procedure will only save that portion of the worksheet that has a named range of Database, and that range must have field names at the top of each column. Here's the procedure:

1. Click on File, Save As.
2. Click on the Options command button in the File, Save As dialog box.
3. In the new dialog box (Figure 15.2), click on the arrow to the right of the File Format field and scroll down through the list until you get to the DBF 3 option. (The DBF 2 and DBF 4 options refer to other versions of dBASE and work in the same fashion.)
4. Click on OK to change the file name extension and return to the File, Save As dialog box. Note that Excel automatically assigns a file name extension of .DBF to make the file usable with dBASE III and IV and dBASE-compatible programs.
5. Click on OK to save the file in dBASE format.

Figure 15.7 illustrates what this data looks like when it is loaded into dBASE III.

Figure 15.7
NAMELIST data in dBASE III

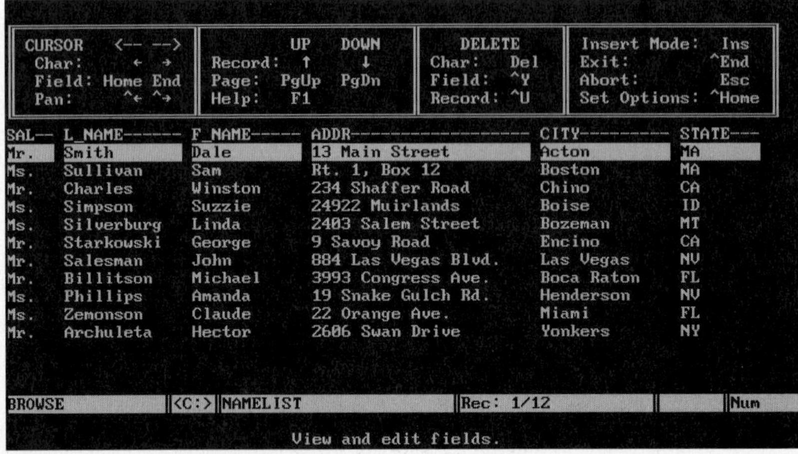

CURSOR <-- -->
Char: ← →
Field: Home End
Pan: ^← ^→

UP DOWN
Record: ↑ ↓
Page: PgUp PgDn
Help: F1

DELETE
Char: Del
Field: ^Y
Record: ^U

Insert Mode: Ins
Exit: ^End
Abort: Esc
Set Options: ^Home

SAL	L_NAME	F_NAME	ADDR	CITY	STATE
Mr.	Smith	Dale	13 Main Street	Acton	MA
Ms.	Sullivan	Sam	Rt. 1, Box 12	Boston	MA
Mr.	Charles	Winston	234 Shaffer Road	Chino	CA
Ms.	Simpson	Suzzie	24922 Muirlands	Boise	ID
Ms.	Silverburg	Linda	2403 Salem Street	Bozeman	MT
Mr.	Starkowski	George	9 Savoy Road	Encino	CA
Mr.	Salesman	John	884 Las Vegas Blvd.	Las Vegas	NV
Mr.	Billitson	Michael	3993 Congress Ave.	Boca Raton	FL
Ms.	Phillips	Amanda	19 Snake Gulch Rd.	Henderson	NV
Ms.	Zemonson	Claude	22 Orange Ave.	Miami	FL
Mr.	Archuleta	Hector	2606 Swan Drive	Yonkers	NY

BROWSE |<C:>|NAMELIST |Rec: 1/12 | |Num

View and edit fields.

Importing from dBASE III and IV Files

Again, like Lotus 1-2-3 files, importing data from a dBASE file is as easy as opening the file with the File, Open command. Use these steps to open a dBASE file:

1. First, close any open files you have been working with.
2. Click on File, Open. Note that by default, Excel inserts a *file mask* in the File Name field. This means that normally you only see files in the list box whose extension starts with XL. Ordinarily you just see worksheets (.XLS), charts (.XLC), macro sheets, (.XLM) and so on in the File, Open dialog box. However, in this case, you also want to see other files out there—namely those with the .DBF file extension.
3. To change the mask in the highlighted File Name field, type ***.DBF** and click on OK. Excel will list only those files that have a .DBF extension, as shown here:

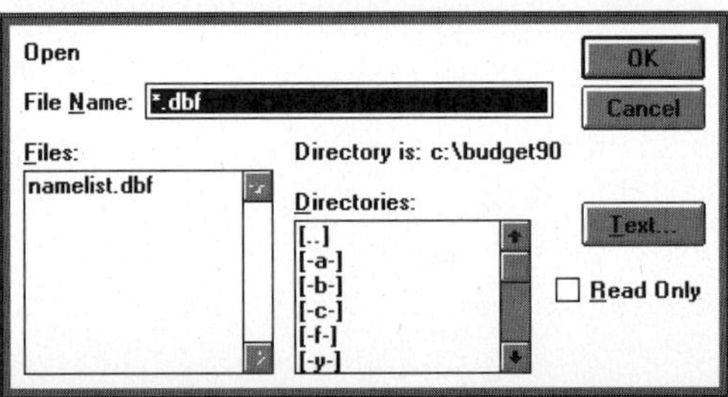

4. Highlight the NAMELIST.DBF file that is shown in the Files list box and click on OK to load it.

Unlike the Lotus file that came into Excel looking quite different than when it left, the dBASE-format file looks virtually identical to the way it went out. Even the appearance of the data is what you would expect since the import procedure uses Excel's default Helvetica 10-point font when it imports the data.

Other File Formats

Although you've now seen how to import and export from the two most popular applications that might have occasion to share data with Excel, there are some other file formats Excel 3.0 supports that you should know about. This section briefly explains those file formats you might use as you move data from one application to another. Each of them is selected in the File Format list box in the File Save As Options dialog box.

Normal

This is Excel's default file format and is the way all regular worksheets are stored. Remember that if you bring data in from another application and you want to save that data for subsequent use as an Excel worksheet, you must use the File, Save As, Normal command so that the data will be stored in the standard Excel format.

By default, files stored in the Normal format will be stored with an .XLS (worksheet), .XLM (macro sheet), .XLC (chart), or .XLW (workspace) file name extension.

Template

Templates were discussed back in Chapter 5. Files saved with this format will have the extension .XLT. Use templates if you want to create an Excel worksheet or macro sheet that will not change at all but will instead be used as a basis for other worksheets that you plan to create.

Excel 2.1

This file format was included for compatibility with earlier versions of Excel. Once you open an Excel 2.1 file with Excel 3.0 and then save it (in Excel's Normal format), it can't be read again by the 2.1 version of Excel. If there is someone else you are sharing data with, and the two of you are using different versions of Excel, use this file format to save files in 2.1 format. Of course, you might find that it's more appropriate to upgrade the other user and avoid the hassle of transferring data between the two formats.

SYLK

SYLK stands for SYmbolic LinK and is included for backward compatibility with earlier Microsoft products such as Multiplan or Excel for the Macintosh version 1.5 or earlier. These files are stored with the extension .SLK. Few applications use this file format today.

Text

This option is useful for saving data in a format that your word processor can use—if, for example, you want to include some portion of a worksheet in a report you are writing.

The only thing that is stored in this type of file is the contents of each cell; that is, formulas and functions are calculated and the *results* are saved. In addition, each column is separated by a tab and each row is terminated with a carriage return. If a cell contains a value that itself contains a comma, those cell contents are surrounded with double quotation marks. Excel stores files in the text format with an extension of .TXT.

Here's what the portion of the NAMELIST.XLS data file looks like when it is saved in Text format:

```
SAL L_NAME   F_NAME   ADDR              CITY   STATE YEARS
Mr. Smith    Dale     13 Main Street    Acton  MA    12
Ms. Sullivan Sam      "Rt. 1, Box 12"   Boston MA    5
Mr. Charles  Winston  234 Shaffer Road  Chino  CA    4
```

CSV

CSV is an acronym for Comma-Separated Values (or sometimes Variables) and is very similar to the Text format except that columns are separated by commas instead of tabs. As with the Text format, if the contents of a cell include a comma, the value is enclosed in double quotation marks. Excel stores these files with the extension .CSV. A portion of the NAMELIST.XLS file stored in CSV format looks like this:

```
SAL,L_NAME,F_NAME,ADDR,CITY,STATE,YEARS
Mr.,Smith,Dale,13 Main Street,Acton,MA,12
Ms.,Sullivan,Sam,"Rt. 1, Box 12",Boston,MA,5
Mr.,Charles,Winston,234 Shaffer Road,Chino,CA,4
Ms.,Simpson,Suzzie,24922 Muirlands,Boise,ID,15
```

DIF

This older file format is an acronym for Data Interchange Format. Once widely used as one way to get data from one program to another, it has fallen out of favor, mostly from disuse rather than technical weaknesses. Use this format if you can't find another file format in common between Excel and the target application. As you might expect, the extension used is .DIF.

Help for the Lotus 1-2-3 User

As mentioned earlier, the Microsoft engineers had to think a lot about the Lotus giant they were taking on back in 1987-1988. Not only did they make their product able to read and write Lotus-format files, but they also took several steps to make it easier for people to transfer their skills from one application to another.

Wooing Lotus users is still a big priority to Microsoft and by the looks of some of the features included in the 3.0 version of Excel, they've done a lot to make life at least tolerable for the Lotus veteran.

In the event that you cut your spreadsheet teeth on Lotus 1-2-3, this section is designed to acquaint you with some of the features available to you as a former Lotus 1-2-3 user.

Selection, Action: The Excel Paradigm

There is one fundamental difference between Lotus 1-2-3 and Excel that takes some effort to overcome: In the Lotus universe, you first tell Lotus what you want to do (action) and then tell it where you want to apply that action (selection). The Excel world is 180 degrees in the other direction: With Excel, you first select the object of your action (selection) and then tell Excel what you want to do to that selection (action). Although this is not difficult to picture or to talk about, it's surprisingly hard to adapt to when you first change from one program to the other.

There is, of course, a logic to the way that Excel does things. Once you select a range (column, row, cell) and then perform an action, that selection usually stays selected. You can then perform another action on the range without having to reselect it.

In contrast, with Lotus, to perform three actions, you would have to state the first action and make the selection, state the second action and make the selection again (the *same* selection, no less), and finally state the third action and make the same selection for the third time—which is a lot of duplicated effort.

Alternate Navigation Keys

Microsoft makes available an option that allows you to change the navigation keys so that they function more as they do in Lotus 1-2-3. Table 15.1

shows the differences between the standard Excel key actions (as shipped) and the alternate navigation-key actions.

Table 15.1 Default Versus Alternate Navigation Key Actions

Key	Default Excel Action	Alternate Action
Right Arrow	Moves right one cell	Moves right one cell
Left Arrow	Moves left one cell	Moves left one cell
Up Arrow	Moves up one cell	Moves up one cell
Down Arrow	Moves down own cell	Moves down own cell
Ctrl-Left Arrow	Goes to next block of data on the left	Moves left one screen
Ctrl-Right Arrow	Goes to next block of data on the right	Moves right one screen
Home	Moves to start of row	Moves to cell A1
End	Moves to rightmost column that contains data	Pressing End then an arrow key (sequentially) moves to next block of data in direction of arrow
PgUp	Moves up one screen	Moves up one screen
PgDn	Moves down one screen	Moves down one screen
F1	Help	Help
F2	Begins formula editing mode	Begins formula editing mode
F5	Formula GoTo command	Moves to specified cell
F9	Recalculates the worksheet	Recalculates the worksheet

In addition, by selecting Alternate Navigation Keys (you'll learn how in a moment), the behavior of some other keys is affected. Table 15.2 describes what those keys do with Alternate Navigation Keys enabled.

Use the following steps to enable the alternate key actions:

1. Close any open worksheets you may have been working with.
2. Click on Options, Workspace.
3. In the dialog box that appears, place an X in the Alternate Navigation Keys checkbox, as shown in Figure 15.8.
4. Click on OK to complete the command.

Table 15.2 **Other Key Actions with Alternate Navigation Keys Enabled**

Key	Action
'	Left-aligns data in the cell
"	Right-aligns data in the cell
^	Centers the data in the cell
\	Repeats the character that follows it across the cell
@	Can be used to start a function or formula
+ – (1-9	Can be used to start a formula

Figure 15.8
Options Workspace dialog box

Getting Help for 1-2-3 Commands

If you are just starting out with Excel and have been using 1-2-3 until this time, you might want to get some additional help with Excel, perhaps in the form of little hints about how to do things. Excel 3.0 has a pretty extensive help facility to help you get started if you are accustomed to Lotus 1-2-3's style of working.

By default, when you press the slash key (/) in Excel you will get the Excel menu bar. This behavior is identical to the Alt key or the F10 key—they all activate Excel's menu bar. This is fine if you've become accustomed to Excel's requirements. Say you just moved over to Excel from 1-2-3, however, and you'd like just a bit more help. Try this:

1. Click on Options, Workspace.
2. Look at the choices available in the dialog box (Figure 15.8) under "Alternate Menu or Help Key." You can have either the slash key (by default) or any other key call up one of two options: the standard Excel menus or a special help facility for Lotus 1-2-3 users. Once you've become more familiar with Excel you'll want to reset this for the standard Excel keys, but in the meantime, choose Lotus 1-2-3 Help.
3. Click on OK to complete the command.
4. Now, back in your worksheet, press the slash key (/) and watch as Excel pops up the special help system. This is illustrated in Figure 15.9.

Figure 15.9
Lotus 1-2-3 help

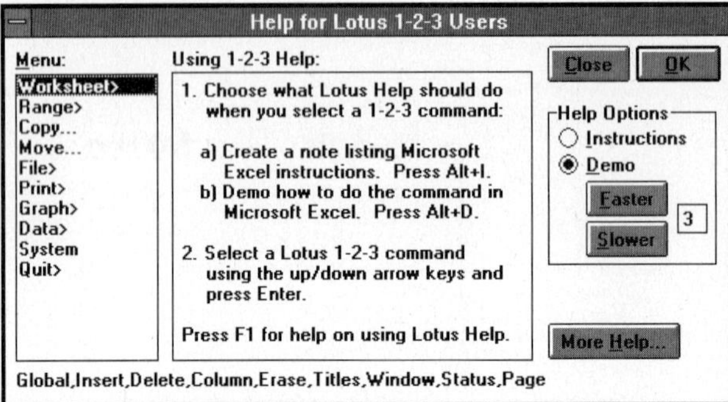

5. Click on the Instructions button.
6. Finally, use the same commands that you would if you were using Lotus 1-2-3 to bring up information about retrieving a file: Type **F**, then **R**. Look at Figure 15.10 and see how Excel has popped up a small screen that contains all the information you need to retrieve a file using Excel's menus.

Translating Macros

Excel includes a separate program called the Macro Translation Assistant to help you make the move from Lotus 1-2-3 to Excel. (Note, however, that the Translation Assistant will not translate macros from Excel to 1-2-3.) Although it isn't completely successful (some macros will need to be modified once you have moved them to Excel worksheets) the Macro Translation Assistant can at least help you to begin the process.

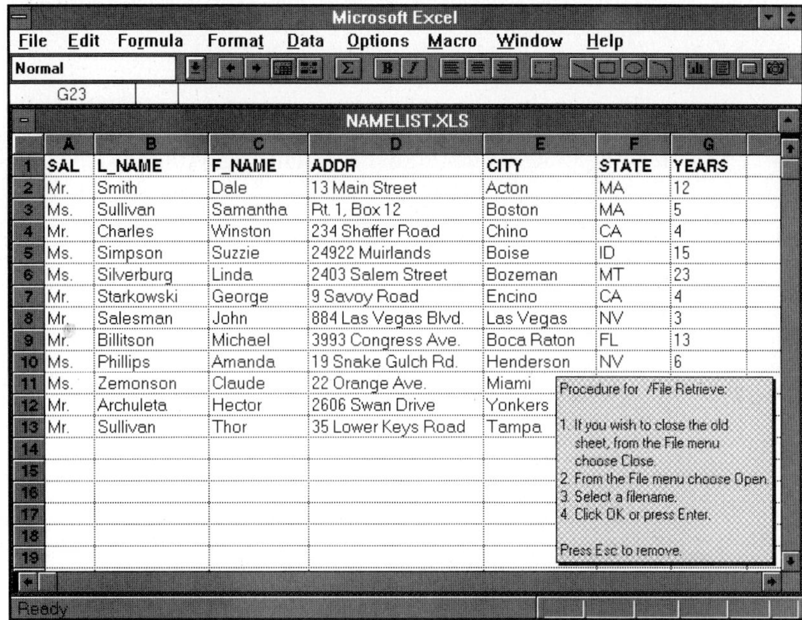

Figure 15.10 Lotus 1-2-3 help note with instructions

You won't be able to try this unless you have a Lotus 1-2-3 spreadsheet with macros in it. If you do, here's how to import macros from Lotus 1-2-3 worksheets into their own Excel macro sheets:

1. Click in the Excel System menu box. It's in the upper-left corner of the Excel window, at the left end of the bar that reads "Microsoft Excel." The System menu appears:

2. Click on the Run option. A dialog box appears.
3. Select the Macro Translator option.
4. Click on OK to complete the command.

5. Click on the Translate, Lotus 1-2-3 option in the resulting dialog box.
6. In the box marked "Select Source Sheet," highlight the worksheets that contain macros you want to translate.
7. Click on OK to accept the list of worksheets.
8. In the box marked "Select Macros To Translate," highlight the macros that you want to translate.
9. Click on OK to begin the translation process.

It's a very good idea to turn on the Verbose option in the Translate Lotus 1-2-3 dialog box because it copies the original text of the Lotus 1-2-3 macro into the translated macro. This is very helpful for those times where the Macro Translation Assistant is unable to completely translate the macro. With the full text, you can see what the original macro did and begin to find an equivalent Excel function.

If the Macro Translation Assistant does not understand a macro that you asked it to translate, it will insert a message in your macro sheet that says what the macro function's purpose was. This gives you a bit more help as you try to find an alternative function.

CHAPTER

16

Data Exchange with the Clipboard and DDE

Using the Clipboard

The Benefits of DDE

Communicating with Other Applications

For Additional Information

EARLIER CHAPTERS HAVE ALLUDED TO SOME OF THE INTERESTING software-integration possibilities within reach of the average end-user using Windows-based programs. Never before in the short but volatile history of the personal computer have we had as much opportunity to integrate applications as we do now with the programs built around the Windows interface. Sadly, this chapter can't begin to do justice to a topic that could take up several volumes. Nevertheless, it should provide the seeds of ideas for future integration projects you might undertake when you realize how feasible they are.

A little background is in order. When Windows was shipped for the first time several years ago, it included a little-known protocol known as Dynamic Data Exchange, or DDE. DDE was a published protocol—a set of rules—that vendors could use to create applications able to integrate with other applications and work with them to share data. DDE made it at least potentially possible for any Windows-based application to communicate with any other Windows-based application.

Unfortunately, DDE at that time fell far short of its potential—primarily because computers then didn't have the requisite horsepower needed to get the optimum performance from DDE. That, coupled with the less-than-universal acceptance of Windows, relegated DDE issues to the back burner. Now, however, with the rising popularity of Windows 3.0, people are beginning to take a serious look at the benefits of Dynamic Data Exchange. Those benefits are explored a little later in the chapter. First, you'll learn more about one of the most useful tools for working with Windows applications, the Clipboard.

Using the Clipboard

It has always been difficult for beginning computer users to successfully transfer data between applications, in spite of the fact that it makes sense for everyone who uses a computer to be able to move data from one program to another.

It used to be that the only way to transfer data and information was to print it out from one program and then retype it into the other application. Surprisingly, many people still believe that they have to do this—that it would be "too hard" to transfer the data any other way than by hand.

Wearying of manually rekeying the data, some people became aware of common file formats. By using such standardized formats as Comma-Separated Values (CSV) and DIF (Data Interchange Format), it was possible to save data from an application in one of these file formats and then import it to another application using the common file format.

When Microsoft Windows come out toward the end of the 1980s, it built on ideas that had until then been unavailable on the IBM-compatible personal computing class of machines. Windows offered both developers and end-users a simple yet usable method of data transfer called the Clipboard.

As previously mentioned, there are two fundamental methods for *inter-program* (between applications) and *interprocess* (within one program) communications, Dynamic Data Exchange (DDE) and the Windows Clipboard.

Of these two, the Clipboard is used much more often. With the Clipboard you can quickly select a range of cells in a spreadsheet (for example), copy them to the Clipboard, and then paste them into another worksheet or perhaps a word processor. Even if the second program was developed by a different vendor, because both applications support the rules of the Clipboard, both products work together well and provide a clean, consistent way to share data.

How the Clipboard Works

The Clipboard is really just a temporary data storage area available from each program—usually through that program's Edit menu. The Windows Clipboard supports several commands whose meanings are consistent from application to application and thus let you operate the Clipboard in the same manner no matter what application you are using.

To use the Clipboard, you must first either move or copy the selected data (using a Cut or Copy command) from one application to the Clipboard. Cutting removes the data from the source application, whereas a copy operation only makes a copy of the data and puts that on the Clipboard. You then move to the target application and place (using the Paste command) the data from the clipboard into the target application.

The Clipboard Within Excel

You have already used the Clipboard within Excel. Back when you were learning about formulas and functions you copied some data from one part of the worksheet to another. Now that you have a bit more perspective on the concept of the Clipboard, you will see how to use it first to transfer data between two worksheets and then for transferring between two different applications.

Use the following instructions to transfer information from one worksheet to another:

1. Open up the BUDGET3.XLS worksheet saved from earlier chapters.
2. Open a new worksheet. Use File, New, Worksheet to create a new one. You should now have two worksheets on your screen, a new, blank one and the one that you've used before.

3. Use Windows, Arrange All to organize the worksheets so that they both appear on the screen. When you finish, your screen should look like Figure 16.1.

Figure 16.1
BUDGET3.XLS and a blank worksheet

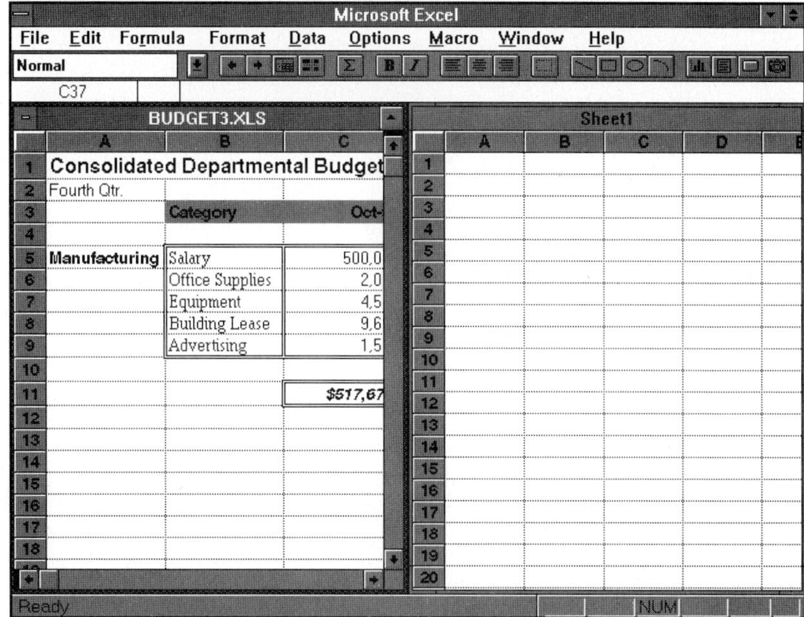

4. If it is not active, activate BUDGET3.XLS by clicking anywhere inside its document window.

5. Highlight the range that you wish to copy from one application to another. For this exercise, highlight B5:B9.

6. Click on Edit, Copy. That data is now copied to the Clipboard. Note that since this was a Copy operation, the data remained in place on the original worksheet.

7. Activate the blank worksheet by clicking anywhere inside it.

8. Highlight the cell that you want to be the upper-left corner of the range that you are about to paste in. Highlight cell C7.

9. Finally, paste in the cells by clicking on Edit, Paste. When you finish, your screen should look like Figure 16.2.

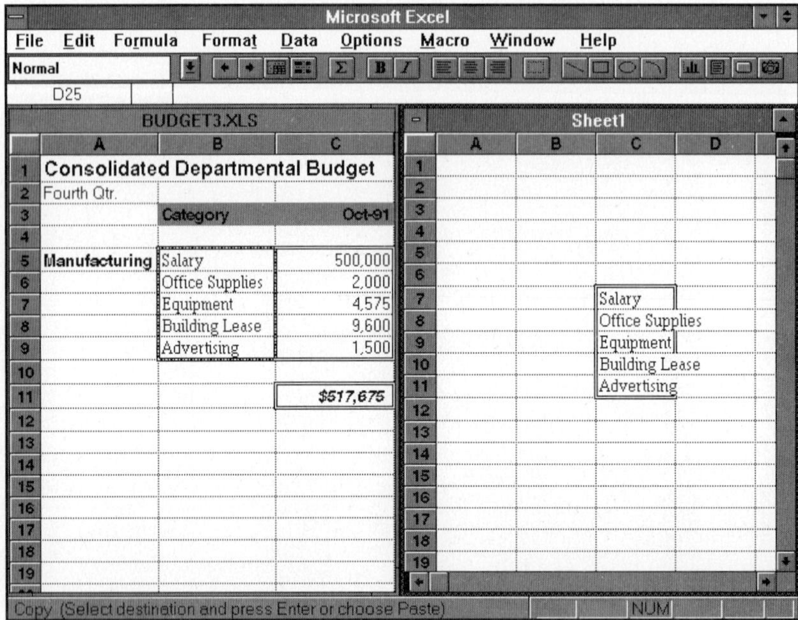

Figure 16.2 Worksheets after performing the Copy operation

The Cut operation is identical to the Copy operation but the data is removed from the source range when it is placed on the Clipboard.

There are a few things to note about the Clipboard. First, only one "item" can be on the Clipboard at a time. Here's how to remember that: Every time you perform either an Edit, Cut or Edit, Copy, whatever was on the Clipboard is replaced by the new cut or copied data. In other words, you can't roam all over your worksheet collecting bits and pieces to put on the Clipboard.

Also, as you've seen in recent chapters, the Clipboard is closely involved with linking. Although the two differ because linking is dynamic and the Clipboard is only good for one operation at a time, it is the Clipboard that places the linking formula into the application. Think of the Clipboard as a one-time data sharing device, whereas DDE and links are semi-permanent.

Using the Clipboard in Other Windows Applications

Using the Clipboard with other Windows programs is very similar to using it within Excel. Certainly you can be assured that the Cut, Copy, and Paste operations work the same from application to application. Whenever you want to transfer data from one Windows application to another, check that application's Edit menu. Chances are you'll see options for Cut, Copy, and Paste.

Here's an example of what you can do with the Clipboard between different Windows applications:

1. Open a new document in a Windows-based word processor such as Word for Windows or the Windows Write program that comes with Windows.
2. Type a few sentences of text into the new document and then place the cursor below the text. This is where you will insert your Excel data.
3. Click on the Minimize button (second from the right in the upper-right corner of the word processing application) to minimize the word processor.
4. If Excel is not already running, start Excel as you normally would.
5. Load your BUDGET1.XLS worksheet.
6. Highlight the range you want to copy to the other application. In this case, highlight the range B5:F9.
7. Click on Edit, Copy to copy the selected range to the Windows Clipboard.
8. Press Ctrl-Esc to bring up the Windows Task Manager. Double-click on the name of the word processor you minimized.
9. Make sure the cursor is where you want it in the word processor, and then click on Edit, Paste from the word processor menu.

Note how the Excel data is immediately pasted from the Clipboard into the word processing application.

The Benefits of DDE

Although the computer industry press has spent a great deal of time and effort describing the benefits of Microsoft Windows as a graphical user interface, much less attention has been paid to the potentially powerful method of data transfer between Windows programs called DDE. Dynamic Data Exchange differs from simple file transfers in that it provides links between two or more programs. As you learned in Chapter 11, these links can shuffle data between the linked programs in real time—as events happen—and not simply when you want the information to be upgraded.

When you created links from one worksheet to another in Chapter 11, you unknowingly used DDE links—Excel created and managed those links on your behalf. In addition, when and if you created the links between Excel and Word for Windows, those were DDE links as well.

Because DDE provides a way for two or more programs from different vendors to communicate, software developers and end-users alike have the ability to devise powerful software solutions to problems that might require more than one application to solve. DDE gives you the ability to create applications that transcend the capabilities of a single application. By allowing programs to share data (or even other programs), vendors can be free to concentrate on building the type of software they know best.

As an example, say your task is to create a report in Word for Windows incorporating data stored in Excel. You would probably agree that it makes sense for the spreadsheet product to excel at numerical analysis and not have a lot of word processing functions. Likewise, Word for Windows doesn't need elaborate financial analysis functions since those are already provided in Excel. DDE permits each of these applications to do what it does best, while enabling you to integrate the best of both worlds.

Perhaps in the future, mature and stable DDE implementations in a graphical user environment will allow a user to purchase program "modules" that serve limited but specific functions. For example, you might purchase a "compute engine" (maybe Excel) for spreadsheet work, a "database engine" to store data, and so on. All data shared among these modules would be shuffled around via DDE or a similar mechanism.

To see how this is happening even now, read on; the next to last section of this chapter describes how you can do some of these things right now.

DDE Command Concepts

Before two programs can transfer data back and forth they must have a "conversation." This is analogous to meeting someone on the street and saying "Hello." If the person answers back with "Hello," your conversation can begin—you've established the protocol for your communication. If the person answers back with "*Buenos dias*," you had better know what to do or the conversation will get nowhere. Either you adapt or they adapt; otherwise the conversation cannot take place.

In the computer world, the program that initiates the conversation with another is called the *client*, and the program receiving the request to initiate a conversation, and providing the data to the client, is called the *server.*

Unfortunately, all of this conversation and subsequent data transfer back and forth between applications is currently still rather difficult for the end-user to program and manage. However, some applications come with macros and programming code for DDE integration already in the package. For example, say you want to compute some real-time stock prices as the stock market changes throughout the day. With Excel and a Windows-based communications program, you could program Excel to initiate a conversation with DynaComm (to pick one of several communications programs). Excel would be the client and DynaComm would be the server.

While DynaComm was linking up with some real-time provider of stock information, Excel would create DDE links between DynaComm and certain cells in the worksheet. Then every time the data changed in DynaComm, that information would be passed back to Excel, and Excel would immediately show the new figures. Because Excel is a spreadsheet, its most productive role is to calculate numbers—not trying to be a communications program. With DDE it doesn't have to be.

Once the conversation is established between the two applications, messages are then passed from one to the other, carrying either data or instructions. There are basically four major types of messages (also called *transactions*) that can be sent via DDE between applications. The following short discussion of these transaction types will give you an idea of the flexibility and potential usefulness of the DDE protocol:

DDE_Advise The DDE_Advise transaction is a request that the server provide information to the client whenever the specified data changes. This function is often called a *hot-link* because any time the data changes, the DDE protocol immediately sends the new information. For instance, if Excel initiated a DDE_Advise with DynaComm, Excel would receive updated information every time the data changed in DynaComm. The graphical financial workstations used in banks and trading operations that use Excel for trading purposes use the DDE_Advise function to keep their graphs and worksheets updated.

DDE_Request A DDE_Request transaction is a one-time request from the client to the server asking for the server to provide some specific information. In the previous example, Excel could request that DynaComm provide a single stock quote.

DDE_Poke The DDE_Poke statement is the opposite of DDE_Request. This statement allows the client application (Excel, in this example) to "poke" information into the server instead of receiving information from it.

DDE_Execute The DDE_Execute statement lets the client application initiate commands on the server. This "remote-control" function has many useful applications. If Excel is the client in our example and DynaComm is the server, Excel could command DynaComm to execute a macro that would log on to the stock service and begin capturing data.

Communicating with Other Applications

If the preceding examples were a bit too complicated, here are two other examples that might be a bit closer to home.

Example: Excel and Word for Windows

I've said that DDE makes sense when there are two different applications that need to share data. Consider the following scenario with Excel and

Microsoft's word processor, Word for Windows. You have a weekly report that you prepare with Word for Windows. Part of the report is a portion of a spreadsheet showing weekly sales figures. Until now, you've been just printing out the spreadsheet and adding the numbers to your report by hand, creating a worksheet-like grid using the Tab key.

With DDE, and using procedures very similar to what you did back in Chapter 11, you can create hot-links between your Excel worksheet and your Word for Windows document such that every time you make a change in the Excel worksheet (presumably once a week), when you open up your report document in Word for Windows, you would have an actual, "live" worksheet—one that was updated every time the numbers in the spreadsheet changed.

This procedure doesn't even require any programming or macro language interaction on your part. As you did in the earlier example (in Chapter 11), you just select the portion of the worksheet you want included in the report document, copy it to the Clipboard, and then perform a Paste, Link where you want the worksheet to appear in your Word for Windows document.

Example: Excel and Q+E

An even more concrete example of the potential for DDE interaction and integration between applications is the way that Excel and a companion product called Q+E work together. Q+E is included with Microsoft Excel 3.0 and is designed for access to external database files. Although Excel provides database features, Q+E is intended for those situations in which you have a database that is too large to fit into Excel's memory and you must store or manipulate records in that database.

Since they use DDE to work together, Q+E and Excel appear almost as one seamless application. Once installed and executed, Q+E seems to just add a few menu items to the Excel menus, and these items function just like any other Excel menu selection.

Under the hood, so to speak, is where Excel and Q+E use DDE to communicate and work together. And, because both Excel and Q+E support DDE, you can link any other application supporting DDE to either Excel or Q+E so that the application's data is updated whenever the data in Q+E changes. Also, of course, Q+E supports the Windows Clipboard, so you also have that option if you want to, for example, move some data out of Q+E and place it in Excel.

For Additional Information

Although it hasn't been feasible here to discuss all the interesting possibilities available when two or more Windows applications can communicate, now that you've been introduced to the concept, you can think about it more and determine if you might be able to use these features. In the context of interapplication integration, the whole is far greater than the sum of its parts.

For further information about using DDE from Excel to other applications, consult the *Microsoft Excel User's Guide* and the *Q+E for Microsoft Excel User's Guide*.

APPENDIX A

The DOS and Windows Environment

This book assumes a basic knowledge of operating within the Microsoft Windows operating environment. It also assumes you are new to the Excel 3.0 spreadsheet program. However, given that many people have not yet worked much with Windows, this appendix is meant to give you a quick overview of the capabilities of Windows and how you can get started using it. At the same time, this appendix is no substitute for the more detailed information you can find in your DOS manual or in the Microsoft Windows User's Guide.

If you have worked with Windows before (or with a Macintosh, for that matter, since the two are very similar), you probably won't need to review this information because you will have worked with these concepts before.

Also in this appendix is a very brief recap of some of the DOS rules for file names and directory conventions. Because the book assumes that you know your way around your hard disk, you'll find some review material on that subject here as well.

A Quick Tour of Windows

Figure A.1 is a view of Microsoft Excel when you first load it. The following paragraphs comprise a brief discussion of the various parts of the window.

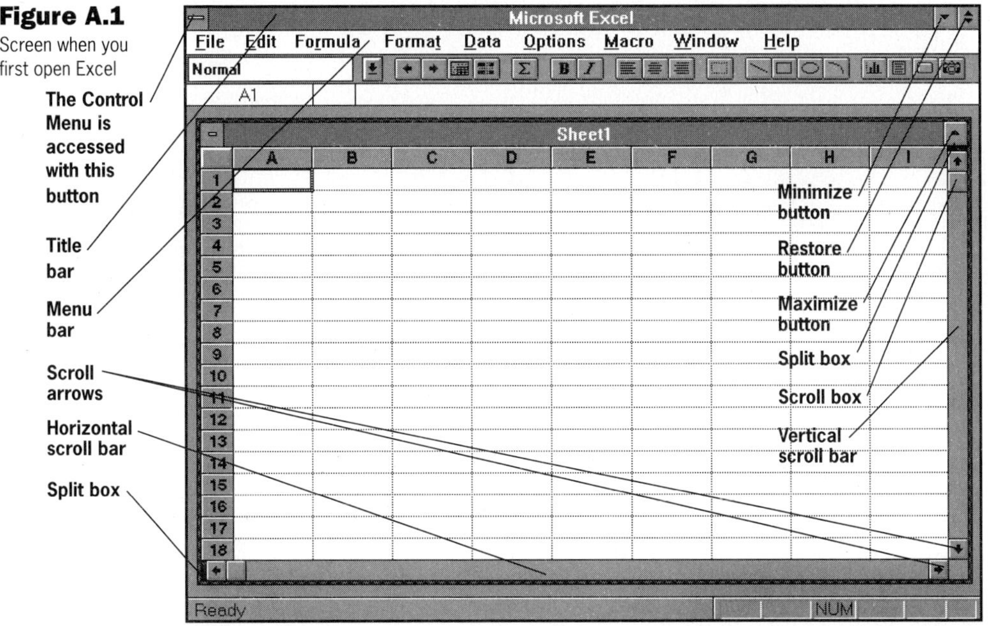

Figure A.1 Screen when you first open Excel

Title Bar The Windows title bar displays the title of the application and often displays the name of the file the application is working with at the time. Under certain circumstances, Excel's title bar will display the name of the active file.

Menu Bar Virtually every Windows application has a menu bar that lists at least a couple commands you can perform.

Control Menu The Control menu is a special menu in an application that controls aspects of the application. Control menus let you maximize, minimize, restore, and close both document windows and whole applications without having to use the mouse. As an example, the Control menu for Excel is shown here:

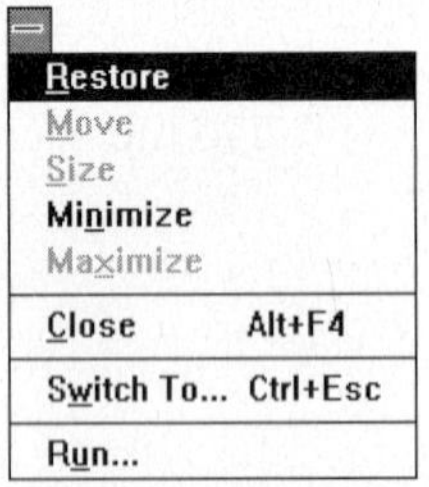

Minimize Button Use this button to cause Excel (or other applications) to shrink down to an icon sitting on the Windows desktop. Note that when you minimize an application it is still running—it is just made smaller so that it doesn't take up much space on the desktop. Some applications (and users) use *iconize* instead of *minimize*.

Maximize Button The Maximize button is the opposite of the Minimize button. It causes the window to grow to the full size of the screen. Use this button when you want as much of the application to show as possible.

Restore Button The Restore button returns a window to the size it was before you maximized it.

Scroll Box This small box, located within each scroll bar, shows the position of the current screen in relation to the size of the entire file. For example, if the scroll box is halfway between the top and the bottom of the scroll bar, you are approximately halfway through the current file. If you click and drag on this box, you can quickly move through the document or worksheet.

Scroll Bars Scroll bars are the vertical and horizontal bars along the right-hand side and lower edge of the Excel screen. Clicking in the shaded area above or below the scroll box moves you one screen at a time in that direction for each click. For example, if you click in the shaded area above the scroll box, you will move up one screen.

Scroll Arrows The scroll arrows are located at the top and bottom of the vertical scroll bar and the right and left ends of the horizontal scroll bar. Use the scroll arrows to move through the worksheet one row or column at a time. Note that this increment varies among different Windows applications. For example, in a word processing document, it might cause your document to scroll one line at a time or one page at a time.

Using the Mouse

As stated earlier in the book, the use of a mouse is highly recommended, and it's assumed that you've at least had an exposure to the mouse and Windows before—if only when you installed Windows on your machine.

Note. Although this book is mouse-oriented, it's important to realize that you can do with the keyboard just about anything that you can do with a mouse—it's just not as easy.

Here are a few terms you should know relating to the use of the mouse:

Click means to position the mouse pointer over an object and press and release the mouse button. This action is used to highlight files, make choices in dialog boxes, and to carry out a command when you click on a command button.

To *double-click* means to hold the mouse pointer over an item and then rapidly click the button twice.

To *drag* a mouse means to position the pointer over an object, press the left mouse button and hold it down, and while holding it down move the mouse elsewhere. Usually, you will do this to move something from one place on the worksheet to another. When you finish, just release the mouse button.

Pointing simply means to move the mouse pointer over a particular object. Note that the Excel mouse pointer is dynamic—that is, it often changes shape depending on the object it points at and the context. The pointer shape will tell you when you've positioned the mouse pointer over a specific area. The different shapes are as follows:

This shape is used to point or highlight when you are in a menu or scroll bar or a chart window. It is also used to select graphic objects.

This shape appears in the worksheet window. With it you can click to select an individual cell or drag to select a range of cells.

After you have selected a graphical tool from the toolbar, this pointer shape allows you to draw an object or place a macro button or text box.

This pointer appears in the formula bar or within a text box in a dialog box when you click to begin inserting characters.

When you place the pointer on the borders between row headings, this shape allows you to adjust the height of the row.

Similar to the preceding shape, this pointer allows you to change the width of a column. Place the pointer on the border between two column headings to do so.

This shape appears when you place the pointer in a window border. You can use it to resize the window either vertically or horizontally.

Appearing at window corners, this pointer allows you to resize a window both horizontally and vertically at the same time.

In Print Preview mode, when you are looking at your pages and layout, you can position this pointer over a section of the worksheet and click to magnify that part.

This is the help pointer—it appears when you press Shift-F1 for context-sensitive help. To get information about a specific area of the screen, simply click there.

In the help system, use this pointer to point to words that are underlined. If the word has a dotted underline, press and hold down the mouse button to see the word's definition. If the word is underlined with a solid rule, you can click on the word to jump to related information.

This shape appears when the pointer is placed on a graphic object that has a macro attached to it. Click once to run the macro.

The hourglass can occur in any context. It means you must wait for the current action or command to be completed.

Window Management

Windows are the heart and foundation of the Windows operating environment. With the ability to move windows around the screen, size them to your liking, and open and close them when you want, you have the opportunity to set up your work area the way you want it to be—not the way some application vendor thinks it should be. The next three sections discuss how to move and resize your windows.

Document Versus Application Windows

Unlike many Windows-based applications, Excel provides the ability to have multiple windows open within the main program window. Although this ability is not unique to Excel, Multiple Document Interface (MDI) gives you maximum flexibility when working with multiple worksheets.

In Excel, the main program window is called the *application window.* This is the window that presents the menu bar, the formula bar, and so on. The application window can be resized and moved like any other Windows application. In fact, if you close down all your worksheets, you can see that your Excel program is little more than a single window, as shown in Figure A.2.

Figure A.2
Excel with all document windows closed

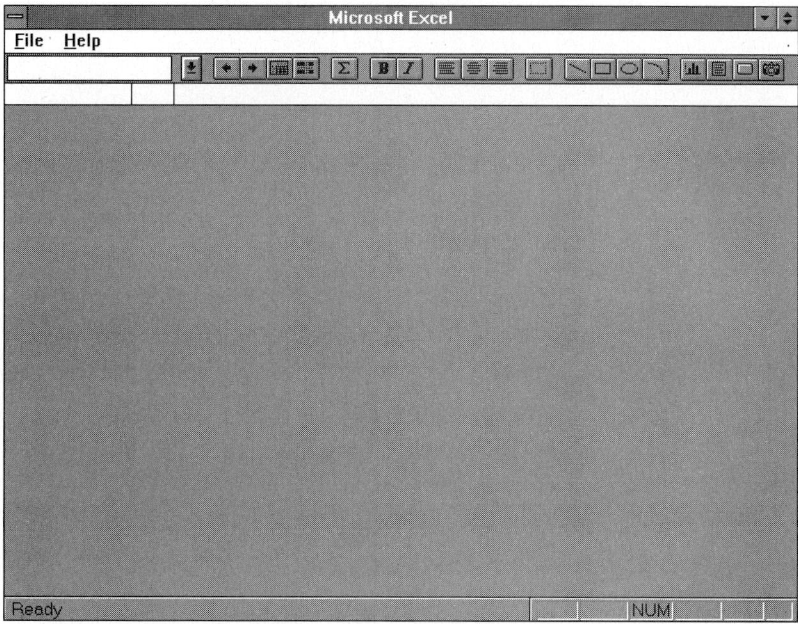

Within the application window, you can have multiple windows active. See Figure A.3 for an illustration of this.

These other windows are called *document windows*, and they can be moved and resized just like any other window. The unique thing about document windows is that, with a few exceptions, they cannot be moved outside of the application window. If you try to move a document window outside the application window, it's as if the document window just disappears behind the main application window.

Sizing Windows

Most windows that you'll encounter—both in Excel and in other Windows-based products—can be resized in several directions. Figure A.4 shows a typical window with the possible points of movement marked. When you move your mouse pointer over the outer borders or corners, the mouse changes shape to indicate that you can then resize the window. In addition, as you drag the borders to resize a window, Microsoft Windows displays an outline so you can tell when the window is the correct size.

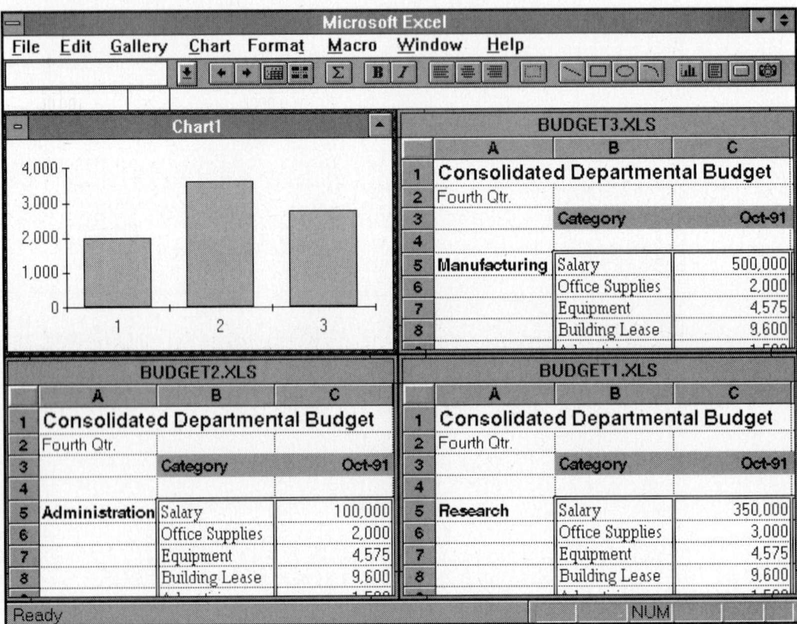

Figure A.3
Document windows displayed inside the application window

Once you start to open multiple document windows in Excel you will appreciate the Window, Arrange All command. If your screen is getting too crowded with windows, and you find yourself getting lost with all the open windows, just go to the Excel menu and click on Window, Arrange All. All of the windows will then be placed on the screen so that no one overlaps another, and you can see each of the windows.

Moving a Window

Moving a window is even easier than resizing it. Just move the mouse into the title bar portion of either the application window or the document window and drag with the mouse until the window is where you want it. Again note that as you're dragging, Windows displays a rectangular outline that shows where the window would be if you were to release the mouse button at that time.

Figure A.4
Excel document window

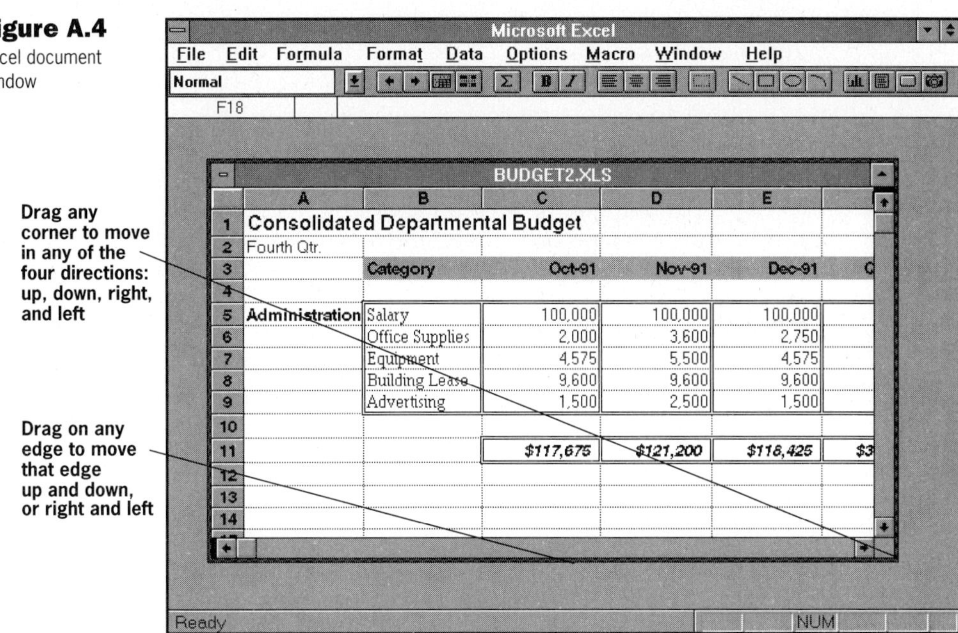

Excel also offers another type of window, called a *pane*. You can split a worksheet horizontally, vertically, or both in order to create up to four panes. By using panes you can view different portions of the same worksheet at the same time. You can even scroll each pane independently.

To divide a sheet into panes, click and drag on one of the split boxes (see Figure A.1) to divide the screen.

Executing Commands in Excel

Excel offers a variety of ways to execute commands. The method you choose will be the one that is most comfortable and easy for you to remember. Excel lets you select commands either by using the mouse or with a series of keyboard selections. Although I'm a strong proponent of using the mouse for this, there are times when it makes sense to use the keyboard—if for no other reason than that you don't have to take your hand off the keyboard.

Choosing Commands with the Mouse

Of the two ways to select and execute commands, the mouse is generally by far the easier. When you want to select a menu item, you just click on it once and the submenu drops down. Then find the item you want on that menu and click on it.

Another way is to click on a main menu item and, keeping the mouse button depressed, move down the menu until you get to the item you want. When the item you want to execute is highlighted, just release the mouse button. Excel will then carry out your command.

Choosing Commands with the Keyboard

It's a credit to the designers of the Windows environment that most (if not all) of the things you can do with the mouse you can also do from the keyboard. It often isn't the most efficient way, nor is it usually mnemonic, but it is possible.

When using the keyboard, generally you start at Excel's menu bar. Note that each of the items on the menu bar has one of its letters underlined. Use either the F10 key or the Alt key in concert with the underlined letter of the command to begin a menu sequence. For example, to display the Format menu, you would press either F10-T or Alt-T. Once you do, the Format menu is displayed (see Figure A.5).

Figure A.5
Excel's Format menu

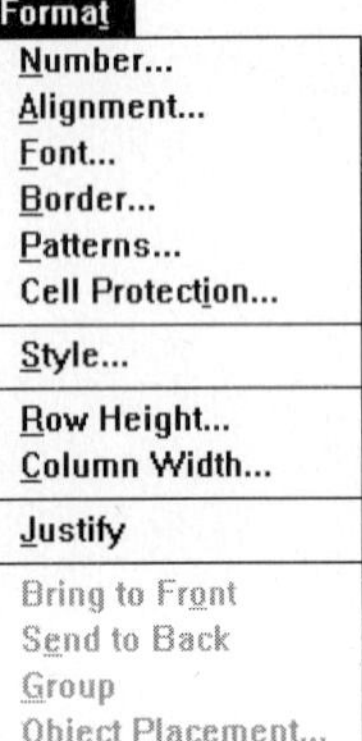

Once the menu is displayed, you can use the arrow keys to move the highlighted bar up or down to your menu choice. Once there, just hit the Enter key to select the menu. Another option is to simply press the underlined letter of your menu choice. For example, to execute the Format, Border command, press Alt-T and then B.

Note that in Figure A.5 there are several menu items that are followed by ellipses. This means there is either a dialog box attached to that menu item or there is another menu below it.

Also note in Figure A.5 that there are several items toward the bottom of the menu that appear in a light shade of gray instead of the normal black of the menu items. Those menu items are said to be *grayed out* or *dimmed* and are not available in this context. Perhaps if a worksheet were open, or if a particular range were highlighted, they would appear as normal menu items. For now, however, they are not available.

Keyboard Shortcuts

In spite of the fact that Excel's keyboard commands are rather terse and often difficult to remember, there are some handy keyboard shortcuts you can use. If you get used to a few of these, they can save you a lot of time in your sessions with Excel. Table A.1 lists Excel's function key shortcuts.

Displaying Short Versus Full Menus

Excel is shipped with the so-called Short Menus enabled. This means that not all options are visible when you first install the product. This was done to avoid confusing novice Excel users, but it comes at the expense of much of the power of the product. For instance, the Data Consolidate, Workspaces, and Formula, Create Names features all are not visible if Short Menus are enabled.

To correct this problem, simply click on Options and look to see what the last entry in the menu is.

If it says "Full Menus," that means you are currently in Short Menus mode. If you click on that option, you will go into Full Menus mode. Table A.2 lists the menu choices that are not available in Short Menus mode.

Table A.1 Function Key Shortcuts

Key	Purpose
Calculation Shortcuts	
F9	Options, Calculate Now
Shift-F9	Options, Calculate Document
Control Options	
Ctrl-F4	Control, Close (active document window)
Alt-F4	Control, Close (active program)
Ctrl-F5	Control, Restore
Ctrl-F7	Control, Move (active document)
Ctrl-F8	Control, Size
Ctrl-F10	Control, Maximize
File Functions	
Alt-F1	File, New (chart)
Alt-Shift-F1	File, New (worksheet)
Alt-Ctrl-F1	File, New (macro sheet)
Alt-F2	File, Save As
Alt-Shift-F2	File, Save
Alt-Ctrl-F2	File, Open
Alt-Ctrl-Shift-F2	File, Print
F11	File, New (chart)
Shift-F11	File, New (worksheet)
Ctrl-F11	File, New (macro sheet)
F12	File, Save As
Shift-F12	File, Save
Ctrl-F12	File, Open

Key	Purpose
Ctrl-Shift-F12	File, Print
Formula Options	
Shift-F2	Formula, Note
F3	Formula, Paste Name
Shift-F3	Formula, Paste Function
Ctrl-F3	Formula, Define Name
Ctrl-Shift-F3	Formula, Create Names
F4	Formula, Reference
F5	Formula, Go To
Shift-F5	Formula, Find (cell with specific contents)
F7	Formula, Find (next cell)
Shift-F7	Formula, Find (previous cell)
Help Shortcuts	
F1	Help
Shift-F1	Context-sensitive help
Selection/Edit Shortcuts	
F2	Begin edit, activate formula bar
F8	Toggles extend mode on/off
Shift-F8	Turns on add mode
F10	Activate menus
Window Options	
Ctrl-F2	Window, Show Information
F6	Next pane
Shift-F6	Previous pane
Ctrl-F6	Next document window
Ctrl-Shift-F6	Previous document window

Table A.2 Additional Options Available on Full Menus

File Menu

Links

Save Workspace

Delete

Edit Menu

Repeat

Paste Special

Paste Link

Fill Workgroup

Formula Menu

Create Names

Apply Names

Replace

Select Special

Show Active Cell

Outline

Goal Seek

Solver

Format Menu

Cell Protection

Justify

Bring to Front

Send to Back

Group

Object Placement

Data Menu

Extract

Delete

Set Extract

Series

Table

Parse

Consolidate

Options Menu

Set Print Titles

Set Page Breaks

Color Palette

Freeze Panes

Protect Document

Workspace

Macro Options

Start Recorder

Set Recorder

Relative Record

Assign to Object

Window Options

Show Info

Workgroup

Hide

Unhide

Working with Dialog Boxes

Figure A.6 shows the Page Setup dialog box within Excel and some of the elements you will need to know how to operate as you work with dialog boxes.

Figure A.6
Page Setup dialog box

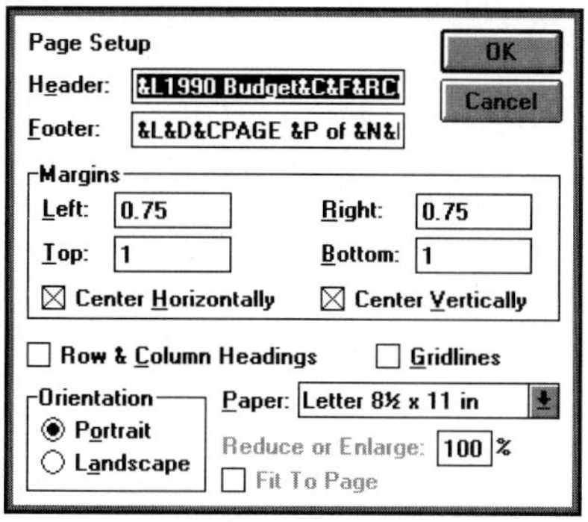

At the top, the boxes labeled "Header" and "Footer" are just editable fields. You can put any text in them that you want.

The Center Horizontally and Center Vertically boxes are examples of *checkboxes*. You enable and disable them (turn them on and off) by clicking in the box. If there is an X in the box, it means the feature is enabled (on). No check means the feature is disabled (off).

In the lower-left corner is a group of *radio buttons*, so called because they resemble the buttons of an old-style car radio. They also share another very interesting characteristic with old car radios: only one button can be "pushed" at a time. Thus, in a Windows application, only one radio button per group can be selected at any given time. Radio buttons are used for items that are mutually exclusive such as, in this case, the orientation of the paper.

Finally, Figure A.6 shows a combo box in the lower-right corner, to the right of "Paper". A combo box is a dialog box element that either presents a list of acceptable values or, if you choose, lets you type in your own value. Figure A.7 shows what happens when you click on the down arrow on the right end of the combo box. You can then either click on one of the menu choices or use the arrow keys to scroll down to the one you want.

How to Get Help

Microsoft builds into each of their products a help system that lets you get information about a particular topic even when you are in the middle of an operation.

Figure A.7
Contents of a combo box

When you need to find something out and you don't want to hunt through the manual (or perhaps you don't have it handy), you can just click on the Help menu item.

Once there, you have several choices, as shown here:

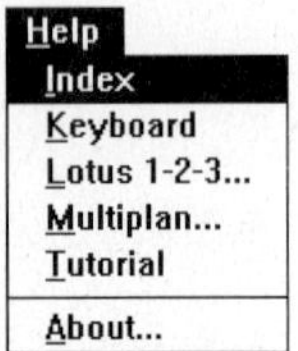

One option is to select Index. Figure A.8 shows what happens when you do so. The Excel help system is actually a separate program from Excel, and what you see in Figure A.8 is the screen from Excel Help.

The underlined text items running down the left of the screen are items you can choose that will take you to other screens. Those screens offer further explanations and often provide still more lists of procedures and features. Figure A.9 is the result of clicking on one of the items.

Look at the button bar at the top of the screen. You can use these menu choices to browse through the help topics, either forwards or backwards (the Browse buttons); go to the index (Index); go back to where you just came from (Back); or search for a specific topic (Search).

Figure A.10 shows what the Search option looks like. Use the list box to search for the topic you want. Once you have found the topic that interests you, click on that topic once to highlight it and then click on the Search command button. Excel will show you subtopics in the bottom part of the dialog box.

Figure A.8
Excel's help system index

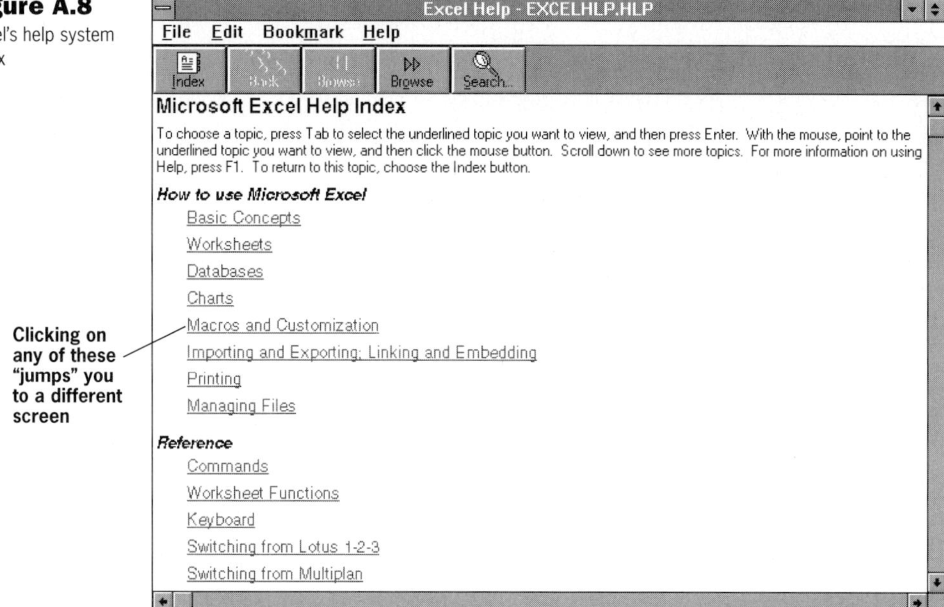

Clicking on any of these "jumps" you to a different screen

Figure A.9
List of detailed procedures

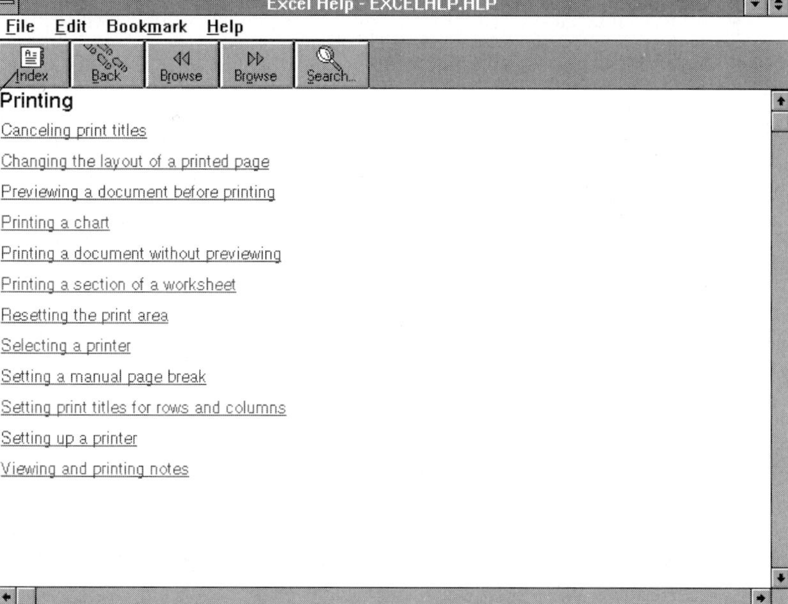

Button bar helps you navigate the help system

Figure A.10
Search dialog box

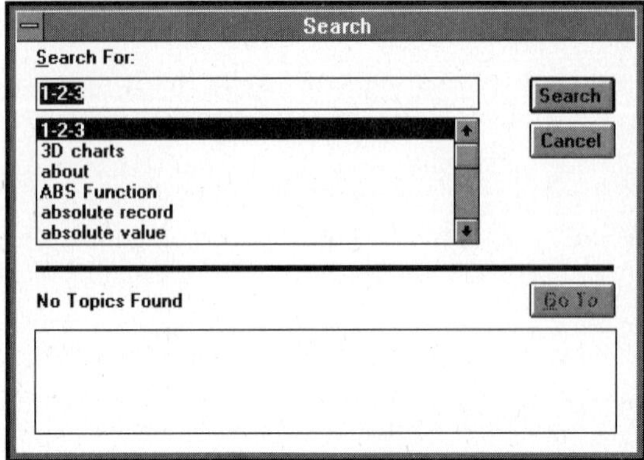

Figure A.11 shows the result of highlighting "canceling options and commands". Once you highlight one of the subtopics, click on Go To. Excel Help will take you right to that topic in the help database.

Figure A.11
Search topics and subtopics

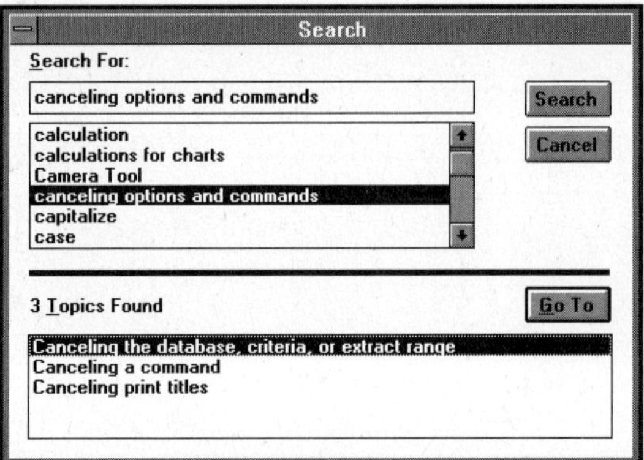

Basic DOS Procedures and Practices

Because Microsoft Windows is an operating environment that runs "on top of" MS-DOS, it is still bound by the rules that govern the use of file names and subdirectories. Virtually all programs that run under DOS have to abide by the same rules, and Windows is no exception. If you've already learned the rules for file names and how subdirectories work, you can bypass this section.

File Name Conventions

Think of a DOS file as you would a file folder—it's a place to store information until you want to use it again. In the case of Excel, all the information you enter on a worksheet eventually must be stored in a file. Failure to do so will result in a loss of data (and a very quick conversion to the religion of daily backups).

With Excel, you first create some information on a worksheet. Then, when you have worked with the data for a while, you decide that it's time to save the data so that a problem with the computer (like the cat chewing through the cord or the two-year-old pulling the plug from the wall) won't cause loss of data. It's at this point that you must decide on a name for the file. It's also the point where DOS's limitations and restrictions rear their heads.

DOS imposes some fairly strict limits on the ways you can name files. Each file designation is composed of two parts: the file name and the extension, separated by a period. The extension is optional and usually the term *file name* is used to refer to both the name and the extension.

The file name must be no more than eight characters long and at least one character long. The "legal" characters in a file are the letters "A" through "Z" (upper or lowercase—DOS doesn't make a distinction), the numbers 0 through 9, and these special characters:

```
_ ^ $ ~ ! # % & - { } ( ) @ ' `
```

File names may not contain spaces, commas, backslashes, forward slashes, or periods other than the one separating the name from the extension.

File name extensions are used to help identify the file contents or type. For example, files with a .COM (command) or .EXE (executable) extension are files that perform some action—they are program files. Other files that are used in special ways by your computer system are those with a .SYS or a .BAT extension.

Your system also has a lot of data files—that is, files that don't necessarily do anything except contain information that a program needs. Into this category fall Excel's worksheet, chart, and macro files. Each type has its own special file extension, which you can use to identify your files. Here's a list of the file extensions Excel uses:

.XLS	Main worksheet
.XLM	Macro sheet
.XLC	Chart file
.XLW	Workspace file

Excel adds these extensions to the files automatically. All you have to do is type the name of the file you want to save or load. Also note that although DOS file names don't have to have extensions, Excel will always add one to a file name.

Here are some examples of valid file names:

BUDGET_1.XLS
COMMAND.COM
CONFIG.SYS
MY-WORK.XLS
EXCEL.EXE

Subdirectories

Today's computers are equipped with monstrous hard drives. Their capacity is often difficult to imagine, let alone keep track of. That's where the concept of subdirectories can help.

Because your hard disk can contain hundreds—and often thousands—of files, it's useful to be able to divide your files based on your choice of categories. You might want to store information according to application or you might choose to store your files based on a project. It's entirely up to you—subdirectories give you that flexibility.

Subdirectories are logical divisions of a hard drive that help you to organize your storage space better. (Subdirectories work on floppy disks, too, but they aren't as useful on a floppy disk as they are on a hard disk.) Consider this partial model of a hard disk:

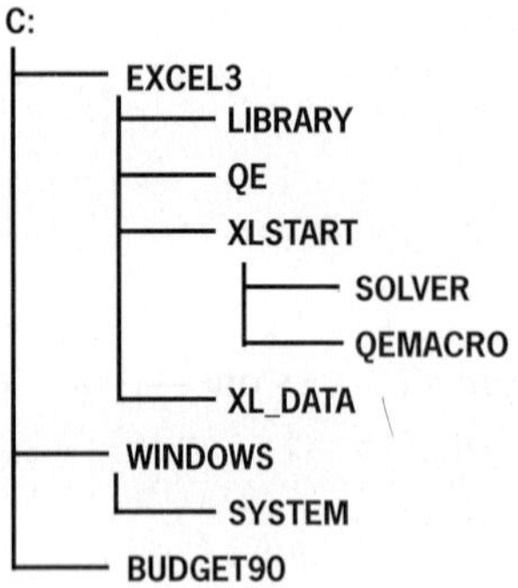

Although this organizational scheme is completely arbitrary, it serves to illustrate how subdirectories work. Notice that there is a subdirectory on this disk called EXCEL3 and beneath that subdirectory there are other subdirectories: LIBRARY, QE, XLSTART, and XL_DATA. There are also two other first-level subdirectories: WINDOWS and BUDGET90. These directories are said to be "on the same level" as EXCEL3.

It's important to understand how subdirectories work within Excel 3.0. Here is the File Save As dialog box showing the directory and file list box:

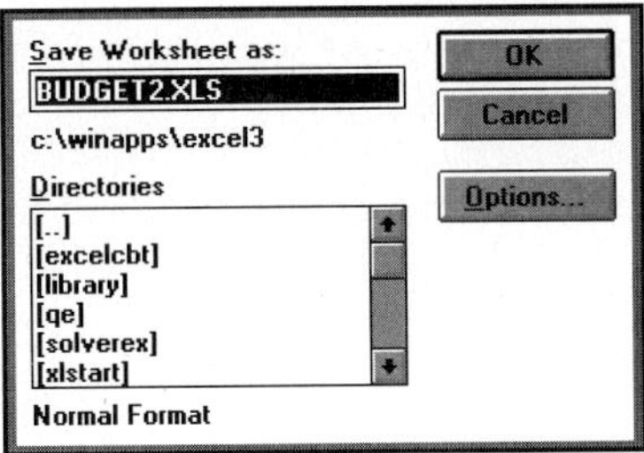

Note the line in the Directories box that looks like two dots in a set of brackets: [..]. That is Excel's way of saying "the directory above this one." If you were to double-click on that line, you would move up the directory structure (or "up the tree," as it's sometimes called). Conversely, if you double-clicked on one of the other lines—the one marked [library], for example—you would be taken to the next level down in the directory structure. Finally, if you scroll all the way down to the bottom of the Directories box, you'll see a listing of the other available drives, as shown here:

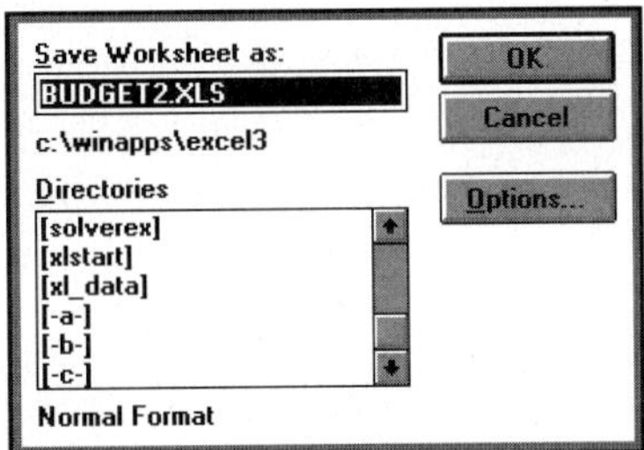

Your list box might look different than this one—it depends on the kind of hardware you have installed on your system—but it will probably have [-a-] and [-b-] drives, and a [-c-] drive, which is probably your hard drive.

Next to the Directories box in most Windows applications is usually a file name box. So when you have found the subdirectory you want, you can then find the name of your file in the companion file name list box.

A P P E N D I X B

Installing Excel 3.0

Many vendors of Windows-based applications these days believe their installation routines to be so surefire that no one will have any problems trying to install the application. That's not been my experience. Nevertheless, Microsoft believes the process to be so foolproof that all of one manual page is devoted to the topic. This brief appendix shows some of the images you'll see during the Excel 3.0 installation process and is meant to answer the questions you may have as you proceed.

Excel 3.0 Requirements

As Windows applications go, Excel 3.0 is on the large side, both in terms of the disk space required and the amount of RAM you'll need to run it efficiently.

Microsoft says that Excel will run on an IBM AT or compatible machine, or higher. From experience, a 386SX is the minimum configuration you should use with Excel. The 286 processor does not really have the horsepower or memory management features to efficiently run Excel, or other large Windows applications (such as PageMaker) for that matter.

Be prepared to give up at least 2.5Mb of hard disk real estate—and that's just for the basic program. If you intend to install all the modules, you'll need to devote a little over 5Mb of hard disk space to Excel.

You'll need some type of graphics card and monitor in order to display Windows and Windows-based applications. A mouse is optional but very highly recommended—all Windows-based applications are much easier to operate with a mouse than without one. Excel 3.0 needs DOS version 3.1 or later, but DOS 5.0 is a better choice for Windows.

Finally, although Microsoft says that 1Mb of RAM is sufficient, you'll want more—perhaps as much as 3 or 4 additional megabytes before Excel performs reasonably well. Excel will load with 1Mb of RAM, but it will not perform very fast in that constricted space.

Installation

Excel 3.0 is shipped on three high-density, 5 1/2-inch floppy disks and two high-density 3 1/2-inch disks. If your machine does not have high-density floppy drives, you can call Microsoft to request low-density disks—there is a request card in the Excel package.

Here's the procedure for installing Excel 3.0 on your computer system:

1. Begin the installation process with the disk marked "Setup" in drive A and the Windows Program Manager on the screen.

2. Double-click in the upper-left corner, on the Program Manager's System Menu icon, to drop down the menu you see here:

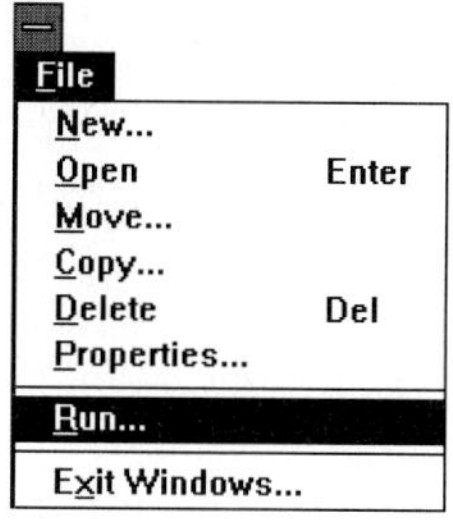

Click on Run. When the resulting dialog box appears, type **a:setup** and then press the Enter key or click on the OK button.

3. If this is the first time you have installed Excel, a dialog box will appear that asks you to enter your full name and affiliation (company name and so on). This information will be encoded on your distribution disks so that it will appear if you pass your copy of Excel on to a friend in order to make an "off-site backup copy" of the program. With copy protection no longer an accepted practice, this is the next best thing. Most companies call it "copy discouragement."

4. Next, Excel will want to know where you'd like to put the program and its related files. You have a lot of options here and it largely depends on how you want your hard disk organized. Many people find it useful to create a directory specifically for Windows applications and then install each application in its own subdirectory. However, for the purposes of this exercise let's assume that you accept the default location (by clicking on Continue in the dialog box shown below). This creates a subdirectory directly off the root directory on the boot drive—usually the C drive. (If you want the program somewhere else, just type in the complete path in the list box labeled "Install to.")

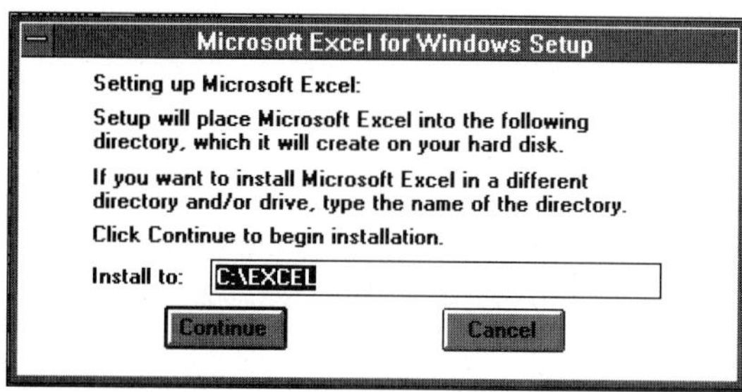

5. Next Excel will ask you what parts of the program you want to install (see Figure B.1). As previously noted, if you choose to install all the program modules, you'll need at least 5.5Mb of hard disk space (actually 5.2Mb and change). Note that Excel also politely displays the amount of space you have left on your hard drive.

Microsoft Excel Setup Options

☒ Microsoft Excel
☒ Microsoft Excel Tutorial
☒ Dialog Editor
☒ Macro Translator
☒ Macro Library Files
☒ Microsoft Excel Solver
☒ Q+E Select Drivers
Space Required: 5,255K
Space Available: 39,848K
Setup Cancel

Figure B.1
Setup Options dialog box

Clicking on the check boxes selects and deselects the options. Note as you do this that Excel keeps track of the amount of disk space required. So, if you're tight on disk space, you can tweak your installation to make sure you've loaded everything you can. See the next section, "Setup Options," for information on each of these options.

6. After you have made all your selections and feel comfortable with your decisions about the portions of the program you intend to load, click on OK and Excel will move on.

7. Next the installation routine asks whether you want Excel configured to be more compatible with Lotus 1-2-3, as shown below. If you have been a Lotus 1-2-3 user, you should probably choose Enable; otherwise select Do Not Enable. Don't worry about being stuck with your decision forever—you can change it back later on in the program. For more information on this feature, see Chapter 15.

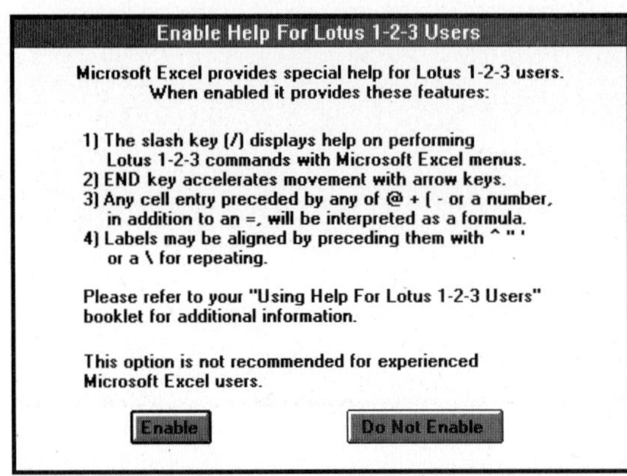

Enable Help For Lotus 1-2-3 Users
Microsoft Excel provides special help for Lotus 1-2-3 users.
When enabled it provides these features:
1) The slash key (/) displays help on performing Lotus 1-2-3 commands with Microsoft Excel menus.
2) END key accelerates movement with arrow keys.
3) Any cell entry preceded by any of @ + (- or a number, in addition to an =, will be interpreted as a formula.
4) Labels may be aligned by preceding them with ^ " ' or a \ for repeating.
Please refer to your "Using Help For Lotus 1-2-3 Users" booklet for additional information.
This option is not recommended for experienced Microsoft Excel users.
Enable
Do Not Enable

After you've answered all of Excel's questions, the installation routine begins to copy program and data files from the floppy disks onto your hard disk. The process is entirely automatic. Excel even displays a "gas gauge" so that you know how much you have left to go. It looks like this:

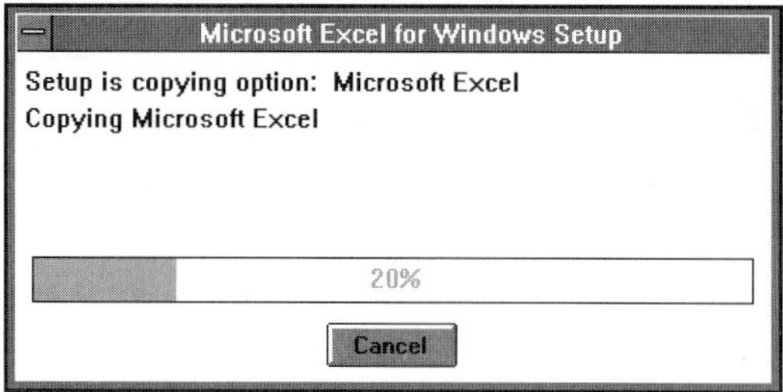

When Excel finishes with one disk, you will be prompted to insert another. Excel will even tell you which disk you should put in, as shown here:

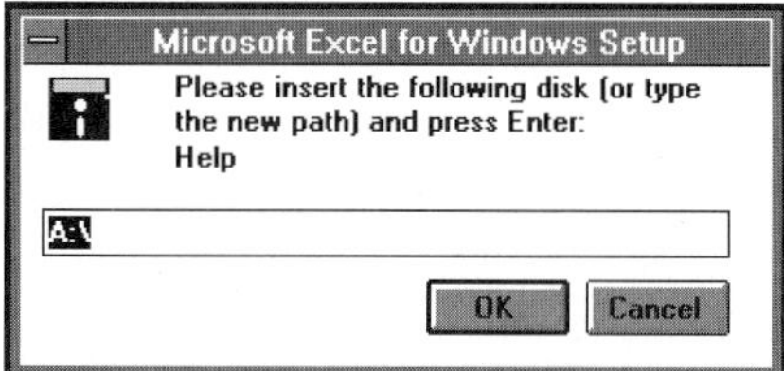

The copying and swapping will proceed for either two disks if you have a 3 1/2-inch drive, or three disks for a 5 1/4-inch drive. When the program is finished with the installation routine, it will automatically create an Excel program group for the Program Manager application, as shown here:

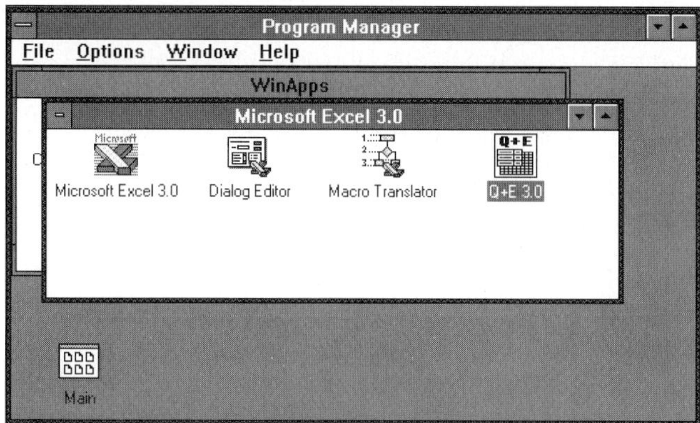

Once you have installed the Excel program on your disk, starting Excel is as easy as double-clicking on the icon marked "MS Excel":

Setup Options

Here is a brief list of what each of the installation options shown in Figure B.1 means:

Microsoft Excel Choose this option to install the minimum file set necessary for using Microsoft Excel 3.0. If this is the first time you are installing Excel 3.0, you must have at least this one option turned on.

Microsoft Excel Tutorial Choose this option to install a series of on-line exercises that provides an interesting and fact-filled way to learn Excel 3.0 interactively.

Dialog Editor Choosing this option installs an application called the Dialog Editor. The Dialog Editor is used to create custom dialog boxes for Microsoft Excel command macros and custom forms for entering database information. This is generally a tool for advanced users.

Macro Translation Assistant Choose this option to install the Macro Translation Assistant, a utility that translates Lotus 1-2-3 macros into Microsoft Excel 3.0 macros. For more information on the Macro Translation Assistant, see Chapter 15. You need this utility if you have macros in Lotus 1-2-3 spreadsheets that you want to convert over to Excel 3.0.

Macro Library Files This option installs a set of sample worksheets and add-in macros that provide ideas about how to use Excel 3.0 efficiently to create powerful worksheet models, charts, and macros.

Microsoft Excel Solver This option installs the Excel Solver. The Solver is a relatively easy-to-use utility that allows you to perform sophisticated mathematical calculations to help you get more and better answers out of your worksheet models. The Solver is discussed more in Chapter 12.

Q+E Finally, this option installs the Q+E companion program, a powerful database add-in program that allows you to manipulate and update database files from a variety of database systems, including dBASE and Microsoft SQL Server. In order to use Q+E with a particular database system, you must first install the corresponding database driver: First choose the Select Driver button (see Figure B.1), and in the dialog box that appears, select the drivers for the databases you want Q+E to connect to. If you want Q+E to start automatically whenever you start Excel 3.0, turn on the Start Q+E with Microsoft Excel check box.

APPENDIX C

Worksheet Function Reference

You learned the basics of working with formulas and functions back in Chapters 3 and 4. This appendix will serve as a reference to all the worksheet functions that Excel provides.

However, because of the scope of this book, this is not intended to be exhaustive. Although all of the functions are listed, only the more frequently used functions are defined and amplified. You will also notice that whereas the function arguments are explained in some detail for most functions, for a few categories the arguments, while shown, are not discussed separately. Again, in those cases, such explanations would have exceeded the scope of the book. Consider this appendix to be both a listing of what Excel is capable of and a resource for the most popular functions. For further information, see the *Microsoft Excel Function Reference.*

The functions are grouped alphabetically by category (as described in Chapter 4) and then alphabetically within each category.

Syntax

The syntax used here to list the functions closely follows the method used in the Microsoft Excel 3.0 documentation. Consider the following example:

```
DDB(cost,salvage,life,period,[factor])
```

In this case, the name of the function is in capital letters. If it were the first item in a formula it would be preceded by an equal sign. Arguments (also called parameters) are set in italics. Finally, if an argument is optional, you will see it enclosed in brackets [ ]. All parameters not optional are required.

To use the above example, DDB() is the name of the function that calculates a double-declining balance method of depreciation. The arguments *cost, salvage, life*, and *period* are all required and must be both present and in the form that Excel expects or you'll get an error message. The argument *factor* is optional.

Database Functions

In all the following database worksheet functions, the required arguments refer to ranges on a worksheet (also see Chapter 14 for more information) and are defined as follows:

database is the range of cells that you have defined as a database within a worksheet. This argument can be either stated as a range (D5:G9, for example) or as a named range. If you use the Data, Set Database command, Excel automatically names the database range Database.

field is how you tell Excel which column you want to use for the function. You may either use the field name as it appears in your database, or you can use a number that describes the relative position of the field. So, if your database contained the fields NAME, AGE, and HEIGHT, NAME would be field 1, AGE would be field 2, and so on.

criteria is the criteria range you use to tell Excel what records to select. Although you must use a valid criterion name in the database functions, the criteria range can be empty. In that case Excel will search through all records in the defined database range.

In the following illustration, the database is the range A1:E8 and has been named Database by the Data, Set Database command. The field names are L_NAME, F_NAME, SALARY, STATE, and HIREDATE. Finally, the criteria range is the range A11:E12 and has been named Criteria by the Data, Set Criteria command.

H18

	A	B	C	D	E	F
1	L_NAME	F_NAME	SALARY	STATE	HIREDATE	
2	Smith	Dale	$54,000	MA	06/12/89	
3	Sullivan	Samantha	$38,445	MA	07/01/86	
4	Charles	Winston	$62,500	CA	03/03/88	
5	Simpson	Suzanne	$100,250	MA	01/15/78	
6	Silverburg	Linda	$73,400	NV	09/21/61	
7	Starkowski	George	$38,000	CA	05/13/39	
8	Salesman	John	$44,700	NV	06/15/61	
9						
10						
11	L_NAME	F_NAME	SALARY	STATE	HIREDATE	
12						

DAVERAGE(*database,field,criteria*)

DAVERAGE() returns the average of the selected *database* entries as specified in the criteria.

For example, if, as shown below, your criteria range defines STATE as MA, then the value of cell B16 is $64,232. This number represents the average salary for those records in which the STATE field equals MA.

database is the range you have defined as the database range. The argument can be expressed as either an explicit range reference (A1:E8) or as a named range. Note that the database range must include the field names at the top of the columns.

field is the name of the field you want to base your selection on. This argument may be expressed as either a field name (the name of the column) or as a relative column number, with 1 being the first column on the left, 2 as the next column, and so on.

B16 =DAVERAGE(Database,3,Criteria)

	A	B	C	D	E	F
1	L_NAME	F_NAME	SALARY	STATE	HIREDATE	
2	Smith	Dale	$54,000	MA	06/12/89	
3	Sullivan	Samantha	$38,445	MA	07/01/86	
4	Charles	Winston	$62,500	CA	03/03/88	
5	Simpson	Suzanne	$100,250	MA	01/15/78	
6	Silverburg	Linda	$73,400	NV	09/21/61	
7	Starkowski	George	$38,000	CA	05/13/39	
8	Salesman	John	$44,700	NV	06/15/61	
9						
10						
11	L_NAME	F_NAME	SALARY	STATE	HIREDATE	
12				MA		
13						
14						
15	Average					
16	Salary-->	$64,232				
17						

criteria is the range you have defined to be the criteria range. This range is used to determine which records in the database range to match. It can be expressed as either an explicit range reference (A11:E12) or as a named range. Note also that the field names must be part of the criteria range.

DCOUNT(*database*,[*field*],*criteria*)

DCOUNT() returns the number of cells that are described by the database and criteria. The *field* parameter is optional, and if you omit it the function will count all the elements in the database that meet the criteria.

In the following illustration, the DCOUNT() function in cell B15 returns the value of 7. Note that since the criteria range is empty, the DCOUNT() function will count all the items in the database range.

database is the range you have defined as the database range. The argument can be expressed as either an explicit range reference (A1:E8) or as a named range. Note that the database range must include the field names at the top of the columns.

field is the name of the field you want to base your selection on. This argument may be expressed as either a field name (the name of the column) or as a relative column number, with 1 being the first column on the left, 2 as the next column, and so on.

criteria is the range you have defined to be the criteria range. This range is used to determine which records in the database range to match. It can be expressed as either an explicit range reference (A11:E12) or as a named range. Note also that the field names must be part of the criteria range.

B15	=DCOUNT(A1:E8,3,Criteria)				
	A	B	C	D	E
1	L_NAME	F_NAME	SALARY	STATE	HIREDATE
2	Smith	Dale	$54,000	MA	06/12/89
3	Sullivan	Samantha	$38,445	MA	07/01/86
4	Charles	Winston	$62,500	CA	03/03/88
5	Simpson	Suzanne	$100,250	MA	01/15/78
6	Silverburg	Linda	$73,400	NV	09/21/61
7	Starkowski	George	$38,000	CA	05/13/39
8	Salesman	John	$44,700	NV	06/15/61
9					
10					
11	L_NAME	F_NAME	SALARY	STATE	HIREDATE
12					
13					
14	Total				
15	Items –>	7			
16					
17					

DCOUNTA(*database,field,criteria*)

DCOUNTA() is the same as DCOUNT(), but it returns the number of non-blank cells from the named database and criteria. Note that the *field* argument is required here.

In the following example there are a few cells in the salary column for which there is missing data. If you want to get an accurate count of the records that have salary information, you would use the DCOUNTA() function. Its syntax would look like this:

```
=DCOUNTA(database,"salary",criteria)
```

Again, the criteria is blank for this example since you want to count the entire database. Note that the above function, in cell B15, returns a value of 4 since there are only four records that match the criteria.

database is the range you have defined as the database range. The argument can be expressed as either an explicit range reference (A1:E8) or as a named range. Note that the database range must include the field names at the top of the columns.

field is the name of the field you want to base your selection on. This argument may be expressed as either a field name (the name of the column) or as a relative column number, with 1 being the first column on the left, 2 as the next column, and so on.

B15 =DCOUNTA(Database,3,Criteria)

	A	B	C	D	E	F
1	L_NAME	F_NAME	SALARY	STATE	HIREDATE	
2	Smith	Dale	$54,000	MA	06/12/89	
3	Sullivan	Samantha	$38,445	MA	07/01/86	
4	Charles	Winston	$62,500	CA	03/03/88	
5	Simpson	Suzanne	$100,250	MA	01/15/78	
6	Silverburg	Linda	$73,400	NV	09/21/61	
7	Starkowski	George	$38,000	CA	05/13/39	
8	Salesman	John	$44,700	NV	06/15/61	
9						
10						
11	L_NAME	F_NAME	SALARY	STATE	HIREDATE	
12						
13	Total					
14	Nonblank					
15	Items -->	7				
16						
17						

criteria is the range you have defined to be the criteria range. This range is used to determine which records in the database range to match. It can be expressed as either an explicit range reference (A11:E12) or as a named range. Note also that the field names must be part of the criteria range.

DGET(*database,field,criteria*)

DGET() returns a single record from the specified database and criteria. Use DGET() to extract a single record from the database that matches the criteria. Note that if more than one record matches the criteria, Excel returns #NUM! error. If this happens, and you want to see all the records that match the criteria, use the Data, Extract command to extract all the matching records to a specified range on your worksheet. If no record matches your criteria, Excel returns a #VALUE! error message.

In the following example, Excel has been asked to show the first name of the person with a salary higher than $100,000 by using the relational operator >100000 in the criteria range.

database is the range you have defined as the database range. The argument can be expressed as either an explicit range reference (A1:E8) or as a named range. Note that the database range must include the field names at the top of the columns.

field is the name of the field you want to base your selection on. This argument may be expressed as either a field name (the name of the column) or as a relative column number, with 1 being the first column on the left, 2 as the next column, and so on.

B15 =DGET(Database,2,Criteria)

	A	B	C	D	E	F
1	L_NAME	F_NAME	SALARY	STATE	HIREDATE	
2	Smith	Dale	$54,000	MA	06/12/89	
3	Sullivan	Samantha	$38,445	MA	07/01/86	
4	Charles	Winston	$62,500	CA	03/03/88	
5	Simpson	Suzanne	$100,250	MA	01/15/78	
6	Silverburg	Linda	$73,400	NV	09/21/61	
7	Starkowski	George	$38,000	CA	05/13/39	
8	Salesman	John	$44,700	NV	06/15/61	
9						
10						
11	L_NAME	F_NAME	SALARY	STATE	HIREDATE	
12			>100000			
13						
14	Highest					
15	Salary-->	Suzanne				
16						
17						

criteria is the range you have defined to be the criteria range. This range is used to determine which records in the database range to match. It can be expressed as either an explicit range reference (A11:E12) or as a named range. Note also that the field names must be part of the criteria range.

DMAX(*database,field,criteria*)

DMAX() returns the largest value from a set of records described by *database* and *criteria*. If the records selected hold 3, 12, and 11, for example, this function will return 12.

The following example shows how Excel will pick out the largest value in a field, in this case, the highest salary for those records where state equals CA. Cell B15 has the following syntax:

```
=DMAX(database,"salary",criteria)
```

Note that you've used the criteria range to narrow down the possibilities. If you had left the criteria range blank, Excel would have returned the highest salary from all the records.

database is the range you have defined as the database range. The argument can be expressed as either an explicit range reference (A1:E8) or as a named range. Note that the database range must include the field names at the top of the columns.

field is the name of the field you want to base your selection on. This argument may be expressed as either a field name (the name of the column) or as a relative column number, with 1 being the first column on the left, 2 as the next column, and so on.

B15 =DMAX(Database,3,Criteria)

	A	B	C	D	E	F
1	L_NAME	F_NAME	SALARY	STATE	HIREDATE	
2	Smith	Dale	$54,000	MA	06/12/89	
3	Sullivan	Samantha	$38,445	MA	07/01/86	
4	Charles	Winston	$62,500	CA	03/03/88	
5	Simpson	Suzanne	$100,250	MA	01/15/78	
6	Silverburg	Linda	$73,400	NV	09/21/61	
7	Starkowski	George	$38,000	CA	05/13/39	
8	Salesman	John	$44,700	NV	06/15/61	
9						
10						
11	L_NAME	F_NAME	SALARY	STATE	HIREDATE	
12				CA		
13						
14	Highest CA					
15	Salary -->	$62,500				
16						
17						

criteria is the range you have defined to be the criteria range. This range is used to determine which records in the database range to match. It can be expressed as either an explicit range reference (A11:E12) or as a named range. Note also that the field names must be a part of the criteria range.

DMIN(*database,field,criteria*)

DMIN() is like DMAX(), but it returns the smallest value from a set of records described by *database* and *criteria.*

In the following example, Excel returns the lowest salary value from those states that do not equal CA. Note the not-equal operator (<>) in the criteria range. If you had not used this selection criteria, Excel would have returned the value of $38,000—the lowest salary in the database.

B15 =DMIN(Database,"salary",Criteria)

	A	B	C	D	E	F
1	L_NAME	F_NAME	SALARY	STATE	HIREDATE	
2	Smith	Dale	$54,000	MA	06/12/89	
3	Sullivan	Samantha	$38,445	MA	07/01/86	
4	Charles	Winston	$62,500	CA	03/03/88	
5	Simpson	Suzanne	$100,250	MA	01/15/78	
6	Silverburg	Linda	$73,400	NV	09/21/61	
7	Starkowski	George	$38,000	CA	05/13/39	
8	Salesman	John	$44,700	NV	06/15/61	
9						
10						
11	L_NAME	F_NAME	SALARY	STATE	HIREDATE	
12				<>CA		
13						
14	Highest CA					
15	Salary -->	$38,445				
16						
17						

database is the range you have defined as the database range. The argument can be expressed as either an explicit range reference (A1:E8) or as a named range. Note that the database range must include the field names at the top of the columns.

field is the name of the field you want to base your selection on. This argument may be expressed as either a field name (the name of the column) or as a relative column number, with 1 being the first column on the left, 2 as the next column, and so on.

criteria is the range you have defined to be the criteria range. This range is used to determine which records in the database range to match. It can be expressed as either an explicit range reference (A11:E12) or as a named range. Note also that the field names must be part of the criteria range.

DPRODUCT(*database,field,criteria*)

DPRODUCT() returns the product of the values described by *database* and *criteria.* If the records selected from the database are 1, 3, and 5, this formula returns the value 15.

database is the range you have defined as the database range. The argument can be expressed as either an explicit range reference (A1:E8) or as a named range. Note that the database range must include the field names at the top of the columns.

field is the name of the field you want to base your selection on. This argument may be expressed as either a field name (the name of the column) or as a relative column number, with 1 being the first column on the left, 2 as the next column, and so on.

criteria is the range you have defined to be the criteria range. This range is used to determine which records in the database range to match. It can be expressed as either an explicit range reference (A11:E12) or as a named range. Note also that the field names must be part of the criteria range.

DSTDEV(*database,field,criteria*)

DSTDEV() returns the estimate of the standard deviation from a sample of the values described by *database* and *criteria.*

database is the range you have defined as the database range. The argument can be expressed as either an explicit range reference (A1:E8) or as a named range. Note that the database range must include the field names at the top of the columns.

field is the name of the field you want to base your selection on. This argument may be expressed as either a field name (the name of the column) or as a relative column number, with 1 being the first column on the left, 2 as the next column, and so on.

criteria is the range you have defined to be the criteria range. This range is used to determine which records in the database range to match. It can be expressed as either an explicit range reference (A11:E12) or as a named range. Note also that the field names must be part of the criteria range.

DSTDEVP(*database,field,criteria*)

DSTDEVP() returns the calculated population standard deviation from the set of records described by *database* and *criteria.*

database is the range you have defined as the database range. The argument can be expressed as either an explicit range reference (A1:E8) or as a named range. Note that the database range must include the field names at the top of the columns.

field is the name of the field you want to base your selection on. This argument may be expressed as either a field name (the name of the column) or as a relative column number, with 1 being the first column on the left, 2 as the next column, and so on.

criteria is the range you have defined to be the criteria range. This range is used to determine which records in the database range to match. It can be expressed as either an explicit range reference (A11:E12) or as a named range. Note also that the field names must be part of the criteria range.

DSUM(*database,field,criteria*)

DSUM() returns a sum of the numbers in the records described by *database* and *criteria.* This is very similar to the normal SUM() function, but the values that are summed are constrained to the database range and selected by the criteria range.

In the following example, you would like to sum the salaries of those employees whose last name starts with "S" and ends with "N". Note the use of the wildcard character here to select all records that start with "S" and end with "N", regardless of what comes in between.

B15	=DSUM(Database,"salary",Criteria)					
	A	B	C	D	E	F
1	L_NAME	F_NAME	SALARY	STATE	HIREDATE	
2	Smith	Dale	$54,000	MA	06/12/89	
3	Sullivan	Samantha	$38,445	MA	07/01/86	
4	Charles	Winston	$62,500	CA	03/03/88	
5	Simpson	Suzanne	$100,250	MA	01/15/78	
6	Silverburg	Linda	$73,400	NV	09/21/61	
7	Starkowski	George	$38,000	CA	05/13/39	
8	Salesman	John	$44,700	NV	06/15/61	
9						
10						
11	L_NAME	F_NAME	SALARY	STATE	HIREDATE	
12	S*N					
13						
14	Total					
15	Salary -->	$183,395				
16						

database is the range you have defined as the database range. The argument can be expressed as either an explicit range reference (A1:E8) or as a named range. Note that the database range must include the field names at the top of the columns.

field is the name of the field you want to base your selection on. This argument may be expressed as either a field name (the name of the column) or as a relative column number, with 1 being the first column on the left, 2 as the next column, and so on.

criteria is the range you have defined to be the criteria range. This range is used to determine which records in the database range to match. It can be expressed as either an explicit range reference (A11:E12) or as a named range. Note also that the field names must be part of the criteria range.

DVAR(*database,field,criteria*)

DVAR() returns an estimated variance from a sample of the values described by *database* and *criteria.*

database is the range you have defined as the database range. The argument can be expressed as either an explicit range reference (A1:E8) or as a named range. Note that the database range must include the field names at the top of the columns.

field is the name of the field you want to base your selection on. This argument may be expressed as either a field name (the name of the column) or as a relative column number, with 1 being the first column on the left, 2 as the next column, and so on.

criteria is the range you have defined to be the criteria range. This range is used to determine which records in the database range to match. It can be expressed as either an explicit range reference (A11:E12) or as a named range. Note also that the field names must be part of the criteria range.

DVARP(*database,field,criteria*)

DVARP() returns the calculated population variance from the values described by *database* and *criteria.*

database is the range you have defined as the database range. The argument can be expressed as either an explicit range reference (A1:E8) or as a named range. Note that the database range must include the field names at the tops of the columns.

field is the name of the field you want to base your selection on. This argument may be expressed as either a field name (the name of the column) or as a relative column number, with 1 being the first column on the left, 2 as the next column, and so on.

criteria is the range you have defined to be the criteria range. This range is used to determine which records in the database range to match. It can be expressed as either an explicit range reference (A11:E12) or as a named range. Note also that the field names must be part of the criteria range.

Date and Time Functions

Excel stores the value of dates and times in a special serial number format. The serial number is made up of an integer portion, which represents the data, and a fractional portion representing the time. In Microsoft Excel 3.0 for Windows and for OS/2, the serial number can range from 0 to 65380. The value 0 represents January 1, 1900, and a serial number value of 65380 represents December 31, 2078.

Because the date and time are maintained in a serial number format, date and time arithmetic is simple. For example, if you subtract the number 1 from a serial number, you will have a new serial number that is one day earlier. The following date and time functions help you maintain dates and times in your worksheet model.

DATE(*year,month,day*)

DATE() returns the serial number of the specified date. For example, =DATE(69,7,20) returns the serial number 25404, which represents the date July 20, 1969. Note that you can add or subtract numbers in order to determine dates in the future or in the past. The following example shows how you can use date arithmetic.

Cell B1 contains =NOW(), which returns today's date as a serial number. Cell B2 contains the function =DATE(69,7,20), which converts July 20, 1969 into a serial number. Both cells have been formatted so that the serial numbers display as dates. Finally, cell B4 contains =B1-B2 and represents the number of days between the ninth of June, 1991 and the first time a man walked on the moon.

B2 | =DATE(69,7,20)

	A	B	C
1	Today's date	14-Jul-91	
2	July 20, 1969	20-Jul-69	
3			
4	**Days Difference ->**	8,029	
5			

year is an integer value between 1900 and 2078. For the years from 1920 to 2019, you can enter the year as a two-digit integer. Otherwise, use all four digits.

month is an integer value representing the month of the year—January is 1, and December is 12.

day is an integer value representing the day of the month: 1 is the first day of the month, 2 is the second day, and so on.

DATEVALUE(*date_text*)

DATEVALUE() converts a textual date value into Excel's serial number date format. This very useful function converts the *date_text* string into a serial number. DATEVALUE("7-20-69") and DATEVALUE("20-Jul-69") both return a serial number of 25404, which corresponds to the date July 20, 1969.

date_text is a quoted text string representing a date. "12-Sep-89" and "8/15/93" are examples of valid date formats.

DAY(*serial_number*)

DAY() converts a serial number to an integer value that represents the day of the month. *serial_number* can be either a serial number or a text string that Excel will convert into a serial number for the purposes of this calculation. The integer value returned is between 1 and 31. For example, DAY ("21-Sep-61") returns 21.

serial_number is Excel's special format for storing dates and times. The serial number format is a real number (with an integer part and a fractional part) from 0 to 65380. It represents dates and times from January 1, 1900 to December 31, 2078.

DAYS360(*start_date,end_date*)

DAYS360() is used to determine the number of days between two dates based on a 360-day year. This function is very useful for certain financial and accounting calculations that are based on the 360-day year. Like the DAY() function, DAYS360() will accept either a serial number or a quoted text string in an acceptable Excel date format.

In the following example, assume that cell B1 contains *start_date*, a serial number that represents today's date, and cell B2 has a serial number corresponding to an end date of September 21, 1961. To calculate the number of days between those two dates based on a 360-day year, use the following syntax:

```
DAYS360(B2,B1)
```

Make sure to place the older date first: If the starting date occurs after the ending date, Excel will display the result as a negative number.

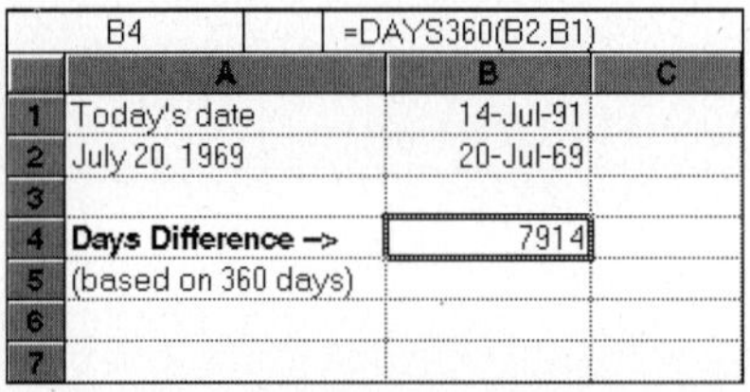

B4 =DAYS360(B2,B1)

	A	B	C
1	Today's date	14-Jul-91	
2	July 20, 1969	20-Jul-69	
3			
4	**Days Difference ->**	7914	
5	(based on 360 days)		
6			
7			

start_date and ***end_date*** are either quoted text strings or serial numbers.

HOUR(*serial_number*)

HOUR() converts a serial number to an integer representing an hour value that is an integer between 0 and 23.

For example, assume that cell C5 contained a serial number that was formatted to show the time as "3:30 PM". In cell C6 the formula =HOUR(C5) would return the integer 15. This number represents the integer number of the hours past midnight, so 12 is noon, 13 is 1:00 PM, 14 is 2:00 PM, and so on.

serial_number is Excel's special format for storing dates and times. The serial number format is a real number (an integer part and a fractional part) from 0 to 65380. It represents dates and times from January 1, 1900 to December 31, 2078.

MINUTE(*serial_number*)

MINUTE() converts a serial number to an integer representing a minute value that is an integer from 0 to 59. This function performs just like HOUR(), but it displays the integer value of the minutes rather than the hour.

serial_number is Excel's special format for storing dates and times. The serial number format is a real number (an integer part and a fractional part) from 0 to 65380. It represents dates and times from January 1, 1900 to December 31, 2078.

MONTH(*serial_number*)

MONTH() converts a serial number to an integer from 1 to 12 that represents the month. For example, 12 is December, and 3 is March. This function works like the HOUR() function, but it determines the integer value of the month and returns that in the cell.

For example, assume cell B11 contains the serial number that represents the date December 25, 1990. The formula =MONTH(B11) in cell B12 would return 12, which corresponds to December.

serial_number is Excel's special format for storing dates and times. The serial number format is a real number (with an integer part and a fractional part) from 0 to 65380. It represents dates and times from January 1, 1900 to December 31, 2078.

NOW()

NOW() returns the serial number of the current date and time. This function is often used to record when a worksheet is printed or calculated. Note, however, that this number is not constantly updated. It is only changed when you recalculate the worksheet.

The NOW() function is one of the few that does not require, nor accept, parameters. It's therefore a very simple function to use. Once you employ the NOW() function in a cell, just format that cell to display the portions of the serial number you want to see. Then you can use the other date and time functions to perform date arithmetic or to perform some action based on the time or date.

SECOND(*serial_number*)

SECOND() converts a serial number to an integer representing the seconds part of the serial number. You may either use a serial number or enter the time as a quoted text string. For example, the formula SECOND("12:53:14") returns the integer value 14.

serial_number is Excel's special format for storing dates and times. The serial number format is a real number (an integer part and a fractional part) from 0 to 65380. It represents dates and times from January 1, 1900 to December 31, 2078.

TIME(*hour,minute,second*)

TIME() is like the DATE() function, but it returns a serial number that corresponds to a particular time value. The part of the serial number that refers to time is to the right of the decimal place. It is a fractional value ranging from 0 to 0.99999999 and represents one full day from 0:00:00 to 11:59:59 PM. For example, the function =TIME(23,22,21) returns the serial number 0.9738542, which represents the serial number for 11:22:21 PM.

hour is a value from 0 to 23 that represents the hour.

minute is a value from 0 to 59 that represents minutes.

second is a value from 0 to 59 that represents seconds.

TIMEVALUE(*time_text*)

TIMEVALUE() converts a time value given as text into a serial number format. This function is analogous to the DATEVALUE() function. The quoted text string may be in any of Excel's acceptable time and date formats. For instance, the function TIMEVALUE("5:10 PM") returns the serial number 0.7152778. Note that any date information in the text string is ignored by Excel. This function is handy if you want to convert a text string into a serial number so that you can do some type of time arithmetic.

time_text is a quoted text string that gives time in one of Excel's acceptable time formats, such as "4:40 PM" or "1:34:48 AM".

TODAY()

TODAY() returns the serial number of today's date. TODAY() is analogous to the NOW() function, but it refers only to the date instead of to both time and date.

In the following example, both cells were formatted to display the serial numbers as a date and a time both. Cell B1 has the TODAY() function, and cell B2 has the NOW() function. Note that although cell B1 does not contain any time information, it will still continue to update every time the spreadsheet recalculates. Obviously, however, since cell B1 only contains date information, it will only change once per day, at the most.

B1 =TODAY()

	A	B	C
1	**TODAY() function ->**	7/14/91 0:00	
2	NOW() function ->	7/14/91 11:11	
3			
4			

WEEKDAY(*serial_number*)

WEEKDAY() displays a serial number as an integer that represents the day of the week. For instance, 1 is Sunday, 2 is Monday, and so on. You may enter the serial number either as a number or as a quoted text string that Excel will translate.

In the following example, cell B1 contains the NOW() function to show today's date and time, and the cell is formatted accordingly. Cell B3 contains the function WEEKDAY(B1) and displays a 1, which corresponds to Sunday (June 9, 1991 was a Sunday).

B3 =WEEKDAY(B1)

	A	B	C
1	Today is ->	7/14/91 11:14	
2			
3	**Weekday ->**	1	
4			
5	(1 is Sunday, 2 is Monday, etc.)		
6			
7			

serial_number is Excel's special format for storing dates and times. The serial number format is a real number (an integer part and a fractional part) from 0 to 65380. It represents dates and times from January 1, 1900 to December 31, 2078.

YEAR(*serial_number*)

YEAR() converts a serial number to an integer that represents a year value. Like many of the other date and time functions, you may enter *serial_number* either as a serial number or as a quoted text string, which Excel will automatically translate into the serial number.

In the following example, cell B1 contains the function NOW(), to show the current date and time, and it is formatted accordingly. Cell B3 contains the function YEAR(B1) and displays the four-digit year value.

B3	=YEAR(B1)		
	A	B	C
1	Today is –>	7/14/91 11:15	
2			
3	Year –>	1991	
4			
5			

serial_number is Excel's special format for storing dates and times. The serial number format is a real number (an integer part and a fractional part) from 0 to 65380. It represents dates and times from January 1, 1900 to December 31, 2078.

Financial Functions

Excel's financial functions are quite useful for performing what would ordinarily be difficult calculations. Far from being limited to esoteric uses, these types of calculations crop up in many aspects of our lives. For example, you may have considered buying a car versus leasing it or tried to decide whether to buy a savings bond or invest the money in your IRA. Or perhaps you run a small business and you need to calculate the depreciation of an asset. All these questions can be resolved with the following set of functions.

DDB(*cost,salvage,life,period,*[*factor*])

DDB() calculates the depreciation of an asset using the double-declining balance method of depreciation.

cost is a value representing the initial cost of an asset.

salvage is a value that represents the value of the asset at the end of the depreciation period. This is also called the *salvage value*.

life is the number of periods over which the asset is depreciated. The unit measure of periods must be the same as *period*.

period is the number of units that represents the period for which you wish to depreciate the asset. This argument must be in the same unit measure as *life*.

factor is the rate at which the balance of the asset declines. If factor is omitted, its value is assumed to be 2.

FV(*rate,nper,pmt,[pv],[type]*)

FV() calculates the future value of those investments that have constant payments over time and a fixed interest rate.

rate is the interest rate per period.

nper is the total number of payment periods in the life of the annuity.

pmt is the payment that is made each period. Normally, the payment includes principal and interest but does not include fees, taxes, or other periodic payments.

pv represents the present value of the annuity. If *pv* is omitted, it is assumed to be 0.

type is a special argument that takes one of two values: 0 means that payments are due at the end of the period, and 1 means that payments are due at the beginning of the period. If *type* is omitted, its value is assumed to be 0.

In the following example, consider an investment where you deposit $2,000 (B6) into a vehicle that earns 7 percent interest per year (B3 is 7 percent divided by 12 to arrive at the monthly interest of .58 percent) and you plan to pay in $200 per month (B5) for 24 months (B4) at the end of each month (B7). The future value of that investment will be $7,435.82.

B1 =FV(B3,B4,B5,B6,B7)

	A	B	C
1	Future Value -->	$7,435.82	
2			
3	Rate	0.58%	
4	Num. of Payments	24	
5	Payment	($200.00)	
6	Present Value	($2,000.00)	
7	Type	0	
8			
9			

Remember that Excel generally requires that outflows of cash (payments that you make) are to be negative numbers. In the above example, cells B5 and B6 contain payments that you make into the investment: B5 is the payment per period and B6 is the initial investment that you made.

IPMT(*rate,per,nper,pv,*[*fv*],[*type*])

IPMT() calculates the interest payments for a loan over a given period of time.

rate is the interest rate per period.

per is the period for which you want to find the interest. This value must be between 1 and the value of *nper.*

nper is the total number of payment periods in the life of the annuity.

pv represents the present value of the annuity. If *pv* is omitted, it is assumed to be 0.

fv is the future value of the annuity. It is the value of the cash balance you want to attain after the last payment is made. If *fv* is omitted, its value is assumed to be 0.

type is a special argument that takes one of two values: 0 means that payments are due at the end of the period, and 1 means that payments are due at the beginning of the period. If *type* is omitted, its value is assumed to be 0.

The following example calculates the interest payment on a loan of $25,000 (B6) at 10 percent interest (B3 is 10 percent divided by 12 to get the monthly interest rate). This loan has a term of three years (B4 shows the number of monthly payments), and you want to determine the interest payment for the 12th month of the loan (B5). In this example, the 12th interest payment would be $151.14. Remember that payments out are negative numbers and moneys you receive are positive numbers.

B1 =IPMT(B3,B4,B5,B6)

	A	B	C
1	Interest Payment–>	($151.14)	
2			
3	Rate	0.83%	
4	Period	12.00	
5	Num. of Payments	36.00	
6	Present Value	$25,000.00	
7	Future Value		
8	Type		
9			
10			

IRR(*values*,[*guess*])

IRR() calculates the internal rate of return for an investment with an uneven cash flow. The IRR calculation is used to determine the rate of return (how well your investment did) based on an initial investment by you and then a series of payments received from that investment.

Cash outflows are negative, and money you receive appears as a positive number. It's important to remember this as you construct a cash-flow range.

values is a range of values that represents a series of cash flows. At least one value in the range must be a positive value, and one must be negative. Usually, the negative value is the amount of money paid into the investment, and the positive numbers are those cash flows that pay back the initial investment and interest.

guess is an initial guess of the result of the IRR calculation. Since the IRR function is an iterative process (that is, Excel tries a number of values until it achieves a certain level of accuracy), you must sometimes include a guess. If *guess* is omitted, its value is assumed to be 10 percent (0.1).

In the following example, consider a rental home that you purchased as a fixer-upper for $50,000. Then you put another $10,000 into the property to upgrade it. Now, six years later, you have totaled the amount of income received from that property and summarized the cash flows in a range on your worksheet. Furthermore, you have named the range CASH_FLOW. The IRR() formula syntax is simple. In cell B1 just place the following command:

```
=IRR(CASH_FLOW)
```

Excel will calculate the rate of return on your initial investments to be -4.85 percent. Even with rising rents, your property isn't doing very well as an investment. Of course, this model doesn't take into account things like tax deductions and so on, so the true rate of return would have to include some other factors.

B1 | =IRR(cash_flow)

	A	B	C
1	Rate of Return -->	-4.85%	
2			
3	Initial Purchase	($50,000.00)	
4	Repair Supplies	($10,000.00)	
5	Total Rent '85	$7,200.00	
6	Total Rent '86	$7,800.00	
7	Total Rent '87	$7,800.00	
8	Total Rent '88	$8,400.00	
9	Total Rent '89	$8,400.00	
10	Total Rent '90	$8,400.00	
11			
12			

MIRR(*values,finance_rate,reinvest_rate*)

MIRR() is similar to the IRR() function, but it takes into account cash flows at different rates of interest.

values is a range of values that represents a series of cash flows. The cash flows do not all have to be positive, but at least one value in the range must be a positive value and one must be a negative value. Usually, the negative value is the amount of money paid into the investment, and the positive numbers are those cash flows that pay back the initial investment.

finance_rate is the interest rate you pay to use the money defined in the *values* range. This is a measure of the cost of funds to you.

reinvest_rate is the interest paid to you when you reinvest your positive cash flows.

NPER(*rate,pmt,pv,[fv],[type]*)

NPER() calculates the number of payments required for a given investment.

In this example, a loan of $3,000 is being paid off at $300 per month, at an interest rate of 10 percent per year (10 percent divided by 12 is 0.83). It will take a little more than ten payments to pay off this obligation.

B1 =NPER(B3,B4,B5)

	A	B	C
1	Number of Payments –>	10.48	
2			
3	Rate	0.83%	
4	Payment	($300.00)	
5	Present Value	$3,000.00	
6			
7			

rate is the interest rate per period.

pmt is the payment that is made each period. Normally, the payment includes principal and interest, but does not include fees, taxes, or other periodic payments.

pv represents the present value of the annuity. If *pv* is omitted, it is assumed to be 0.

fv is the future value of the annuity. It is the value of the cash balance that you want to attain after the last payment is made. If *fv* is omitted, its value is assumed to be 0.

type is a special argument that takes one of two values: 0 means that payments are due at the end of the period, and 1 means that payments are due at the beginning. If *type* is omitted, its value is assumed to be 0.

NPV(*rate,value1,[value2],...*)

NPV() calculates the net present value of an investment based on a series of cash flows and a discount rate. The value returned by the NPV() function reflects the value of an investment today based on the cash flows at the indicated discount rate.

rate is the discount rate per period.

value1, value2,... are from 1 to 13 arguments that represent the payments out and income generated. Each argument can be either a numeric value, an explicit range reference, or a named range.

PMT(*rate,nper,pv,[fv],[type]*)

PMT() calculates the periodic payments required to achieve a certain return based on a known interest rate.

This example shows that the monthly payment required to pay off a $25,000 obligation in ten months at 10 percent annual interest is $2,616.

B1 =PMT(B3,B4,B5)

	A	B	C
1	Payment–>	($2,616)	
2			
3	Rate	0.83%	
4	Number of Paym	10.00	
5	Present Value	$25,000.00	
6	Future Value		
7	Type		
8			
9			

rate is the interest rate per period.

nper is the total number of payment periods in the life of the annuity.

pv represents the present value of the annuity. If *pv* is omitted, it is assumed to be 0.

fv is the future value of the annuity. It is the value of the cash balance that you want to attain after the last payment is made. If *fv* is omitted, its value is assumed to be 0.

type is a special argument that takes one of two values: 0 means that payments are due at the end of the period, and 1 means payments are due at the beginning of the period. If *type* is omitted, its value is assumed to be 0.

PPMT(*rate,per,nper,pv,[fv],[type]*)

PPMT() returns the payment on the principal for a given investment over time. It is similar to PMT() but only calculates the principal.

rate is the interest rate per period.

per is the period for which you want to find the payment amount. This value must be between 1 and the value of *nper.*

nper is the total number of payment periods in the life of the annuity.

pv represents the present value of the annuity. If *pv* is omitted, it is assumed to be 0.

fv is the future value of the annuity. It is the value of the cash balance that you want to attain after the last payment is made. If *fv* is omitted, its value is assumed to be 0.

type is a special argument that takes one of two values: 0 means that payments are due at the end of the period, and 1 means payments are due at the beginning of the period. If *type* is omitted, its value is assumed to be 0.

PV(*rate,nper,pmt,[fv],[type]*)

PV() calculates the present value of an investment. The present value of an investment is the future value that a set of cash flows is worth today. In other words, the present value of an investment is the amount of money that you must invest today in order to achieve a desired level of return (the *rate* argument). This function is often used to measure the attractiveness of an investment.

Consider the following example: Say that you are offered an investment opportunity that paid out $2,500 per year for the next 10 years. In order to get this investment (also referred to here as an *annuity*), you must pay $10,000. Are you willing to pay out $10,000 in return for $25,000?

The *rate* argument is the rate that you believe you can make on the $2,500 per year that you receive from the annuity. In the following example, assuming that you can earn 9.5 percent on the money you receive, it would be an attractive investment for you even if you paid as much as $15,697. (Remember that money that you pay out is negative and money that you receive is positive.) It's an attractive investment because you were given the opportunity to receive a total of $25,000 in exchange for $10,000 now.

B1 =PV(B3,B4,B5,B6,B7)

	A	B	C
1	Present Value –>	($15,697)	
2			
3	Rate	9.50%	
4	Number of Payments	10	
5	Payment	$2,500.00	
6	Future Value		
7	Type		
8			

rate is the interest rate per period.

nper is the total number of payment periods in the life of the annuity.

pmt is the payment that is made each period. Normally, the payment includes principal and interest but does not include fees, taxes, or other periodic payments.

fv is the future value of the annuity. It is a value of the cash balance that you want to attain after the last payment is made. If *fv* is omitted, its value is assumed to be 0.

type is a special argument that takes one of two values: 0 means that payments are due at the end of the period, and 1 means payments are due at the beginning of the period. If *type* is omitted, its value is assumed to be 0.

RATE(*nper*,pmt,*pv*,[*fv*],[*type*],[*guess*])

RATE() calculates the interest rate on a periodic basis for a given investment. Use this function to determine the amount of interest per period for an annuity given the present value of the investment, the number of periods, and the payment information.

nper is the total number of payment periods in the life of the annuity.

pmt is the payment that is made each period. Normally, the payment includes principal and interest but does not include fees, taxes, or other periodic payments.

pv represents the present value of the annuity. If *pv* is omitted, it is assumed to be 0.

fv is the future value of the annuity. It is a value of the cash balance that you want to attain after the last payment is made. If *fv* is omitted, its value is assumed to be 0.

type is a special argument that takes one of two values: 0 means that payments are due at the end of the period, and 1 means payments are due at the beginning of the period. If *type* is omitted, its value is assumed to be 0.

guess is what you believe the rate will be. If *guess* is omitted, its value is assumed to be 10 percent (0.1).

SLN(*cost,salvage,life*)

SLN() calculates the depreciation of an asset using the straight-line method of depreciation.

cost is a value representing the initial cost of an asset.

salvage is a value that represents the value of the asset at the end of the depreciation period. This is also called the *salvage value*.

life is the number of periods over which the asset is depreciated.

SYD(*cost,salvage,life,per*)

SYD() calculates the depreciation of an asset by using the sum-of-years'-digits method of depreciation.

cost is a value representing the initial cost of an asset.

salvage is a value that represents the value of the asset at the end of the depreciation period. This is also called the *salvage value*.

life is the number of periods over which the asset is depreciated. The unit measure of periods must be the same as it is for *per*.

per is the period for which you want to find the interest.

VDB(*cost,salvage,life,start_period,end_period,*[*factor*], [*no_switch*])

VDB() calculates the depreciation of an asset by using a declining balance method.

cost is a value representing the initial cost of an asset.

salvage is a value that represents the value of the asset at the end of the depreciation period. This is also called the *salvage value*.

life is the number of periods over which the asset is depreciated. The unit measure of life must be the same as *start_period* and *end_period*.

start_period is the starting period for which you want to calculate the depreciation. Make sure that *start_period* is expressed in the same unit terms as *life* and *end_period*. For example, if you use months as the unit measure for *life*, *start_period* must be expressed in months as well.

end_period is the ending period for which you want to calculate the depreciation. Make sure that *end_period* uses the same unit measurement as *start_-period* and *life*. For example, if you use months as the unit measure for *life*, *end_period* must be expressed in months as well.

factor is the optional rate at which the balance declines. If you omit *factor*, Excel assumes it to be 2, which signifies the double-declining balance method of depreciation.

no_switch is an optional logical value (TRUE or FALSE) that specifies whether Excel should switch to the straight-line method of depreciation when that depreciation would be greater than with the double-declining balance method of calculation. *no_switch* can take one of two values:

- If *no_switch* is TRUE, Excel will not switch to straight-line depreciation, even when the depreciation is greater than the double-declining balance calculation.
- If *no_switch* is FALSE or omitted, Excel will switch to a straight-line depreciation calculation when the depreciation is greater than the double-declining balance calculation.

Informational Functions

The informational functions are mostly those that return some type of information about the worksheet. In some cases they are useful for beginning to intermediate users, but mostly they are useful for complex worksheets and intricate models.

ADDRESS(*row_num*,*column_num*,[*abs_num*],[*a1*], [*sheet_text*])

ADDRESS() is used to create an address (reference) based on the textual contents of a cell.

row_num is the row number to use in the reference.

col_num is the column number to use in the reference.

abs_num represents the type of reference to return. If you omit *abs_num*, it defaults to 1, which means an absolute reference ($A$1). The value 2 means absolute row and relative column (A$1); 3 means relative row and absolute column ($A1); and 4 means a relative reference (A1).

a1 is a logical value (TRUE or FALSE) that specifies either the A1 or the R1C1 style of addressing. If *a1* is TRUE or is omitted, the A1 style of addressing is used.

sheet_text is the name of another worksheet or macro sheet that you want to refer to in the address.

AREAS(*reference*)

AREAS() calculates the number of areas in a given reference. (Here, *area* is synonymous with *range*.)

reference refers to a cell or range of cells.

CELL(*info_type*,[*reference*])

CELL() returns a wide variety of information in a cell such as its formatting, type, contents, and so on.

info_type is a text value that determines what type of information Excel returns about the cell. (See the *Microsoft Excel Function Reference* for more information about allowable arguments.)

reference refers to a cell or range of cells.

COLUMN([*reference*])

COLUMN() returns the column number of a given reference, for example COLUMN(B4) would return 2.

reference refers to a cell or range of cells.

COLUMNS(*array*)

COLUMNS() calculates the number of columns in an array or reference.

array is a reference to an array or an array formula.

INDIRECT(*ref_text*,[*a1*])

INDIRECT() returns a reference as given in a textual value.

ref_text is a reference to a cell using either the R1C1 or the A1 addressing format.

a1 is a logical value that specifies either the A1 or the R1C1 style of addressing. If *a1* is TRUE or is omitted, the A1 style of addressing is used.

INFO(*type_num*)

INFO() is similar to the CELL() function, but it returns information about the operating system and operating environment of the host computer.

type_num is a quoted text string that defines what information you want to know about the operating system and hardware environment of the host computer.

ISBLANK(*value*)

ISBLANK() returns TRUE if *value* is blank.

value is either a blank cell, error value, logical value, text value, numeric value, or reference value that you want to test for the presence of, depending on the context in which *value* is used.

For example, ISBLANK(D5) would return TRUE if cell D5 is blank. This function is very useful for those times when you want to check to see if a cell is blank before putting some other value there. For instance, recall that a database extract will overwrite whatever data is in a cell. You can avoid this disaster by first checking to see if the cells in the extract range are empty with the ISBLANK worksheet function.

ISERR(*value*)

ISERR() returns TRUE if *value* is any error value other than #N/A.

value is either a blank cell, error value, logical value, text value, numeric value, or reference value that you want to test for the presence of, depending on the context in which *value* is used.

ISERROR(*value*)

ISERROR() returns TRUE if *value* contains any error value or condition.

value is either a blank cell, error value, logical value, text value, numeric value, or reference value that you want to test for the presence of, depending on the context in which *value* is used.

ISLOGICAL(*value*)

ISLOGICAL() returns TRUE if *value* is a logical value.

value is either a blank cell, error value, logical value, text value, numeric value, or reference value that you want to test for the presence of, depending on the context in which *value* is used.

ISNA(*value*)

ISNA() returns TRUE if *value* is #N/A.

value is either a blank cell, error value, logical value, text value, numeric value, or reference value that you want to test for the presence of, depending on the context in which *value* is used.

ISNOTEXT(*value*)

ISNOTEXT() returns TRUE if *value* is not a text entry.

value is either a blank cell, error value, logical value, text value, numeric value, or reference value that you want to test for the presence of, depending on the context in which *value* is used.

ISNUMBER(*value*)

ISNUMBER() returns TRUE only if *value* is a number.

value is either a blank cell, error value, logical value, text value, numeric value, or reference value that you want to test for the presence of, depending on the context in which *value* is used.

ISREF(*value*)

ISREF() returns TRUE if *value* is a reference to another cell.

value is either a blank cell, error value, logical value, text value, numeric value, or reference value that you want to test for the presence of, depending on the context in which *value* is used.

ISTEXT(*value*)

ISTEXT() returns TRUE only if *value* is text.

value is either a blank cell, error value, logical value, text value, numeric value, or reference value that you want to test for the presence of, depending on the context in which *value* is used.

N(*value*)

N() converts a value to a number depending on the contents of a cell. It's used mostly for compatibility and interoperability with other spreadsheet products.

value is either a blank cell, error value, logical value, text value, numeric value, or reference value that you want to test for the presence of, depending on the context in which *value* is used.

NA()

NA() places the string "#N/A" in a cell.

OFFSET(*reference,rows,cols,*[*height*],[*width*])

OFFSET() returns the offset address (reference) from the specified address.

reference is the cell reference from which you want to base the offset. Note that *reference* can only be a single selection—multiple selections will return a #VALUE! error.

rows is the positive or negative number of rows that you want the upper-left corner of the reference to refer to. Positive numbers denote that number of rows down, whereas negative numbers refer to rows up.

cols is the positive or negative number of columns that you want the upper-left corner of the reference to refer to. Positive numbers refer to columns to the right of *reference*, and negative numbers refer to columns to the left of *reference*.

height is an optional number that refers to the height you want the returned reference to have. Unlike *rows* and *cols*, *height* must be a positive number.

width is an optional width, stated in number of columns, that you want the returned reference to have. Unlike *rows* and *cols*, *width* must be a positive number.

ROW([*reference*])

ROW() returns the row number of the reference. This is similar to the COLUMN() function.

reference refers to a cell or range of cells.

ROWS(*array*)

Like the COLUMNS() function, ROWS() returns the number of rows in a reference.

array is a reference to an array or to an array formula.

T(*value*)

T() returns the text referred to by *value*. This function is mostly used to ensure compatibility with other spreadsheet programs. In most Excel situations, T() is not needed.

value is either a blank cell, error value, logical value, text value, numeric value, or reference value that you want to test for the presence of, depending on the context in which *value* is used.

TYPE(*value*)

TYPE() returns an integer value that corresponds to the data type of *value*. The value that TYPE() returns is 1 for a number, 2 for text, 4 for a logical value, 8 for a formula, 16 for an error value, and 64 for an array.

value is either a blank cell, error value, logical value, text value, numeric value, or reference value that you want to test for the presence of, depending on the context in which *value* is used.

Logical Functions

The group of logical functions will become very important to your models because they have the ability to influence the action of your model. With the logical functions, you can test whether one value is equal to another and then take appropriate action depending on the outcome of the test.

AND(*logical1*,[*logical2*],...)

AND() performs a logical AND on the arguments. It returns TRUE only if all the arguments are TRUE. For instance, the following formula returns TRUE:

```
AND(1+2=3,1+5>2,4<>5)
```

***logical1*, *logical2*,...** are the logical conditions that you want to test. You can test up to 14 logical conditions at one time.

FALSE()

FALSE() inserts the value of FALSE into a cell. It's useful for looping structures in macros.

IF(*logical_test*,*value_if_true*,*value_if_false*)

IF() performs a logical test, then returns one of two values, depending on the result of the test. This is a very useful function for handling decision logic as you begin to build more complex models.

logical_test is any value or expression that Excel can evaluate to either a TRUE or FALSE result. For example, 5=4 is a logical text that returns FALSE, but 6>3 returns TRUE.

value_if_true is the optional value to return if the result of the logical test is TRUE. If this argument is omitted and the value of *logical_test* is TRUE, Excel returns TRUE.

value_if_false is the optional value to return if the result of the logical test is FALSE. If this argument is omitted and the value of *logical_test* is FALSE, Excel returns FALSE.

For example, assume that cell A5 contains your age and cell A7 contains this function:

```
=IF(A5>=30,"You're over the hill","You're still young")
```

If the value of cell A5 is greater than or equal to 30, then cell A7 will contain the message "You're over the hill", otherwise the cell will salute your youth.

NOT(*logical*)

NOT() reverses the logic of the argument, that is, NOT(TRUE) returns = FALSE.

logical is a value or expression that can be evaluated to either TRUE or FALSE.

OR(*logical1*,[*logical2*],...)

OR() performs a logical test of the arguments and returns TRUE if any of the arguments are true. Compare this with the AND() function.

logical1, logical2,... are the logical conditions that you want to test. You can test up to 14 logical conditions at one time.

TRUE()

TRUE() inserts the value of TRUE into a cell.

Lookup Functions

The lookup functions let you reference information stored in lists in an Excel worksheet. The tables are quite useful for things like tax tables, where you first have to find someone's income in a table and then find out what the appropriate tax bracket is. The lookup functions are usually reserved for specialized applications. For that reason, explanations of the arguments have been omitted.

CHOOSE(*index_num*,*value1*,[*value2*],...)

CHOOSE() selects one item from a list of several values.

HLOOKUP(*lookup_value*,*table_array*,*row_index_num*)

HLOOKUP() performs a search of an array for *lookup_value* in the top row of the array and then looks down to find the referenced item.

INDEX (*reference,row_num,column_num,*[*area_num*]) or (*array,*[*row_num*],[*column_num*])

INDEX() returns the value of a cell at the intersection of specified rows and columns.

LOOKUP (*lookup_value,*array) or (*lookup_value,lookup_vector,result_vector*)

LOOKUP() performs searches in specific arrays or references and returns values based on the search.

MATCH(*lookup_value,lookup_array,*[*match_type*])

MATCH() returns the position (instead of the contents) of a cell containing *lookup_value.*

VLOOKUP(*lookup_value,table_array,col_index_num*)

VLOOKUP() is similar to HLOOKUP() but performs a search for *lookup_value* in the column to the right or left of the data that you want to search.

Mathematical Functions

The mathematical functions handle computationally difficult calculations for you. Although it's possible to create formulas and functions that perform any of these calculations, Excel provides these for you. They have already been tested and are reliable.

ABS(*number*)

ABS( ) calculates the absolute value of *number.*

number is a real number that you want acted on by the function.

EXP(*number*)

EXP( ) calculates the base of the natural logarithm (e) raised to a certain power (*number*).

number is a real number that you want acted on by the function.

FACT(*number*)

FACT() calculates the factorial of *number*. For example, FACT(3) equals 1*2*3=6.

number is a real number that you want acted on by the function.

INT(*number*)

INT() returns the integer portion of *number*. It's useful for rounding to the nearest whole integer.

number is a real number that you want acted on by the function.

LN(*number*)

LN() calculates the natural logarithm of *number*.

number is a real number that you want acted on by the function.

LOG(*number,base*)

LOG() calculates the logarithm of *number* to the specified *base*.

number is a real number that you want acted on by the function.

base is the base of the logarithm. If you omit base, Excel assumes it is 10.

LOG10(*number*)

LOG10() calculates the base 10 logarithm of *number*.

number is a real number that you want acted on by the function.

MOD(*number,divisor*)

MOD() returns the *modulo* (remainder) of *number*, after dividing it by *divisor*.

number is a real number that you want acted on by the function.

divisor is the number you divide into *number*.

PI()

PI() inserts the value of pi to 15 digits into the cell.

PRODUCT(*number1*,[*number2*],...)

PRODUCT() multiplies the arguments together.

number is a real number that you want acted on by the function. Note that *number* can be a single value or a reference to a range.

RAND()

RAND() returns a random number between 0 and 1.

ROUND(*number,num_digits*)

ROUND() rounds *number* off to the number of digits specified.

number is a real number that you want acted on by the function.

num_digits is the number of digits you want *number* rounded to. For values greater than zero, *number* is rounded to that number of decimal places. If the value is 0, the ROUND function rounds the number to the nearest integer. If the value is less than zero, the number is rounded to the left of the decimal place.

SIGN(*number*)

SIGN() returns the sign of a number—negative or positive.

number is a real number that you want acted on by the function.

SQRT(*number*)

SQRT() calculates the square root of *number.*

number is a real number that you want acted on by the function.

SUM(*number1*,[*number2*],...)

SUM() performs the summation of the arguments.

number is a real number that you want acted on by the function. Note that *number* can be a single value or a reference to a range.

TRUNC(*number*,[*num_digits*])

TRUNC() cuts off (truncates) *number* to the specified number of digits. Note that this is different from ROUND().

number is a real number that you want acted on by the function.

num_digits is the number of digits you want the number truncated to. If *num_digits* is omitted, TRUNC will truncate all the values to the right of the decimal place.

Matrix Functions

The matrix functions facilitate complex matrix mathematical calculations on arrays and matrices within Excel. Unless you know that you have a need for these functions, you probably won't have to worry about them.

MDETERM(*array*)

MDETERM() calculates the matrix determinant of *array*.

array can be either a cell range, an array reference, or a named reference to an array. The array must have an equal number of rows and columns.

MINVERSE(*array*)

MINVERSE() calculates the matrix inverse of *array*.

array can be either a cell range, an array reference, or a named reference to an array. The array must have an equal number of rows and columns.

MMULT(*array1*,*array2*)

MMULT() multiplies the two arrays together.

array1*, *array2 can be either cell ranges, array references, or named references to arrays. Each array must have an equal number of rows and columns.

SUMPRODUCT(*array1*,*array2*,...)

SUMPRODUCT() multiplies the corresponding values in each of the arguments and then adds them together.

array1, array2,... can be either cell ranges, array references, or named references to arrays. Each array must have an equal number of rows and columns.

TRANSPOSE(*array*)

TRANSPOSE() calculates the transpose of *array.*

array can be either a cell range, an array reference, or a named reference to an array. The array must have an equal number of rows and columns.

Statistical Functions

Excel includes a number of functions that are designed to make statistical calculations easier. One of them, AVERAGE(), you've used before.

Despite that, some of these functions are quite complicated and difficult to use. For example, you probably won't have much use for the multiple regression tools such as LOGEST(), TREND(), and LINEST(). The arguments for these more-complex functions have been omitted.

AVERAGE(*number1*,[*number2*],...)

AVERAGE() calculates the arithmetic mean (average) of the arguments. Excel first counts the number of items in the ranges or individual cells defined by *number* and then sums the items. Finally, the function divides by the total number of items.

number1, number2,... are the arguments that you want to work with; you can use up to 14 arguments at one time. These arguments can be actual values, range references, or named ranges.

COUNT(*value1*,[*value2*],...)

COUNT() totals the number of values in the arguments. However, only cells containing numbers are counted.

value1, value2,... refer to cells that contain most of the valid data types within Excel (text, logical values, numbers). You can use from 1 to 14 arguments with the COUNT() function.

COUNTA(*value1*,[*value2*],...)

COUNTA() is just like COUNT(), but it only counts all cells that are not blank. This is a complementary function to COUNT(). This function is useful for counting nonblank cells in a range—that is, those cells that have something in them.

value1, value2,... refer to cells that contain any of the valid data types within Excel (text, logical values, numbers). However, only cells containing data are counted—those that are empty are ignored. You can use from 1 to 14 arguments with the COUNTA() function.

GROWTH(*known_y's*,[*known_x's*],[*new_x's*],[*const*])

GROWTH() calculates values along an exponential trend by fitting an exponential curve.

LINEST(*known_y's*,[*known_x's*],[*const*],[*stats*])

LINEST() calculates the parameters and predicts the values along a linear-trend line.

LOGEST(*known_y's*,[*known_x's*],[*const*],[*stats*])

LOGEST() calculates the parameters and predicts the values along an exponential-trend line.

MAX(*number1*,[*number2*],...)

MAX() calculates the largest value in a list of arguments.

number1, number2,... are the arguments that you want to work with; you can use up to 14 arguments at one time. These arguments can be actual values, range references, or named ranges.

MEDIAN(*number1*,[*number2*],...)

MEDIAN() calculates the median value in a list of arguments. Remember that the median value is that value in a list below which fall half of the numbers. That is, half the numbers occur above the median and half below it.

number1, number2,... are the arguments that you want to work with; you can use up to 14 arguments at one time. These arguments can be actual values, range references, or named ranges.

MIN(*number1*,[*number2*],...)

MIN() calculates the smallest value in a list of arguments.

number1, number2,... are the arguments that you want to work with; you can use up to 14 arguments at one time. These arguments can be actual values, range references, or named ranges.

STDEV(*number1*,[*number2*],...)

STDEV() calculates the sample standard deviation of a list of arguments.

number1, number2,... are the arguments that you want to work with; you can use up to 14 arguments at one time. These arguments can be actual values, range references, or named ranges.

STDEVP(*number1*,[*number2*],...)

STDEVP() calculates the population standard deviation of a list of arguments.

number1, number2,... are the arguments that you want to work with; you can use up to 14 arguments at one time. These arguments can be actual values, range references, or named ranges.

TREND(*known_y's*,[*known_x's*],[*new_x's*],[*const*])

TREND() calculates the parameters and predicts the values of items on a linear-trend line.

VAR(*number1*,[*number2*],...)

VAR() calculates the sample variance of a list of arguments.

number1, number2,... are the arguments that you want to work with; you can use up to 14 arguments at one time. These arguments can be actual values, range references, or named ranges.

VARP(*number1*,[*number2*],...)

VARP() calculates the population variance of a list of arguments.

number1, number2,... are the arguments that you want to work with; you can use up to 14 arguments at one time. These arguments can be actual values, range references, or named ranges.

String (Text) Functions

Aside from the date and time functions, the string functions are probably the most useful. If you do any type of textual application with Excel, you will find that the string functions can be very helpful.

CHAR(*number*)

CHAR() returns the code specified by *number.* This function is helpful for entering special characters and symbols into a worksheet. (See Chapter 6 for more information on special characters.) For example, the function =CHAR(165) displays a Japanese yen symbol in the cell.

number is a numeric value between 1 and 255 that represents the character you want to display in the cell. The character this function displays is based on the character set in your computer. For Windows, the ANSI Windows character set is used.

CLEAN(*text*)

CLEAN() removes special (control) characters from the specified *text.* You will only really use this function if you import text from other applications that might have inserted control characters into the text. Use the CLEAN() function to remove any nonprinting characters from the text string.

text is a cell or a range of cells that contain textual information along with nonprinting characters that you want to remove.

CODE(*text*)

CODE() returns the code for the first character in *text.* This is the opposite of the CHAR() function. For example, =CODE(Apple) returns 65, the ASCII value for a capital "A."

text is a cell or a text string for which you want the first character code. This is the textual information you want to act on. The code this function displays is based on the character set in your computer. For Windows, the ANSI Windows character set is used.

DOLLAR(*number*,[*decimals*])

DOLLAR() formats a number and converts it to a text value. For instance, the function =DOLLAR(1244) returns the value $1,244.00. Note that the value returned by the DOLLAR() function is a textual value and will not work in mathematical calculations.

number is either a cell or a range of cells that contain numeric data.

decimals is an optional numeric value that represents how many digits should be displayed to the right of the decimal place.

EXACT(*text1,text2*)

EXACT() compares two strings of text. This function returns TRUE if the two strings are identical, in both spelling and case. For example, the function EXACT("smith","smith") returns TRUE, but EXACT("smith","Smith") returns FALSE because of the capital "S."

text1 is the first string of text you want to compare. Note that this can be a cell that contains numeric information.

text2 is the second string of text that you want to compare. Note that this can be a cell that contains numeric information.

FIND(*find_text,within_text,*[*start_at_num*])

FIND() searches for one text value within another one. This function is case-sensitive. *find_text* is the text you want to find in the string *within_text.* Optionally, you can add the *start_at_num* parameter to specify which character in *within_text* to start the search with.

This function returns the beginning position number of the search string within the target string. For example, =FIND("a","Santa Claus") returns 2.

find_text is a text string that contains the text you want to search for.

within_text is a text string containing the text you want to find.

start_at_num represents the optional character position at which you want to begin the search. If this value is omitted, Excel assumes it to be 1. That is, the search begins at the first character of the *within_text* string.

FIXED(*number,*[*decimals*])

FIXED() formats a number to a text value with a fixed number of decimals. This function is very similar to the DOLLAR() function, except that it formats the number to an optional fixed number of decimal places. For example, the function =FIXED(1244,3) returns 1,244.000 and converts it to a text value.

number is either a cell or a range of cells that contains numeric data.

decimals is an optional numeric value that represents how many digits should be displayed to the right of the decimal place.

LEFT(*text*,[*num_chars*])

LEFT() returns the leftmost character(s) from a string of text. Use this function to return a portion of a text string. If you omit the *num_chars* parameter, Excel will just return the first character of the string.

For example, the function =LEFT("Easter Bunny",4) returns the text string "East".

text is the textual information from which you want to extract some portion of text.

num_chars refers to the number of characters you want to obtain from the left end of *text*.

LEN(*text*)

LEN() returns the length of a string of text. For example, if cell A2 contains the text string "Abe Lincoln" then the function =LEN(A2) in cell A3 would return 11 as the length of the text string (including the spaces).

text represents a cell or a quoted text string that contains textual information for which you want to determine the length.

LOWER(*text*)

LOWER() converts a string of text to lowercase. For example, the function =LOWER("This is A MIX") returns the text string "this is a mix".

text is the textual information that you want to convert to lowercase.

MID(*text*,*start_num*,*num_chars*)

MID() returns a portion of text extracted from the middle of another text string. *text* is the target text string; *start_num* is the starting position of the text you want to extract; and *num_chars* is the number of characters you want to extract.

This function is similar to the LEFT() function but MID() returns a substring from the middle of the target string. For example, the function =MID("Final Test Results",7,4) returns the string "Test".

text refers to the cell or quoted text string that you want to extract some text from.

start_num is the character position where you want to begin extracting the substring from *text.*

num_chars is the number of characters you want the extracted string to be.

PROPER(*text*)

PROPER() formats a string of text to have initial capital letters. *text* is the string you want to convert. For example, if cell B3 contains the text string "the raIn in spAin" then the function =PROPER(B3) in cell B5 returns the text string "The Rain In Spain" This is a useful function for working with proper names.

text is the textual information you want to have the initial capitalization.

REPLACE(*old_text,start_num,num_chars,new_text*)

REPLACE() replaces old text from within a text string with new text. *old_text* is the string that contains the text that you want to replace; *start_num* is the position within *old_text* where you want to new text to go; and *num_chars* is the number of characters to replace with *new_text.*

old_text is the textual information that you want to change.

start_num is the position of the character where *new_text* begins replacing *old_text.*

num_chars is the number of characters from *old_text* that you want to replace with the new text.

new_text is the new text that you want to replace the old text.

REPT(*text,number_times*)

REPT() repeats the *text* value a specified number of times. For example, the function =REPT("+-",4) returns "+-+-+-+-" in the cell where you place the function.

text is the text that you want to repeat a certain number of times.

number_times is the number of times that you want to repeat the *text* value. This must be a positive number.

RIGHT(*text*,[*num_chars*])

Right( ) returns the rightmost character(s) from a string of text. Use this function to return a portion of a text string. If you omit the *num_chars* parameter, Excel will just return the last character of the string.

For example, the function =RIGHT("Welcome to California",18) returns the text string "come to California".

text is the textual information from which you want to extract the some portion of text.

num_chars refers to the number of characters you want to obtain from the right end of *text*.

SEARCH([*find_text*],*within_text*,[*start_num*])

SEARCH( ) looks for one text value within another one and returns the number of the character where the search text is found in the source text.

This function is similar to the FIND( ) function, but it is not case-sensitive.

find_text is the cell or the quoted text string containing the text that you want to search for in *within_text*.

within_text is the cell or quoted text string that contains the text you want to find.

start_num is the optional character number, counting from the left, where you want to begin the search.

SUBSTITUTE(*text*,*old_text*,*new_text*,[*instance_num*])

SUBSTITUTE( ) replaces old characters in a text string with new text. This function is similar to the REPLACE( ) function, but SUBSTITUTE( ) looks for *old_text* within *text* and then replaces *old_text* with *new_text*.

For example, the function =SUBSTITUTE("ice cream","cream","milk") returns the text string "ice milk".

text is the cell or the quoted text string in which you want to substitute characters.

old_text is the text that you want to find and replace with the new text.

new_text is the text that you want to take the place of the old text.

instance_num is the optional value that determines which of the values of *old_text* (if there is more than one) you wish to replace.

TEXT(*value,format_text*)

TEXT() formats a number and converts it to a text value.

value is a number or a cell containing a numeric value.

format_text is text formatted with a number format from the list of formats available in the Format Number dialog box.

TRIM(*text*)

TRIM() removes extra spaces from a string of text. This is a useful function if you have a worksheet model that prompts users for information. Since you can't control how many extra spaces they might add to an input line, just use the TRIM() function to clean up the line before you store it in the model.

For example, the function =TRIM("Big   holes   here") returns the text string "Big holes here".

text is the quoted text string, cell, or range reference that contains the textual information you want to trim.

UPPER(*text*)

UPPER() formats a string of text to all uppercase letters. This is the opposite of LOWER()—it converts text strings to all uppercase. For example, the function =UPPER("Bay Bank") returns the text string "BAY BANK".

text is the quoted text string, cell, or range reference that contains the textual information you want to convert to all uppercase.

VALUE(*text*)

VALUE() converts a text argument into a number. This is the opposite of the TEXT() function.

text is the textual version of any valid Excel number or date and time format that you want to convert to a number. This function is normally not used since Excel already understands to convert text into numbers when necessary.

Trigonometric Functions

Last but not least are the trigonometric functions. If you can still remember high school trigonometry, these functions will help you to calculate the heights of buildings and telephone poles. Since so few models use these functions, however, they are presented here in abbreviated form.

ACOS(*number*)

ACOS() calculates the arccosine of *number.*

ACOSH(*number*)

ACOSH() calculates the inverse hyperbolic cosine of *number.*

ASIN(*number*)

ASIN() calculates the arcsine of *number.*

ASINH(*number*)

ASINH() calculates the inverse hyperbolic sine of *number.*

ATAN(*number*)

ATAN() calculates the arctangent of *number.*

ATAN2(*x_num,y_num*)

ATAN2() calculates the arctangent from x and y coordinates (*x_num, y_num*).

ATANH(*number*)

ATANH() calculates the inverse hyperbolic tangent of *number.*

COS(*number*)

COS() calculates the cosine of *number.*

COSH(*number*)

COSH() calculates the hyperbolic cosine of *number.*

SIN(*number*)

SIN() calculates the sine of *number.*

SINH(*number*)

SINH() calculates the hyperbolic sine of *number.*

TAN(*number*)

TAN() calculates the tangent of *number.*

TANH(*number*)

TANH() calculates the hyperbolic tangent of *number.*

INDEX

A

B

C

D

K

L

M

P

Q

R

S

X

Y

Z